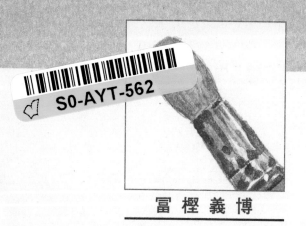

冨樫義博

About the how-to-draw-manga guide *Jump Ryu:* it was more difficult than I thought to draw while answering questions from someone behind me. I probably sounded like an idiot because my responses were so slow. Please, have a heart.

Yoshihiro Togashi

Yoshihiro Togashi's manga career began in 1986 at the age of 20, when he won the coveted Ōsamu Tezuka Award for new manga artists. He debuted in the Japanese **Weekly Shonen Jump** magazine in 1989 with the romantic comedy **Tende Shôwaru Cupid**. From 1990 to 1994 he wrote and drew the hit manga **YuYu Hakusho**, which was followed by the dark comedy science-fiction series **Level E**, and finally this adventure series, **Hunter x Hunter**, available from VIZ Media's SHONEN JUMP Advanced imprint. In 1999 he married the manga artist Naoko Takeuchi.

HUNTER X HUNTER Volume 33
SHONEN JUMP ADVANCED Manga Edition

STORY AND ART BY
YOSHIHIRO TOGASHI

English Adaptation & Translation/Lillian Olsen
Touch-up Art & Lettering/Mark McMurray
Design/Matt Hinrichs
Editor/Urian Brown

HUNTERxHUNTER © POT (Yoshihiro Togashi) 2014, 2016
All rights reserved. First published in Japan in 2014, 2016 by SHUEISHA
Inc., Tokyo. English translation rights arranged by SHUEISHA Inc.

The stories, characters and incidents mentioned in this publication are
entirely fictional.

Printed in the U.S.A.

Published by VIZ Media, LLC
P.O. Box 77010
San Francisco, CA 94107

10 9 8 7 6 5 4 3 2 1
First printing, March 2017

SHONEN JUMP ADVANCED MANGA

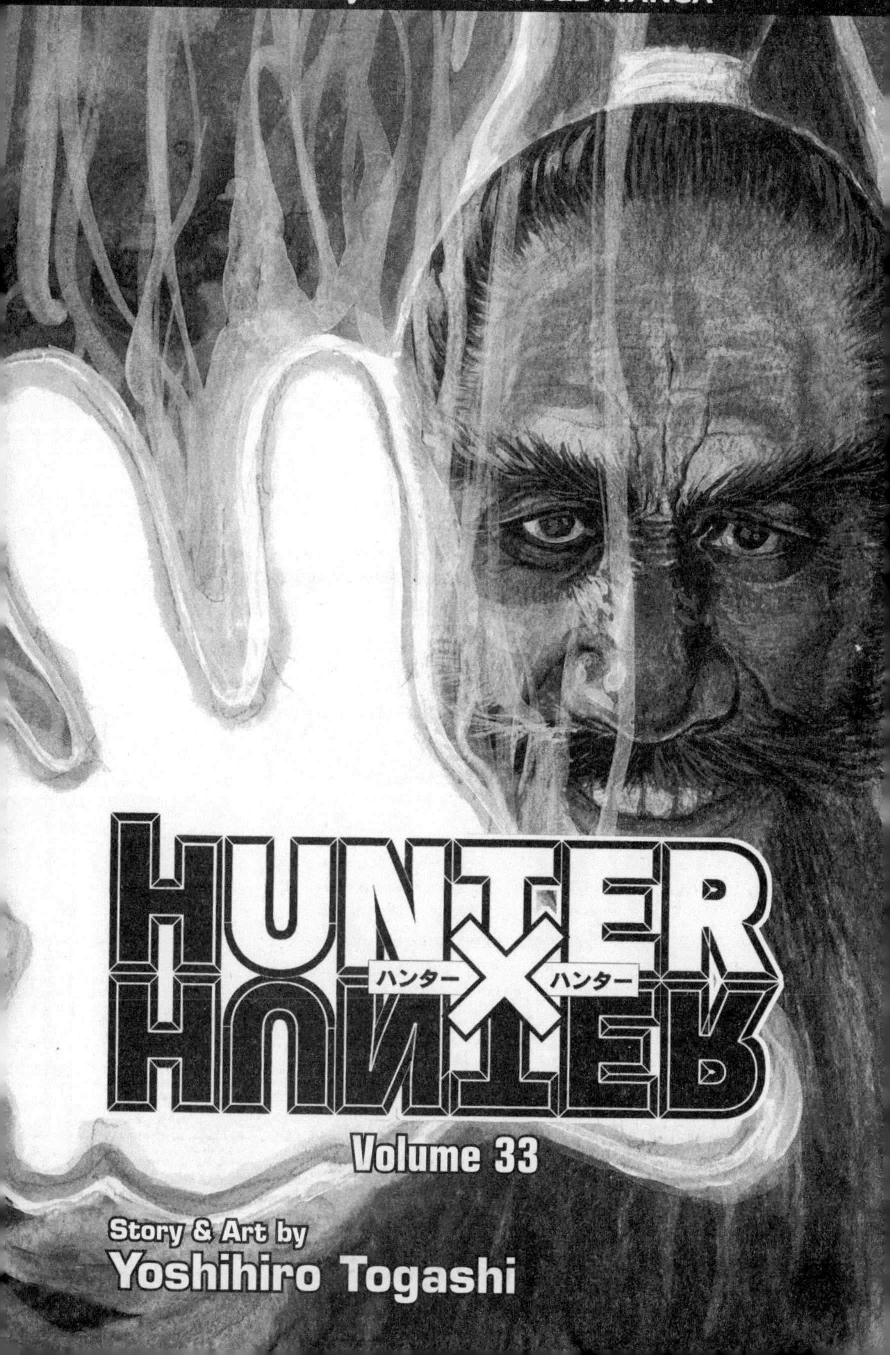

HUNTER × HUNTER

ハンター × ハンター

Volume 33

Story & Art by

Yoshihiro Togashi

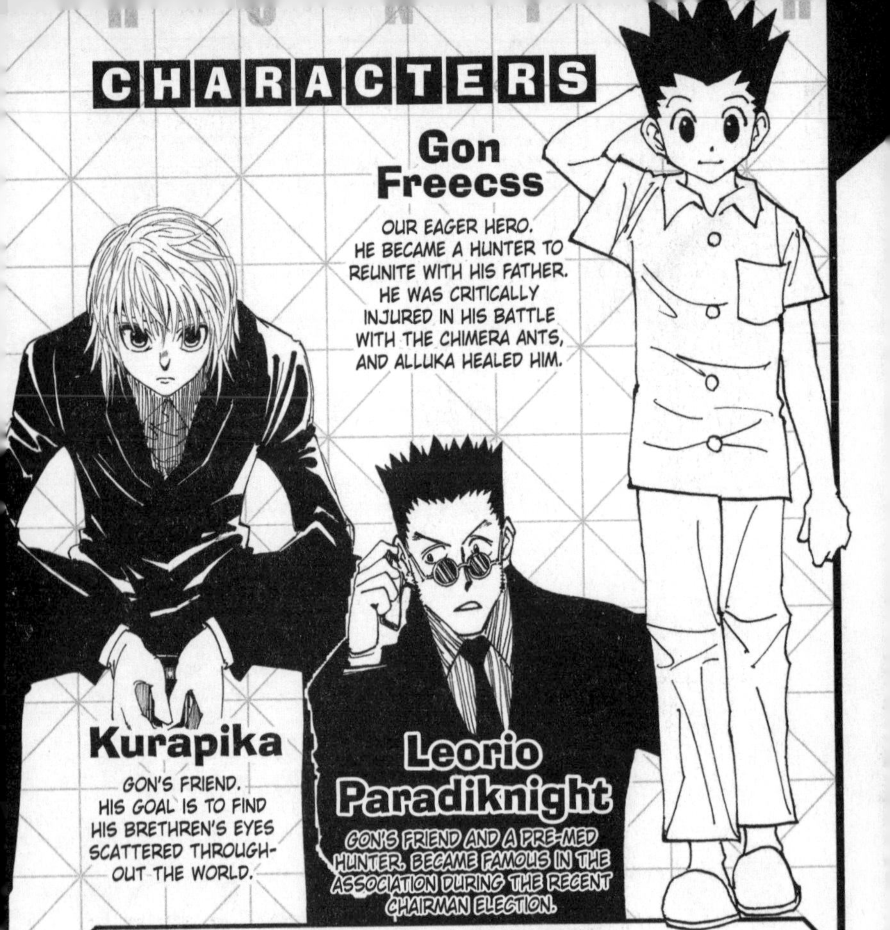

CHARACTERS

Gon Freecss

OUR EAGER HERO. HE BECAME A HUNTER TO REUNITE WITH HIS FATHER. HE WAS CRITICALLY INJURED IN HIS BATTLE WITH THE CHIMERA ANTS, AND ALLUKA HEALED HIM.

Kurapika

GON'S FRIEND. HIS GOAL IS TO FIND HIS BRETHREN'S EYES SCATTERED THROUGHOUT THE WORLD.

Leorio Paradiknight

GON'S FRIEND AND A PRE-MED HUNTER. BECAME FAMOUS IN THE ASSOCIATION DURING THE RECENT CHAIRMAN ELECTION.

The Story Thus Far

GON DREAMS OF BEING A HUNTER LIKE THE FATHER HE HARDLY REMEMBERS, THE GREAT GING FREECSS.

GON REUNITES WITH GING'S OLD FRIEND KITE AND STARTS ON AN ADVENTURE IN NGL, WHERE AN ENCOUNTER WITH THE CHIMERA ANTS RESULTS IN KITE'S CAPTURE WHEN HE TRIES TO PROTECT GON. FINALLY, THE KING ANT IS BORN, AND HE IS A VICIOUS CREATURE WHO WOULD EVEN EAT HIS OWN KIND. OUR HEROES STORM THE PALACE IN EAST GORTEAU TO DEFEAT THE ANTS. MANKIND IS VICTORIOUS, BUT AT THE COST OF HUNTER ASSOCIATION CHAIRMAN NETERO'S LIFE, AND GON IS CRITICALLY WOUNDED.

AN ELECTION IS HELD TO PICK THE NEXT HUNTER ASSOCIATION CHAIRMAN, AND CHEEDLE OF THE ZODIACS IS PICKED. GON IS HEALED BY ALLUKA, KILLUA'S SISTER.

NETERO'S SON, BEYOND, ANNOUNCES A VOYAGE TO THE DARK CONTINENT TO THE ENTIRE WORLD. THE HUNTER ASSOCIATION IS ORDERED TO HUNT BEYOND...

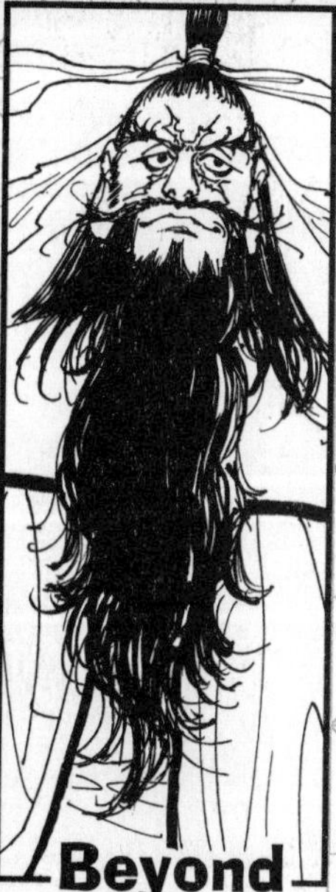

Beyond Netero

NETERO'S SON. PLANNING THE FORBIDDEN JOURNEY TO THE DARK CONTINENT.

Pariston

FORMER HUNTER ASSOCIATION VICE CHAIRMAN AND FORMERLY ONE OF THE ZODIACS. INTRICATELY INVOLVED IN BEYOND'S JOURNEY PLANS.

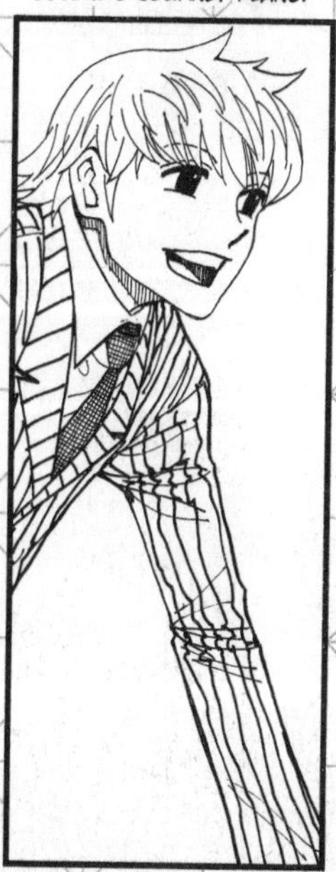

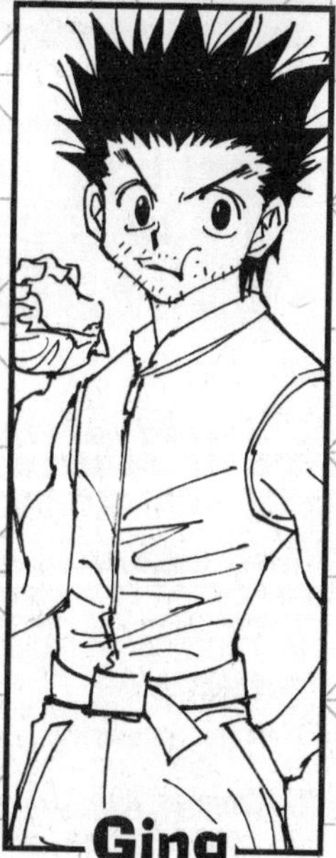

Ging

GON'S FATHER, ONE OF THE TOP FIVE NEN USERS IN THE WORLD. WITHDREW FROM THE HUNTER ASSOCIATION ZODIACS.

The Zodiacs

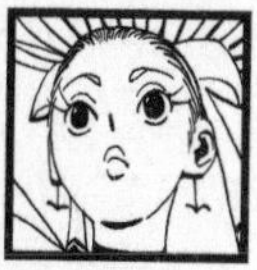

CLUCK (BIRD)

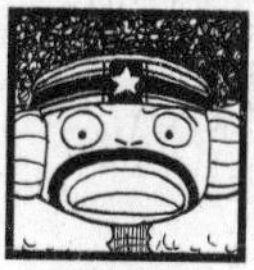

GINTA (RAM)

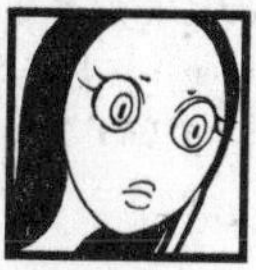

GEL (SNAKE)

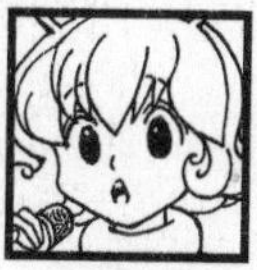

PYON (RABBIT)

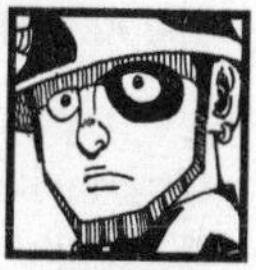

MIZAISTOM (COW)

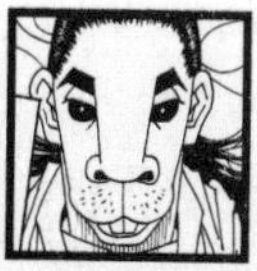

SATCHO (HORSE)

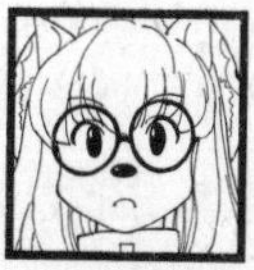

CHEADLE (DOG)

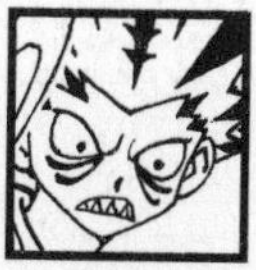

KANZAI (TIGER)

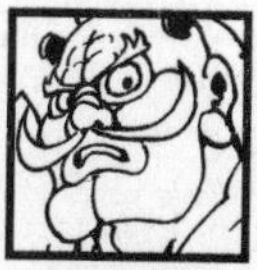

BOTOBAI (DRAGON)

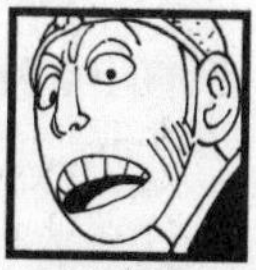

SAIYU (MONKEY)

HUNTER×HUNTER

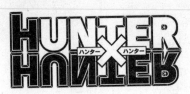

Volume 33

CONTENTS

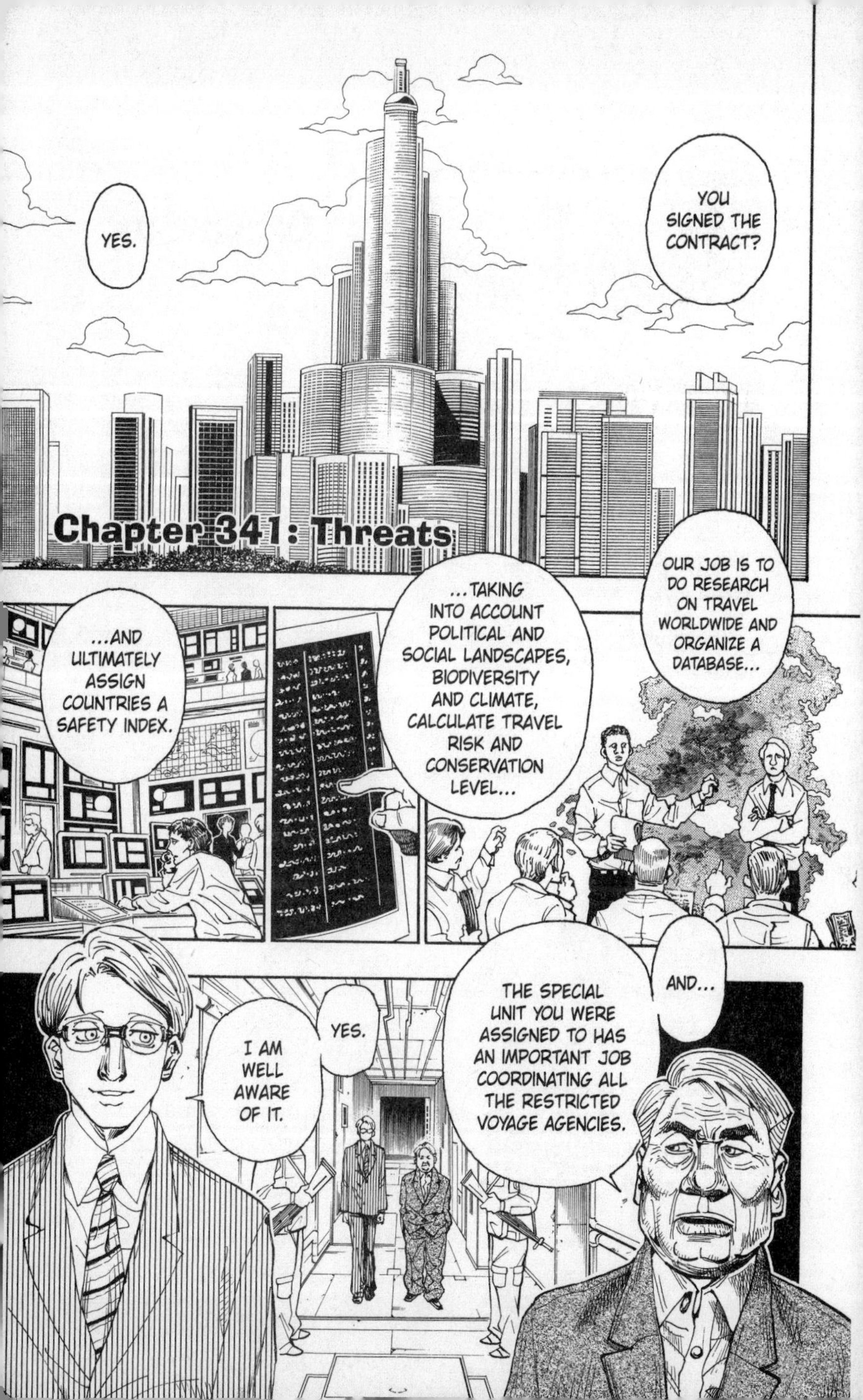
YOU SIGNED THE CONTRACT?
YES.
Chapter 341: Threats
OUR JOB IS TO DO RESEARCH ON TRAVEL WORLDWIDE AND ORGANIZE A DATABASE...
...TAKING INTO ACCOUNT POLITICAL AND SOCIAL LANDSCAPES, BIODIVERSITY AND CLIMATE, CALCULATE TRAVEL RISK AND CONSERVATION LEVEL...
...AND ULTIMATELY ASSIGN COUNTRIES A SAFETY INDEX.
AND...
THE SPECIAL UNIT YOU WERE ASSIGNED TO HAS AN IMPORTANT JOB COORDINATING ALL THE RESTRICTED VOYAGE AGENCIES.
YES.
I AM WELL AWARE OF IT.

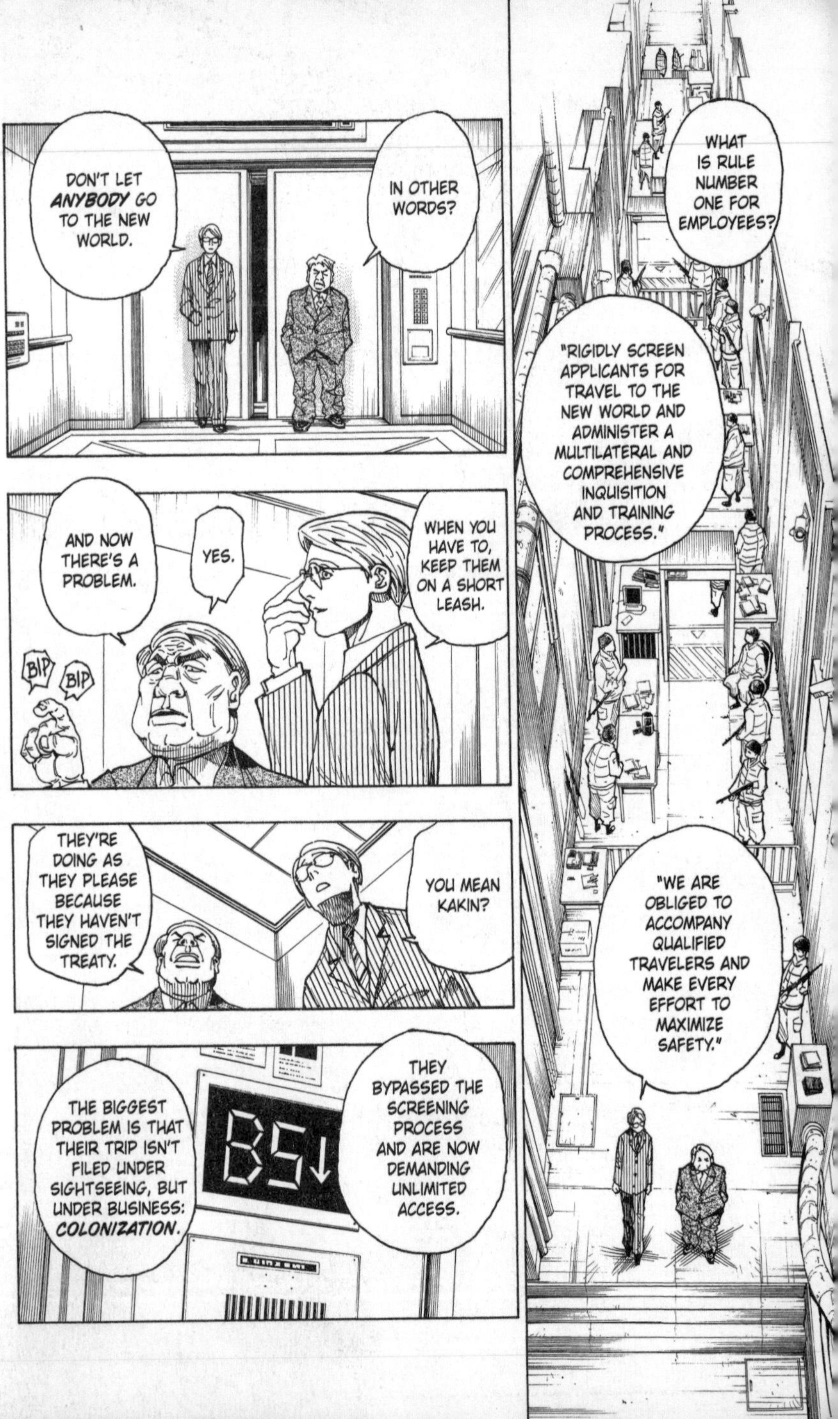
WHAT IS RULE NUMBER ONE FOR EMPLOYEES?
"RIGIDLY SCREEN APPLICANTS FOR TRAVEL TO THE NEW WORLD AND ADMINISTER A MULTILATERAL AND COMPREHENSIVE INQUISITION AND TRAINING PROCESS."
"WE ARE OBLIGED TO ACCOMPANY QUALIFIED TRAVELERS AND MAKE EVERY EFFORT TO MAXIMIZE SAFETY."
IN OTHER WORDS?
DON'T LET ***ANYBODY*** GO TO THE NEW WORLD.
WHEN YOU HAVE TO, KEEP THEM ON A SHORT LEASH.
YES.
AND NOW THERE'S A PROBLEM.
BIP
BIP
YOU MEAN KAKIN?
THEY'RE DOING AS THEY PLEASE BECAUSE THEY HAVEN'T SIGNED THE TREATY.
THEY BYPASSED THE SCREENING PROCESS AND ARE NOW DEMANDING UNLIMITED ACCESS.
B5↓
THE BIGGEST PROBLEM IS THAT THEIR TRIP ISN'T FILED UNDER SIGHTSEEING, BUT UNDER BUSINESS: ***COLONIZATION***.

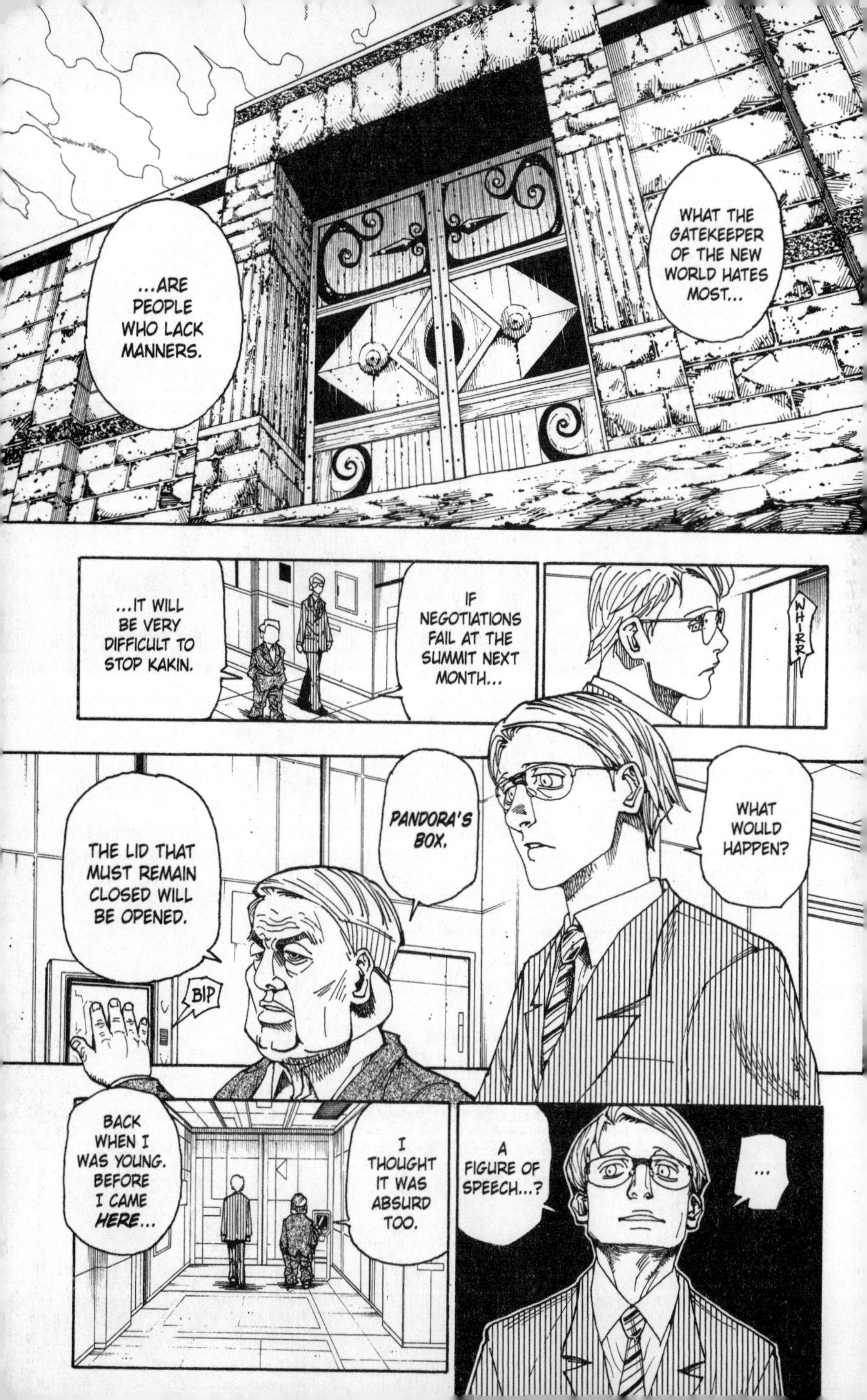
WHAT THE GATEKEEPER OF THE NEW WORLD HATES MOST...
...ARE PEOPLE WHO LACK MANNERS.
WHIRR
IF NEGOTIATIONS FAIL AT THE SUMMIT NEXT MONTH...
...IT WILL BE VERY DIFFICULT TO STOP KAKIN.
WHAT WOULD HAPPEN?
PANDORA'S BOX.
THE LID THAT MUST REMAIN CLOSED WILL BE OPENED.
BIP
A FIGURE OF SPEECH...?
...
I THOUGHT IT WAS ABSURD TOO.
BACK WHEN I WAS YOUNG. BEFORE I CAME *HERE*...

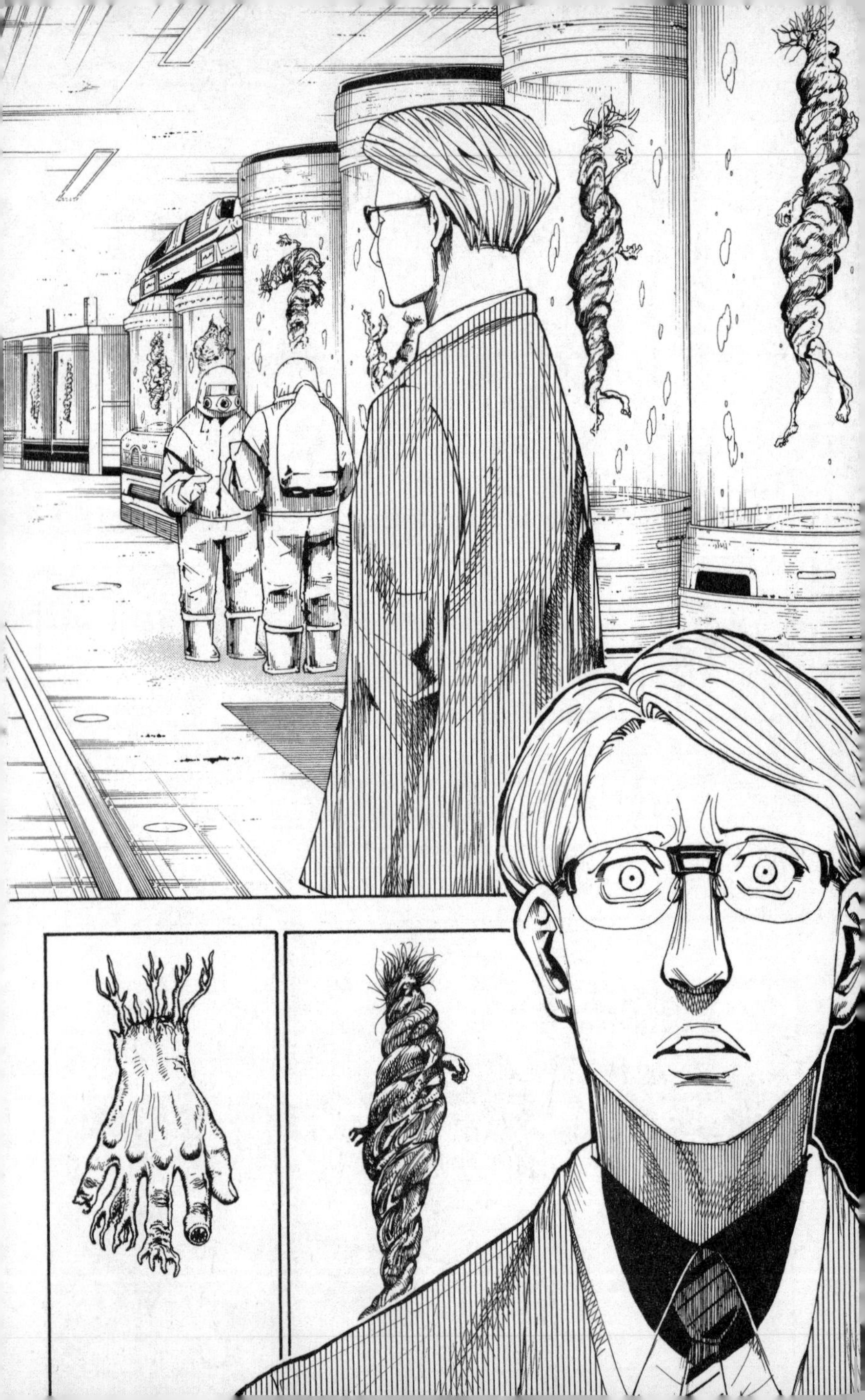

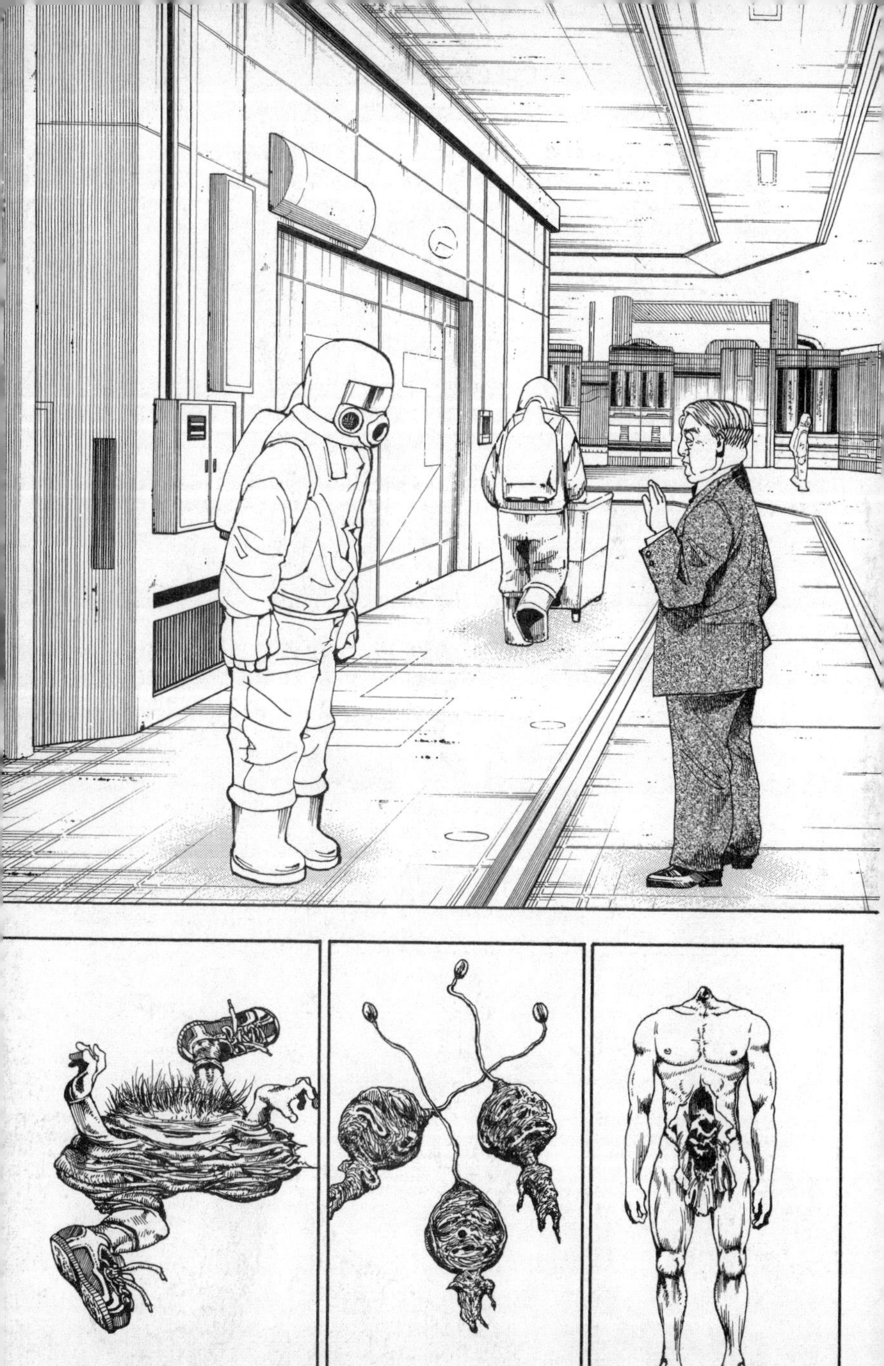

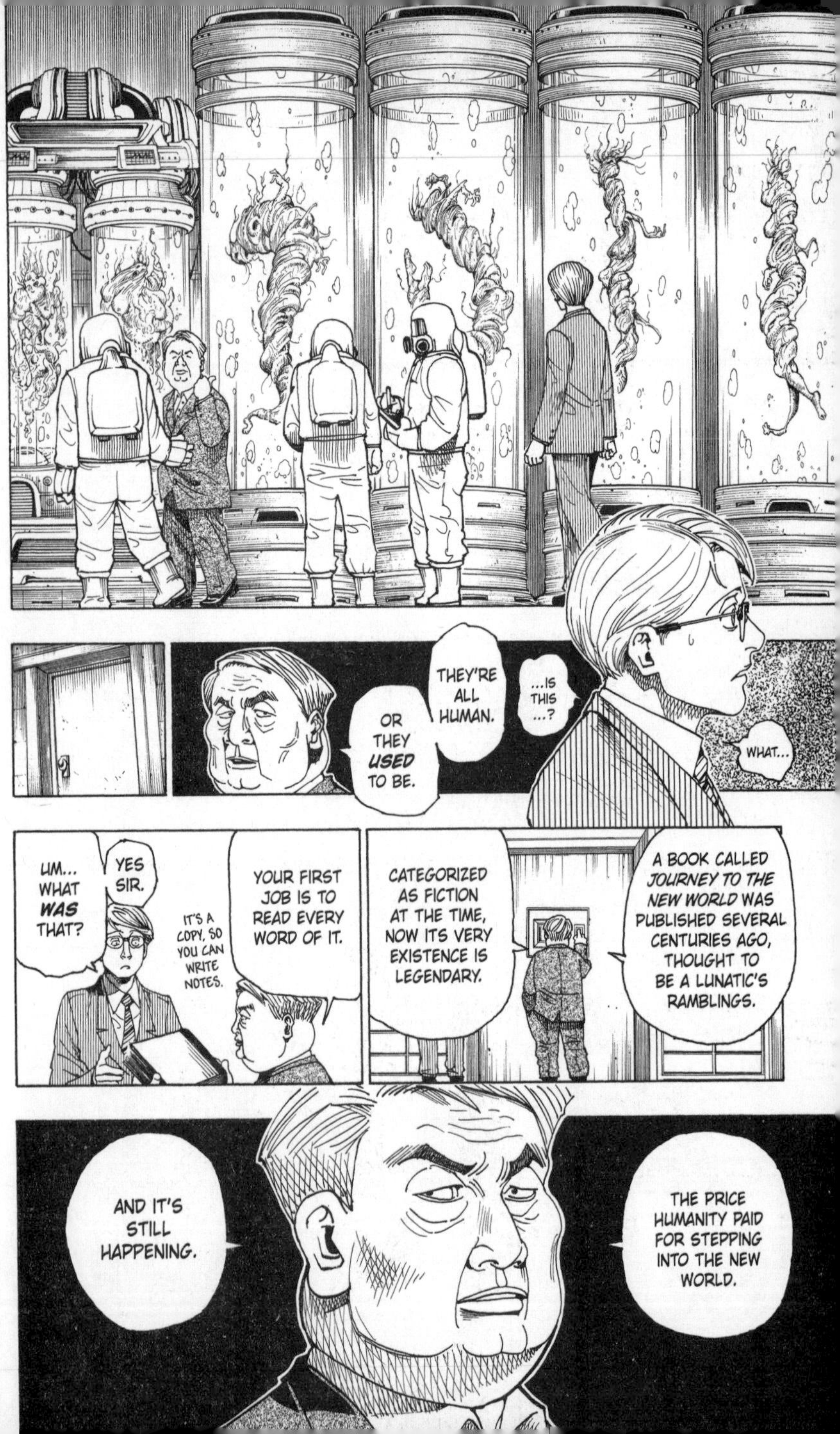
WHAT...
...IS THIS ...?
THEY'RE ALL HUMAN.
OR THEY *USED* TO BE.
A BOOK CALLED *JOURNEY TO THE NEW WORLD* WAS PUBLISHED SEVERAL CENTURIES AGO, THOUGHT TO BE A LUNATIC'S RAMBLINGS.
CATEGORIZED AS FICTION AT THE TIME, NOW ITS VERY EXISTENCE IS LEGENDARY.
YOUR FIRST JOB IS TO READ EVERY WORD OF IT.
IT'S A COPY, SO YOU CAN WRITE NOTES.
YES SIR.
UM... WHAT *WAS* THAT?
THE PRICE HUMANITY PAID FOR STEPPING INTO THE NEW WORLD.
AND IT'S STILL HAPPENING.

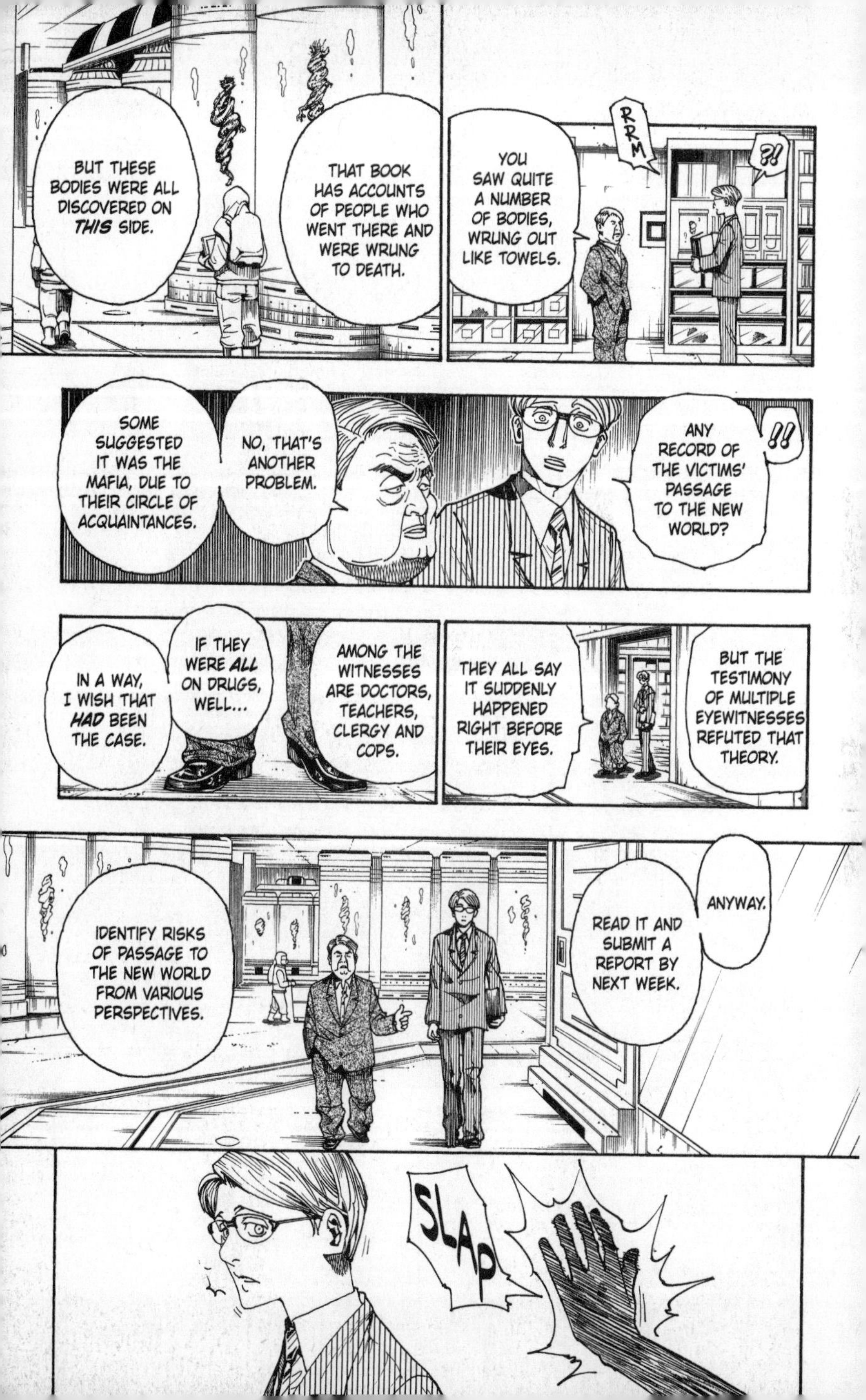
RRM
?!
YOU SAW QUITE A NUMBER OF BODIES, WRUNG OUT LIKE TOWELS.
THAT BOOK HAS ACCOUNTS OF PEOPLE WHO WENT THERE AND WERE WRUNG TO DEATH.
BUT THESE BODIES WERE ALL DISCOVERED ON *THIS* SIDE.
!!
ANY RECORD OF THE VICTIMS' PASSAGE TO THE NEW WORLD?
NO, THAT'S ANOTHER PROBLEM.
SOME SUGGESTED IT WAS THE MAFIA, DUE TO THEIR CIRCLE OF ACQUAINTANCES.
BUT THE TESTIMONY OF MULTIPLE EYEWITNESSES REFUTED THAT THEORY.
THEY ALL SAY IT SUDDENLY HAPPENED RIGHT BEFORE THEIR EYES.
AMONG THE WITNESSES ARE DOCTORS, TEACHERS, CLERGY AND COPS.
IF THEY WERE *ALL* ON DRUGS, WELL...
IN A WAY, I WISH THAT *HAD* BEEN THE CASE.
ANYWAY.
READ IT AND SUBMIT A REPORT BY NEXT WEEK.
IDENTIFY RISKS OF PASSAGE TO THE NEW WORLD FROM VARIOUS PERSPECTIVES.
SLAP

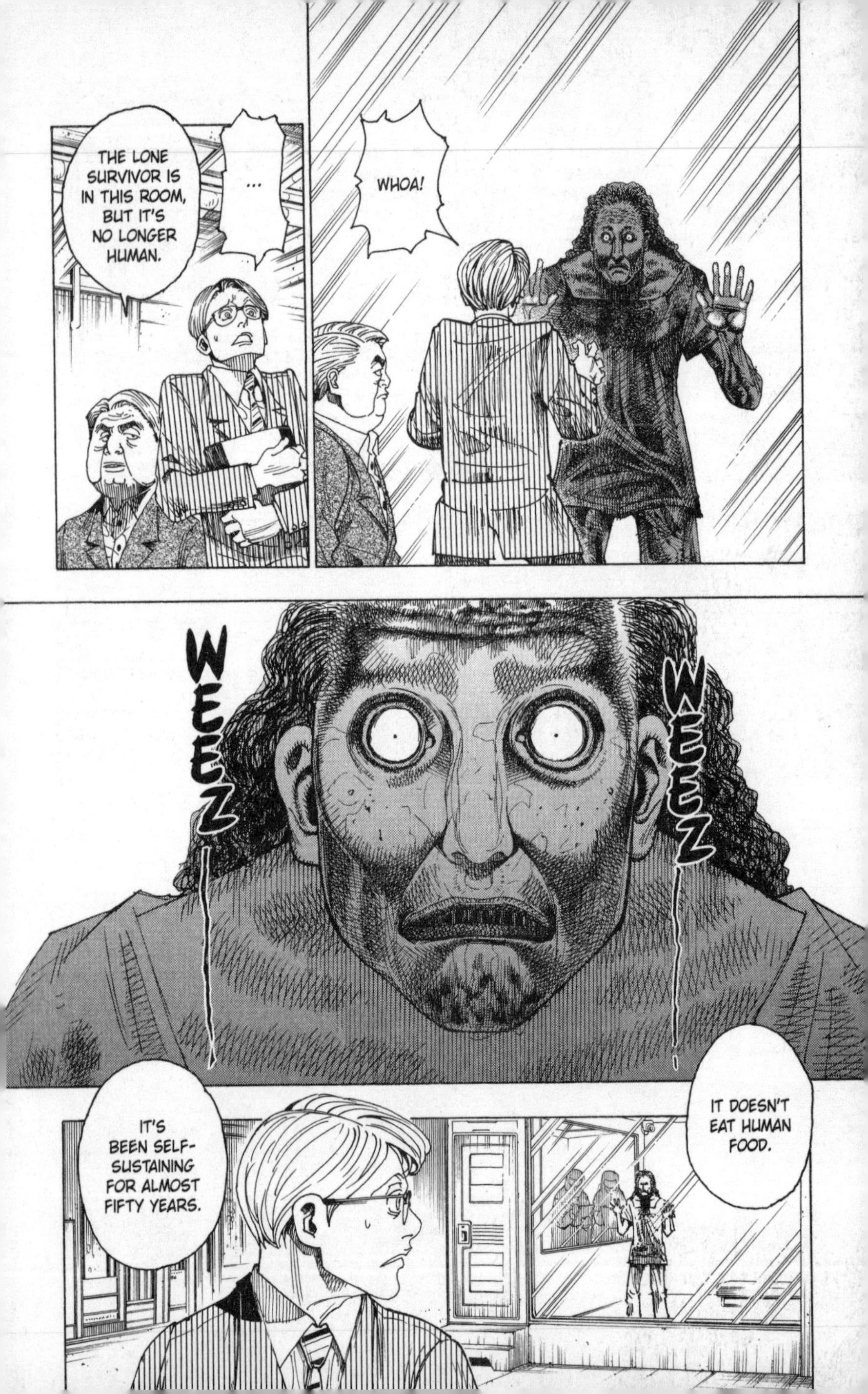
WHOA!
...
THE LONE SURVIVOR IS IN THIS ROOM, BUT IT'S NO LONGER HUMAN.
WEEZ
WEEZ
IT DOESN'T EAT HUMAN FOOD.
IT'S BEEN SELF-SUSTAINING FOR ALMOST FIFTY YEARS.

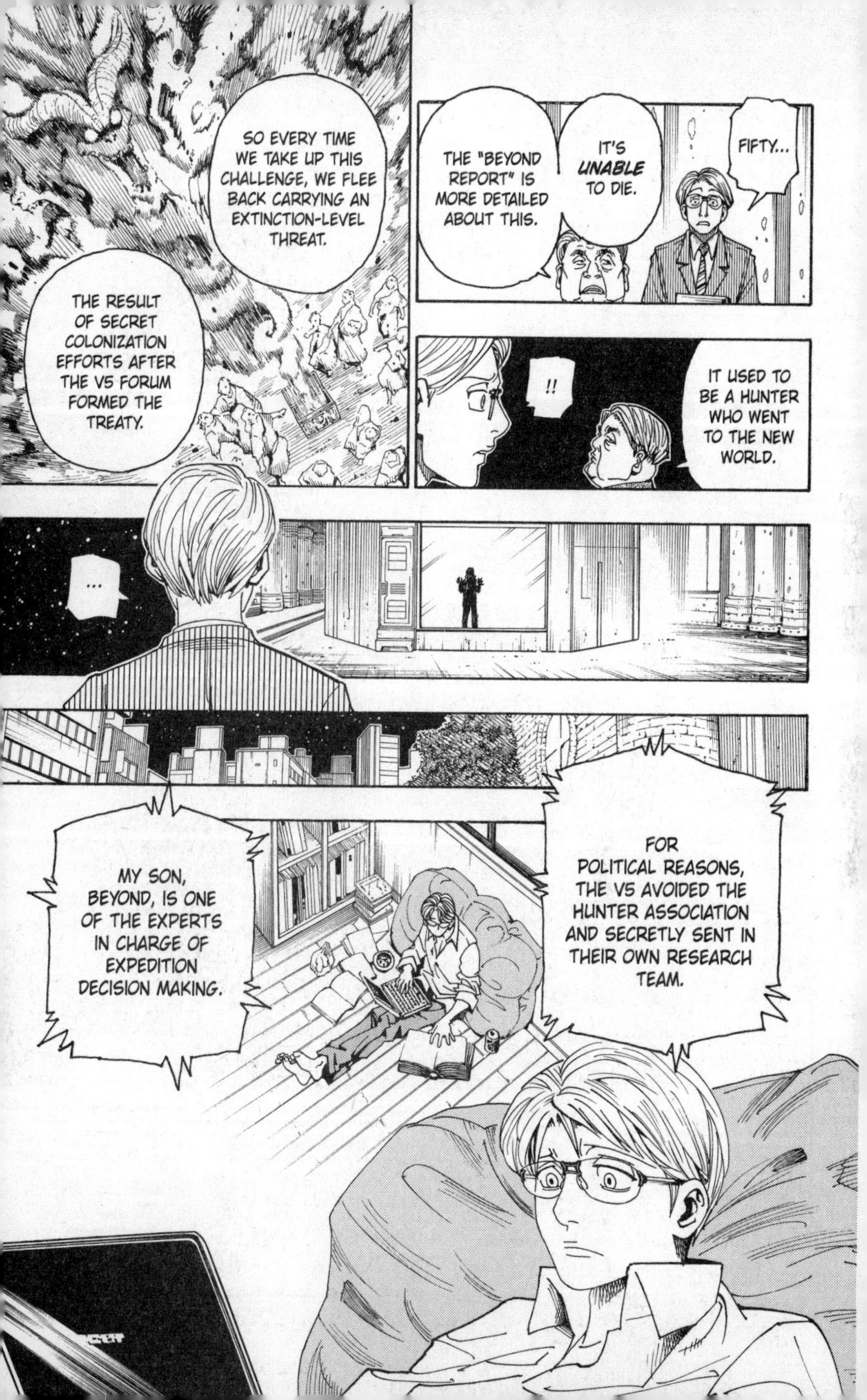
FIFTY...
IT'S *UNABLE* TO DIE.
THE "BEYOND REPORT" IS MORE DETAILED ABOUT THIS.
IT USED TO BE A HUNTER WHO WENT TO THE NEW WORLD.
!!
SO EVERY TIME WE TAKE UP THIS CHALLENGE, WE FLEE BACK CARRYING AN EXTINCTION-LEVEL THREAT.
THE RESULT OF SECRET COLONIZATION EFFORTS AFTER THE V5 FORUM FORMED THE TREATY.
...
FOR POLITICAL REASONS, THE V5 AVOIDED THE HUNTER ASSOCIATION AND SECRETLY SENT IN THEIR OWN RESEARCH TEAM.
MY SON, BEYOND, IS ONE OF THE EXPERTS IN CHARGE OF EXPEDITION DECISION MAKING.

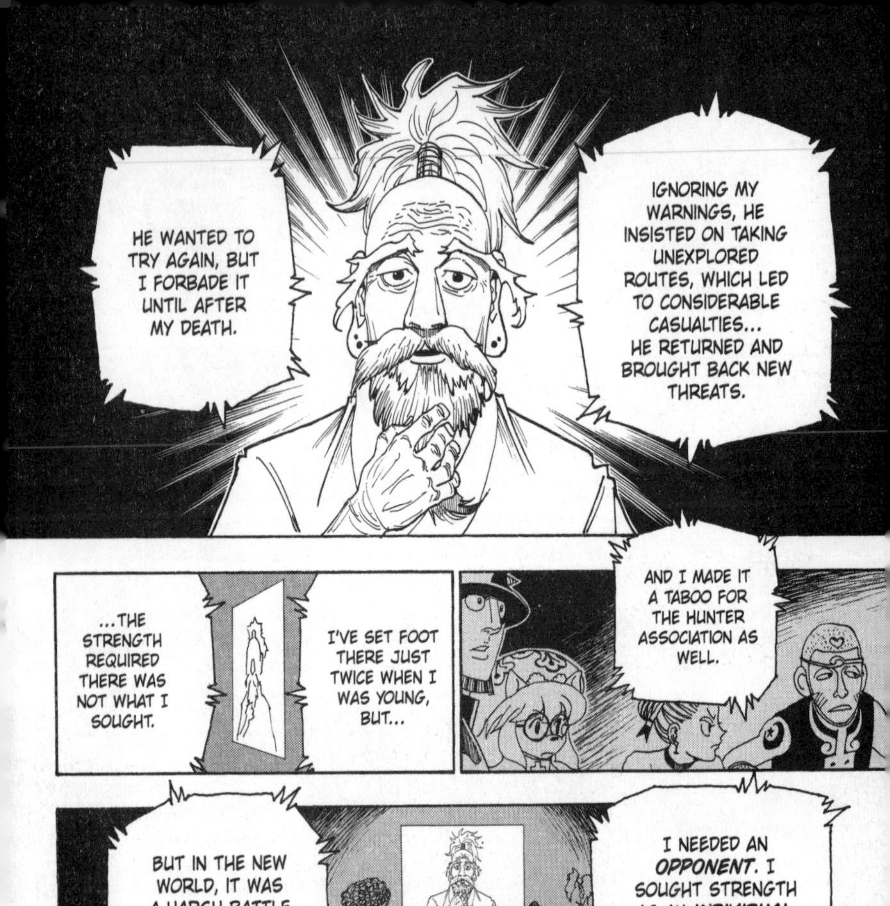
IGNORING MY WARNINGS, HE INSISTED ON TAKING UNEXPLORED ROUTES, WHICH LED TO CONSIDERABLE CASUALTIES... HE RETURNED AND BROUGHT BACK NEW THREATS.
HE WANTED TO TRY AGAIN, BUT I FORBADE IT UNTIL AFTER MY DEATH.
AND I MADE IT A TABOO FOR THE HUNTER ASSOCIATION AS WELL.
I'VE SET FOOT THERE JUST TWICE WHEN I WAS YOUNG, BUT...
...THE STRENGTH REQUIRED THERE WAS NOT WHAT I SOUGHT.
I NEEDED AN *OPPONENT*. I SOUGHT STRENGTH AS AN *INDIVIDUAL*, WITH EITHER VICTORY OR DEFEAT AS AN OUTCOME.
BUT IN THE NEW WORLD, IT WAS A HARSH BATTLE AGAINST MOTHER NATURE, WHERE NO VICTOR EXISTS.
THE STRENGTH MY SON DESIRED WAS FORMIDABLE AND ESSENTIAL TO EXPLORING THERE.
IF ANYTHING, HE'S PROBABLY MORE SUITED TO BEING A HUNTER THAN I.

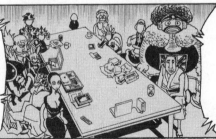

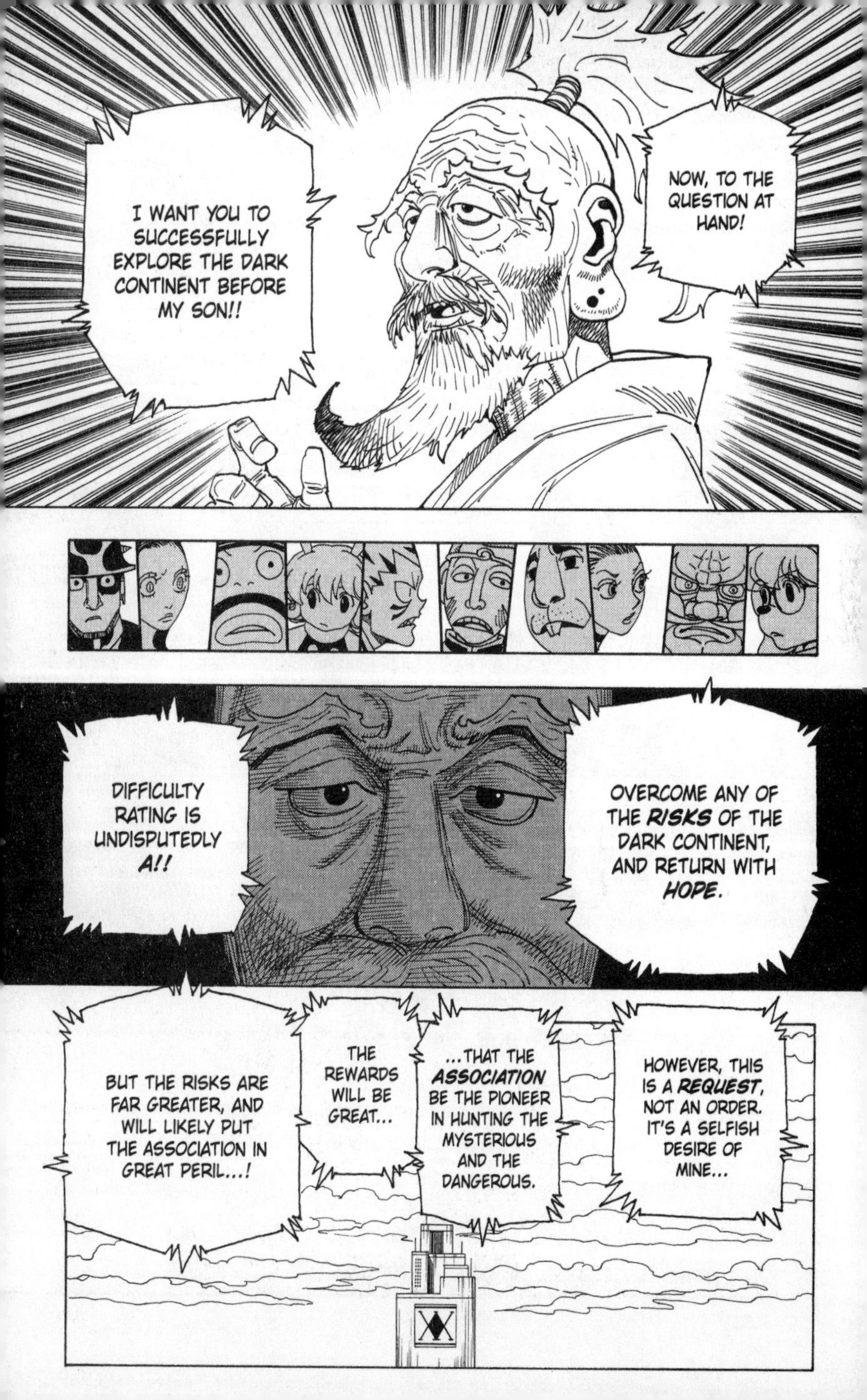
NOW, TO THE QUESTION AT HAND!
I WANT YOU TO SUCCESSFULLY EXPLORE THE DARK CONTINENT BEFORE MY SON!!
OVERCOME ANY OF THE ***RISKS*** OF THE DARK CONTINENT, AND RETURN WITH ***HOPE***.
DIFFICULTY RATING IS UNDISPUTEDLY ***A!!***
HOWEVER, THIS IS A ***REQUEST***, NOT AN ORDER. IT'S A SELFISH DESIRE OF MINE...
...THAT THE ***ASSOCIATION*** BE THE PIONEER IN HUNTING THE MYSTERIOUS AND THE DANGEROUS.
THE REWARDS WILL BE GREAT...
BUT THE RISKS ARE FAR GREATER, AND WILL LIKELY PUT THE ASSOCIATION IN GREAT PERIL...!

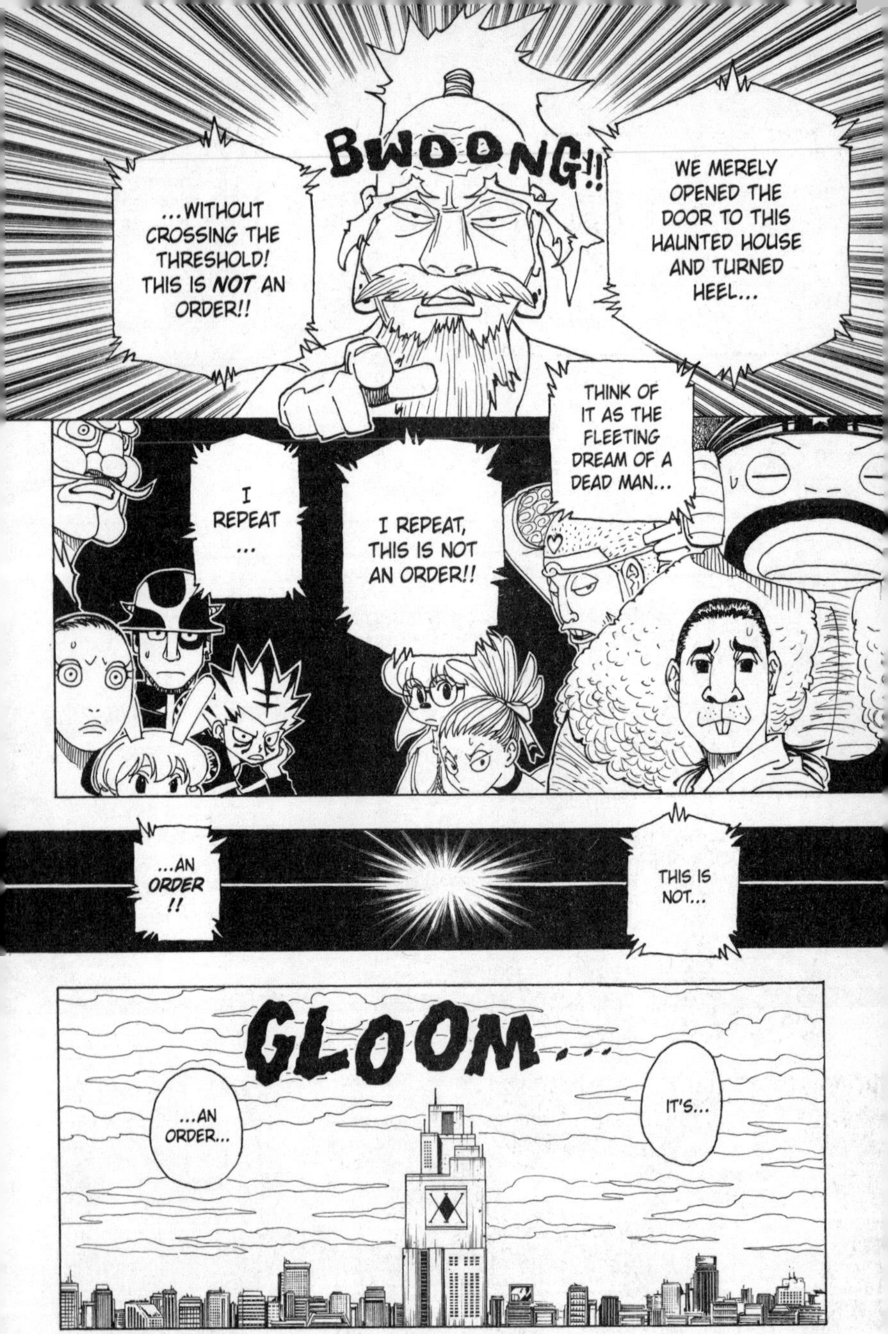
WE MERELY OPENED THE DOOR TO THIS HAUNTED HOUSE AND TURNED HEEL...
BWOONG!!
...WITHOUT CROSSING THE THRESHOLD! THIS IS NOT AN ORDER!!
THINK OF IT AS THE FLEETING DREAM OF A DEAD MAN...
I REPEAT, THIS IS NOT AN ORDER!!
I REPEAT ...
THIS IS NOT...
...AN ORDER !!
GLOOM...
IT'S...
...AN ORDER...

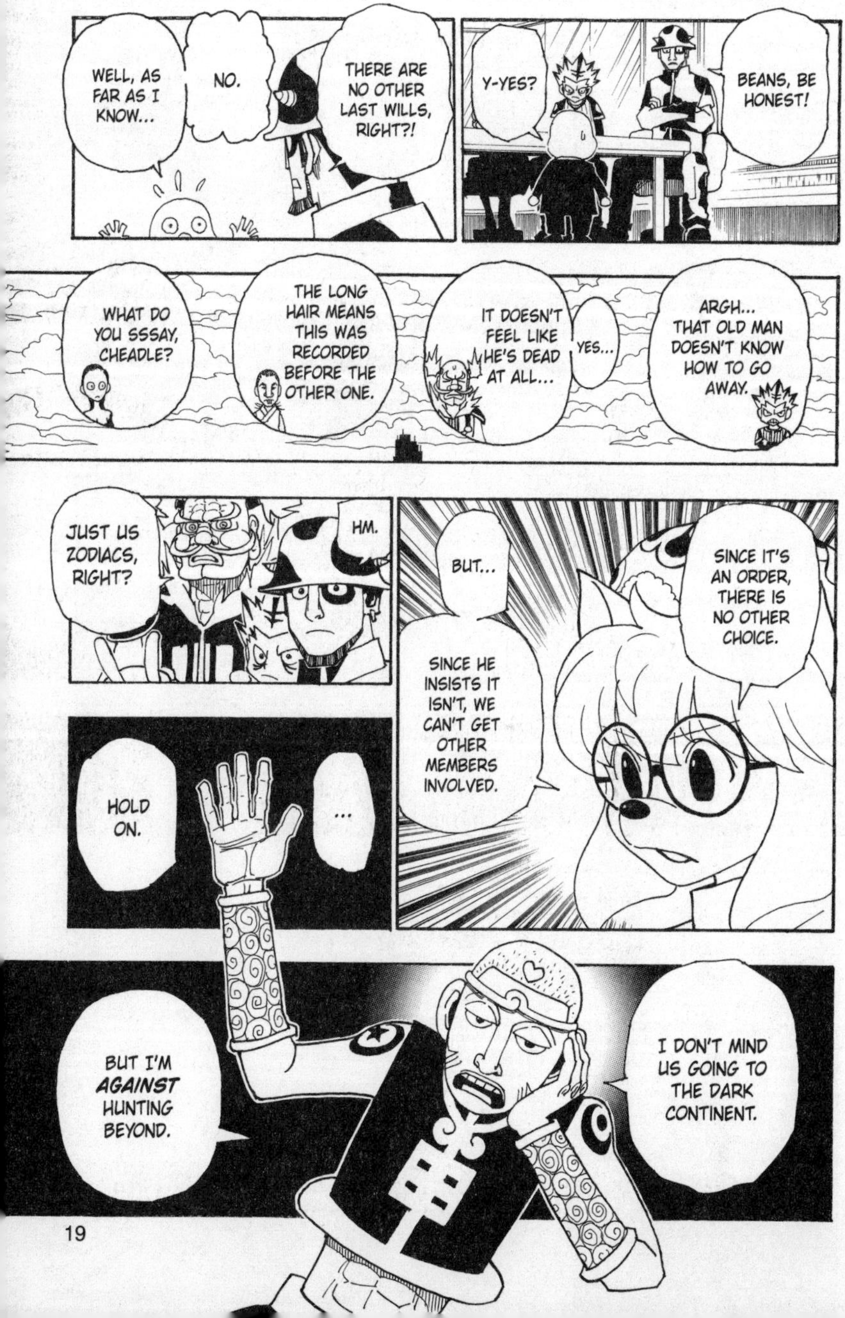
BEANS, BE HONEST!
Y-YES?
THERE ARE NO OTHER LAST WILLS, RIGHT?!
NO.
WELL, AS FAR AS I KNOW...
ARGH... THAT OLD MAN DOESN'T KNOW HOW TO GO AWAY.
YES...
IT DOESN'T FEEL LIKE HE'S DEAD AT ALL...
THE LONG HAIR MEANS THIS WAS RECORDED BEFORE THE OTHER ONE.
WHAT DO YOU SSSAY, CHEADLE?
SINCE IT'S AN ORDER, THERE IS NO OTHER CHOICE.
BUT...
SINCE HE INSISTS IT ISN'T, WE CAN'T GET OTHER MEMBERS INVOLVED.
HM.
JUST US ZODIACS, RIGHT?
...
HOLD ON.
I DON'T MIND US GOING TO THE DARK CONTINENT.
BUT I'M *AGAINST* HUNTING BEYOND.

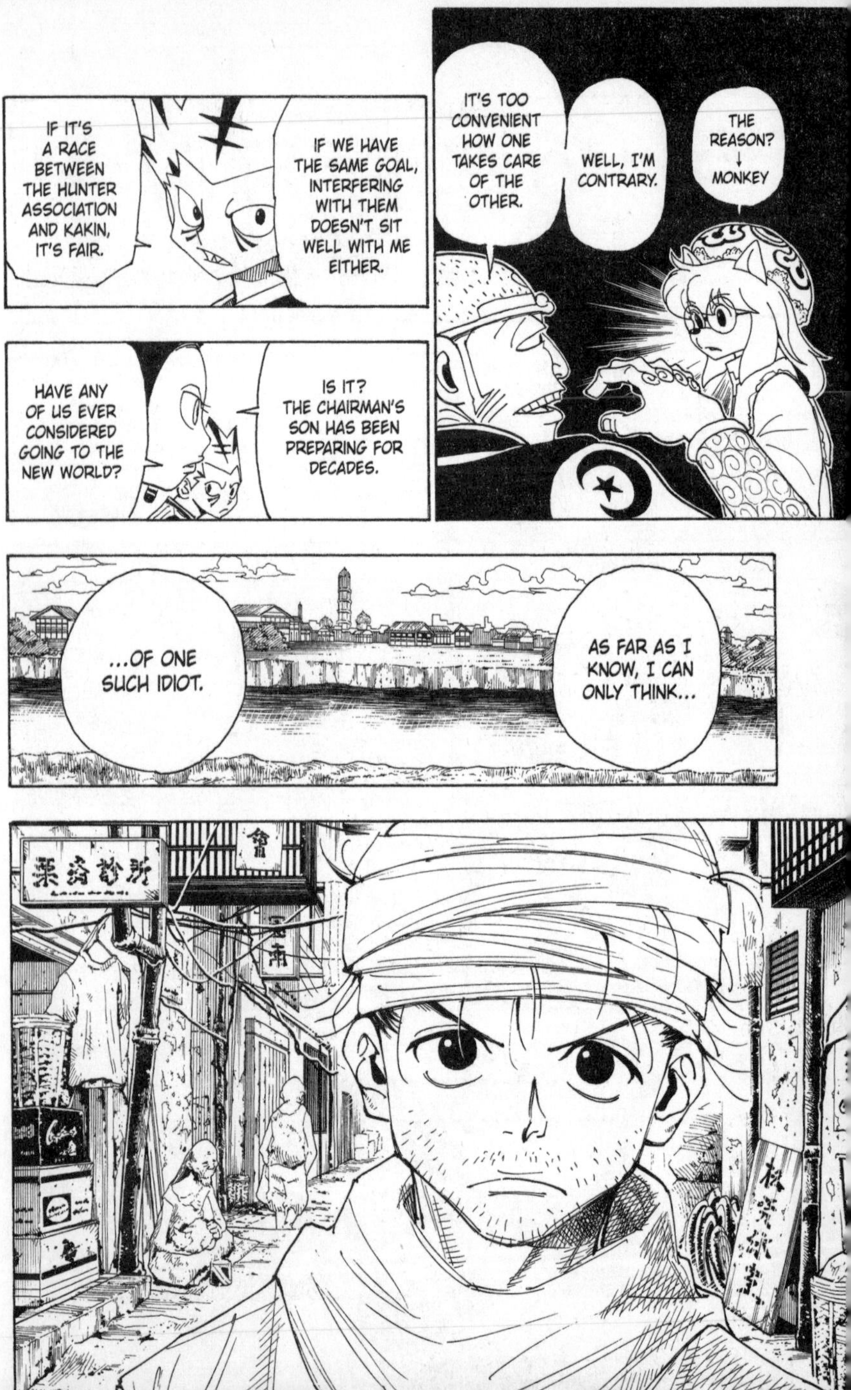
THE REASON? ↓ MONKEY
WELL, I'M CONTRARY.
IT'S TOO CONVENIENT HOW ONE TAKES CARE OF THE OTHER.
IF WE HAVE THE SAME GOAL, INTERFERING WITH THEM DOESN'T SIT WELL WITH ME EITHER.
IF IT'S A RACE BETWEEN THE HUNTER ASSOCIATION AND KAKIN, IT'S FAIR.
IS IT? THE CHAIRMAN'S SON HAS BEEN PREPARING FOR DECADES.
HAVE ANY OF US EVER CONSIDERED GOING TO THE NEW WORLD?
AS FAR AS I KNOW, I CAN ONLY THINK...
...OF ONE SUCH IDIOT.

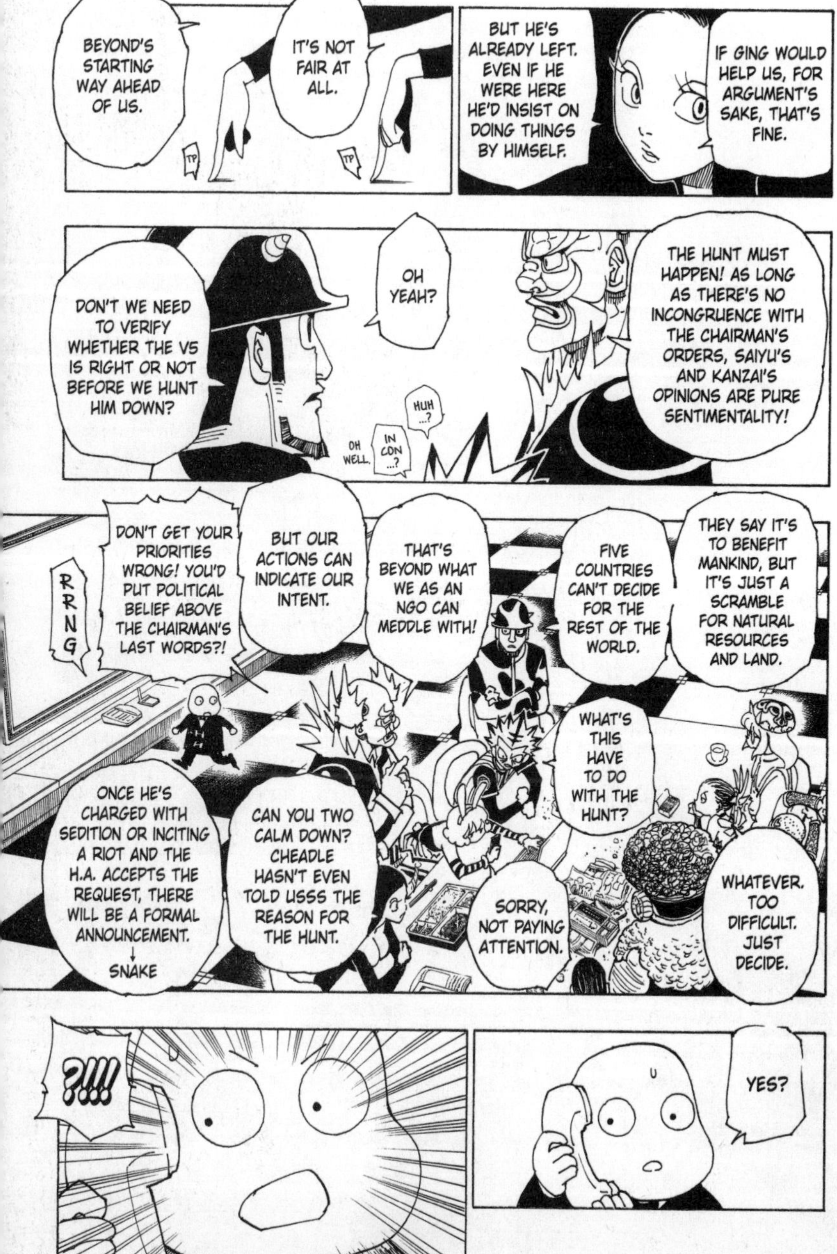
IF GING WOULD HELP US, FOR ARGUMENT'S SAKE, THAT'S FINE.
BUT HE'S ALREADY LEFT. EVEN IF HE WERE HERE HE'D INSIST ON DOING THINGS BY HIMSELF.
IT'S NOT FAIR AT ALL.
TP
BEYOND'S STARTING WAY AHEAD OF US.
TP
THE HUNT MUST HAPPEN! AS LONG AS THERE'S NO INCONGRUENCE WITH THE CHAIRMAN'S ORDERS, SAIYU'S AND KANZAI'S OPINIONS ARE PURE SENTIMENTALITY!
OH YEAH?
DON'T WE NEED TO VERIFY WHETHER THE V5 IS RIGHT OR NOT BEFORE WE HUNT HIM DOWN?
HUH ...?
IN CON ...?
OH WELL.
THEY SAY IT'S TO BENEFIT MANKIND, BUT IT'S JUST A SCRAMBLE FOR NATURAL RESOURCES AND LAND.
FIVE COUNTRIES CAN'T DECIDE FOR THE REST OF THE WORLD.
THAT'S BEYOND WHAT WE AS AN NGO CAN MEDDLE WITH!
BUT OUR ACTIONS CAN INDICATE OUR INTENT.
DON'T GET YOUR PRIORITIES WRONG! YOU'D PUT POLITICAL BELIEF ABOVE THE CHAIRMAN'S LAST WORDS?!
RRNG
WHAT'S THIS HAVE TO DO WITH THE HUNT?
WHATEVER. TOO DIFFICULT. JUST DECIDE.
SORRY, NOT PAYING ATTENTION.
CAN YOU TWO CALM DOWN? CHEADLE HASN'T EVEN TOLD USSS THE REASON FOR THE HUNT.
ONCE HE'S CHARGED WITH SEDITION OR INCITING A RIOT AND THE H.A. ACCEPTS THE REQUEST, THERE WILL BE A FORMAL ANNOUNCEMENT.
↓
SNAKE
YES?
?!!!

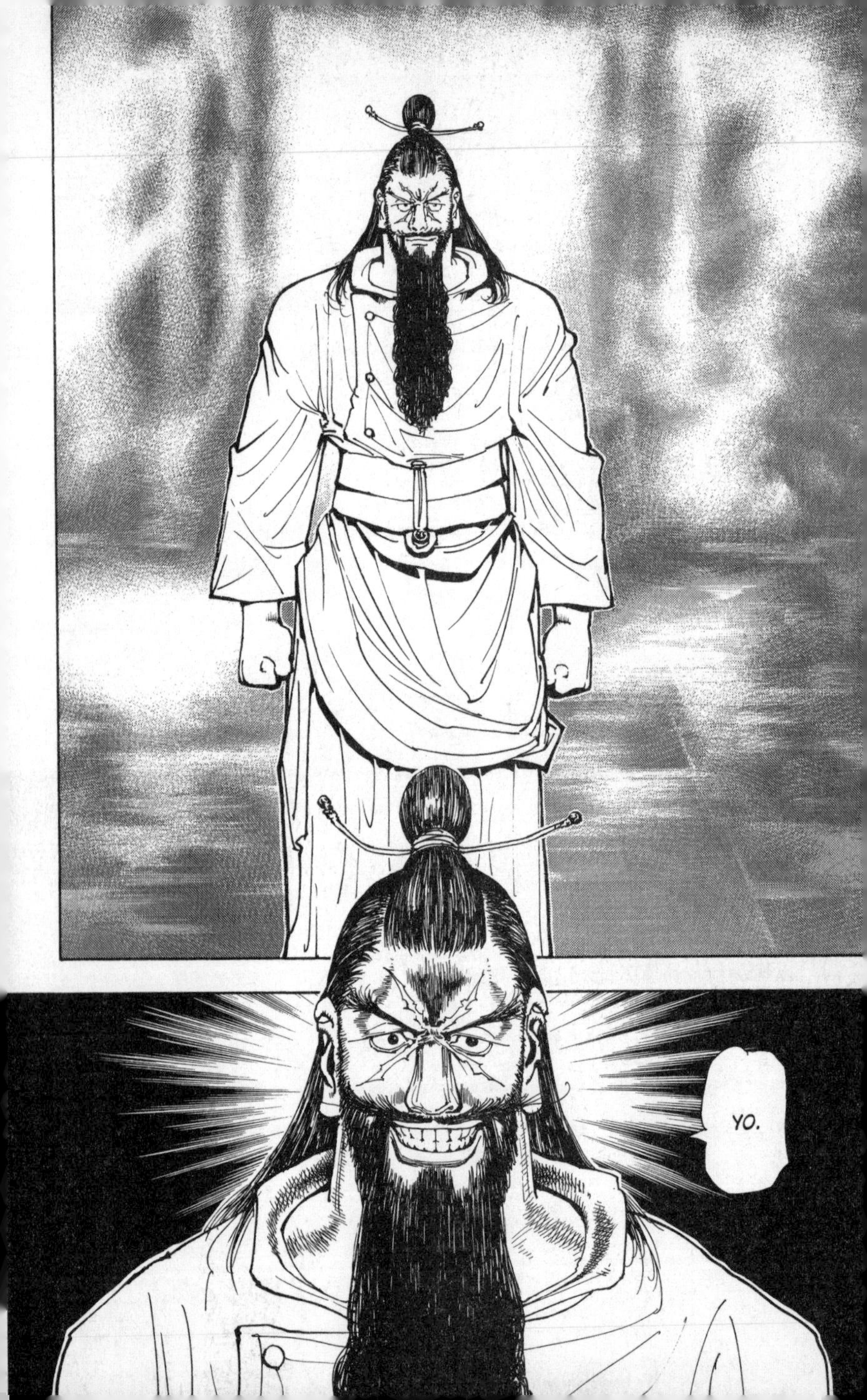
YO.

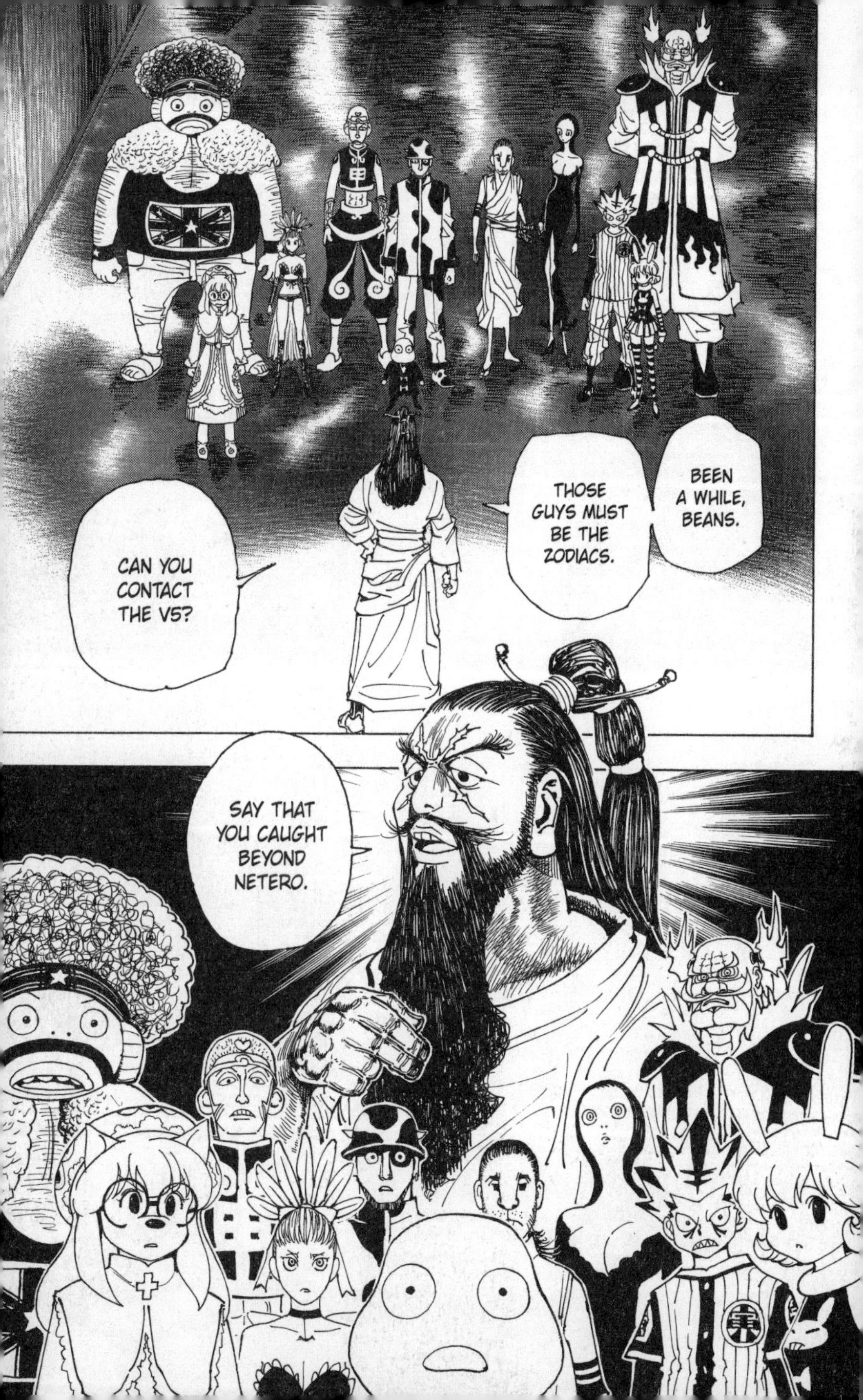
BEEN A WHILE, BEANS.
THOSE GUYS MUST BE THE ZODIACS.
CAN YOU CONTACT THE V5?
SAY THAT YOU CAUGHT BEYOND NETERO.

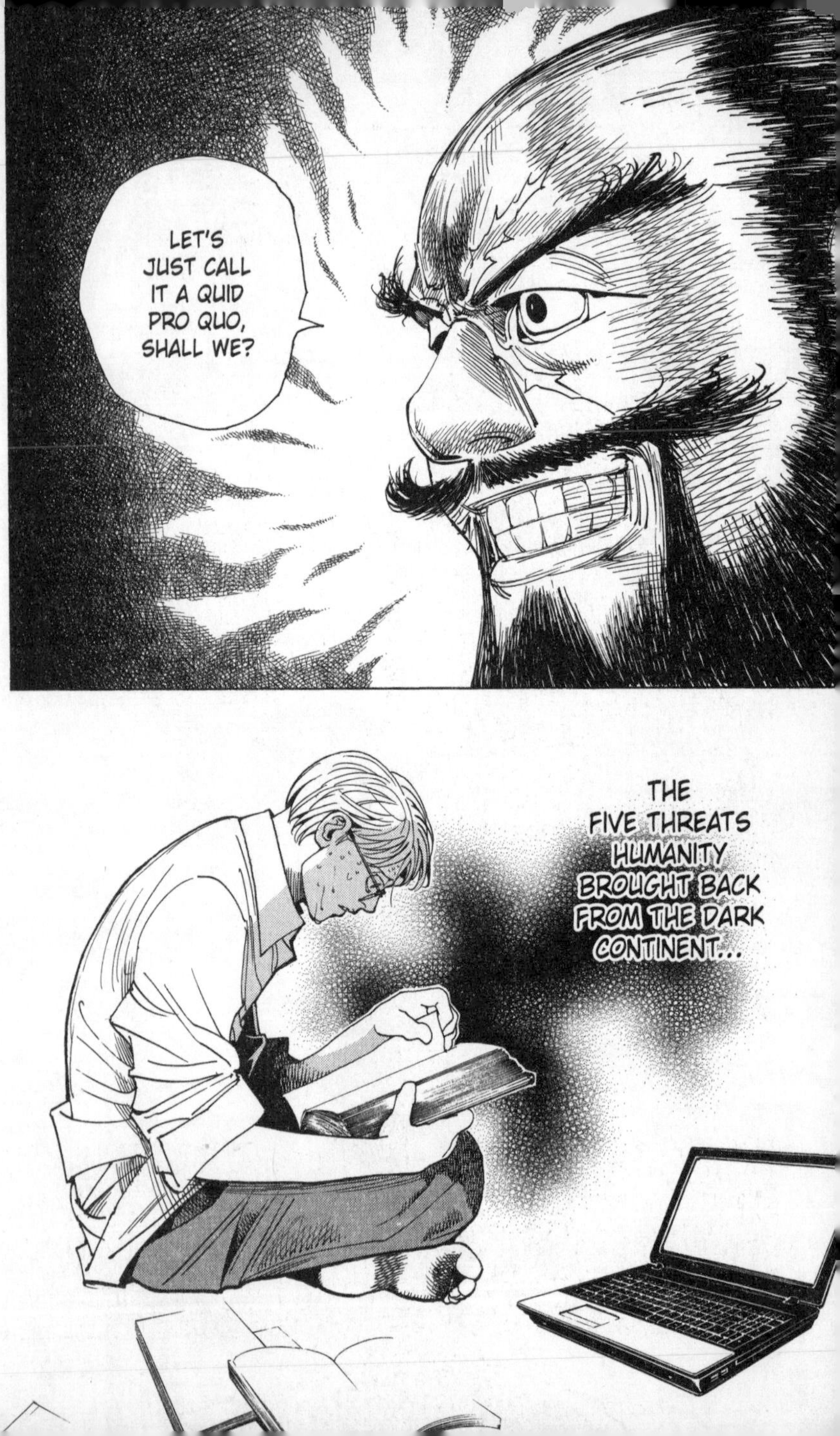
LET'S JUST CALL IT A QUID PRO QUO, SHALL WE?
THE FIVE THREATS HUMANITY BROUGHT BACK FROM THE DARK CONTINENT...

READ THIS WAY

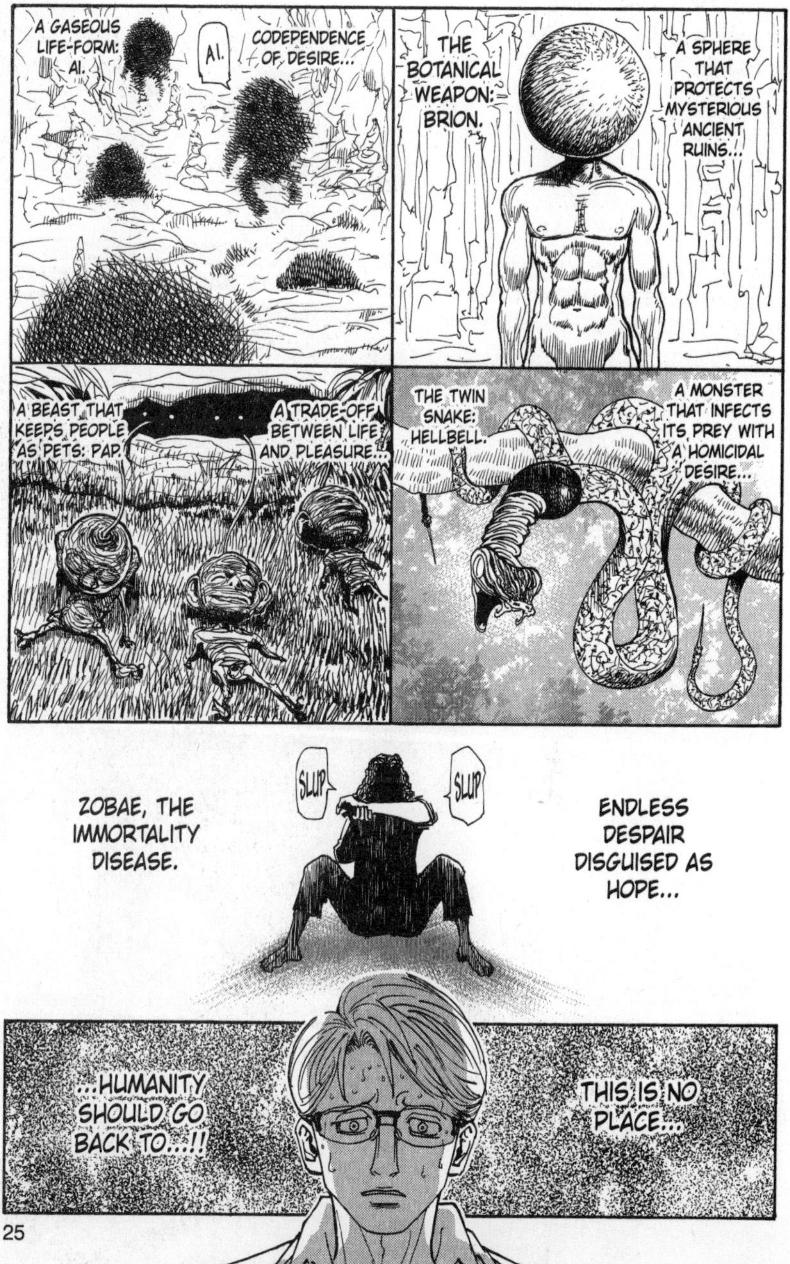

A SPHERE THAT PROTECTS MYSTERIOUS ANCIENT RUINS...
THE BOTANICAL WEAPON: BRION.
CODEPENDENCE OF DESIRE...
AI.
A GASEOUS LIFE-FORM: AI.
A MONSTER THAT INFECTS ITS PREY WITH A HOMICIDAL DESIRE...
THE TWIN SNAKE: HELLBELL.
A TRADE-OFF BETWEEN LIFE AND PLEASURE...
A BEAST THAT KEEPS PEOPLE AS PETS: PAP.
ENDLESS DESPAIR DISGUISED AS HOPE...
SLUP
SLUP
ZOBAE, THE IMMORTALITY DISEASE.
THIS IS NO PLACE...
...HUMANITY SHOULD GO BACK TO...!!

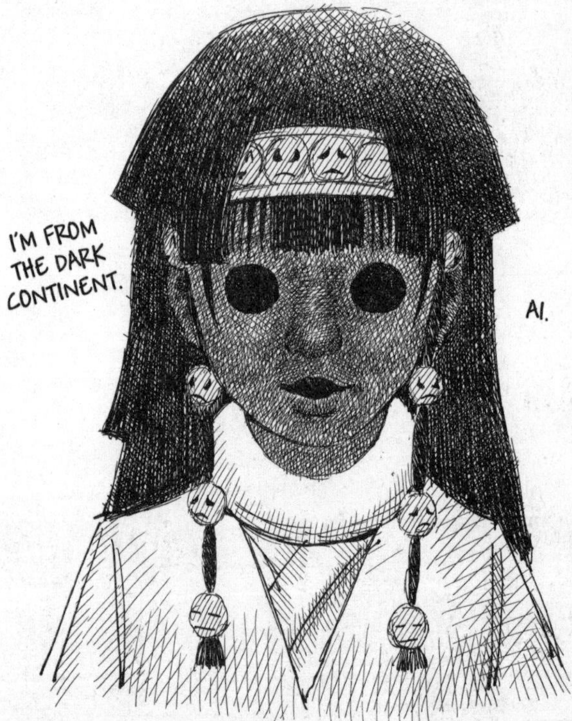
I'M FROM THE DARK CONTINENT.
AI.

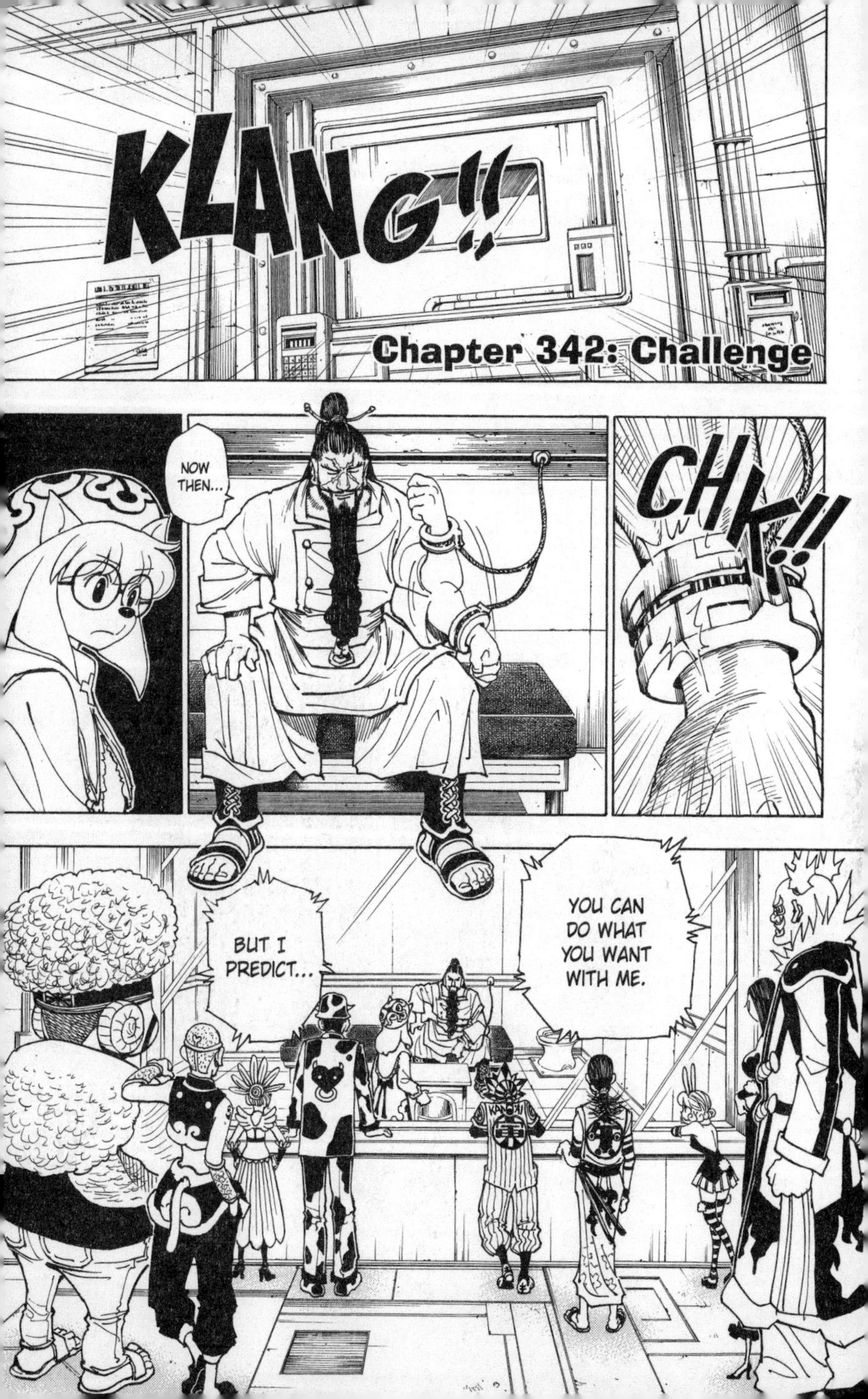
KLANG!!
Chapter 342: Challenge
CHK!!
NOW THEN...
YOU CAN DO WHAT YOU WANT WITH ME.
BUT I PREDICT...

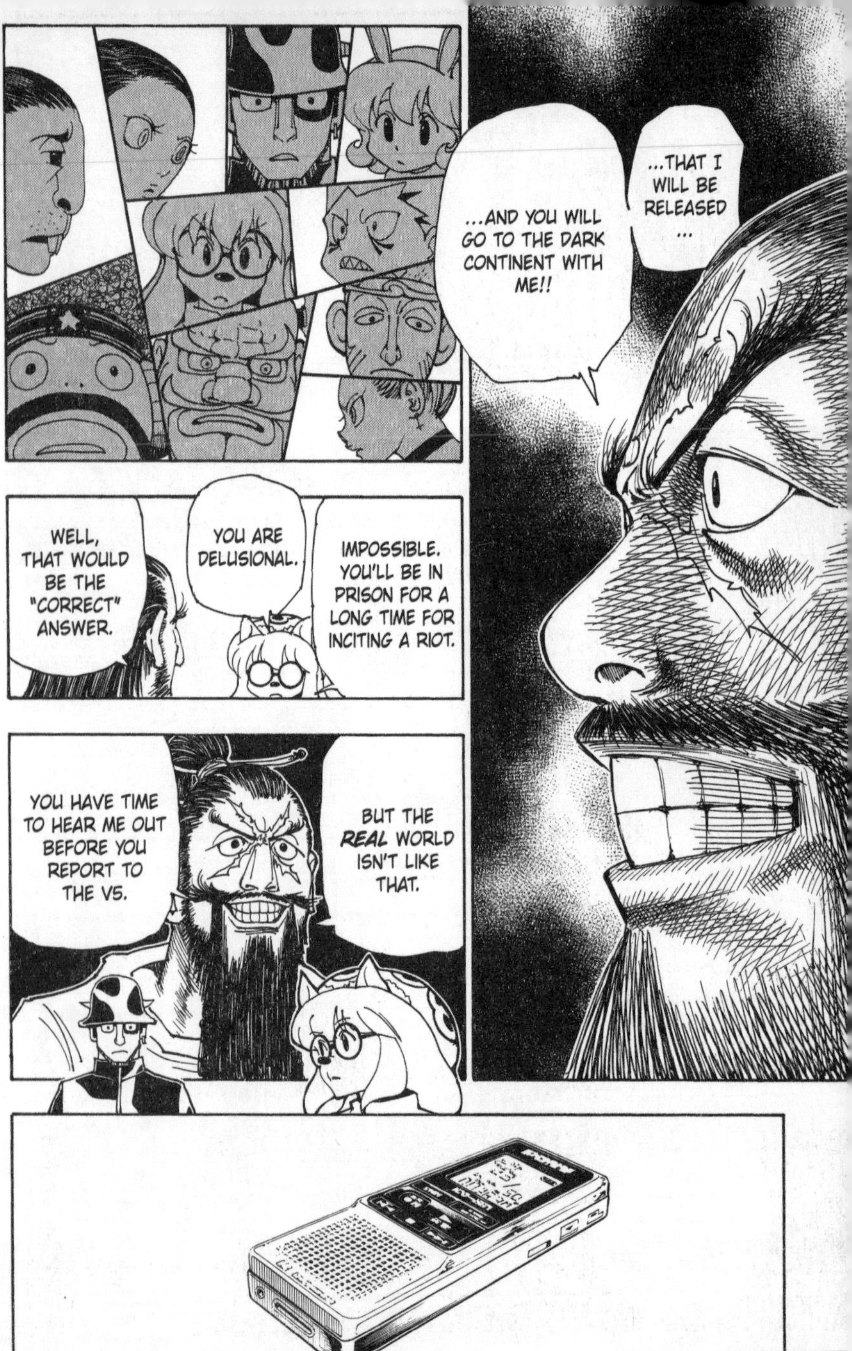
...THAT I WILL BE RELEASED ...
...AND YOU WILL GO TO THE DARK CONTINENT WITH ME!!
IMPOSSIBLE. YOU'LL BE IN PRISON FOR A LONG TIME FOR INCITING A RIOT.
YOU ARE DELUSIONAL.
WELL, THAT WOULD BE THE "CORRECT" ANSWER.
BUT THE *REAL* WORLD ISN'T LIKE THAT.
YOU HAVE TIME TO HEAR ME OUT BEFORE YOU REPORT TO THE V5.

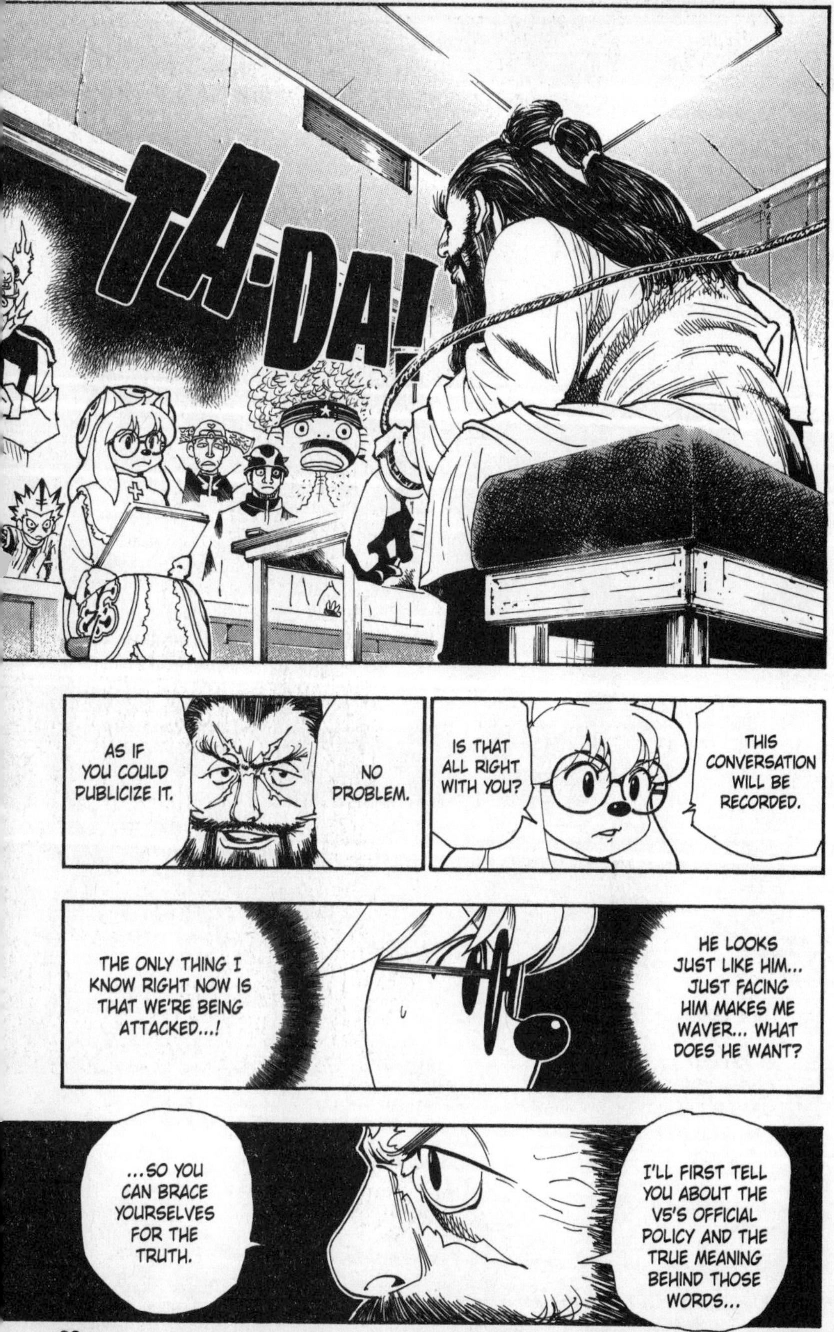
TA-DA!
THIS CONVERSATION WILL BE RECORDED.
IS THAT ALL RIGHT WITH YOU?
NO PROBLEM.
AS IF YOU COULD PUBLICIZE IT.
HE LOOKS JUST LIKE HIM... JUST FACING HIM MAKES ME WAVER... WHAT DOES HE WANT?
THE ONLY THING I KNOW RIGHT NOW IS THAT WE'RE BEING ATTACKED...!
I'LL FIRST TELL YOU ABOUT THE V5'S OFFICIAL POLICY AND THE TRUE MEANING BEHIND THOSE WORDS...
...SO YOU CAN BRACE YOURSELVES FOR THE TRUTH.

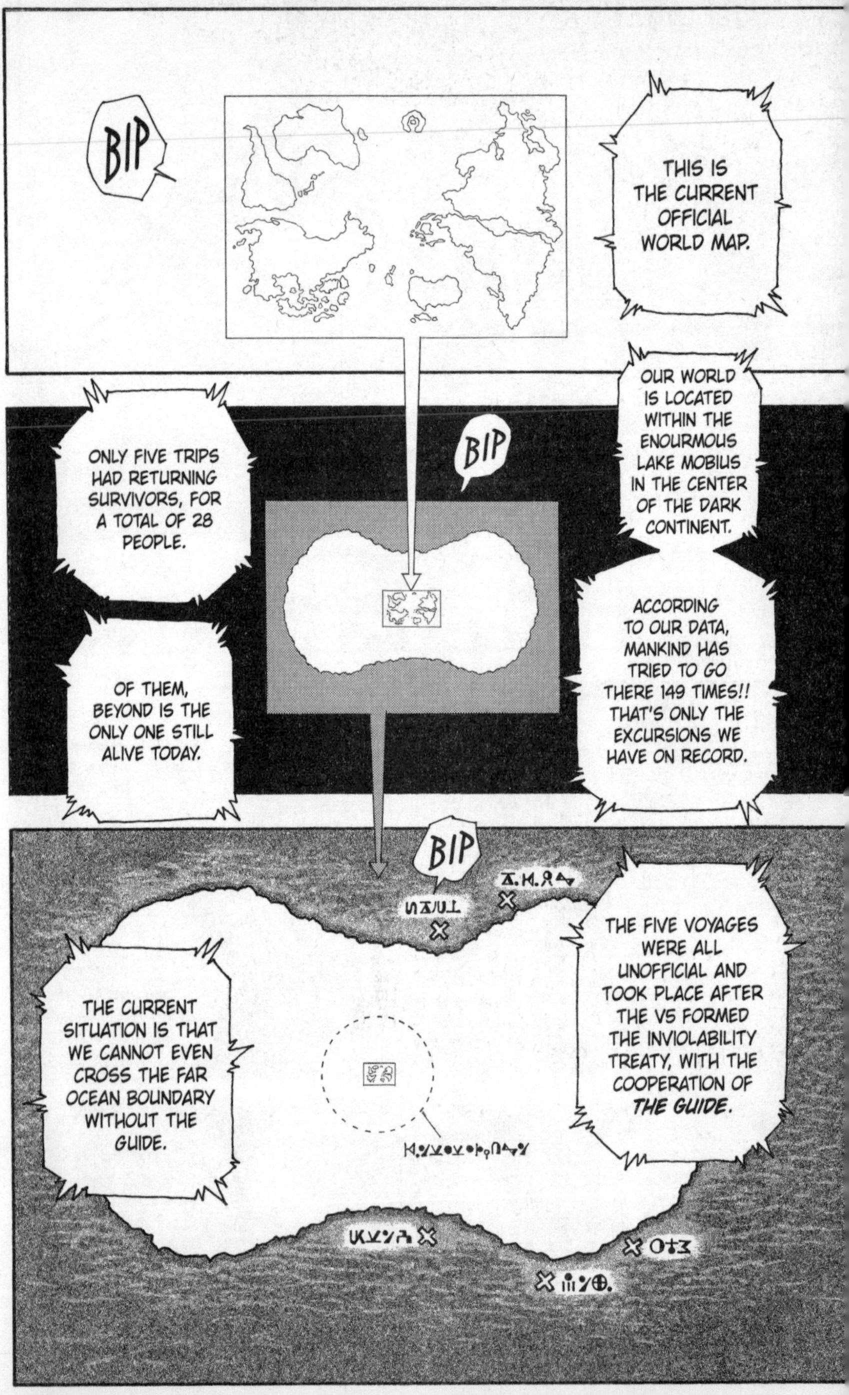
THIS IS THE CURRENT OFFICIAL WORLD MAP.
BIP
OUR WORLD IS LOCATED WITHIN THE ENOURMOUS LAKE MOBIUS IN THE CENTER OF THE DARK CONTINENT.
ACCORDING TO OUR DATA, MANKIND HAS TRIED TO GO THERE 149 TIMES!! THAT'S ONLY THE EXCURSIONS WE HAVE ON RECORD.
BIP
ONLY FIVE TRIPS HAD RETURNING SURVIVORS, FOR A TOTAL OF 28 PEOPLE.
OF THEM, BEYOND IS THE ONLY ONE STILL ALIVE TODAY.
BIP
THE FIVE VOYAGES WERE ALL UNOFFICIAL AND TOOK PLACE AFTER THE V5 FORMED THE INVIOLABILITY TREATY, WITH THE COOPERATION OF *THE GUIDE*.
THE CURRENT SITUATION IS THAT WE CANNOT EVEN CROSS THE FAR OCEAN BOUNDARY WITHOUT THE GUIDE.

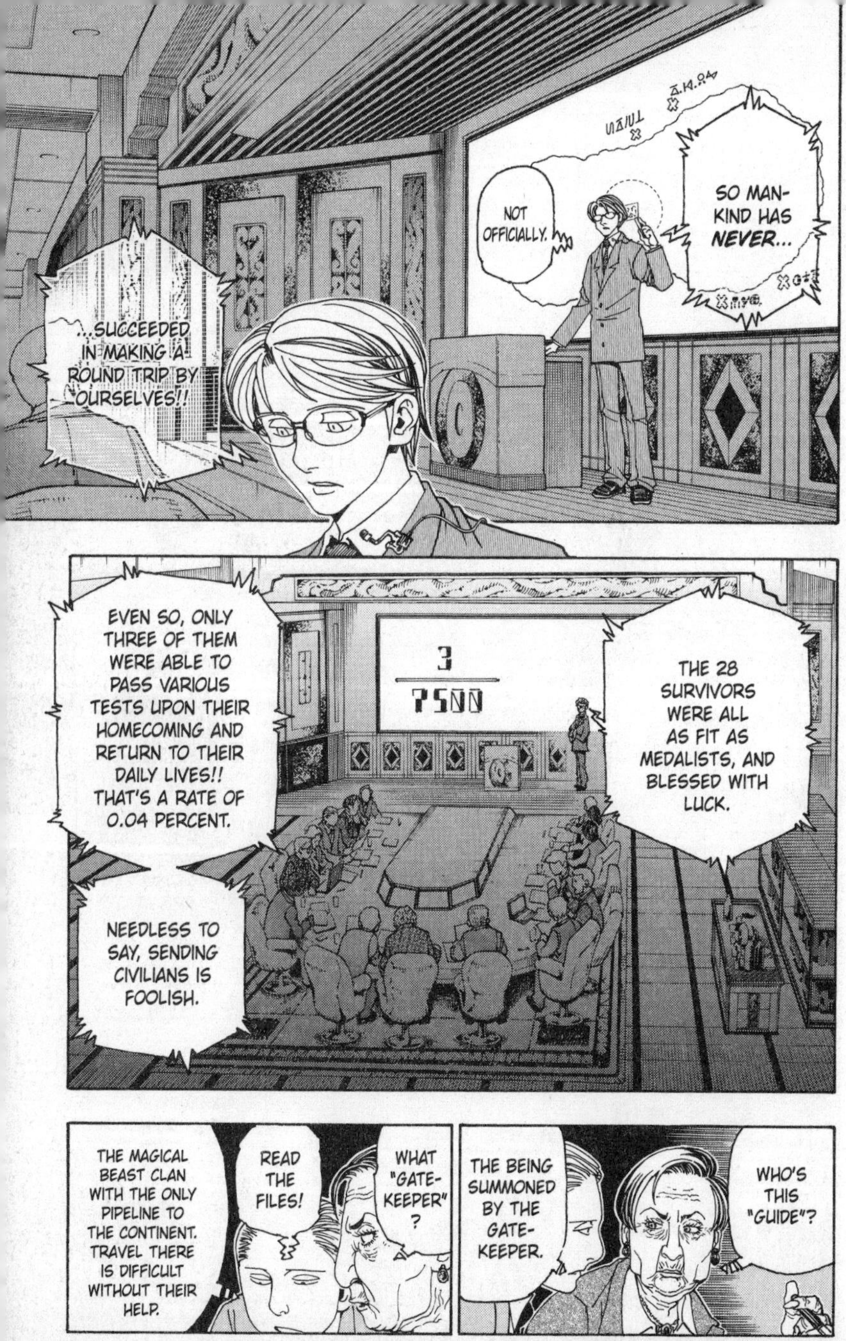
SO MAN-KIND HAS **NEVER...**
NOT OFFICIALLY.
...SUCCEEDED IN MAKING A ROUND TRIP BY OURSELVES!!
THE 28 SURVIVORS WERE ALL AS FIT AS MEDALISTS, AND BLESSED WITH LUCK.
3
7500
EVEN SO, ONLY THREE OF THEM WERE ABLE TO PASS VARIOUS TESTS UPON THEIR HOMECOMING AND RETURN TO THEIR DAILY LIVES!! THAT'S A RATE OF 0.04 PERCENT.
NEEDLESS TO SAY, SENDING CIVILIANS IS FOOLISH.
WHO'S THIS "GUIDE"?
THE BEING SUMMONED BY THE GATE-KEEPER.
WHAT "GATE-KEEPER"?
READ THE FILES!
THE MAGICAL BEAST CLAN WITH THE ONLY PIPELINE TO THE CONTINENT. TRAVEL THERE IS DIFFICULT WITHOUT THEIR HELP.

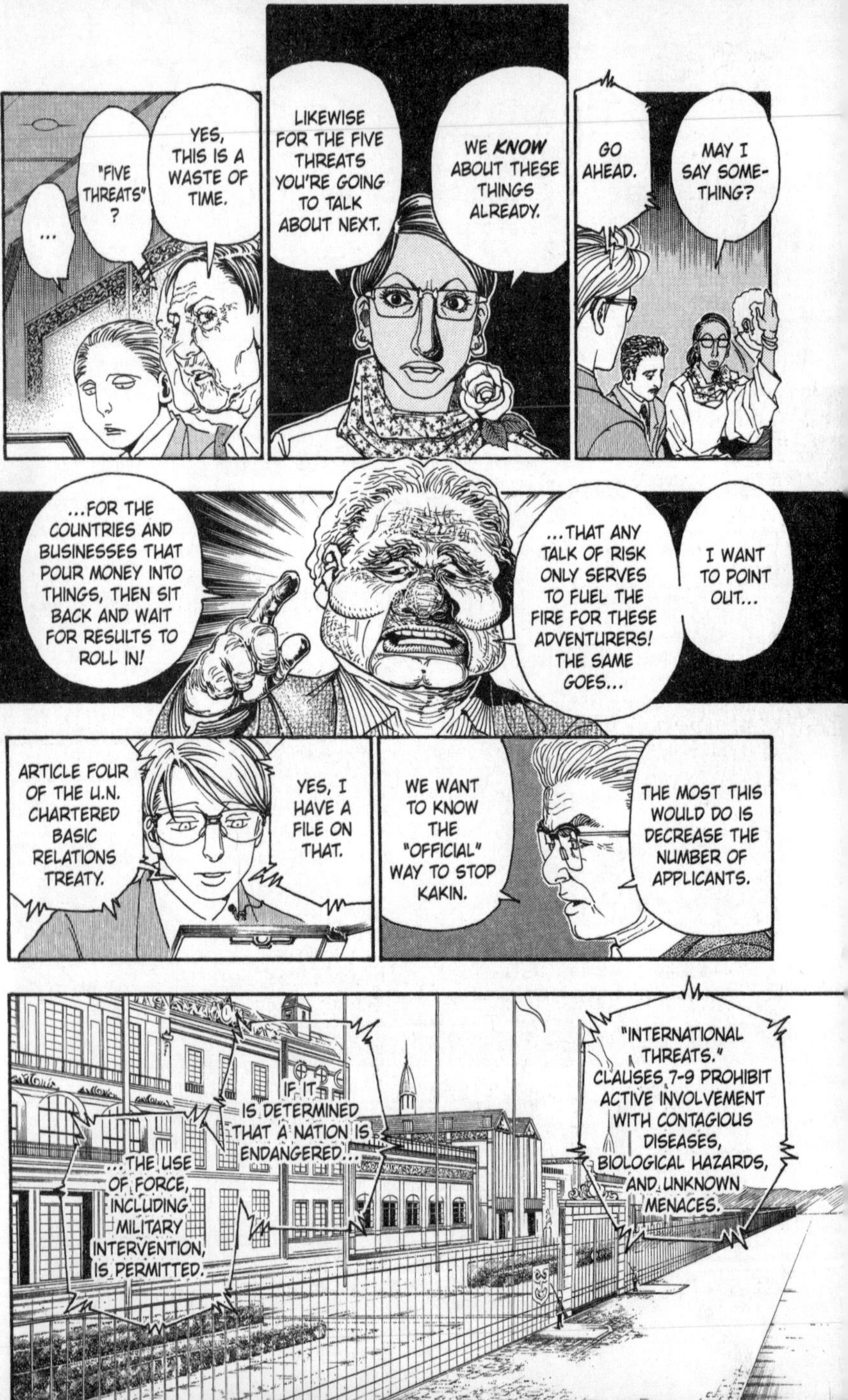
MAY I SAY SOME-THING?
GO AHEAD.
WE *KNOW* ABOUT THESE THINGS ALREADY.
LIKEWISE FOR THE FIVE THREATS YOU'RE GOING TO TALK ABOUT NEXT.
YES, THIS IS A WASTE OF TIME.
"FIVE THREATS" ?
...
I WANT TO POINT OUT...
...THAT ANY TALK OF RISK ONLY SERVES TO FUEL THE FIRE FOR THESE ADVENTURERS! THE SAME GOES...
...FOR THE COUNTRIES AND BUSINESSES THAT POUR MONEY INTO THINGS, THEN SIT BACK AND WAIT FOR RESULTS TO ROLL IN!
THE MOST THIS WOULD DO IS DECREASE THE NUMBER OF APPLICANTS.
WE WANT TO KNOW THE "OFFICIAL" WAY TO STOP KAKIN.
YES, I HAVE A FILE ON THAT.
ARTICLE FOUR OF THE U.N. CHARTERED BASIC RELATIONS TREATY.
"INTERNATIONAL THREATS." CLAUSES 7-9 PROHIBIT ACTIVE INVOLVEMENT WITH CONTAGIOUS DISEASES, BIOLOGICAL HAZARDS, AND UNKNOWN MENACES.
IF IT IS DETERMINED THAT A NATION IS ENDANGERED...
...THE USE OF FORCE, INCLUDING MILITARY INTERVENTION, IS PERMITTED.

READ THIS WAY

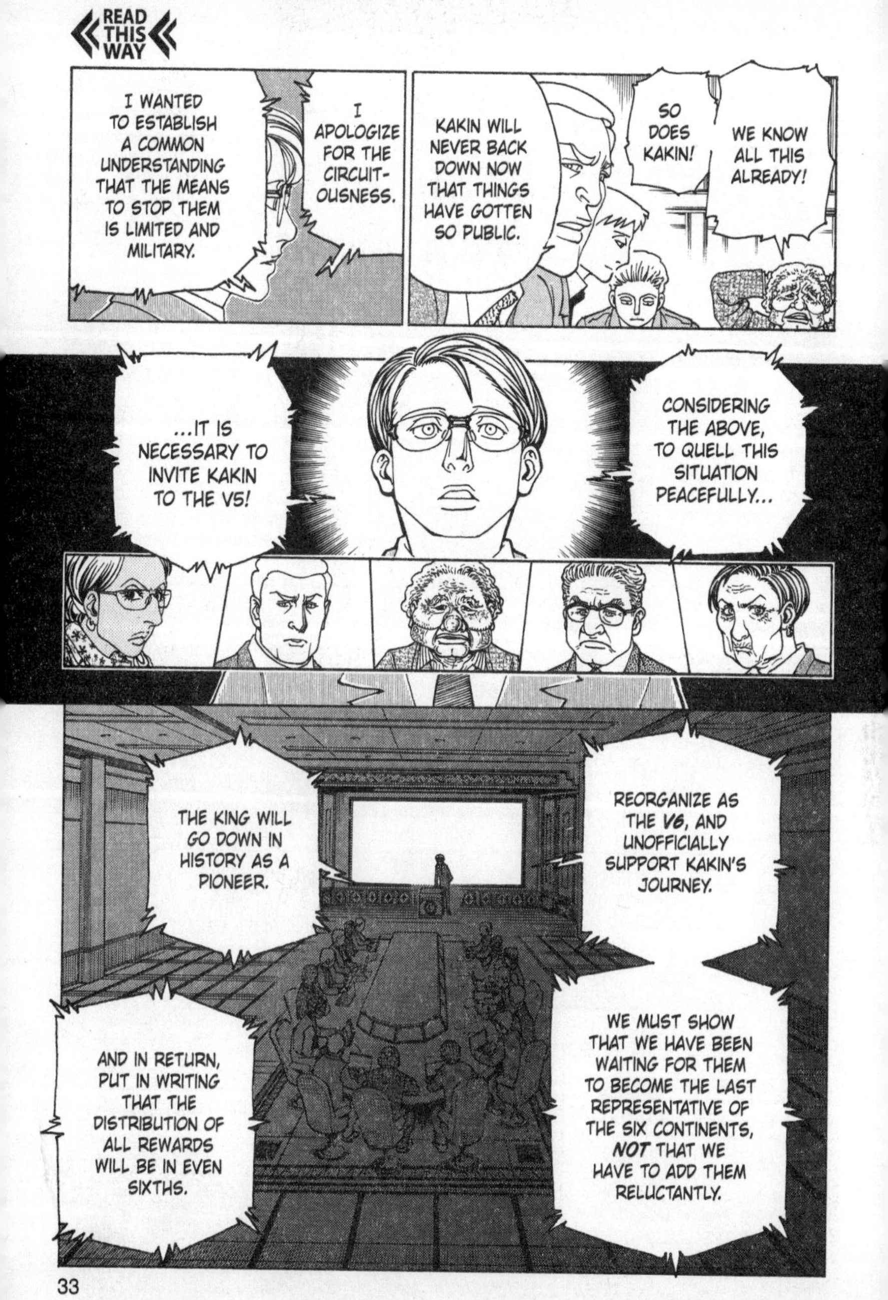
WE KNOW ALL THIS ALREADY!
SO DOES KAKIN!
KAKIN WILL NEVER BACK DOWN NOW THAT THINGS HAVE GOTTEN SO PUBLIC.
I APOLOGIZE FOR THE CIRCUIT-OUSNESS.
I WANTED TO ESTABLISH A COMMON UNDERSTANDING THAT THE MEANS TO STOP THEM IS LIMITED AND MILITARY.
CONSIDERING THE ABOVE, TO QUELL THIS SITUATION PEACEFULLY...
...IT IS NECESSARY TO INVITE KAKIN TO THE V5!
REORGANIZE AS THE *V6*, AND UNOFFICIALLY SUPPORT KAKIN'S JOURNEY.
THE KING WILL GO DOWN IN HISTORY AS A PIONEER.
WE MUST SHOW THAT WE HAVE BEEN WAITING FOR THEM TO BECOME THE LAST REPRESENTATIVE OF THE SIX CONTINENTS, ***NOT*** THAT WE HAVE TO ADD THEM RELUCTANTLY.
AND IN RETURN, PUT IN WRITING THAT THE DISTRIBUTION OF ALL REWARDS WILL BE IN EVEN SIXTHS.

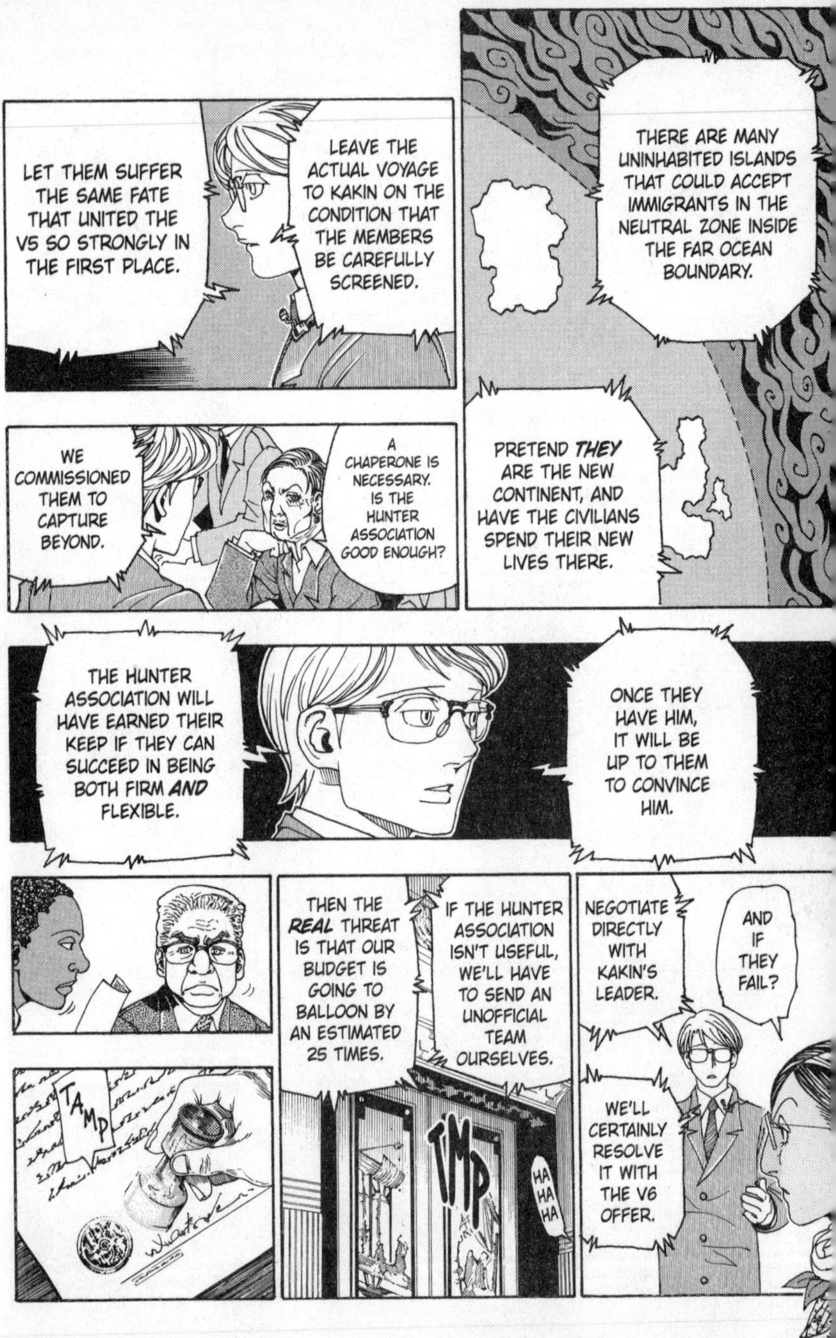
THERE ARE MANY UNINHABITED ISLANDS THAT COULD ACCEPT IMMIGRANTS IN THE NEUTRAL ZONE INSIDE THE FAR OCEAN BOUNDARY.
PRETEND *THEY* ARE THE NEW CONTINENT, AND HAVE THE CIVILIANS SPEND THEIR NEW LIVES THERE.
LEAVE THE ACTUAL VOYAGE TO KAKIN ON THE CONDITION THAT THE MEMBERS BE CAREFULLY SCREENED.
LET THEM SUFFER THE SAME FATE THAT UNITED THE V5 SO STRONGLY IN THE FIRST PLACE.
A CHAPERONE IS NECESSARY. IS THE HUNTER ASSOCIATION GOOD ENOUGH?
WE COMMISSIONED THEM TO CAPTURE BEYOND.
ONCE THEY HAVE HIM, IT WILL BE UP TO THEM TO CONVINCE HIM.
THE HUNTER ASSOCIATION WILL HAVE EARNED THEIR KEEP IF THEY CAN SUCCEED IN BEING BOTH FIRM *AND* FLEXIBLE.
AND IF THEY FAIL?
NEGOTIATE DIRECTLY WITH KAKIN'S LEADER.
WE'LL CERTAINLY RESOLVE IT WITH THE V6 OFFER.
IF THE HUNTER ASSOCIATION ISN'T USEFUL, WE'LL HAVE TO SEND AN UNOFFICIAL TEAM OURSELVES.
THEN THE *REAL* THREAT IS THAT OUR BUDGET IS GOING TO BALLOON BY AN ESTIMATED 25 TIMES.
TMP
HA HA HA
TAMP

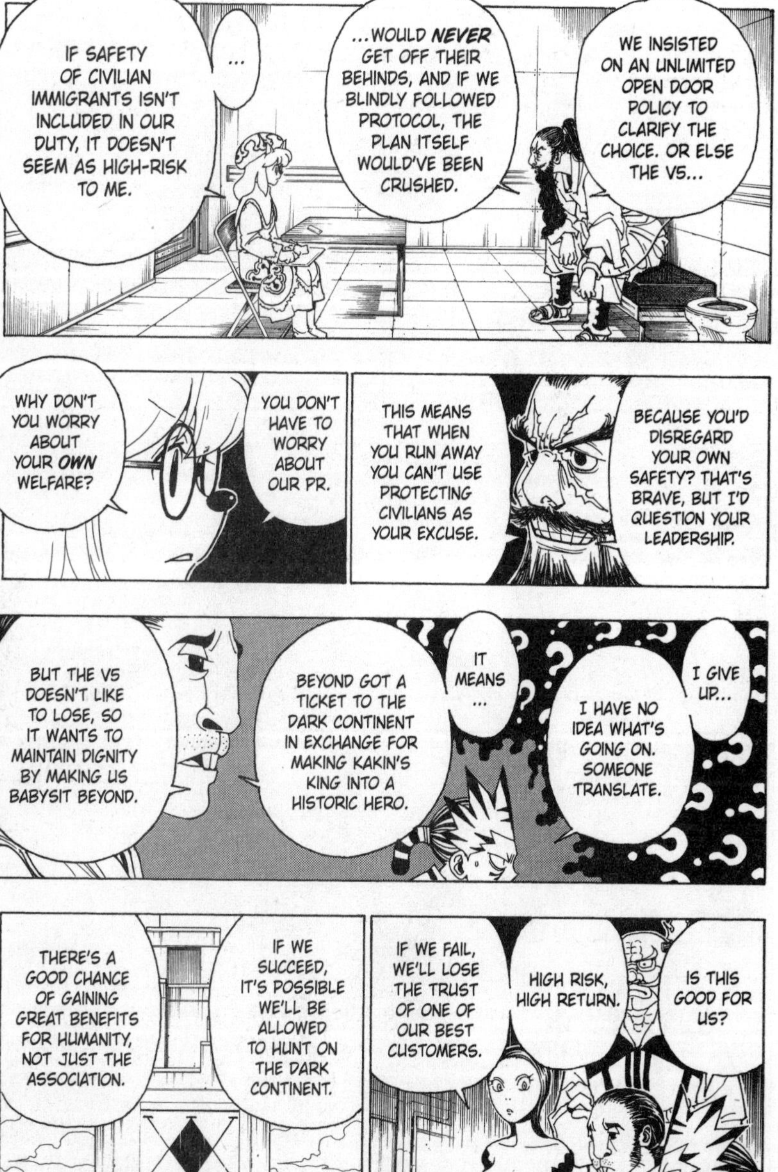
WE INSISTED ON AN UNLIMITED OPEN DOOR POLICY TO CLARIFY THE CHOICE. OR ELSE THE V5...
...WOULD **NEVER** GET OFF THEIR BEHINDS, AND IF WE BLINDLY FOLLOWED PROTOCOL, THE PLAN ITSELF WOULD'VE BEEN CRUSHED.
...
IF SAFETY OF CIVILIAN IMMIGRANTS ISN'T INCLUDED IN OUR DUTY, IT DOESN'T SEEM AS HIGH-RISK TO ME.
BECAUSE YOU'D DISREGARD YOUR OWN SAFETY? THAT'S BRAVE, BUT I'D QUESTION YOUR LEADERSHIP.
THIS MEANS THAT WHEN YOU RUN AWAY YOU CAN'T USE PROTECTING CIVILIANS AS YOUR EXCUSE.
YOU DON'T HAVE TO WORRY ABOUT OUR PR.
WHY DON'T YOU WORRY ABOUT YOUR ***OWN*** WELFARE?
I GIVE UP...
I HAVE NO IDEA WHAT'S GOING ON. SOMEONE TRANSLATE.
IT MEANS ...
BEYOND GOT A TICKET TO THE DARK CONTINENT IN EXCHANGE FOR MAKING KAKIN'S KING INTO A HISTORIC HERO.
BUT THE V5 DOESN'T LIKE TO LOSE, SO IT WANTS TO MAINTAIN DIGNITY BY MAKING US BABYSIT BEYOND.
IS THIS GOOD FOR US?
HIGH RISK, HIGH RETURN.
IF WE FAIL, WE'LL LOSE THE TRUST OF ONE OF OUR BEST CUSTOMERS.
IF WE SUCCEED, IT'S POSSIBLE WE'LL BE ALLOWED TO HUNT ON THE DARK CONTINENT.
THERE'S A GOOD CHANCE OF GAINING GREAT BENEFITS FOR HUMANITY, NOT JUST THE ASSOCIATION.

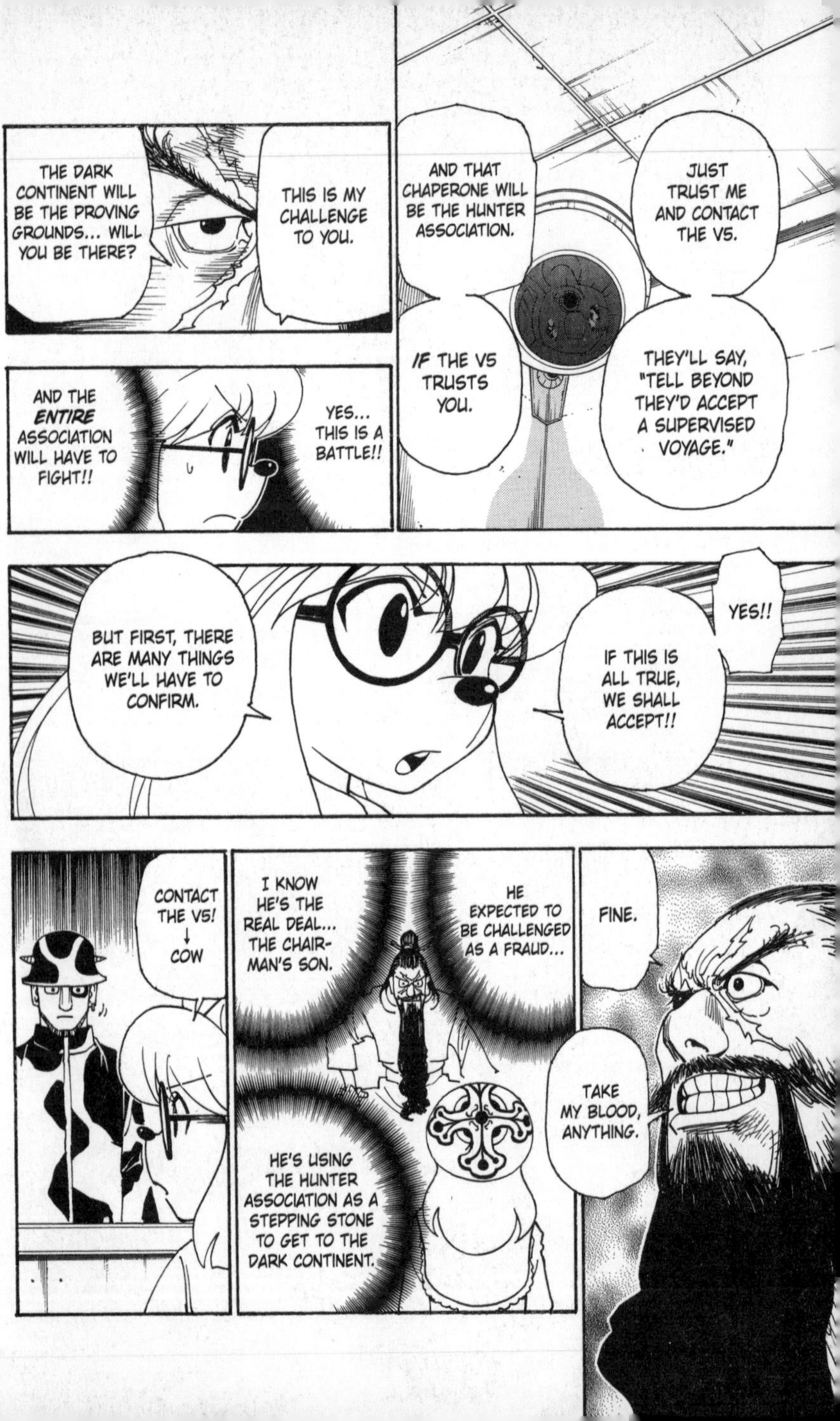
JUST TRUST ME AND CONTACT THE V5.
THEY'LL SAY, "TELL BEYOND THEY'D ACCEPT A SUPERVISED VOYAGE."
AND THAT CHAPERONE WILL BE THE HUNTER ASSOCIATION.
IF THE V5 TRUSTS YOU.
THIS IS MY CHALLENGE TO YOU.
THE DARK CONTINENT WILL BE THE PROVING GROUNDS... WILL YOU BE THERE?
YES... THIS IS A BATTLE!!
AND THE ***ENTIRE*** ASSOCIATION WILL HAVE TO FIGHT!!
YES!!
IF THIS IS ALL TRUE, WE SHALL ACCEPT!!
BUT FIRST, THERE ARE MANY THINGS WE'LL HAVE TO CONFIRM.
FINE.
TAKE MY BLOOD, ANYTHING.
HE EXPECTED TO BE CHALLENGED AS A FRAUD...
I KNOW HE'S THE REAL DEAL... THE CHAIR-MAN'S SON.
HE'S USING THE HUNTER ASSOCIATION AS A STEPPING STONE TO GET TO THE DARK CONTINENT.
CONTACT THE V5!
↓
COW

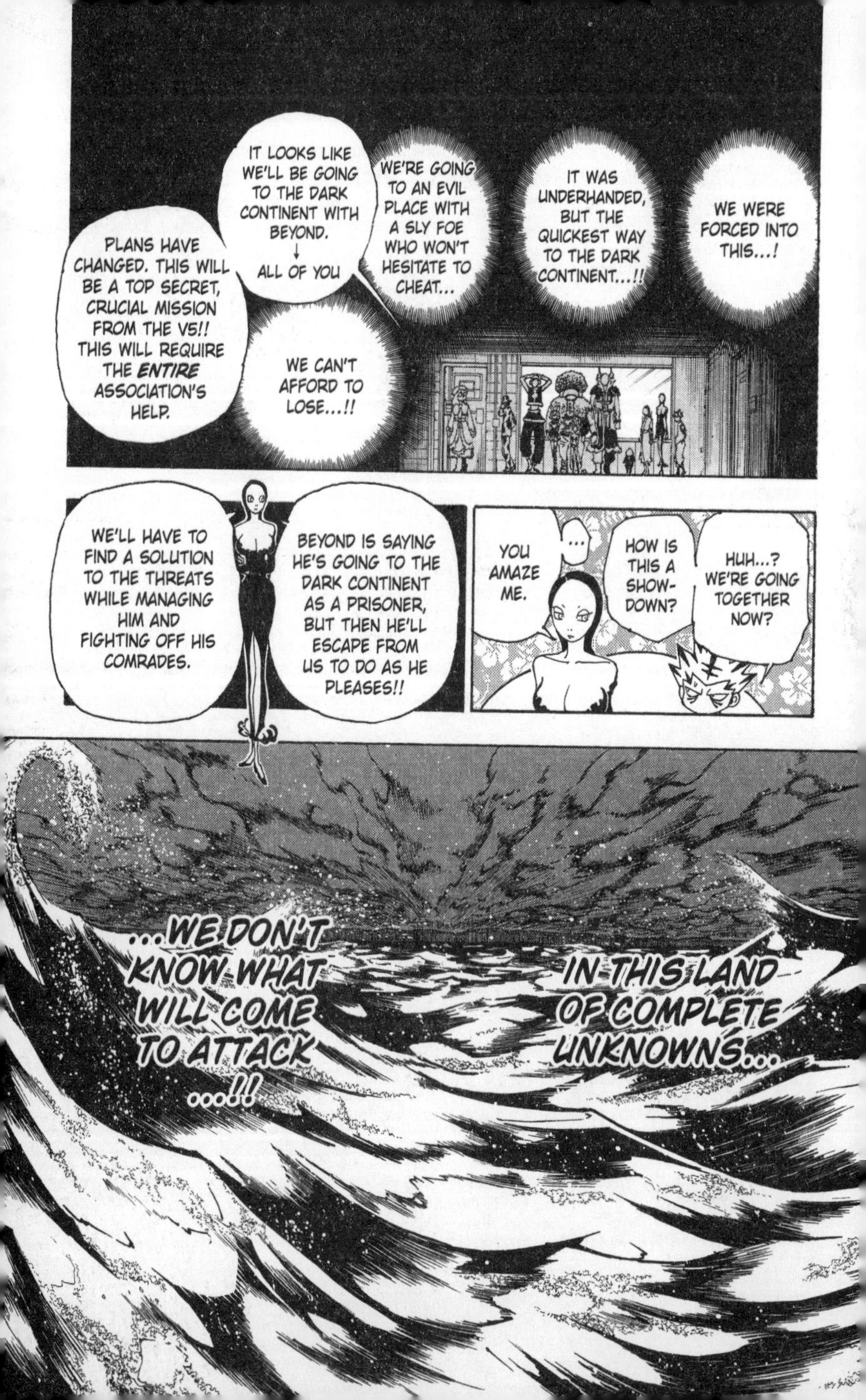
WE WERE FORCED INTO THIS...!
IT WAS UNDERHANDED, BUT THE QUICKEST WAY TO THE DARK CONTINENT...!!
WE'RE GOING TO AN EVIL PLACE WITH A SLY FOE WHO WON'T HESITATE TO CHEAT...
IT LOOKS LIKE WE'LL BE GOING TO THE DARK CONTINENT WITH BEYOND. ↓ ALL OF YOU
WE CAN'T AFFORD TO LOSE...!!
PLANS HAVE CHANGED. THIS WILL BE A TOP SECRET, CRUCIAL MISSION FROM THE V5!! THIS WILL REQUIRE THE *ENTIRE* ASSOCIATION'S HELP.
HUH...? WE'RE GOING TOGETHER NOW?
HOW IS THIS A SHOW-DOWN?
...
YOU AMAZE ME.
BEYOND IS SAYING HE'S GOING TO THE DARK CONTINENT AS A PRISONER, BUT THEN HE'LL ESCAPE FROM US TO DO AS HE PLEASES!!
WE'LL HAVE TO FIND A SOLUTION TO THE THREATS WHILE MANAGING HIM AND FIGHTING OFF HIS COMRADES.
IN THIS LAND OF COMPLETE UNKNOWNS...
...WE DON'T KNOW WHAT WILL COME TO ATTACK ...!!

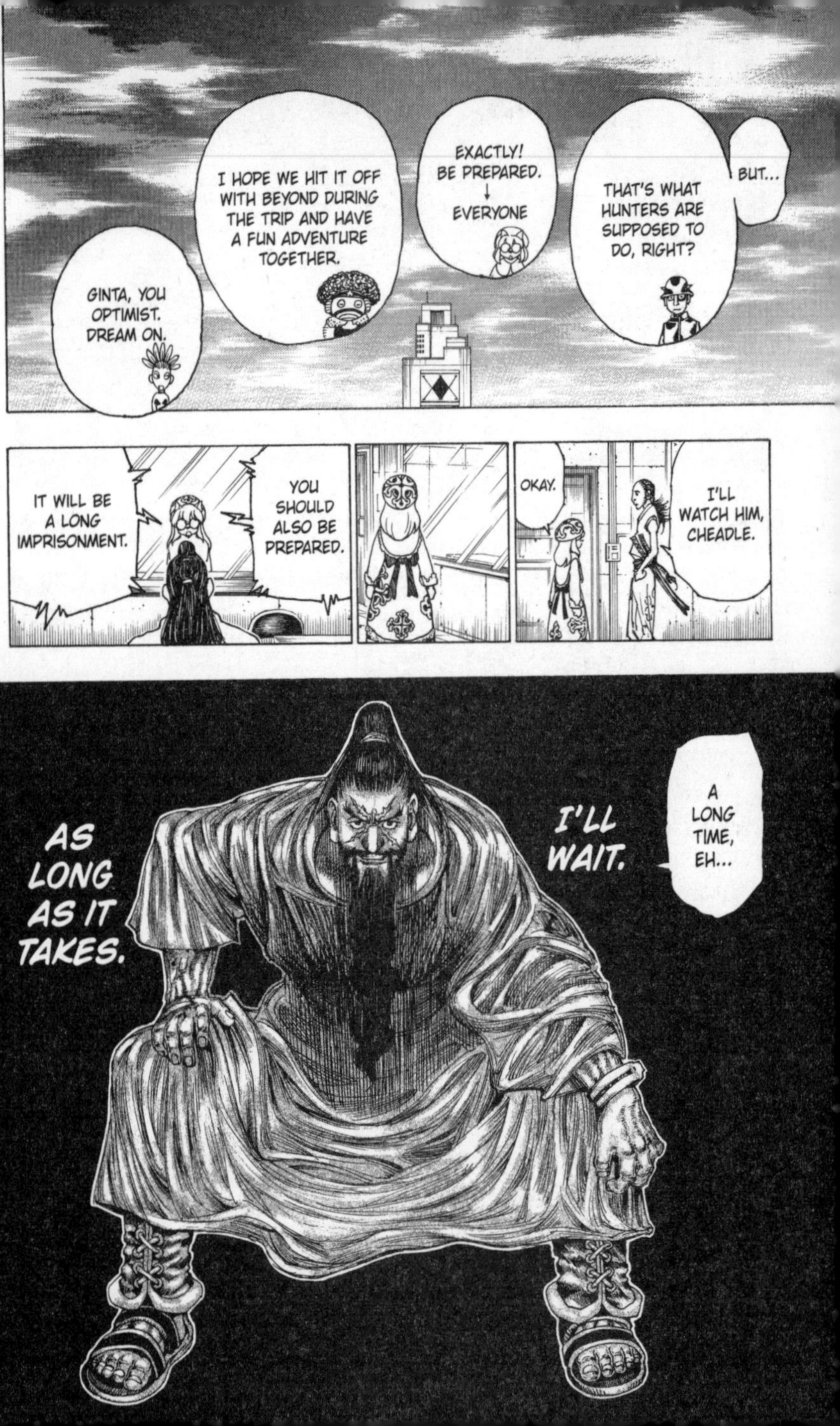
BUT...
THAT'S WHAT HUNTERS ARE SUPPOSED TO DO, RIGHT?
EXACTLY! BE PREPARED.
↓
EVERYONE
I HOPE WE HIT IT OFF WITH BEYOND DURING THE TRIP AND HAVE A FUN ADVENTURE TOGETHER.
GINTA, YOU OPTIMIST. DREAM ON.
I'LL WATCH HIM, CHEADLE.
OKAY.
YOU SHOULD ALSO BE PREPARED.
IT WILL BE A LONG IMPRISONMENT.
A LONG TIME, EH...
I'LL WAIT.
AS LONG AS IT TAKES.

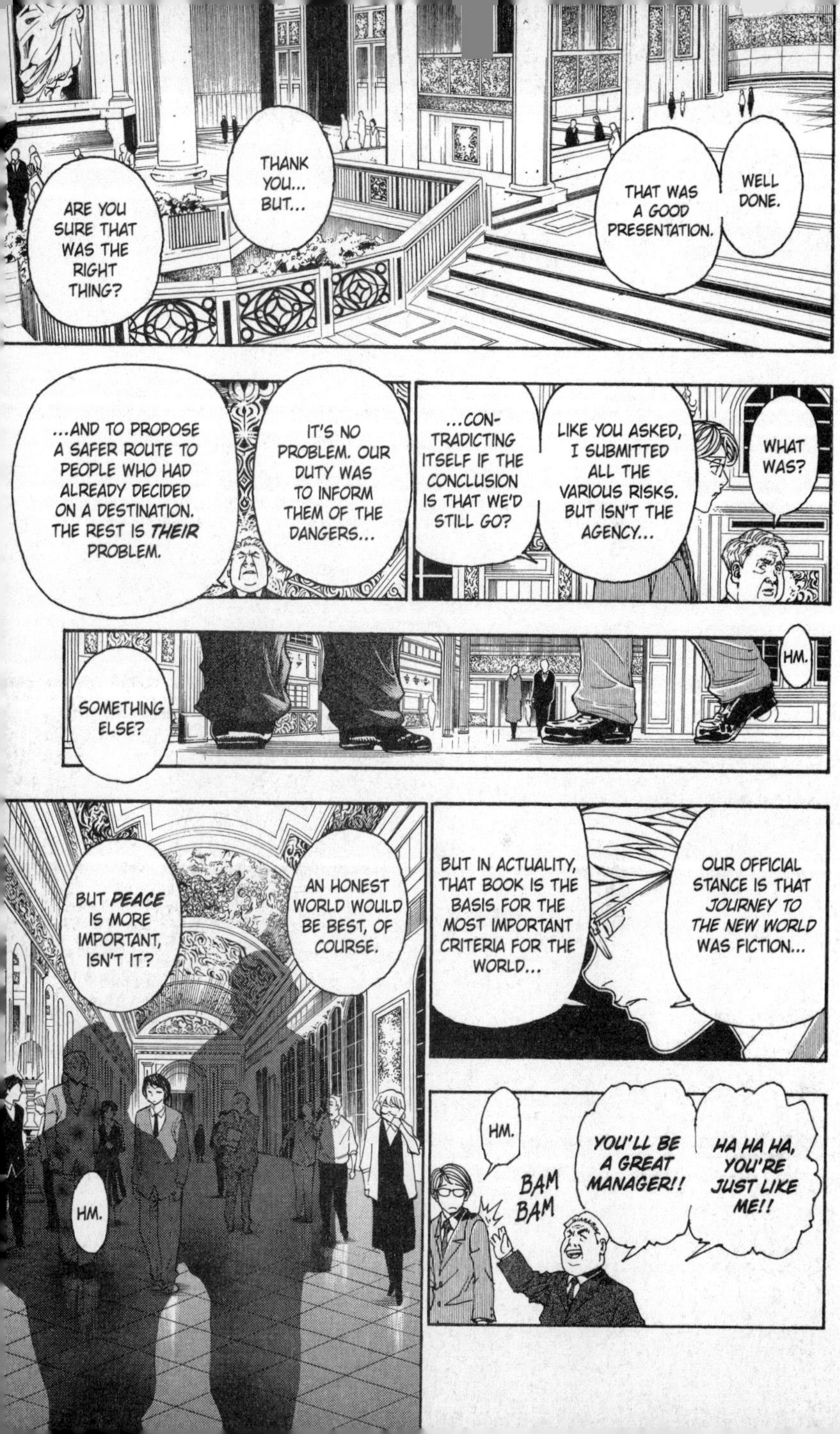
WELL DONE.
THAT WAS A GOOD PRESENTATION.
THANK YOU... BUT...
ARE YOU SURE THAT WAS THE RIGHT THING?
WHAT WAS?
LIKE YOU ASKED, I SUBMITTED ALL THE VARIOUS RISKS. BUT ISN'T THE AGENCY...
...CON-TRADICTING ITSELF IF THE CONCLUSION IS THAT WE'D STILL GO?
IT'S NO PROBLEM. OUR DUTY WAS TO INFORM THEM OF THE DANGERS...
...AND TO PROPOSE A SAFER ROUTE TO PEOPLE WHO HAD ALREADY DECIDED ON A DESTINATION. THE REST IS *THEIR* PROBLEM.
HM.
SOMETHING ELSE?
OUR OFFICIAL STANCE IS THAT *JOURNEY TO THE NEW WORLD* WAS FICTION...
BUT IN ACTUALITY, THAT BOOK IS THE BASIS FOR THE MOST IMPORTANT CRITERIA FOR THE WORLD...
HA HA HA, YOU'RE JUST LIKE ME!!
YOU'LL BE A GREAT MANAGER!!
BAM BAM
HM.
AN HONEST WORLD WOULD BE BEST, OF COURSE.
BUT *PEACE* IS MORE IMPORTANT, ISN'T IT?
HM.

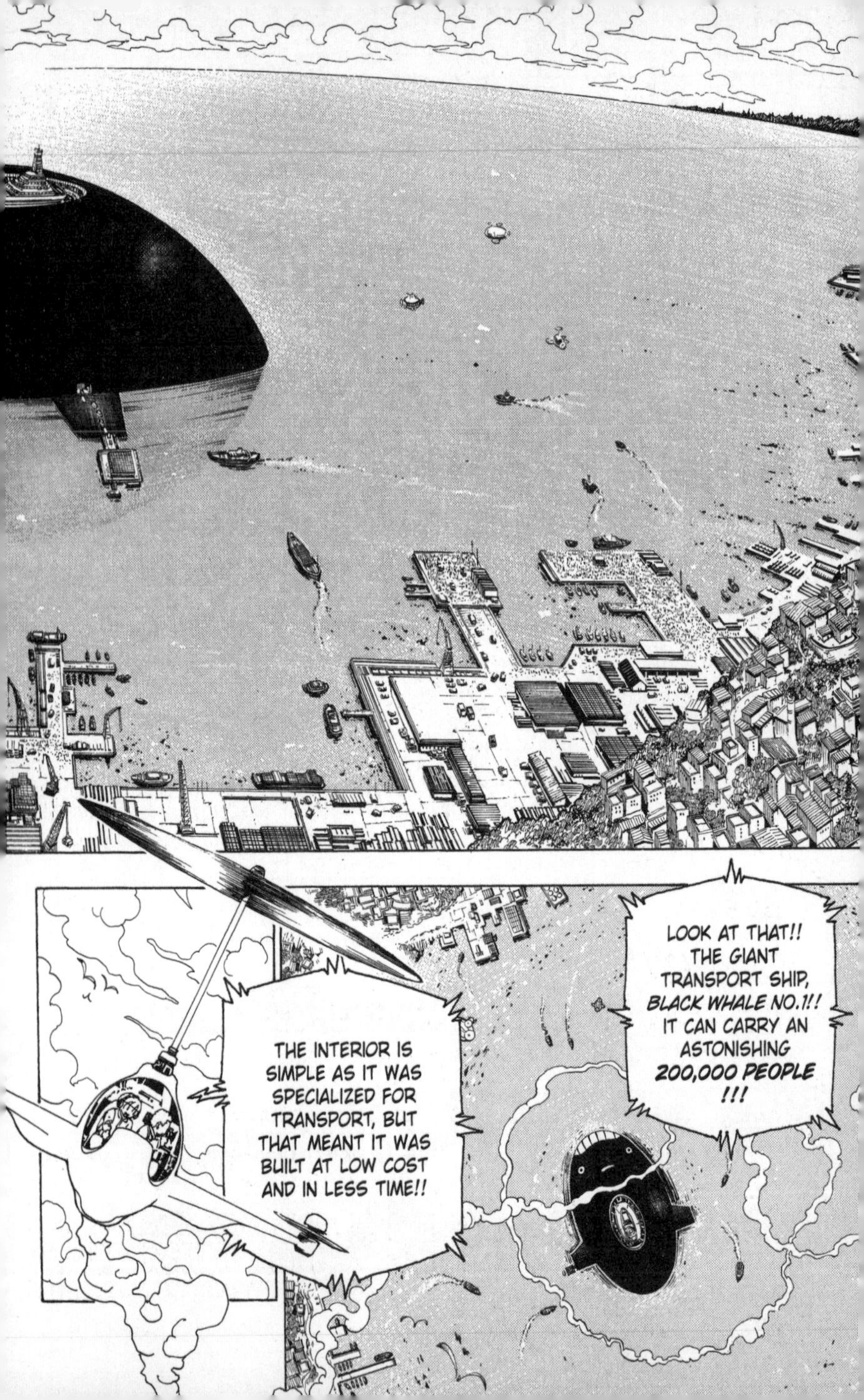
LOOK AT THAT!! THE GIANT TRANSPORT SHIP, *BLACK WHALE NO.1!!* IT CAN CARRY AN ASTONISHING **200,000 PEOPLE !!!**
THE INTERIOR IS SIMPLE AS IT WAS SPECIALIZED FOR TRANSPORT, BUT THAT MEANT IT WAS BUILT AT LOW COST AND IN LESS TIME!!

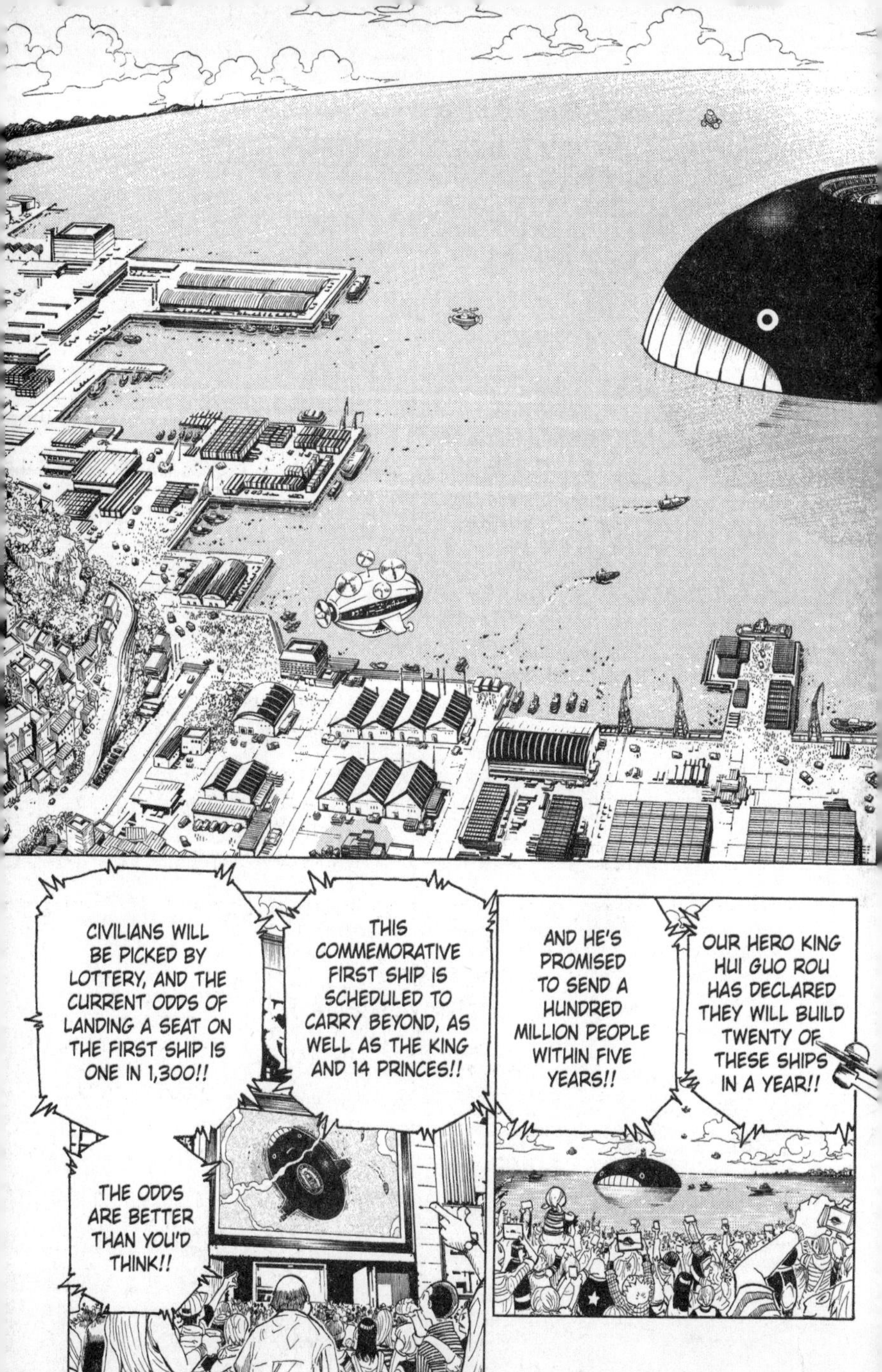
OUR HERO KING HUI GUO ROU HAS DECLARED THEY WILL BUILD TWENTY OF THESE SHIPS IN A YEAR!!
AND HE'S PROMISED TO SEND A HUNDRED MILLION PEOPLE WITHIN FIVE YEARS!!
THIS COMMEMORATIVE FIRST SHIP IS SCHEDULED TO CARRY BEYOND, AS WELL AS THE KING AND 14 PRINCES!!
CIVILIANS WILL BE PICKED BY LOTTERY, AND THE CURRENT ODDS OF LANDING A SEAT ON THE FIRST SHIP IS ONE IN 1,300!!
THE ODDS ARE BETTER THAN YOU'D THINK!!

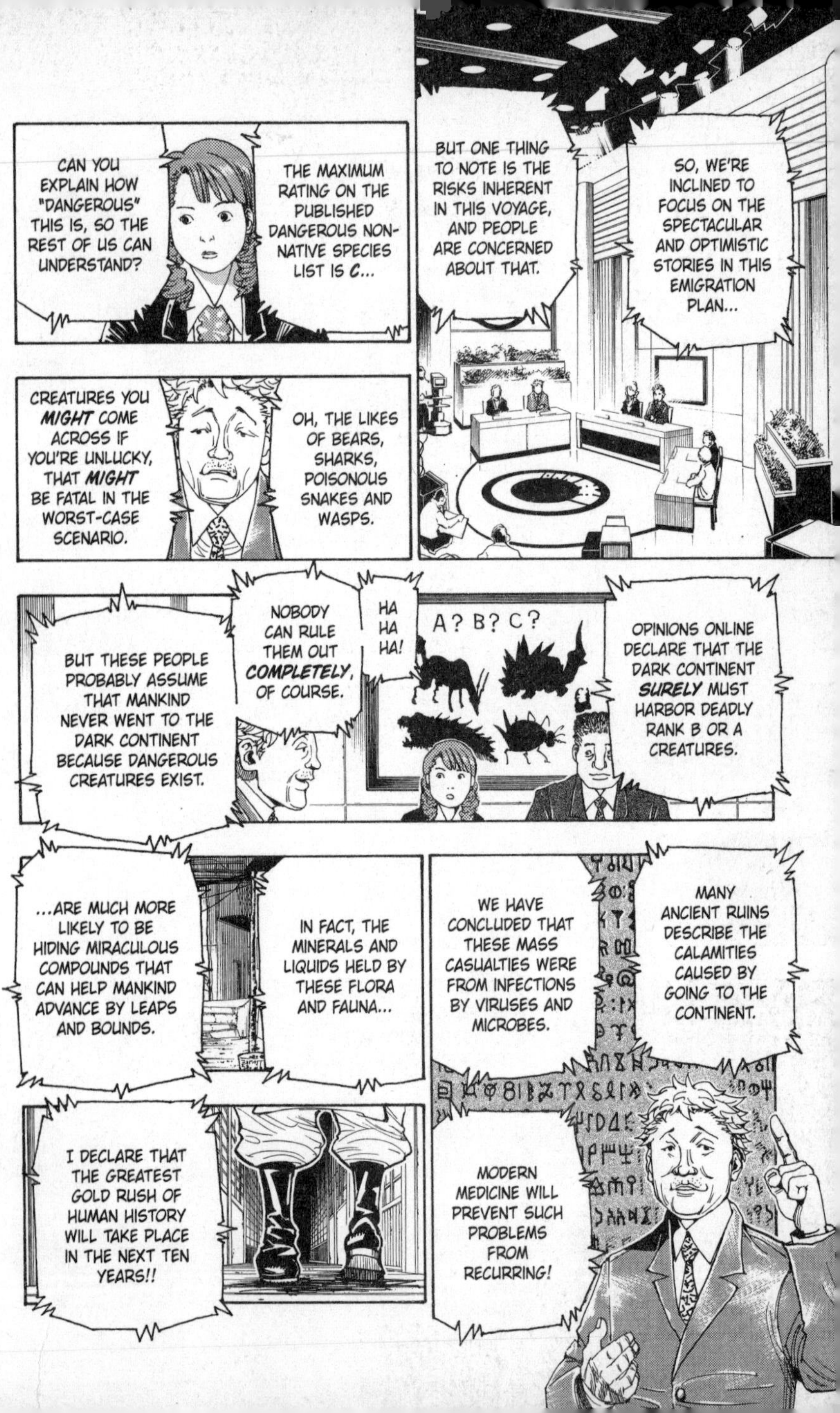
SO, WE'RE INCLINED TO FOCUS ON THE SPECTACULAR AND OPTIMISTIC STORIES IN THIS EMIGRATION PLAN...
BUT ONE THING TO NOTE IS THE RISKS INHERENT IN THIS VOYAGE, AND PEOPLE ARE CONCERNED ABOUT THAT.
THE MAXIMUM RATING ON THE PUBLISHED DANGEROUS NON-NATIVE SPECIES LIST IS C...
CAN YOU EXPLAIN HOW "DANGEROUS" THIS IS, SO THE REST OF US CAN UNDERSTAND?
OH, THE LIKES OF BEARS, SHARKS, POISONOUS SNAKES AND WASPS.
CREATURES YOU MIGHT COME ACROSS IF YOU'RE UNLUCKY, THAT MIGHT BE FATAL IN THE WORST-CASE SCENARIO.
OPINIONS ONLINE DECLARE THAT THE DARK CONTINENT SURELY MUST HARBOR DEADLY RANK B OR A CREATURES.
A? B? C?
HA HA HA!
NOBODY CAN RULE THEM OUT COMPLETELY, OF COURSE.
BUT THESE PEOPLE PROBABLY ASSUME THAT MANKIND NEVER WENT TO THE DARK CONTINENT BECAUSE DANGEROUS CREATURES EXIST.
MANY ANCIENT RUINS DESCRIBE THE CALAMITIES CAUSED BY GOING TO THE CONTINENT.
WE HAVE CONCLUDED THAT THESE MASS CASUALTIES WERE FROM INFECTIONS BY VIRUSES AND MICROBES.
MODERN MEDICINE WILL PREVENT SUCH PROBLEMS FROM RECURRING!
IN FACT, THE MINERALS AND LIQUIDS HELD BY THESE FLORA AND FAUNA...
...ARE MUCH MORE LIKELY TO BE HIDING MIRACULOUS COMPOUNDS THAT CAN HELP MANKIND ADVANCE BY LEAPS AND BOUNDS.
I DECLARE THAT THE GREATEST GOLD RUSH OF HUMAN HISTORY WILL TAKE PLACE IN THE NEXT TEN YEARS!!

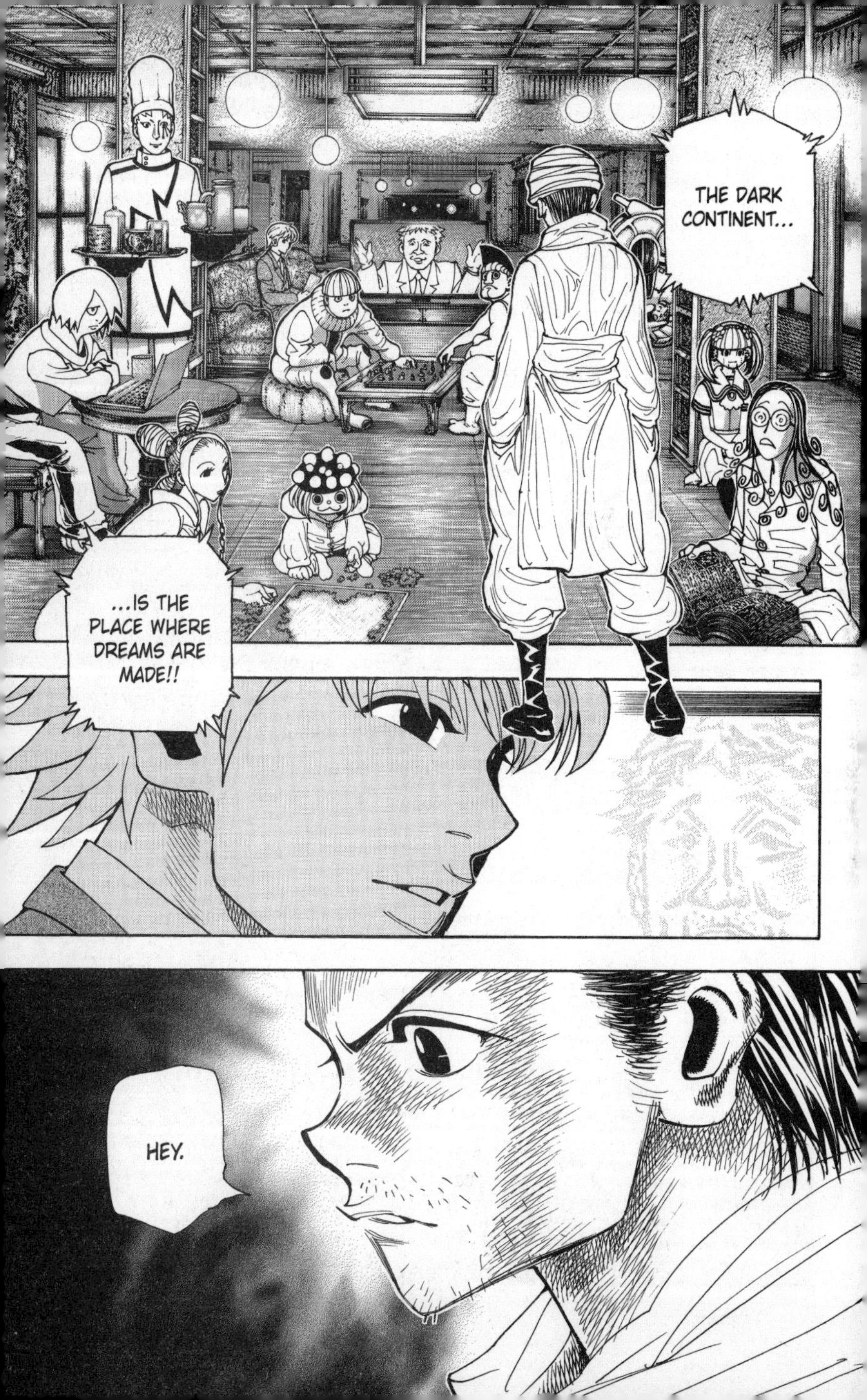
THE DARK CONTINENT...
...IS THE PLACE WHERE DREAMS ARE MADE!!
HEY.

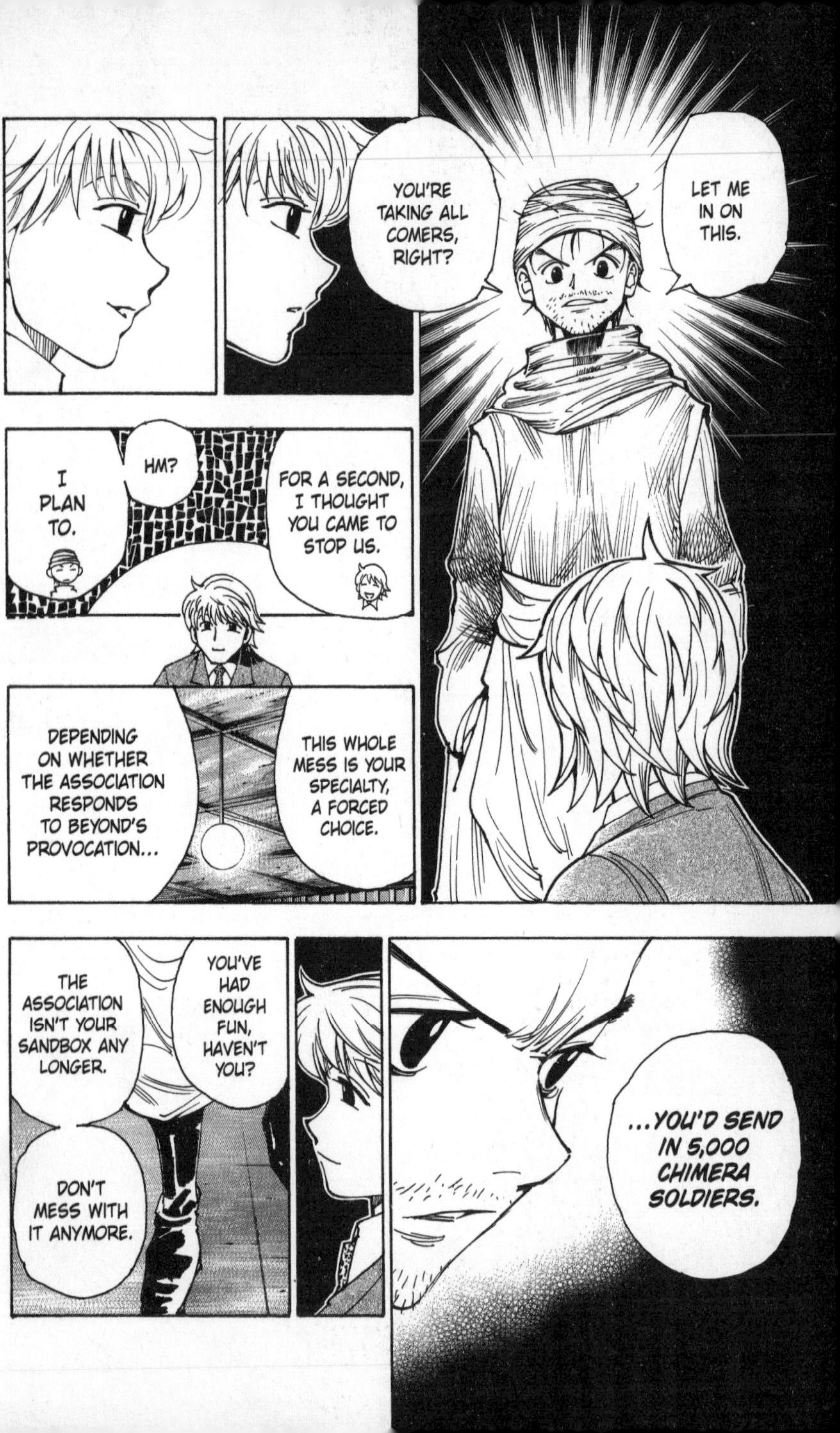
LET ME IN ON THIS.
YOU'RE TAKING ALL COMERS, RIGHT?
FOR A SECOND, I THOUGHT YOU CAME TO STOP US.
HM?
I PLAN TO.
THIS WHOLE MESS IS YOUR SPECIALTY, A FORCED CHOICE.
DEPENDING ON WHETHER THE ASSOCIATION RESPONDS TO BEYOND'S PROVOCATION...
...YOU'D SEND IN 5,000 CHIMERA SOLDIERS.
YOU'VE HAD ENOUGH FUN, HAVEN'T YOU?
THE ASSOCIATION ISN'T YOUR SANDBOX ANY LONGER.
DON'T MESS WITH IT ANYMORE.

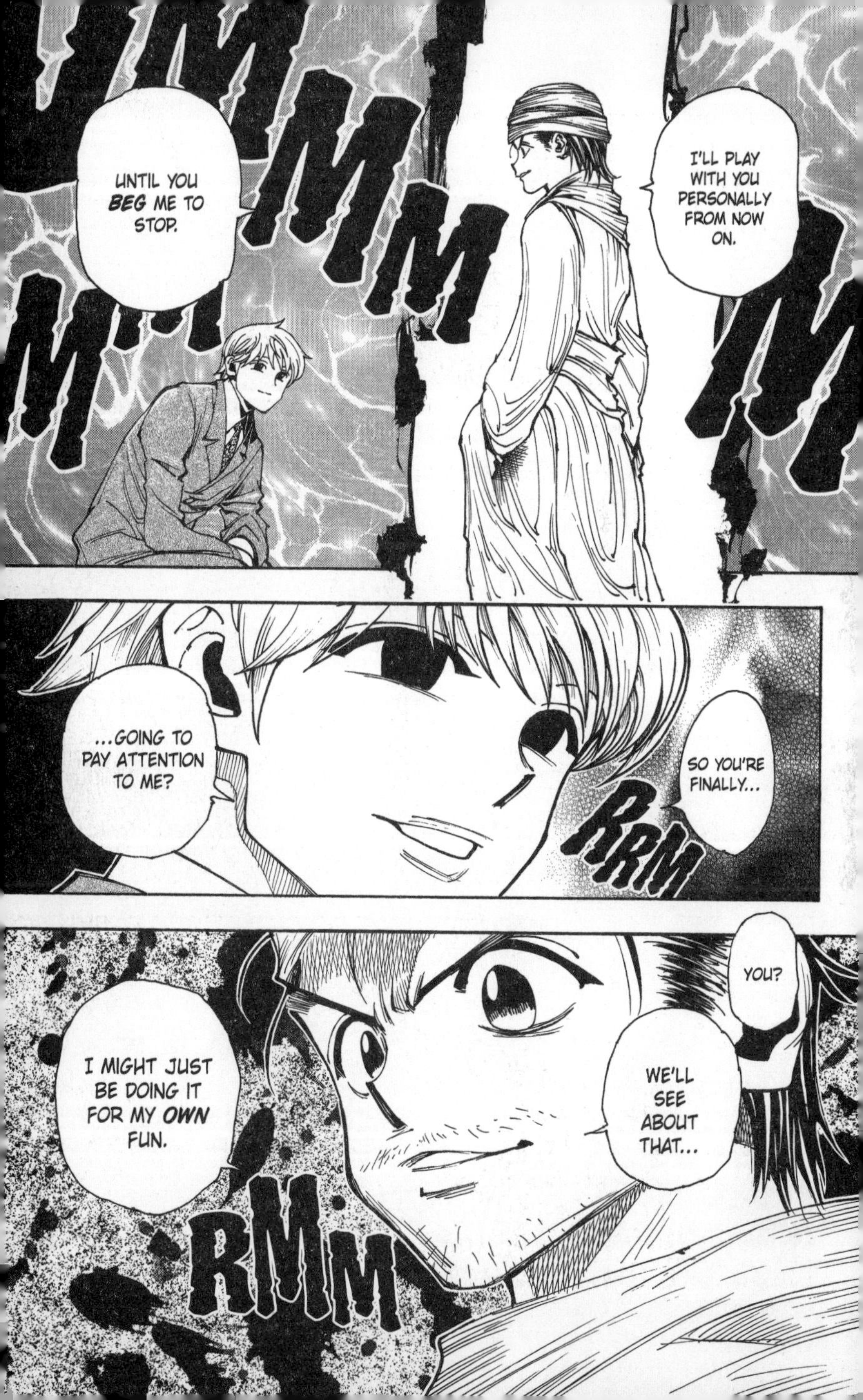
I'LL PLAY WITH YOU PERSONALLY FROM NOW ON.
UNTIL YOU *BEG* ME TO STOP.
SO YOU'RE FINALLY...
RRM
...GOING TO PAY ATTENTION TO ME?
YOU?
WE'LL SEE ABOUT THAT...
I MIGHT JUST BE DOING IT FOR MY *OWN* FUN.
RMM

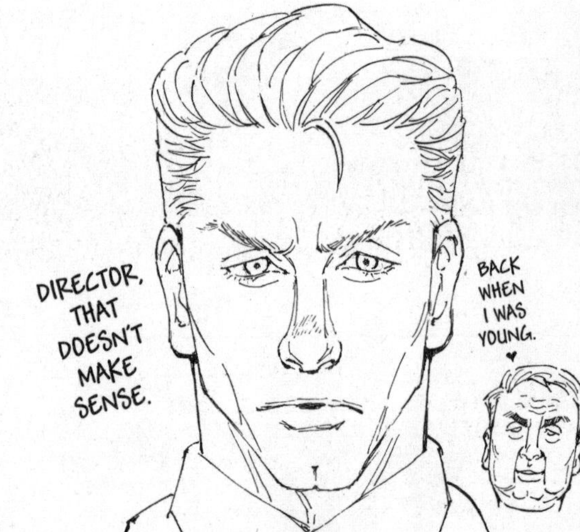
DIRECTOR, THAT DOESN'T MAKE SENSE.
BACK WHEN I WAS YOUNG. ♥

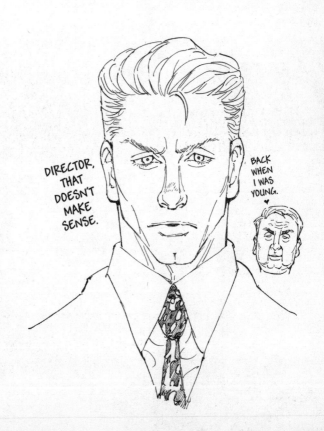

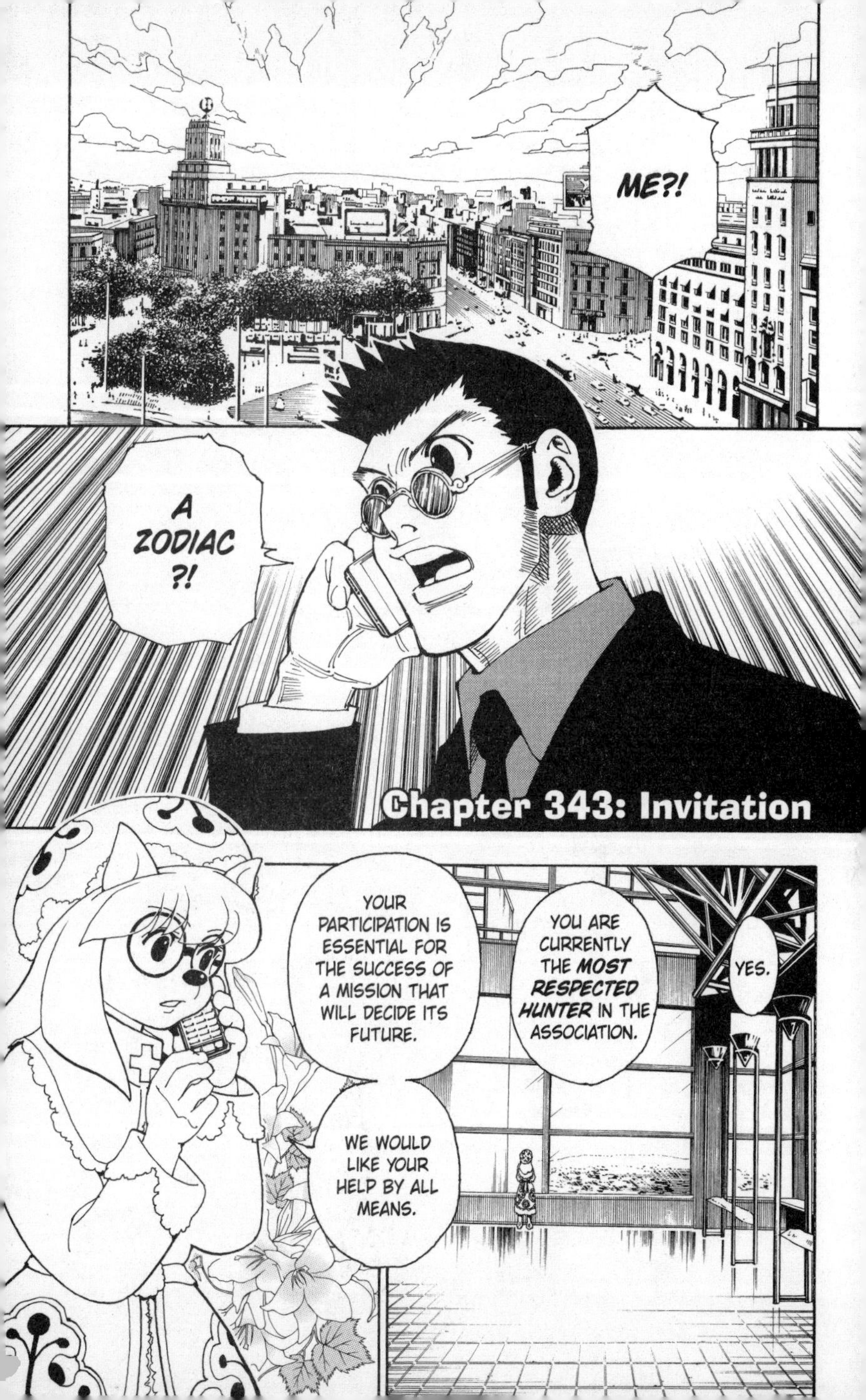
ME?!
A ZODIAC ?!
Chapter 343: Invitation
YES.
YOU ARE CURRENTLY THE MOST RESPECTED HUNTER IN THE ASSOCIATION.
YOUR PARTICIPATION IS ESSENTIAL FOR THE SUCCESS OF A MISSION THAT WILL DECIDE ITS FUTURE.
WE WOULD LIKE YOUR HELP BY ALL MEANS.

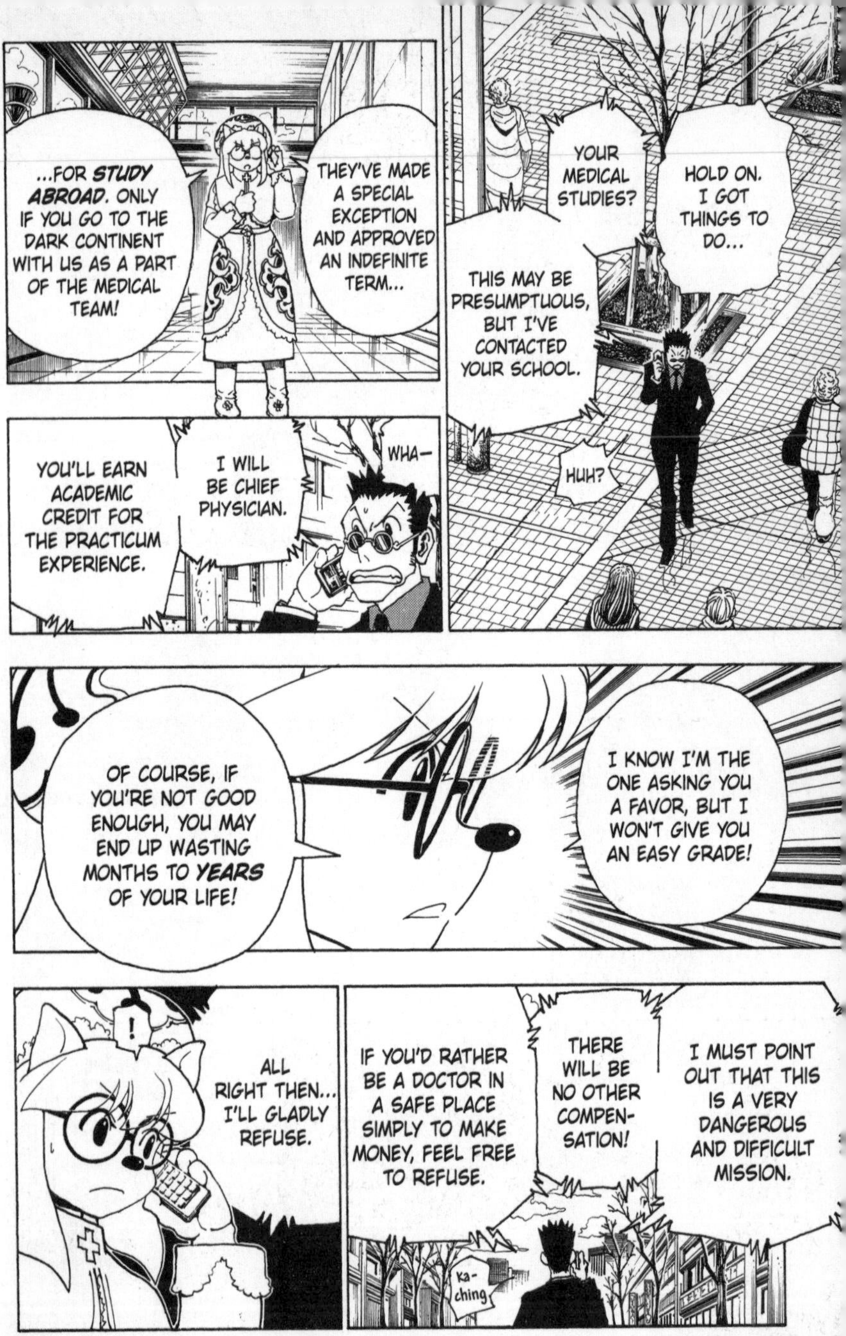
HOLD ON. I GOT THINGS TO DO...
YOUR MEDICAL STUDIES?
THIS MAY BE PRESUMPTUOUS, BUT I'VE CONTACTED YOUR SCHOOL.
HUH?
THEY'VE MADE A SPECIAL EXCEPTION AND APPROVED AN INDEFINITE TERM...
...FOR STUDY ABROAD. ONLY IF YOU GO TO THE DARK CONTINENT WITH US AS A PART OF THE MEDICAL TEAM!
WHA-
I WILL BE CHIEF PHYSICIAN.
YOU'LL EARN ACADEMIC CREDIT FOR THE PRACTICUM EXPERIENCE.
I KNOW I'M THE ONE ASKING YOU A FAVOR, BUT I WON'T GIVE YOU AN EASY GRADE!
OF COURSE, IF YOU'RE NOT GOOD ENOUGH, YOU MAY END UP WASTING MONTHS TO YEARS OF YOUR LIFE!
I MUST POINT OUT THAT THIS IS A VERY DANGEROUS AND DIFFICULT MISSION.
THERE WILL BE NO OTHER COMPEN-SATION!
IF YOU'D RATHER BE A DOCTOR IN A SAFE PLACE SIMPLY TO MAKE MONEY, FEEL FREE TO REFUSE.
Ka-ching
!
ALL RIGHT THEN... I'LL GLADLY REFUSE.

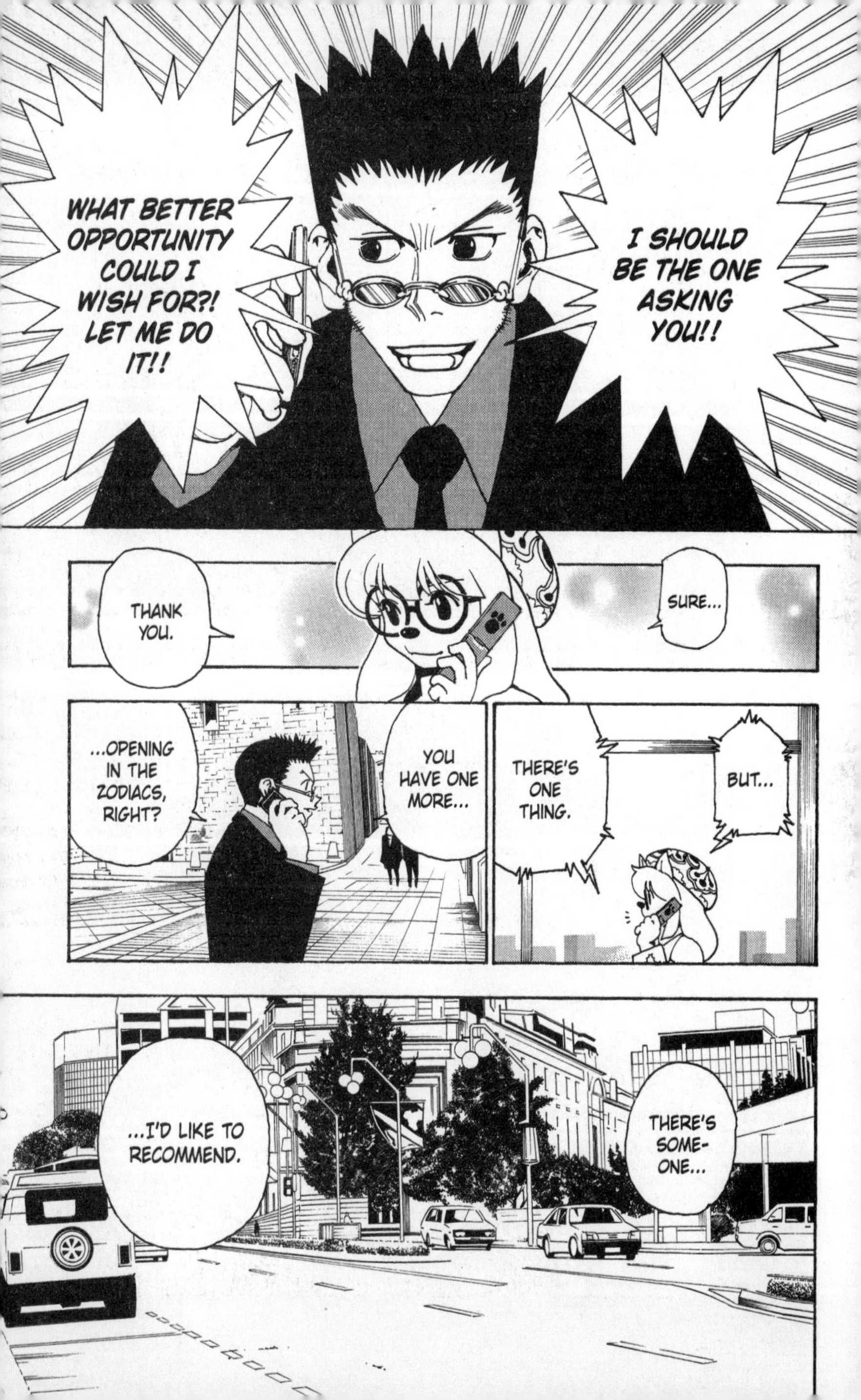
I SHOULD BE THE ONE ASKING YOU!!
WHAT BETTER OPPORTUNITY COULD I WISH FOR?! LET ME DO IT!!
SURE...
THANK YOU.
BUT...
THERE'S ONE THING.
YOU HAVE ONE MORE...
...OPENING IN THE ZODIACS, RIGHT?
THERE'S SOME-ONE...
...I'D LIKE TO RECOMMEND.

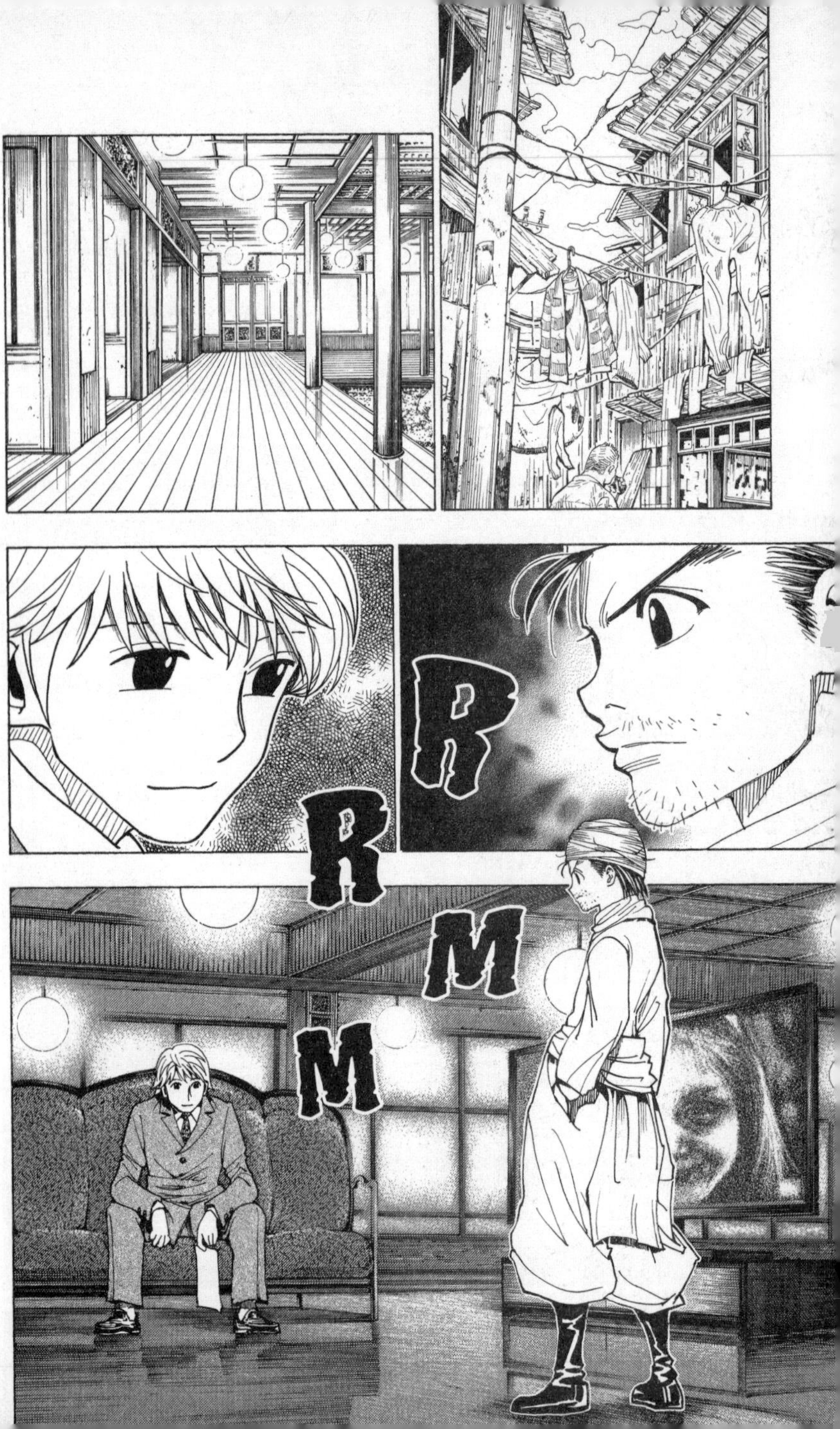
RRMM

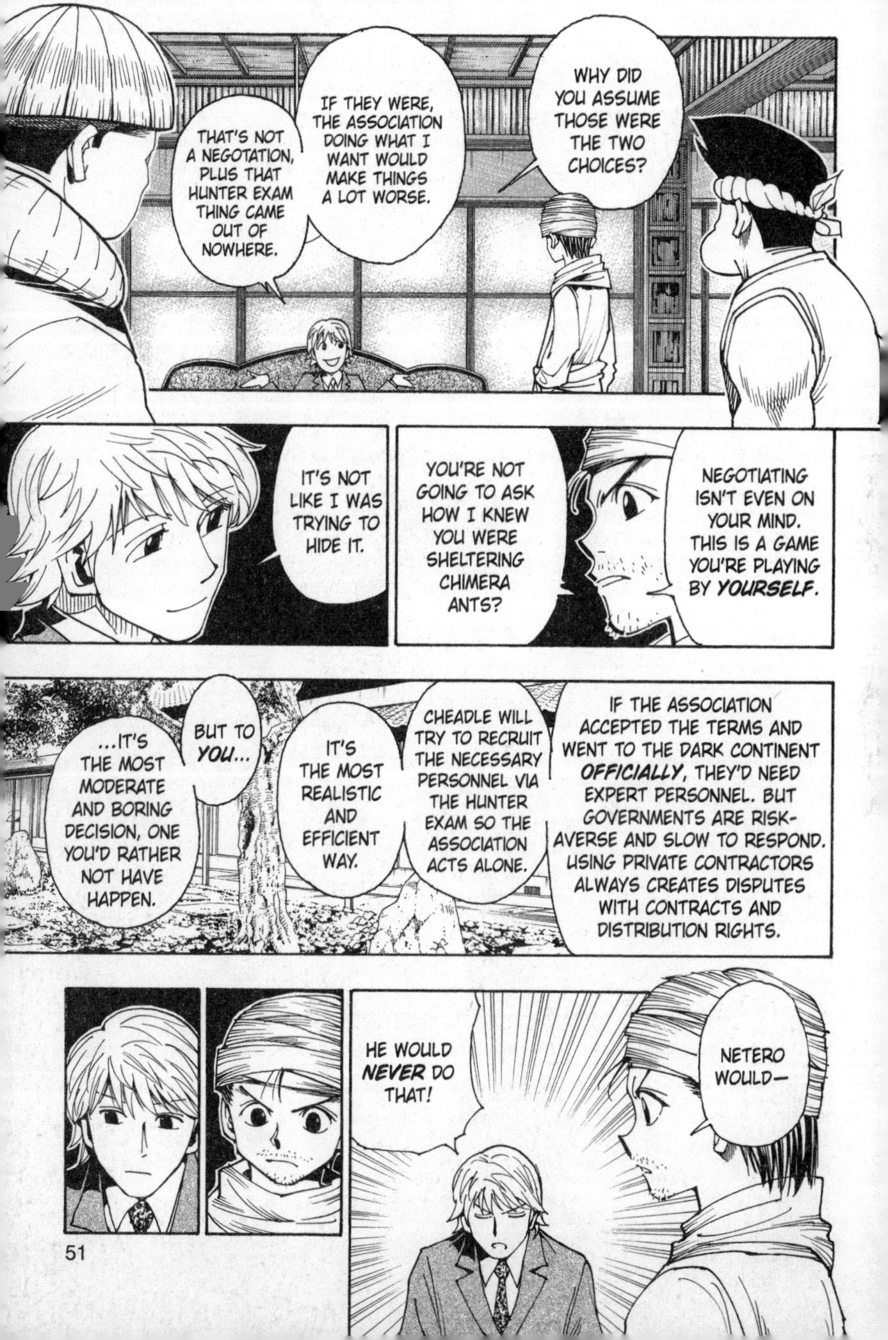
WHY DID YOU ASSUME THOSE WERE THE TWO CHOICES?
IF THEY WERE, THE ASSOCIATION DOING WHAT I WANT WOULD MAKE THINGS A LOT WORSE.
THAT'S NOT A NEGOTATION, PLUS THAT HUNTER EXAM THING CAME OUT OF NOWHERE.
NEGOTIATING ISN'T EVEN ON YOUR MIND. THIS IS A GAME YOU'RE PLAYING BY ***YOURSELF***.
YOU'RE NOT GOING TO ASK HOW I KNEW YOU WERE SHELTERING CHIMERA ANTS?
IT'S NOT LIKE I WAS TRYING TO HIDE IT.
IF THE ASSOCIATION ACCEPTED THE TERMS AND WENT TO THE DARK CONTINENT ***OFFICIALLY***, THEY'D NEED EXPERT PERSONNEL. BUT GOVERNMENTS ARE RISK-AVERSE AND SLOW TO RESPOND. USING PRIVATE CONTRACTORS ALWAYS CREATES DISPUTES WITH CONTRACTS AND DISTRIBUTION RIGHTS.
CHEADLE WILL TRY TO RECRUIT THE NECESSARY PERSONNEL VIA THE HUNTER EXAM SO THE ASSOCIATION ACTS ALONE.
IT'S THE MOST REALISTIC AND EFFICIENT WAY.
BUT TO ***YOU***...
...IT'S THE MOST MODERATE AND BORING DECISION, ONE YOU'D RATHER NOT HAVE HAPPEN.
NETERO WOULD—
HE WOULD ***NEVER*** DO THAT!

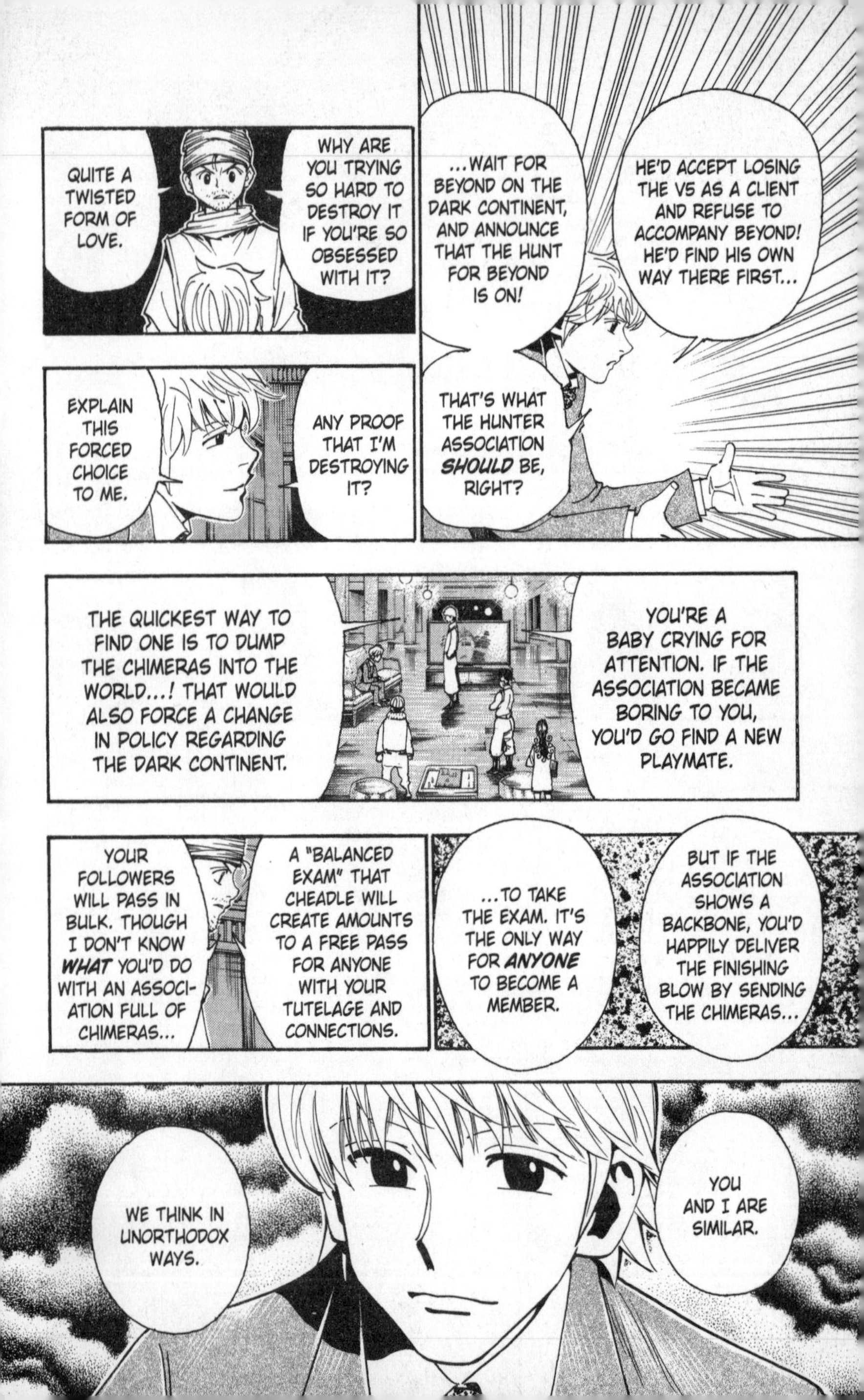

HE'D ACCEPT LOSING THE V5 AS A CLIENT AND REFUSE TO ACCOMPANY BEYOND! HE'D FIND HIS OWN WAY THERE FIRST...
...WAIT FOR BEYOND ON THE DARK CONTINENT, AND ANNOUNCE THAT THE HUNT FOR BEYOND IS ON!
THAT'S WHAT THE HUNTER ASSOCIATION SHOULD BE, RIGHT?
WHY ARE YOU TRYING SO HARD TO DESTROY IT IF YOU'RE SO OBSESSED WITH IT?
QUITE A TWISTED FORM OF LOVE.
ANY PROOF THAT I'M DESTROYING IT?
EXPLAIN THIS FORCED CHOICE TO ME.
YOU'RE A BABY CRYING FOR ATTENTION. IF THE ASSOCIATION BECAME BORING TO YOU, YOU'D GO FIND A NEW PLAYMATE.
THE QUICKEST WAY TO FIND ONE IS TO DUMP THE CHIMERAS INTO THE WORLD...! THAT WOULD ALSO FORCE A CHANGE IN POLICY REGARDING THE DARK CONTINENT.
BUT IF THE ASSOCIATION SHOWS A BACKBONE, YOU'D HAPPILY DELIVER THE FINISHING BLOW BY SENDING THE CHIMERAS...
...TO TAKE THE EXAM. IT'S THE ONLY WAY FOR ANYONE TO BECOME A MEMBER.
A "BALANCED EXAM" THAT CHEADLE WILL CREATE AMOUNTS TO A FREE PASS FOR ANYONE WITH YOUR TUTELAGE AND CONNECTIONS.
YOUR FOLLOWERS WILL PASS IN BULK. THOUGH I DON'T KNOW WHAT YOU'D DO WITH AN ASSOCIATION FULL OF CHIMERAS...
YOU AND I ARE SIMILAR.
WE THINK IN UNORTHODOX WAYS.

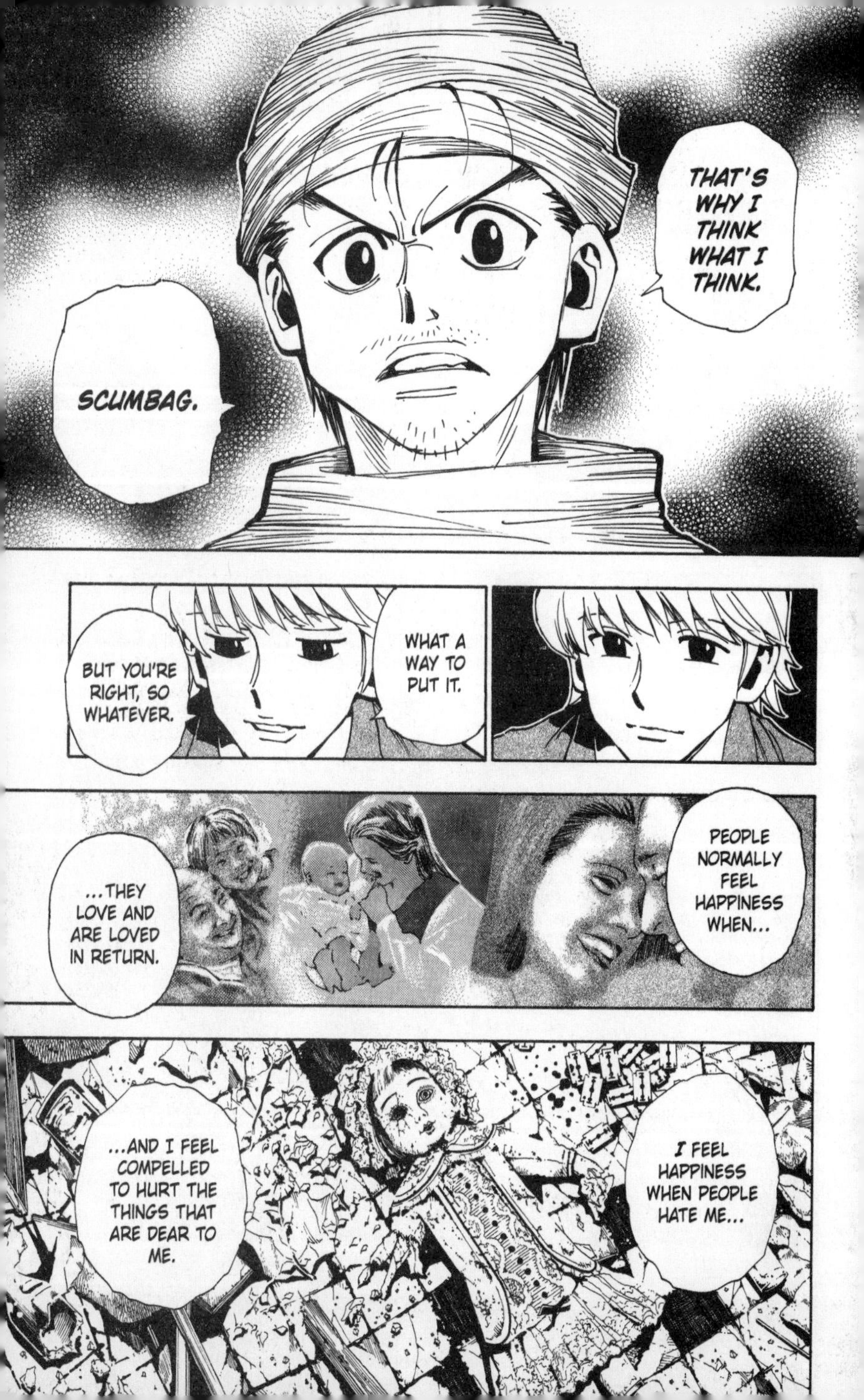
THAT'S WHY I THINK WHAT I THINK.
SCUMBAG.
WHAT A WAY TO PUT IT.
BUT YOU'RE RIGHT, SO WHATEVER.
PEOPLE NORMALLY FEEL HAPPINESS WHEN...
...THEY LOVE AND ARE LOVED IN RETURN.
I FEEL HAPPINESS WHEN PEOPLE HATE ME...
...AND I FEEL COMPELLED TO HURT THE THINGS THAT ARE DEAR TO ME.

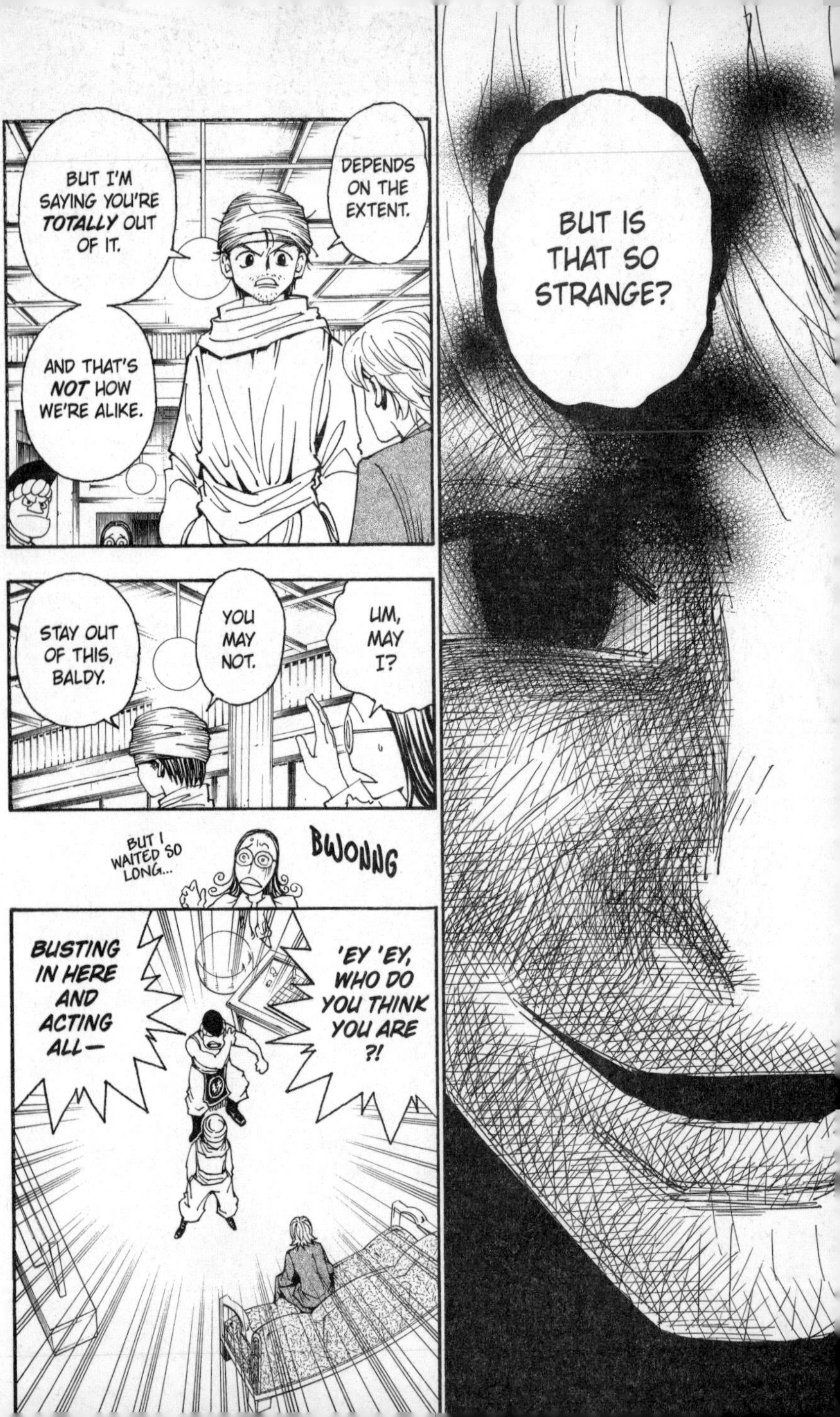
BUT IS THAT SO STRANGE?
DEPENDS ON THE EXTENT.
BUT I'M SAYING YOU'RE TOTALLY OUT OF IT.
AND THAT'S NOT HOW WE'RE ALIKE.
UM, MAY I?
YOU MAY NOT.
STAY OUT OF THIS, BALDY.
BWONNG
BUT I WAITED SO LONG...
'EY 'EY, WHO DO YOU THINK YOU ARE?!
BUSTING IN HERE AND ACTING ALL—

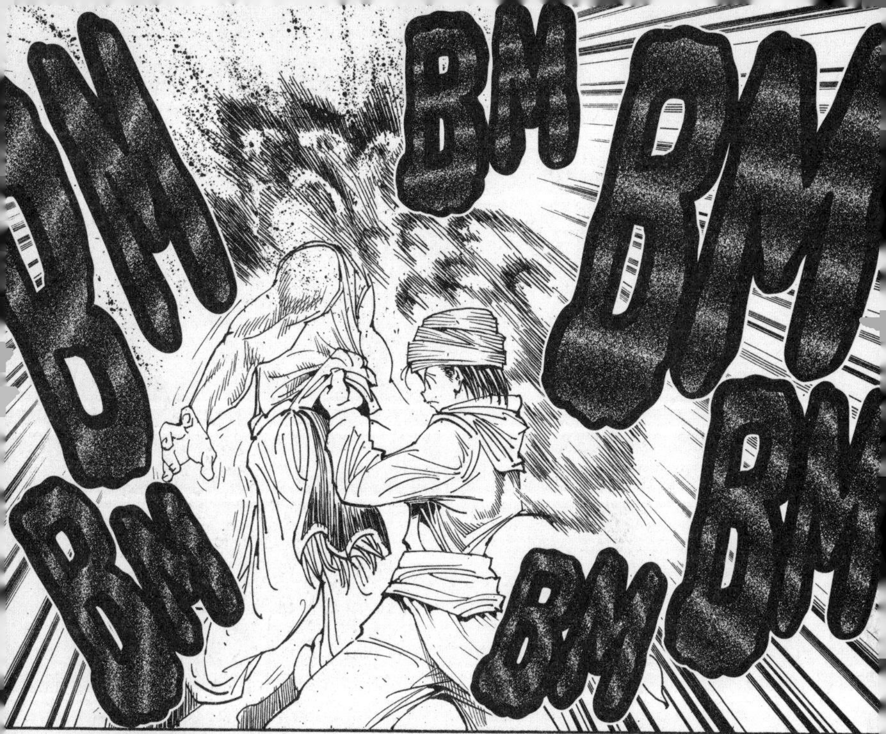
BM
BM
BM
BM
BM
BM
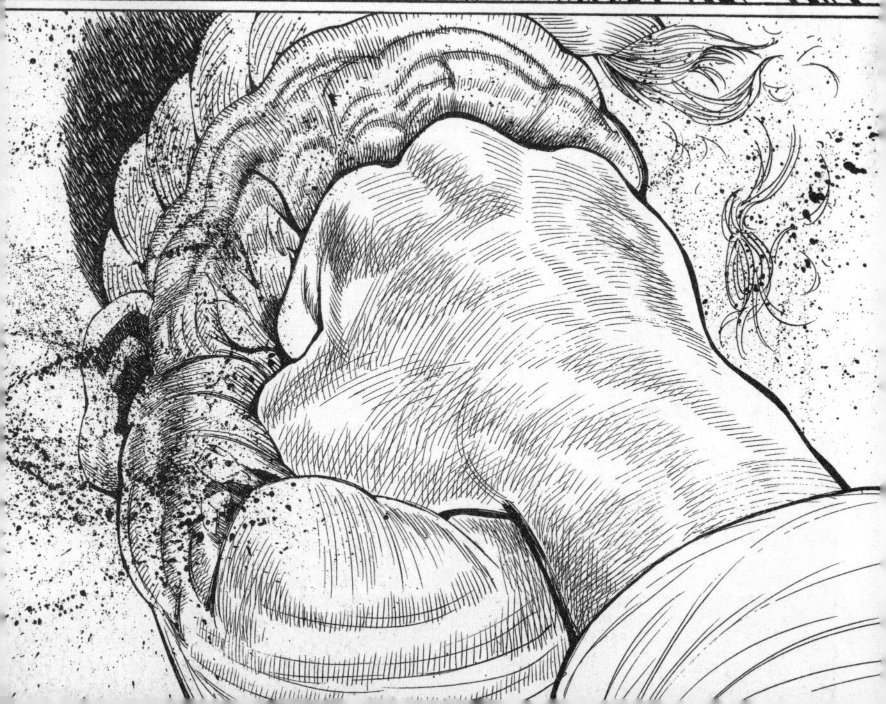

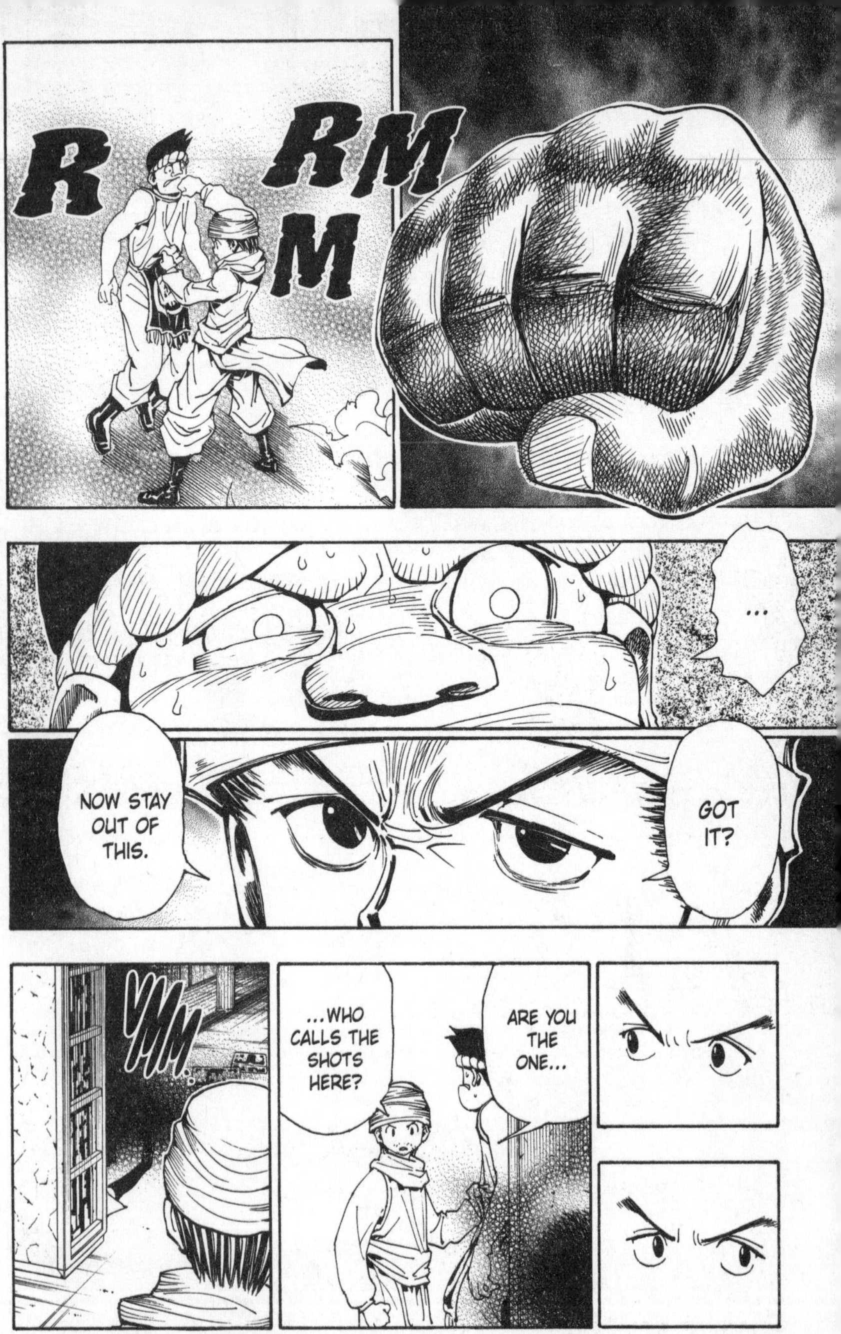
RRMM
...
GOT IT?
NOW STAY OUT OF THIS.
ARE YOU THE ONE...
...WHO CALLS THE SHOTS HERE?
VMM

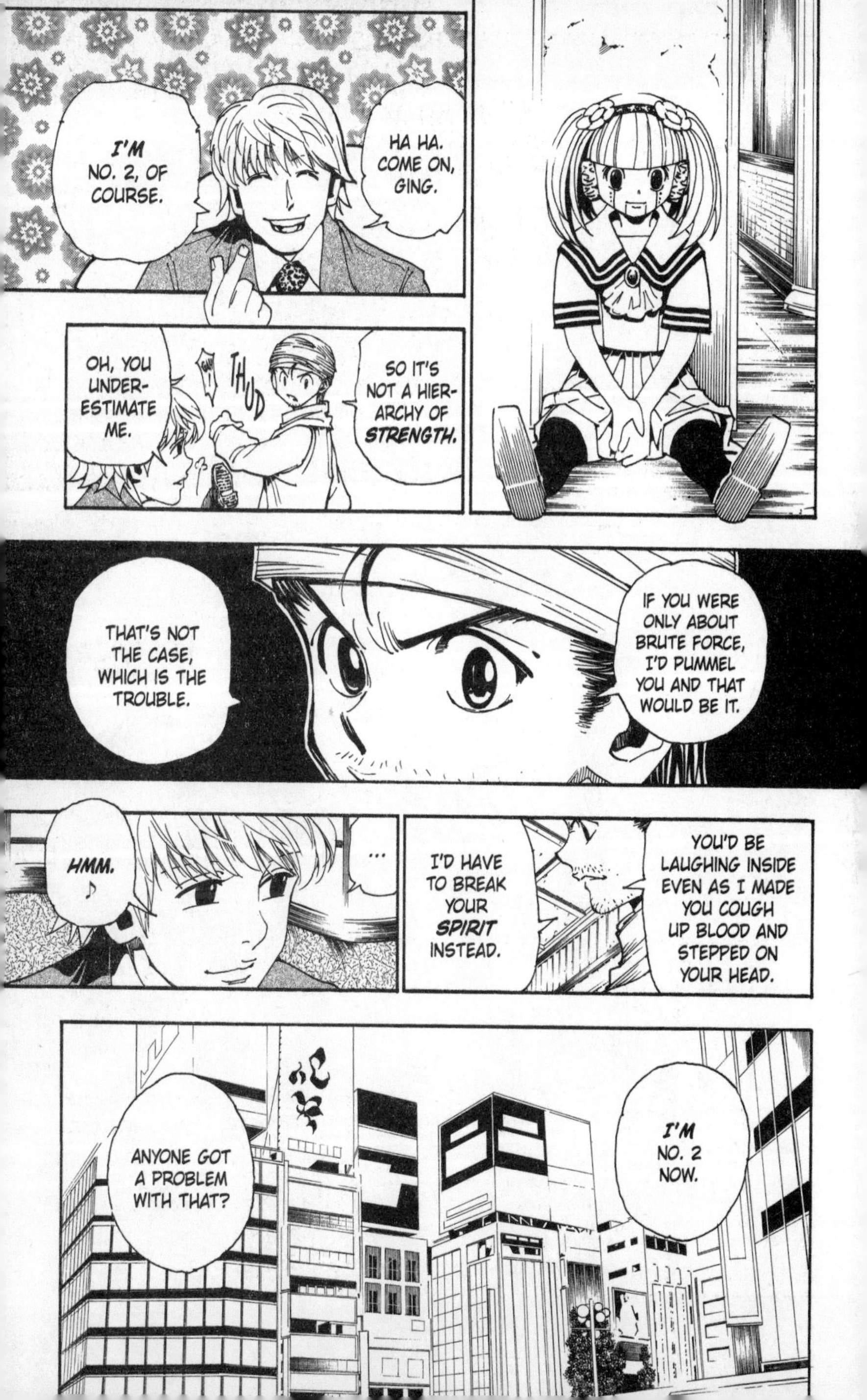
HA HA. COME ON, GING.
I'M NO. 2, OF COURSE.
SO IT'S NOT A HIERARCHY OF STRENGTH.
THUD
OH, YOU UNDERESTIMATE ME.
IF YOU WERE ONLY ABOUT BRUTE FORCE, I'D PUMMEL YOU AND THAT WOULD BE IT.
THAT'S NOT THE CASE, WHICH IS THE TROUBLE.
YOU'D BE LAUGHING INSIDE EVEN AS I MADE YOU COUGH UP BLOOD AND STEPPED ON YOUR HEAD.
I'D HAVE TO BREAK YOUR SPIRIT INSTEAD.
...
HMM. ♪
I'M NO. 2 NOW.
ANYONE GOT A PROBLEM WITH THAT?

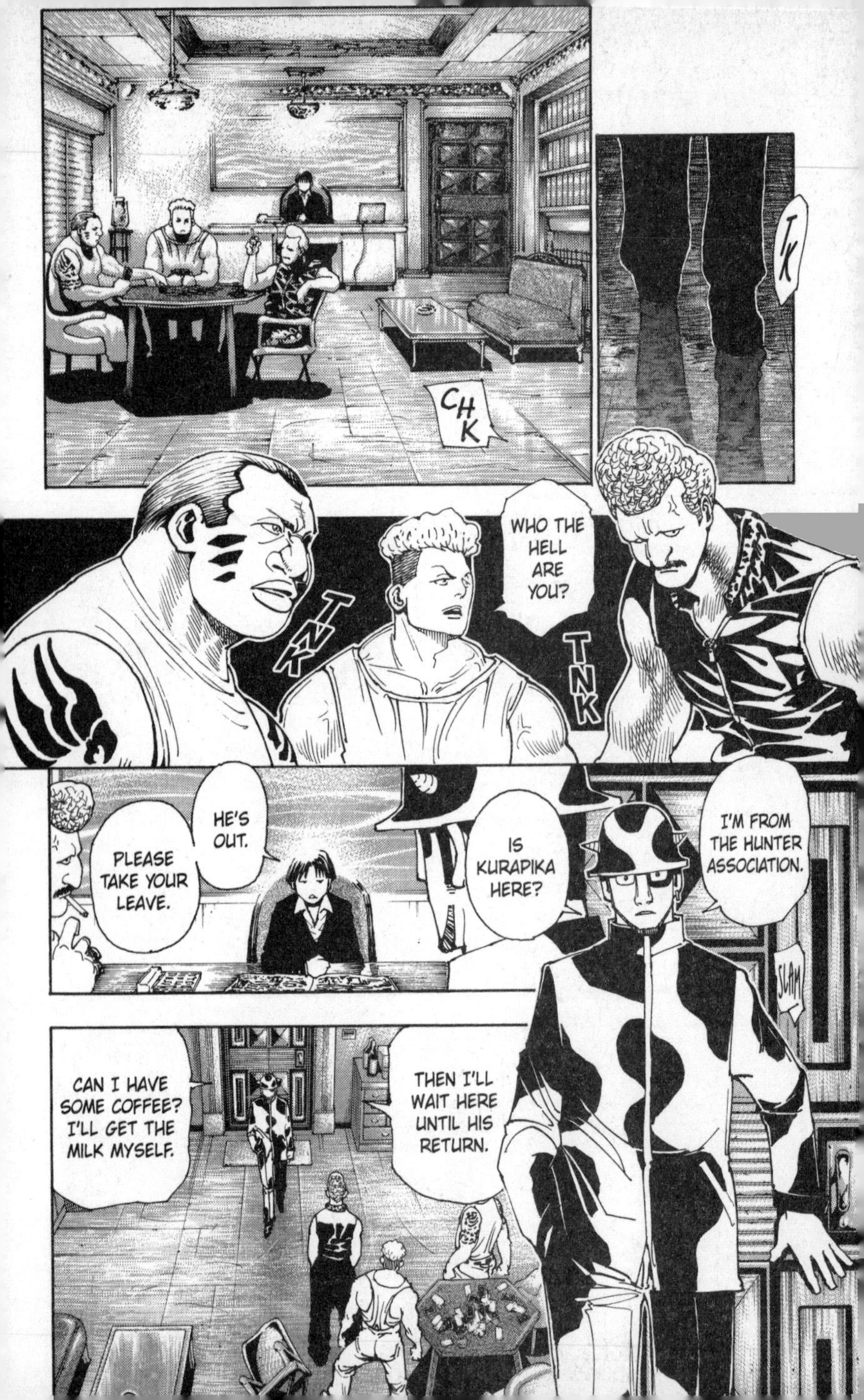
TK
CHK
WHO THE HELL ARE YOU?
TNK
TNK
SLAM
I'M FROM THE HUNTER ASSOCIATION.
IS KURAPIKA HERE?
HE'S OUT.
PLEASE TAKE YOUR LEAVE.
THEN I'LL WAIT HERE UNTIL HIS RETURN.
CAN I HAVE SOME COFFEE? I'LL GET THE MILK MYSELF.

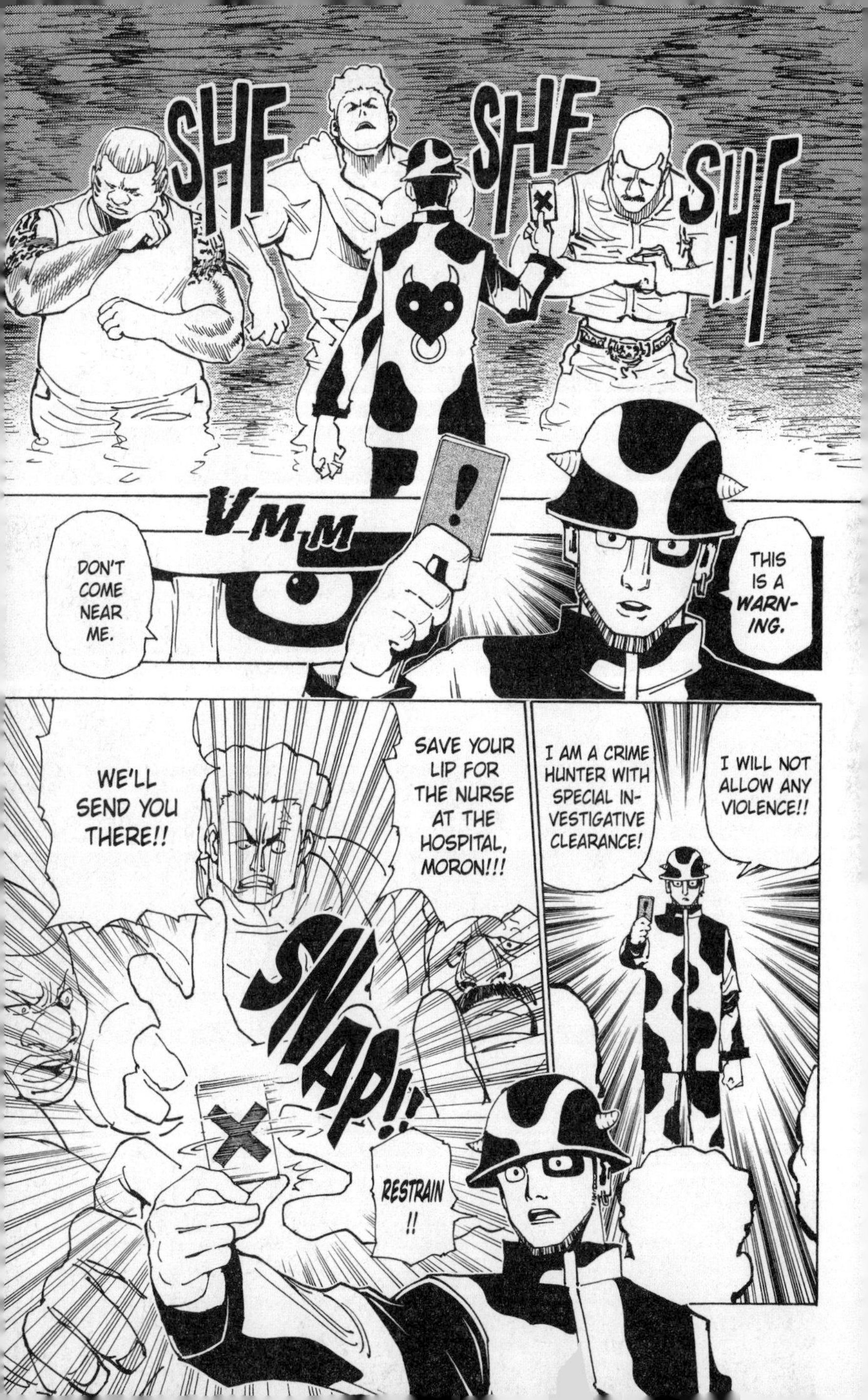
SHF
SHF
SHF
THIS IS A WARN-ING.
VMM
DON'T COME NEAR ME.
I WILL NOT ALLOW ANY VIOLENCE!!
I AM A CRIME HUNTER WITH SPECIAL IN-VESTIGATIVE CLEARANCE!
SAVE YOUR LIP FOR THE NURSE AT THE HOSPITAL, MORON!!!
WE'LL SEND YOU THERE!!
SNAP!!
RESTRAIN!!

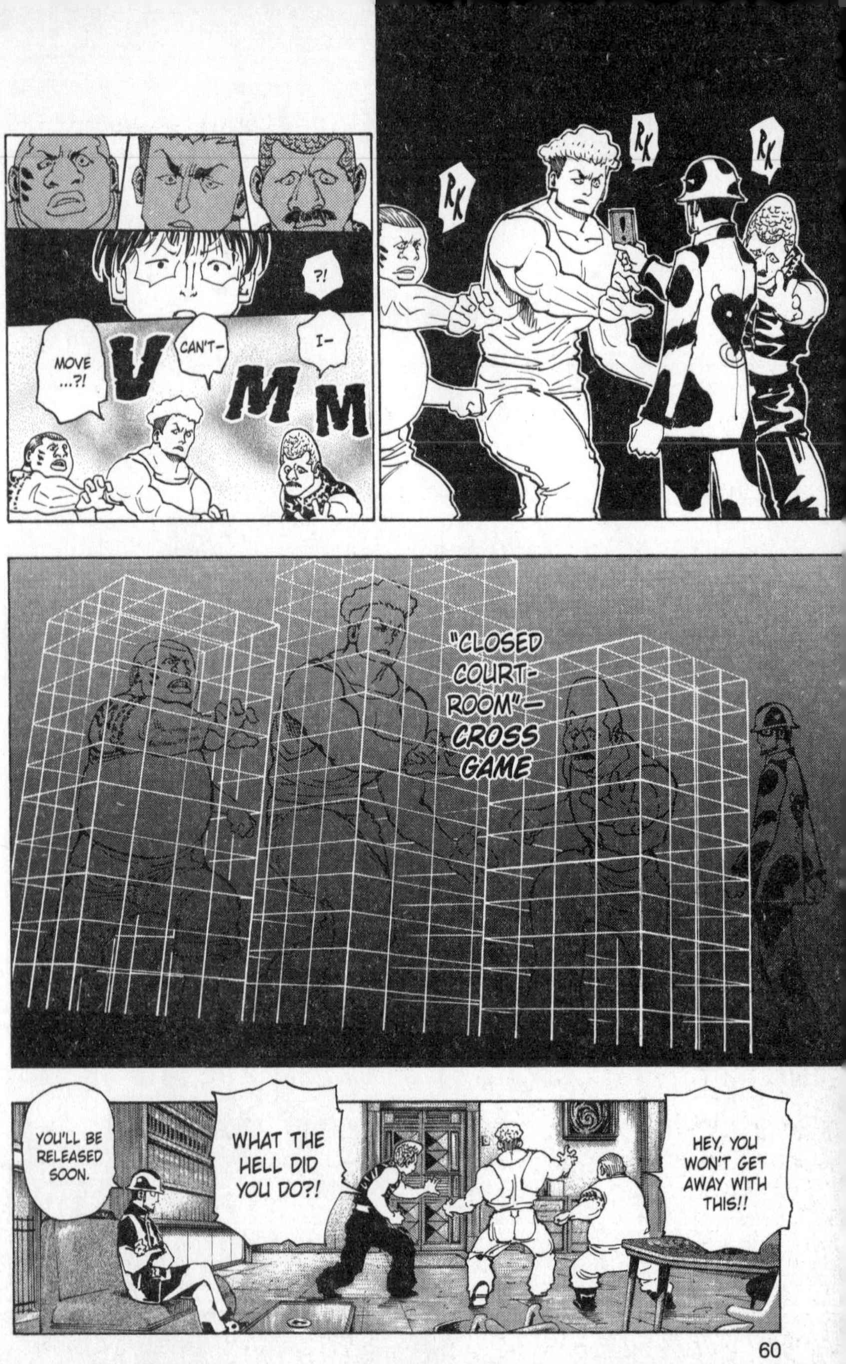
RK
RK
RK
?!
I-
CAN'T-
MOVE ...?!
VMM
"CLOSED COURT-ROOM"—CROSS GAME
HEY, YOU WON'T GET AWAY WITH THIS!!
WHAT THE HELL DID YOU DO?!
YOU'LL BE RELEASED SOON.

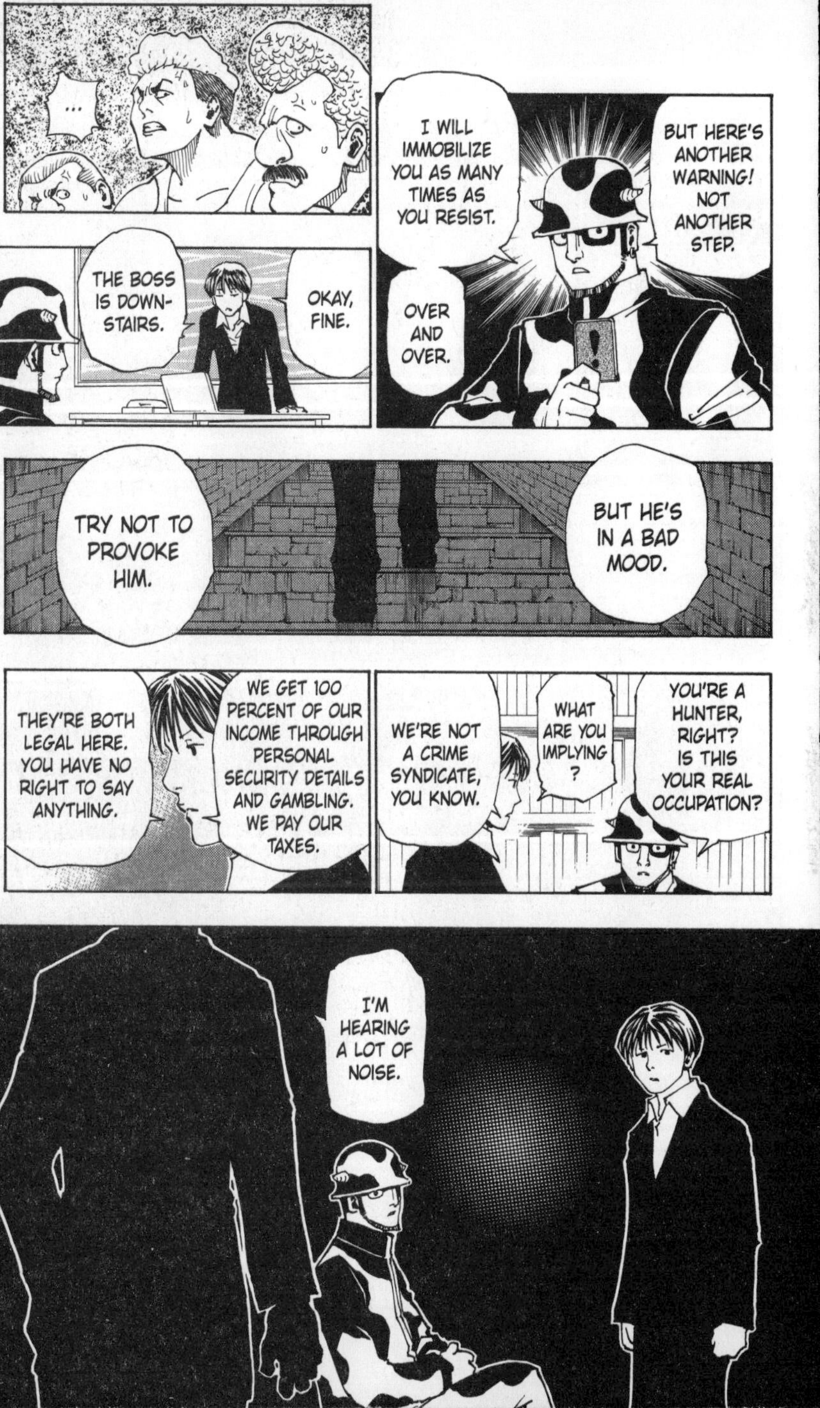
BUT HERE'S ANOTHER WARNING! NOT ANOTHER STEP.
I WILL IMMOBILIZE YOU AS MANY TIMES AS YOU RESIST.
OVER AND OVER.
...
OKAY, FINE.
THE BOSS IS DOWN-STAIRS.
BUT HE'S IN A BAD MOOD.
TRY NOT TO PROVOKE HIM.
YOU'RE A HUNTER, RIGHT? IS THIS YOUR REAL OCCUPATION?
WHAT ARE YOU IMPLYING?
WE'RE NOT A CRIME SYNDICATE, YOU KNOW.
WE GET 100 PERCENT OF OUR INCOME THROUGH PERSONAL SECURITY DETAILS AND GAMBLING. WE PAY OUR TAXES.
THEY'RE BOTH LEGAL HERE. YOU HAVE NO RIGHT TO SAY ANYTHING.
I'M HEARING A LOT OF NOISE.

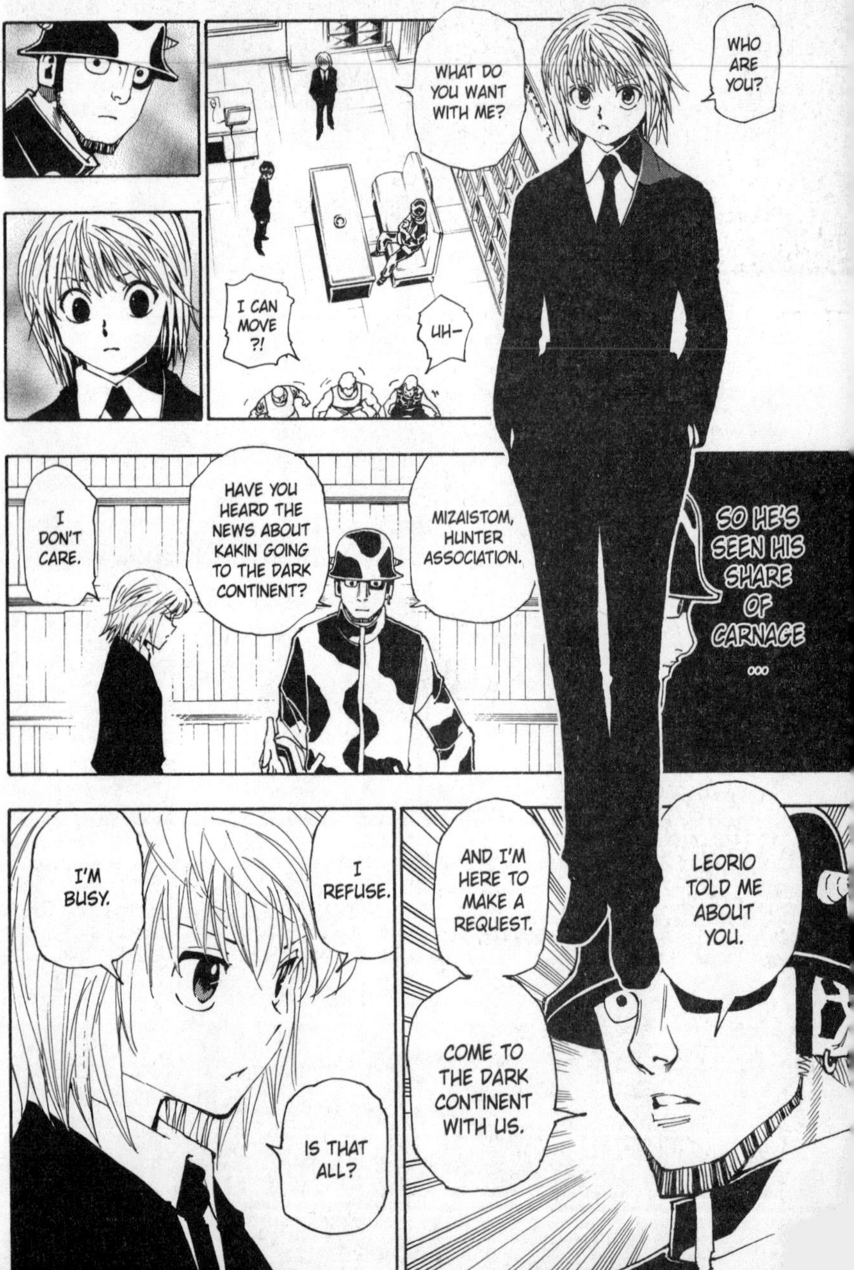
WHO ARE YOU?
WHAT DO YOU WANT WITH ME?
UH-
I CAN MOVE ?!
SO HE'S SEEN HIS SHARE OF CARNAGE...
MIZAISTOM, HUNTER ASSOCIATION.
HAVE YOU HEARD THE NEWS ABOUT KAKIN GOING TO THE DARK CONTINENT?
I DON'T CARE.
LEORIO TOLD ME ABOUT YOU.
AND I'M HERE TO MAKE A REQUEST.
COME TO THE DARK CONTINENT WITH US.
I REFUSE.
I'M BUSY.
IS THAT ALL?

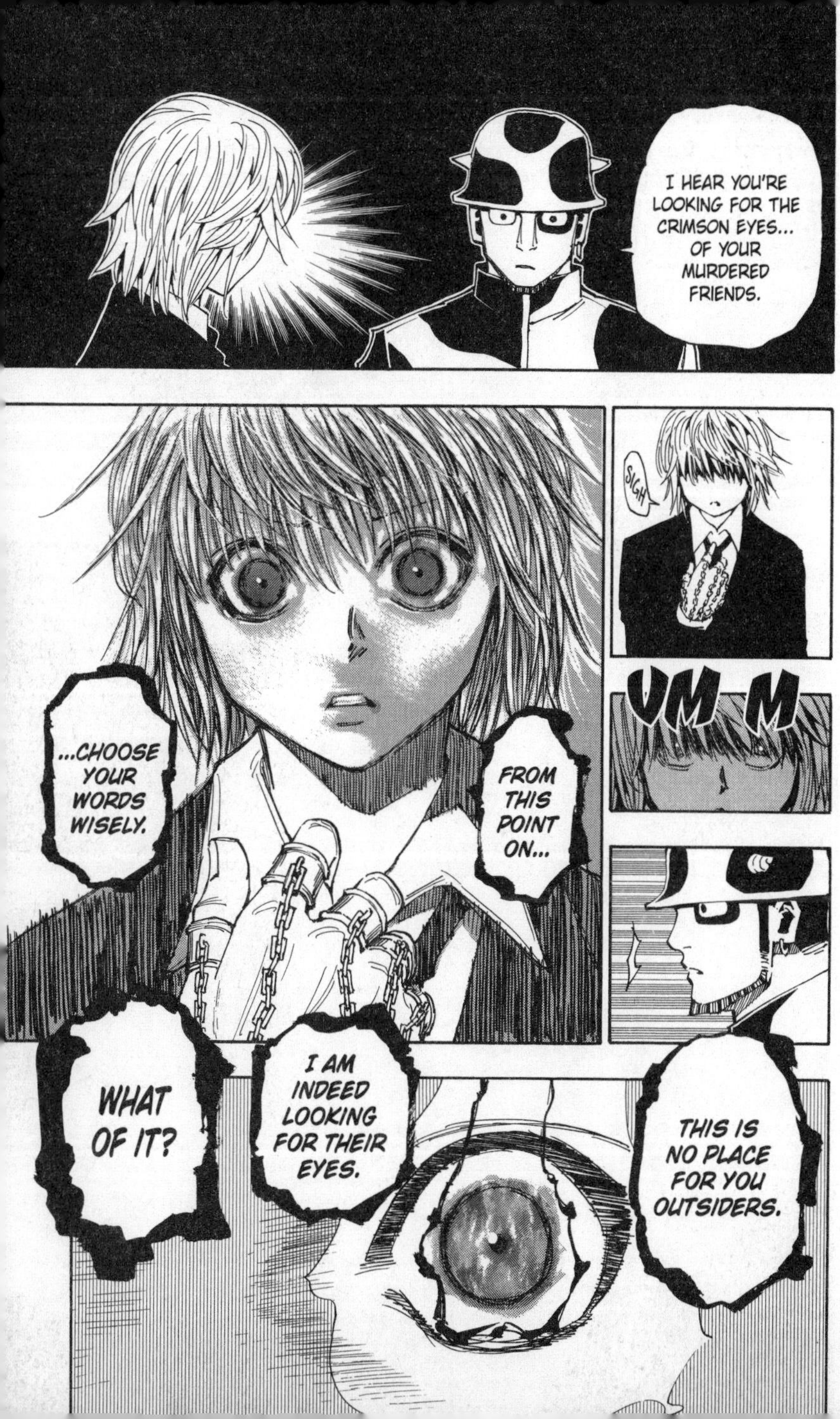

I HEAR YOU'RE LOOKING FOR THE CRIMSON EYES... OF YOUR MURDERED FRIENDS.
SIGH
UMM
FROM THIS POINT ON...
...CHOOSE YOUR WORDS WISELY.
THIS IS NO PLACE FOR YOU OUTSIDERS.
I AM INDEED LOOKING FOR THEIR EYES.
WHAT OF IT?

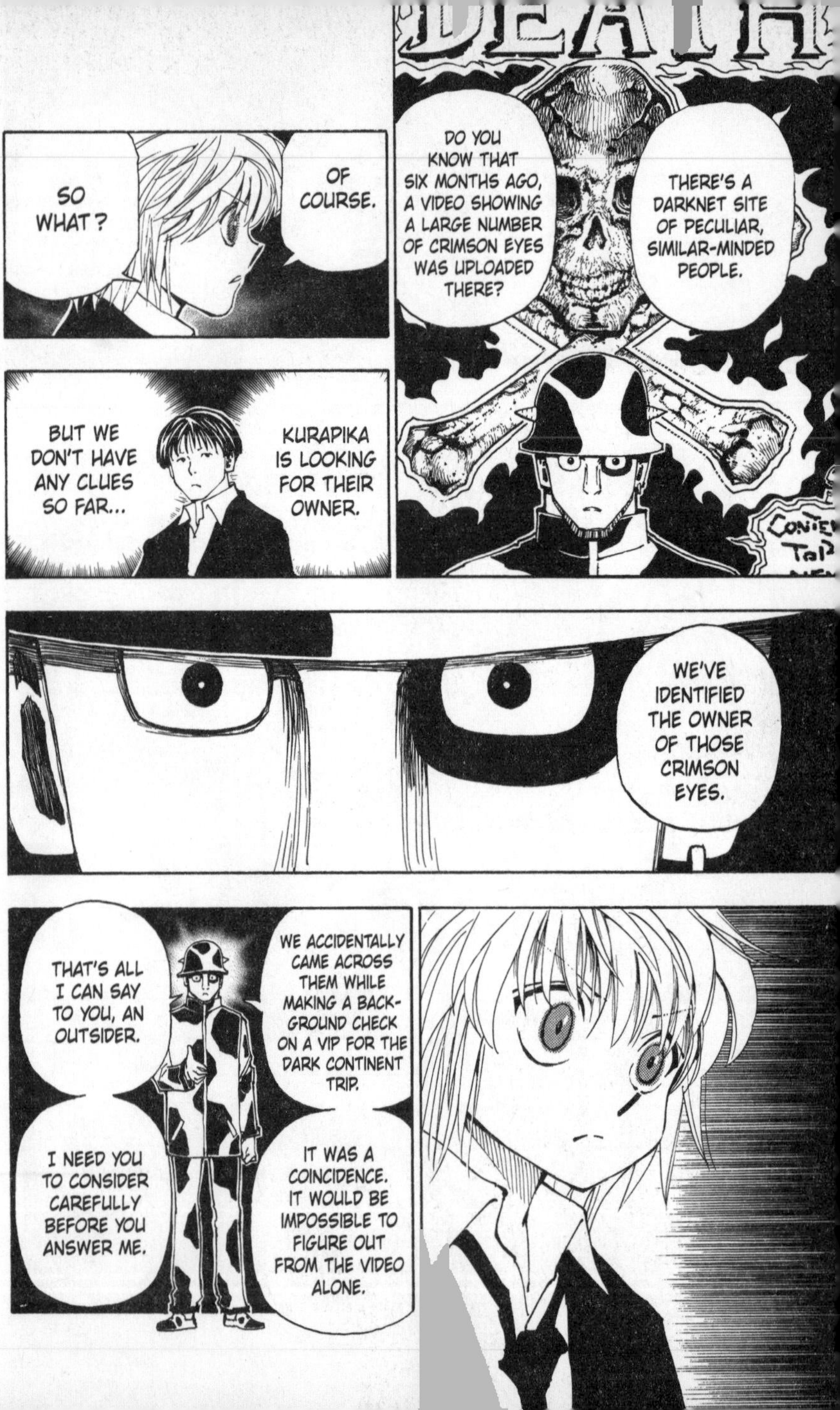
DEATH
THERE'S A DARKNET SITE OF PECULIAR, SIMILAR-MINDED PEOPLE.
DO YOU KNOW THAT SIX MONTHS AGO, A VIDEO SHOWING A LARGE NUMBER OF CRIMSON EYES WAS UPLOADED THERE?
OF COURSE.
SO WHAT?
KURAPIKA IS LOOKING FOR THEIR OWNER.
BUT WE DON'T HAVE ANY CLUES SO FAR...
WE'VE IDENTIFIED THE OWNER OF THOSE CRIMSON EYES.
WE ACCIDENTALLY CAME ACROSS THEM WHILE MAKING A BACK-GROUND CHECK ON A VIP FOR THE DARK CONTINENT TRIP.
THAT'S ALL I CAN SAY TO YOU, AN OUTSIDER.
IT WAS A COINCIDENCE. IT WOULD BE IMPOSSIBLE TO FIGURE OUT FROM THE VIDEO ALONE.
I NEED YOU TO CONSIDER CAREFULLY BEFORE YOU ANSWER ME.

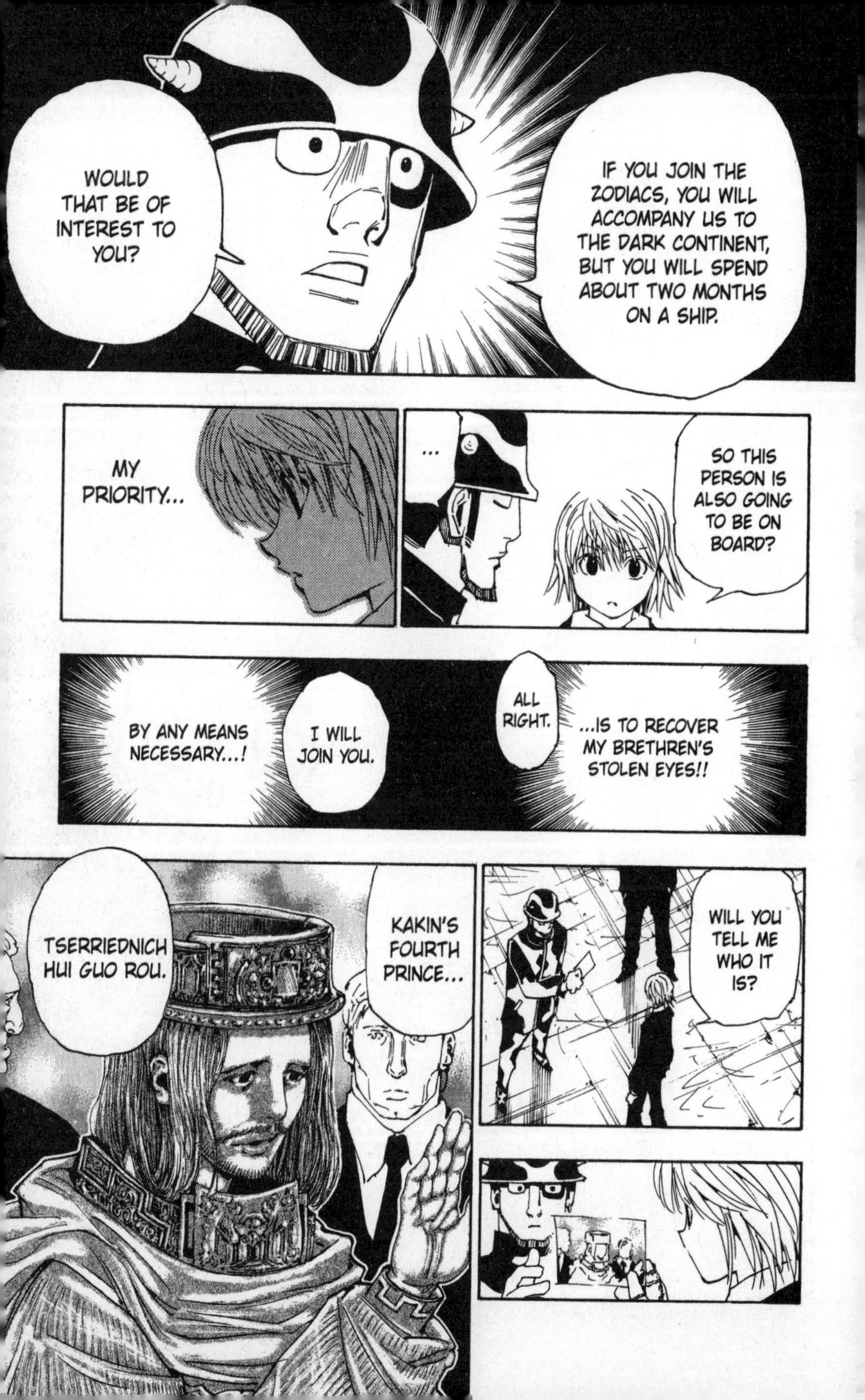
IF YOU JOIN THE ZODIACS, YOU WILL ACCOMPANY US TO THE DARK CONTINENT, BUT YOU WILL SPEND ABOUT TWO MONTHS ON A SHIP.
WOULD THAT BE OF INTEREST TO YOU?
SO THIS PERSON IS ALSO GOING TO BE ON BOARD?
...
MY PRIORITY...
...IS TO RECOVER MY BRETHREN'S STOLEN EYES!!
ALL RIGHT.
I WILL JOIN YOU.
BY ANY MEANS NECESSARY...!
WILL YOU TELL ME WHO IT IS?
KAKIN'S FOURTH PRINCE...
TSERRIEDNICH HUI GUO ROU.

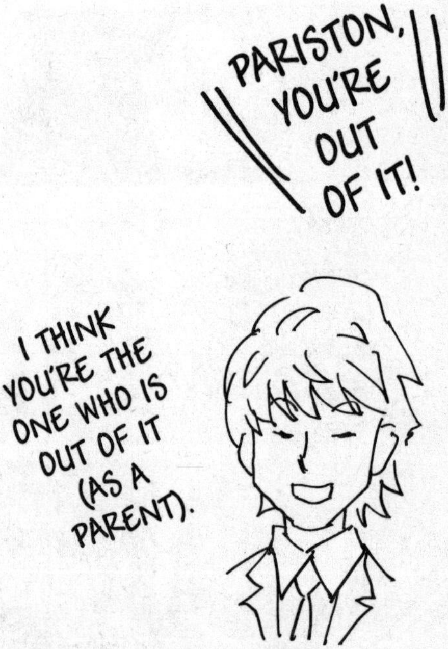
PARISTON, YOU'RE OUT OF IT!
I THINK YOU'RE THE ONE WHO IS OUT OF IT (AS A PARENT).

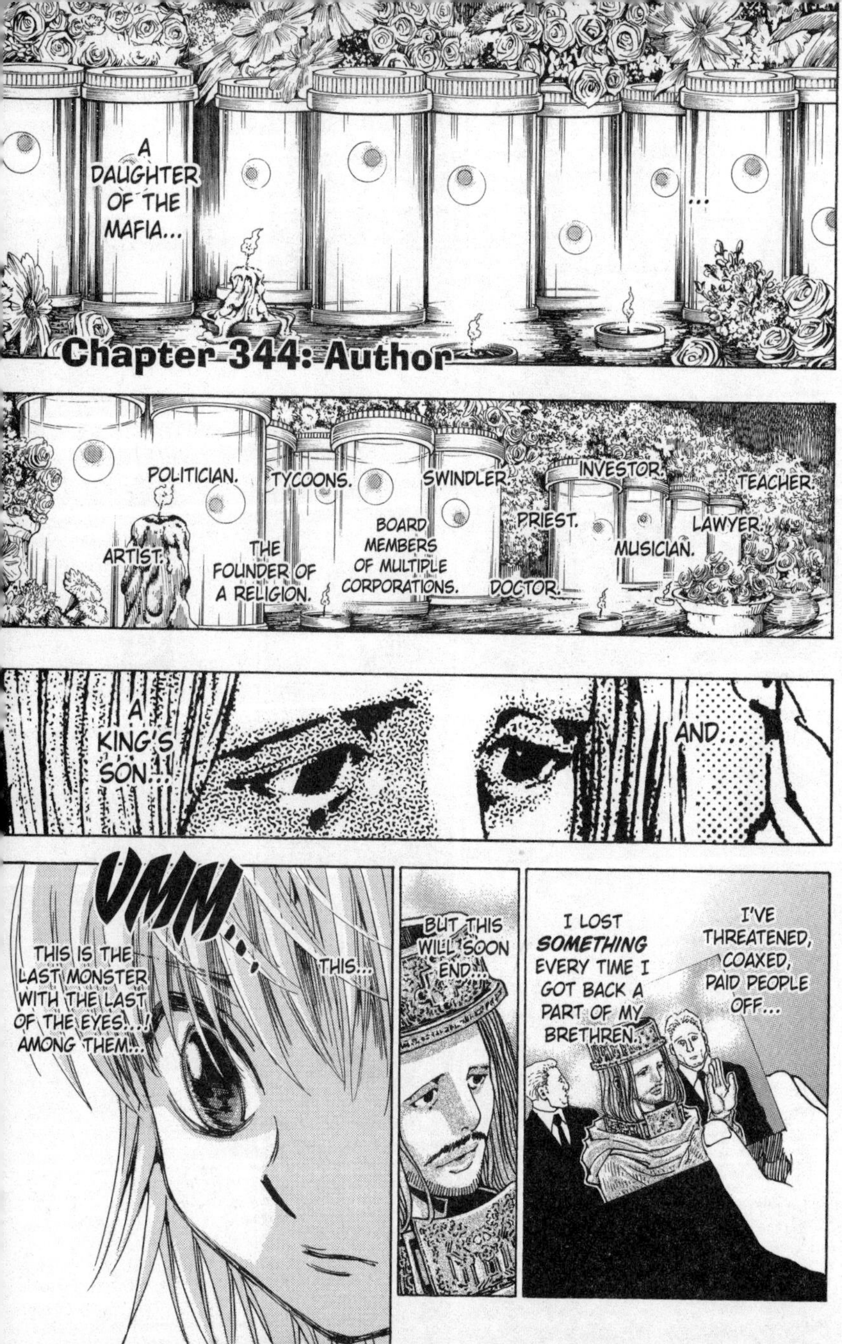
A DAUGHTER OF THE MAFIA...
...
Chapter 344: Author
TEACHER.
INVESTOR.
LAWYER.
MUSICIAN.
PRIEST.
DOCTOR.
SWINDLER.
BOARD MEMBERS OF MULTIPLE CORPORATIONS.
TYCOONS.
THE FOUNDER OF A RELIGION.
POLITICIAN.
ARTIST.
A KING'S SON...
AND...
I'VE THREATENED, COAXED, PAID PEOPLE OFF...
I LOST SOMETHING EVERY TIME I GOT BACK A PART OF MY BRETHREN.
BUT THIS WILL SOON END...
UMM...
THIS...
THIS IS THE LAST MONSTER WITH THE LAST OF THE EYES...! AMONG THEM...

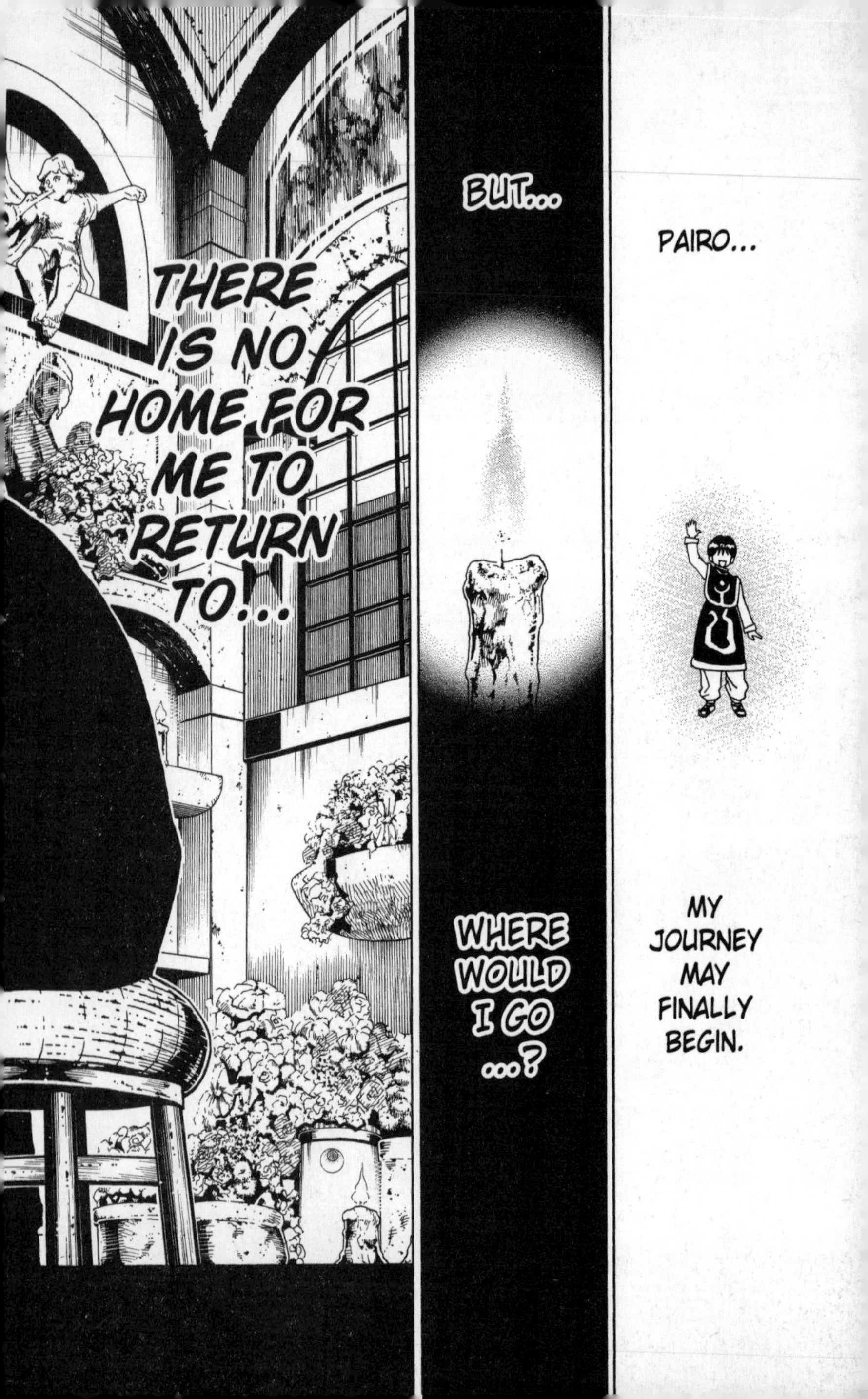
PAIRO...
MY JOURNEY MAY FINALLY BEGIN.
BUT...
WHERE WOULD I GO ...?
THERE IS NO HOME FOR ME TO RETURN TO!...

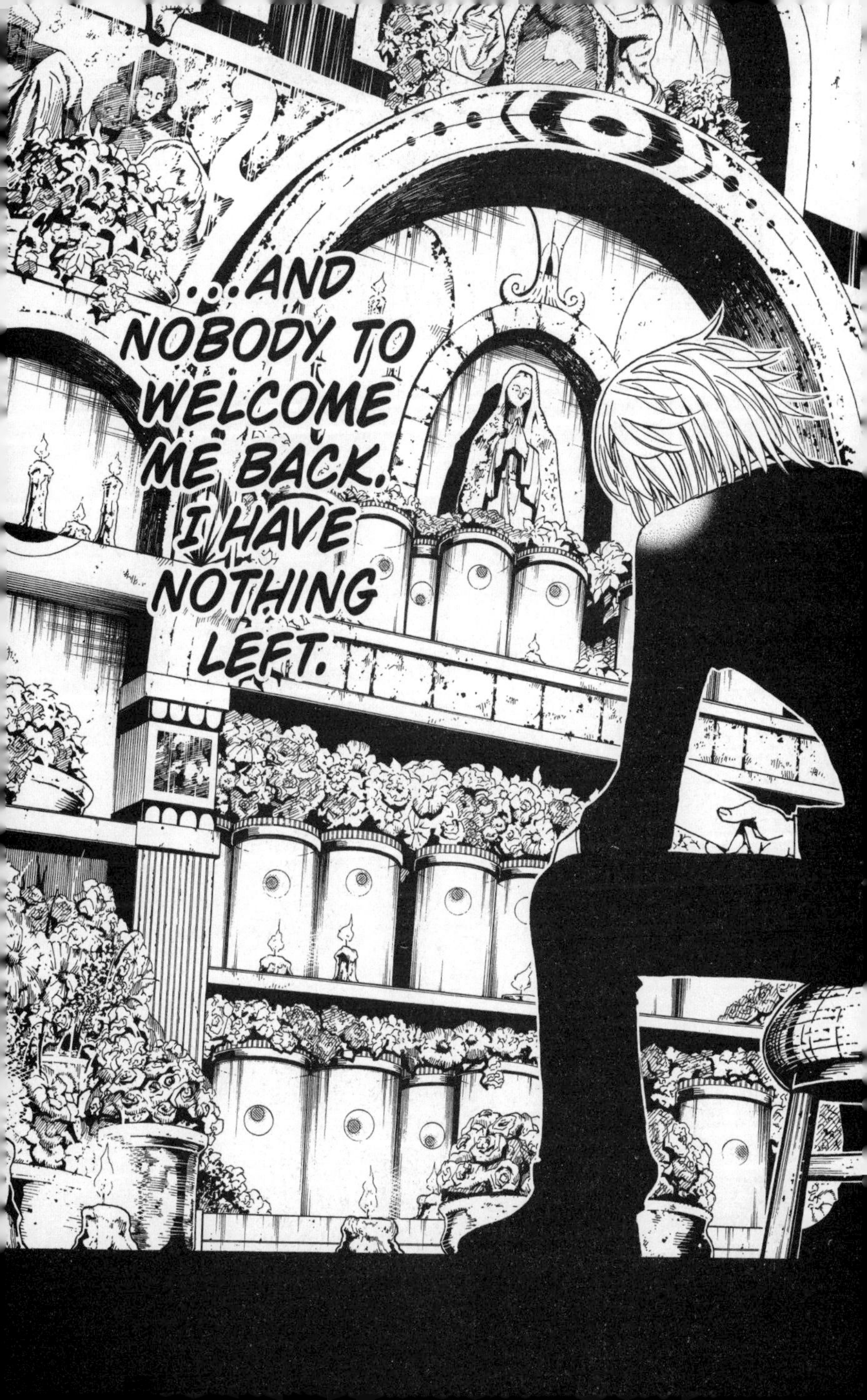
...AND NOBODY TO WELCOME ME BACK. I HAVE NOTHING LEFT.

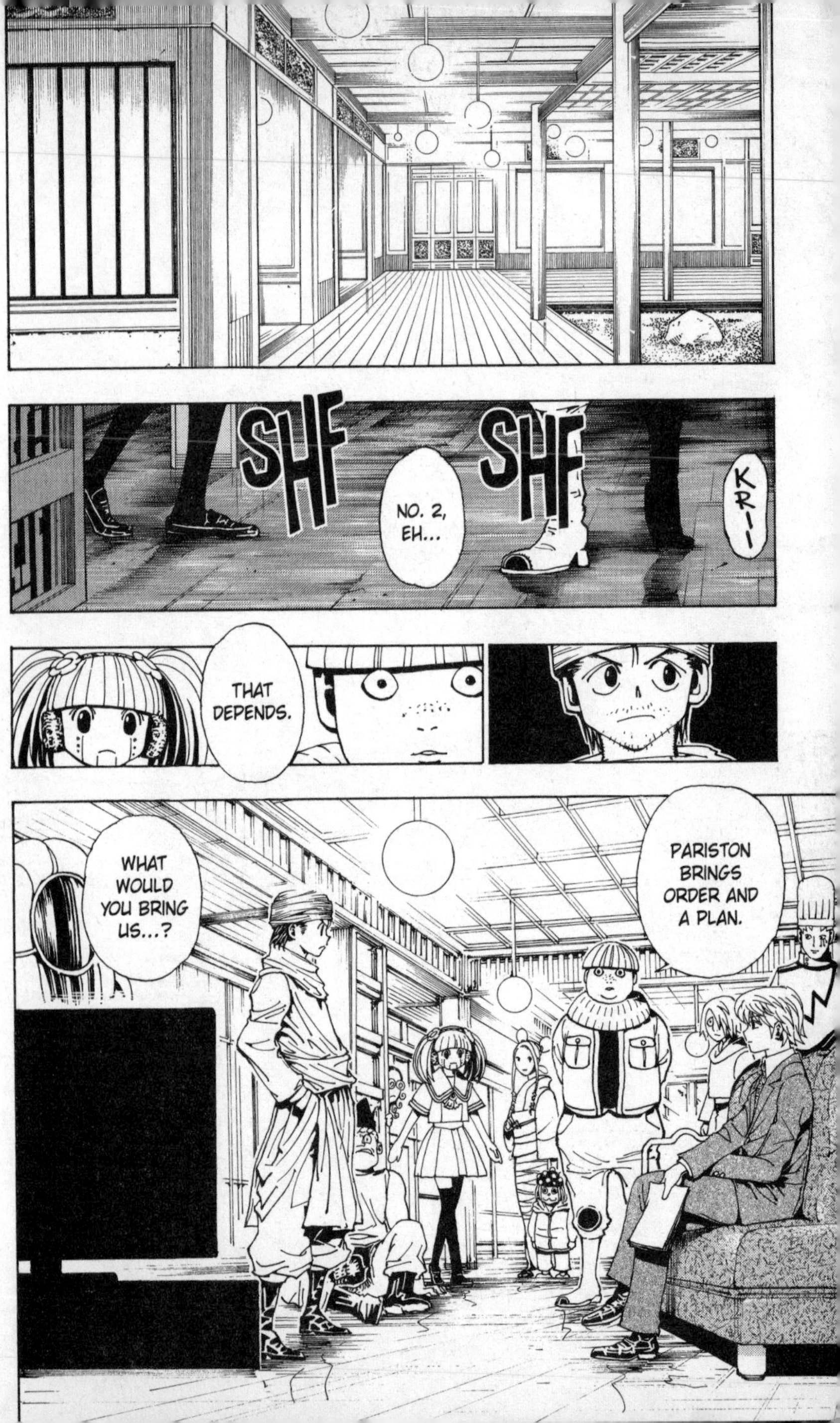
KRI—
SHF
NO. 2, EH...
SHF
THAT DEPENDS.
PARISTON BRINGS ORDER AND A PLAN.
WHAT WOULD YOU BRING US...?

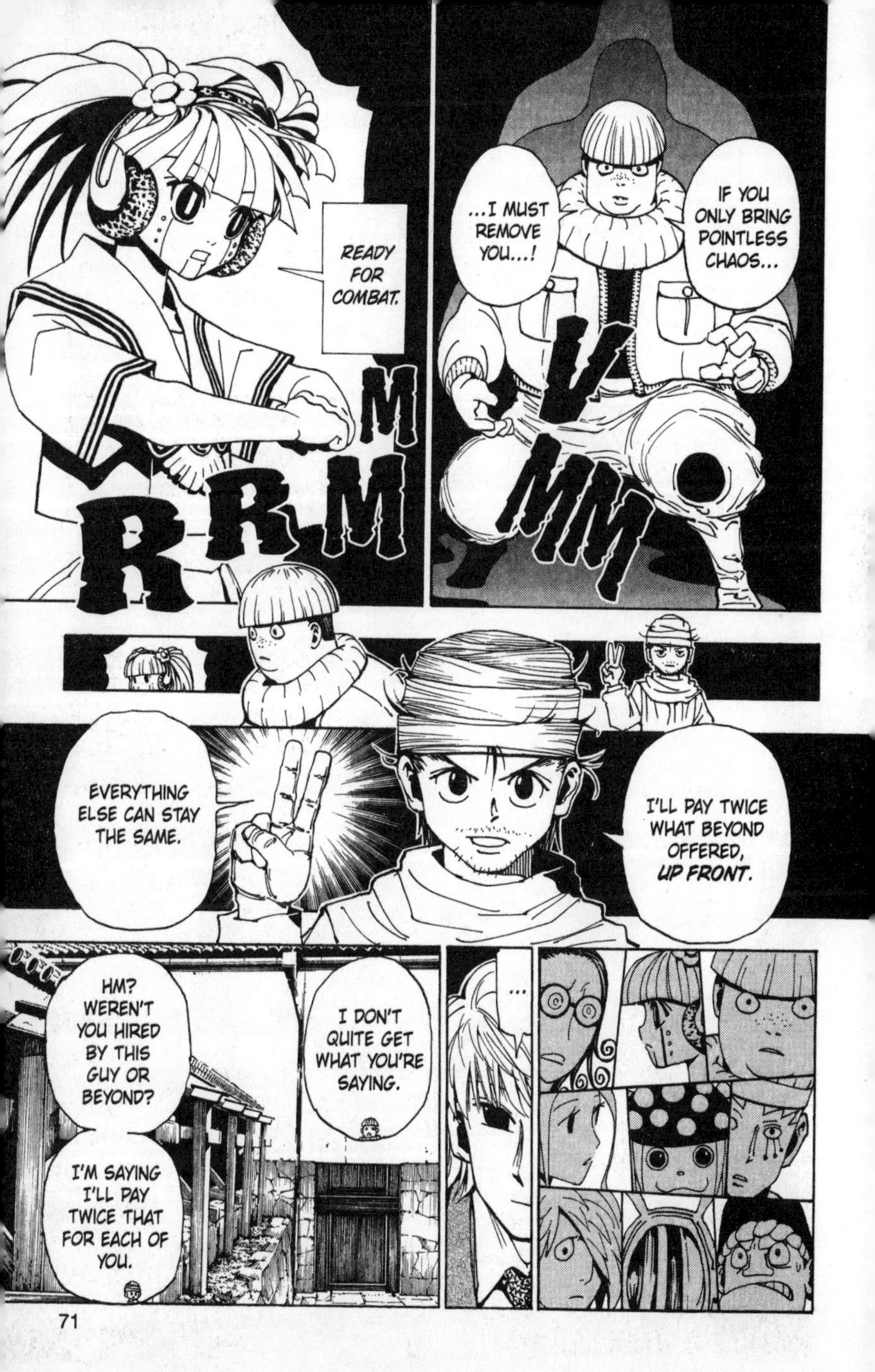
IF YOU ONLY BRING POINTLESS CHAOS...
...I MUST REMOVE YOU...!
VMM
READY FOR COMBAT.
RRMMM
I'LL PAY TWICE WHAT BEYOND OFFERED, *UP FRONT*.
EVERYTHING ELSE CAN STAY THE SAME.
...
I DON'T QUITE GET WHAT YOU'RE SAYING.
HM? WEREN'T YOU HIRED BY THIS GUY OR BEYOND?
I'M SAYING I'LL PAY TWICE THAT FOR EACH OF YOU.

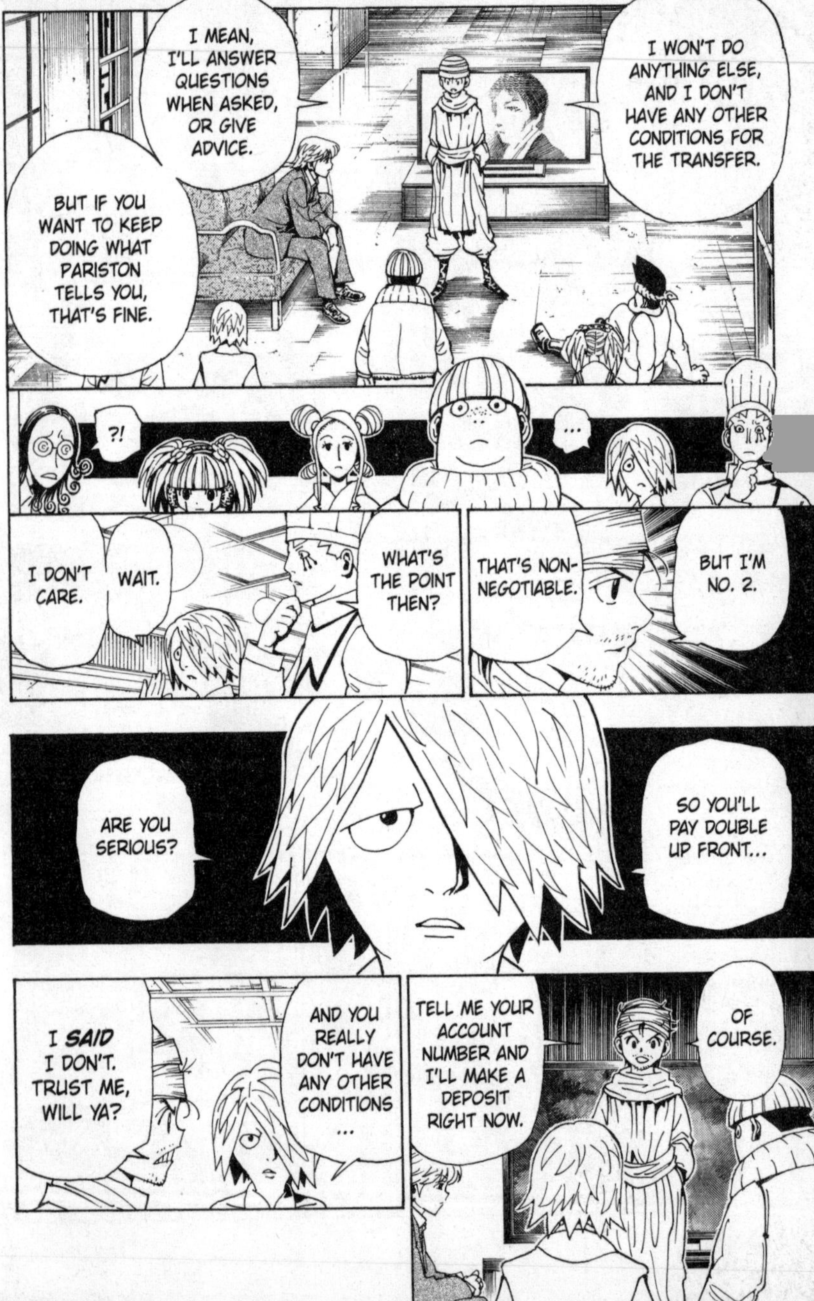
I WON'T DO ANYTHING ELSE, AND I DON'T HAVE ANY OTHER CONDITIONS FOR THE TRANSFER.
I MEAN, I'LL ANSWER QUESTIONS WHEN ASKED, OR GIVE ADVICE.
BUT IF YOU WANT TO KEEP DOING WHAT PARISTON TELLS YOU, THAT'S FINE.
...
?!
BUT I'M NO. 2.
THAT'S NON-NEGOTIABLE.
WHAT'S THE POINT THEN?
WAIT.
I DON'T CARE.
SO YOU'LL PAY DOUBLE UP FRONT...
ARE YOU SERIOUS?
OF COURSE.
TELL ME YOUR ACCOUNT NUMBER AND I'LL MAKE A DEPOSIT RIGHT NOW.
AND YOU REALLY DON'T HAVE ANY OTHER CONDITIONS ...
I *SAID* I DON'T. TRUST ME, WILL YA?

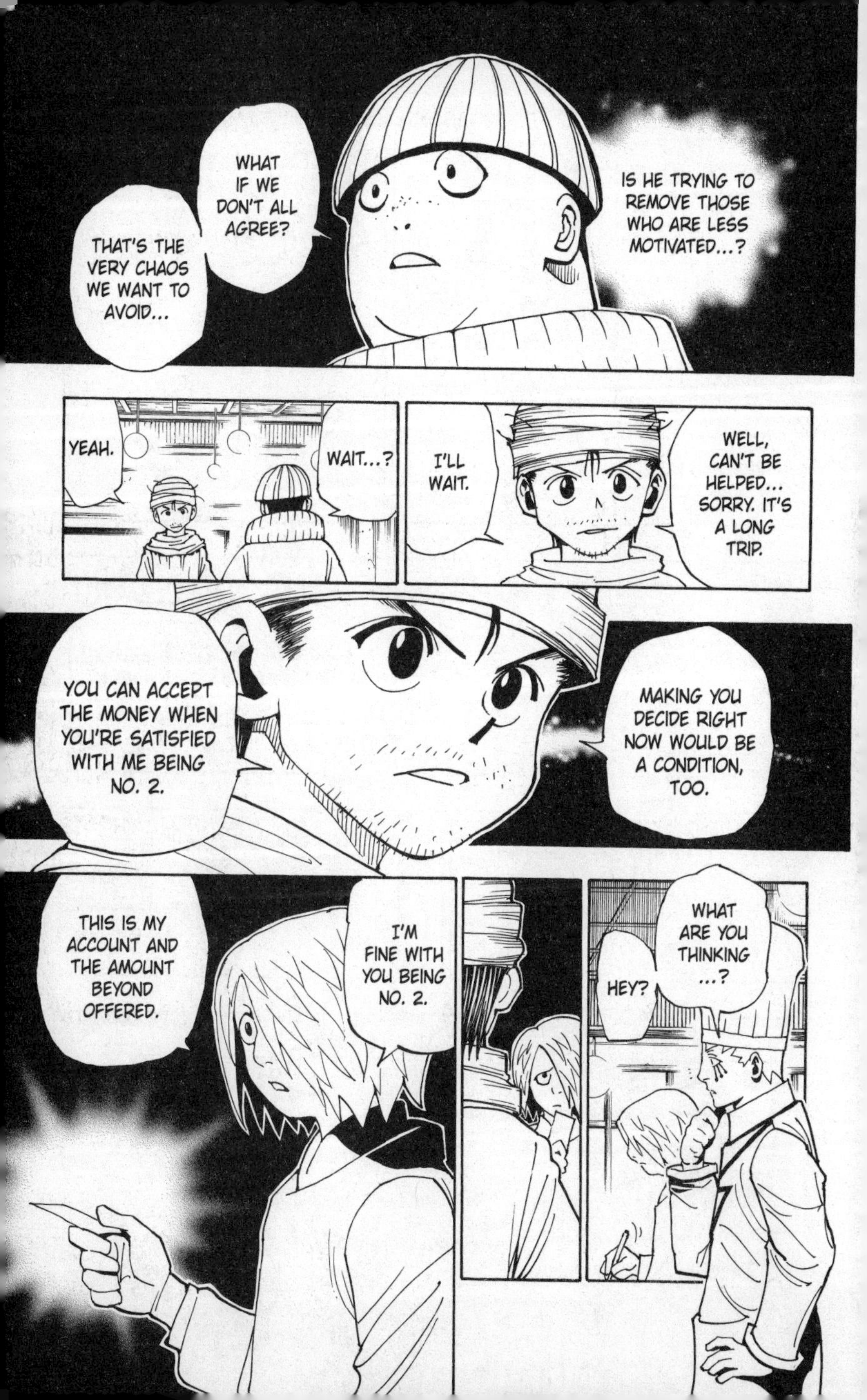
IS HE TRYING TO REMOVE THOSE WHO ARE LESS MOTIVATED...?
WHAT IF WE DON'T ALL AGREE?
THAT'S THE VERY CHAOS WE WANT TO AVOID...
WELL, CAN'T BE HELPED... SORRY. IT'S A LONG TRIP.
I'LL WAIT.
WAIT...?
YEAH.
MAKING YOU DECIDE RIGHT NOW WOULD BE A CONDITION, TOO.
YOU CAN ACCEPT THE MONEY WHEN YOU'RE SATISFIED WITH ME BEING NO. 2.
WHAT ARE YOU THINKING...?
HEY?
I'M FINE WITH YOU BEING NO. 2.
THIS IS MY ACCOUNT AND THE AMOUNT BEYOND OFFERED.

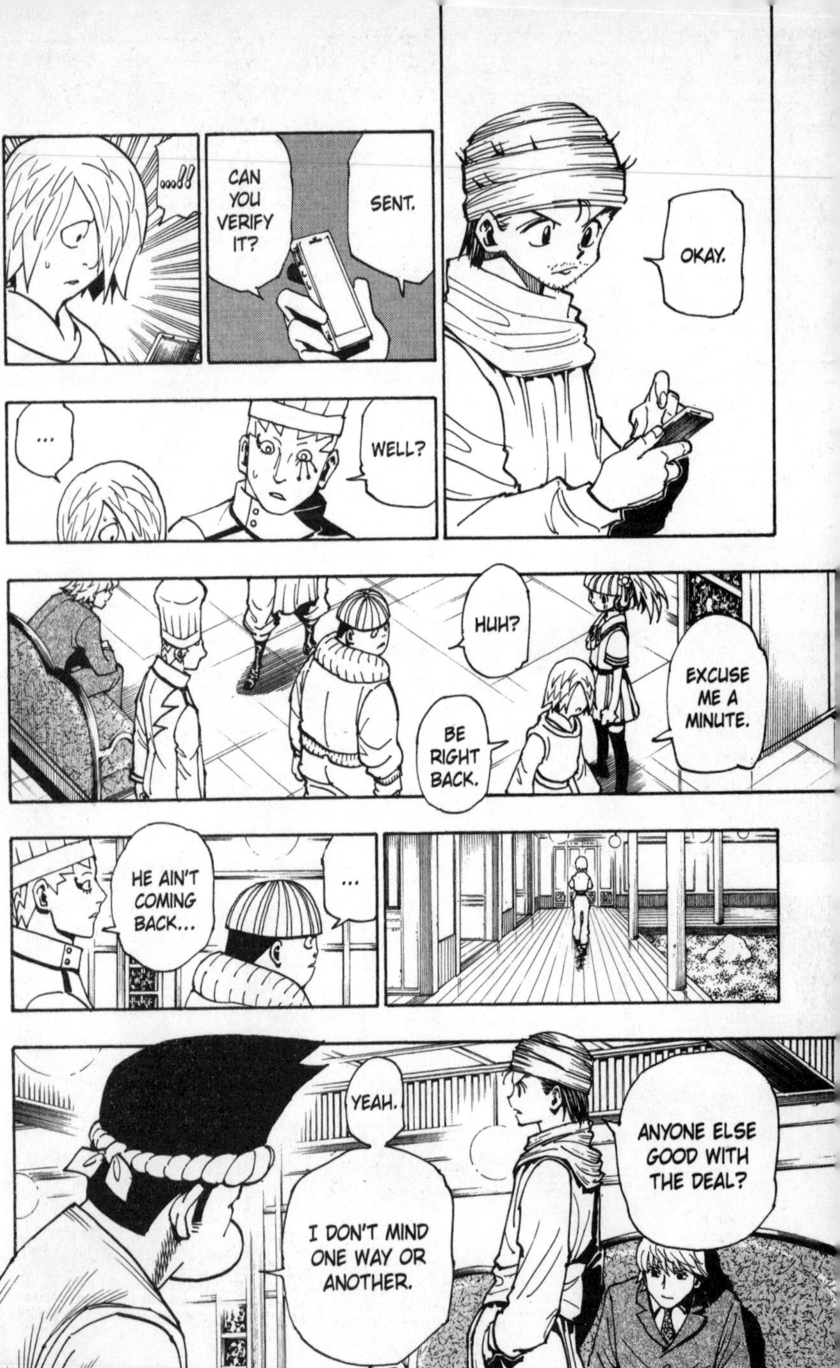
OKAY.
SENT.
CAN YOU VERIFY IT?
...!!
WELL?
...
EXCUSE ME A MINUTE.
HUH?
BE RIGHT BACK.
...
HE AIN'T COMING BACK...
ANYONE ELSE GOOD WITH THE DEAL?
YEAH.
I DON'T MIND ONE WAY OR ANOTHER.

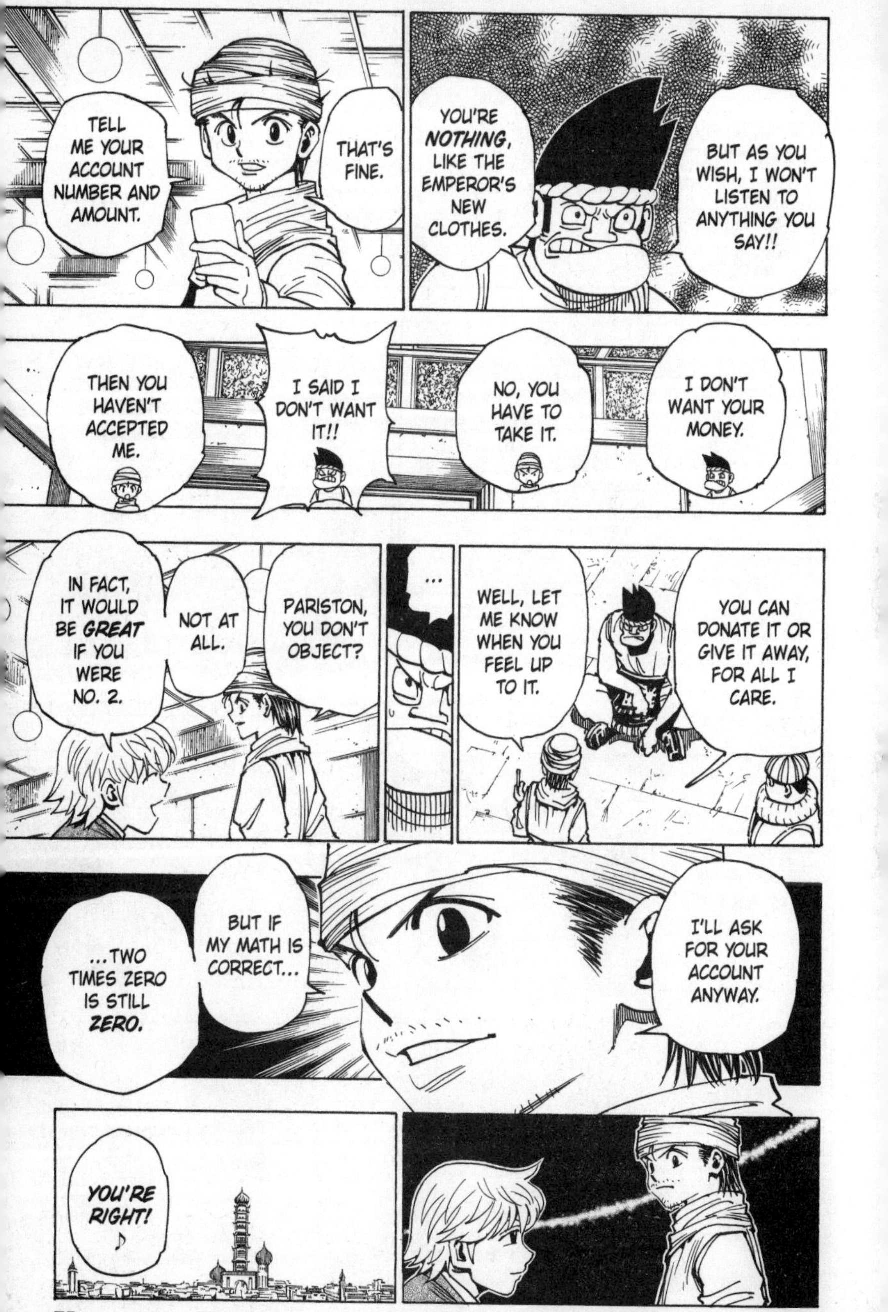
BUT AS YOU WISH, I WON'T LISTEN TO ANYTHING YOU SAY!!
YOU'RE *NOTHING*, LIKE THE EMPEROR'S NEW CLOTHES.
THAT'S FINE.
TELL ME YOUR ACCOUNT NUMBER AND AMOUNT.
I DON'T WANT YOUR MONEY.
NO, YOU HAVE TO TAKE IT.
I SAID I DON'T WANT IT!!
...
THEN YOU HAVEN'T ACCEPTED ME.
YOU CAN DONATE IT OR GIVE IT AWAY, FOR ALL I CARE.
WELL, LET ME KNOW WHEN YOU FEEL UP TO IT.
...
PARISTON, YOU DON'T OBJECT?
NOT AT ALL.
IN FACT, IT WOULD BE *GREAT* IF YOU WERE NO. 2.
I'LL ASK FOR YOUR ACCOUNT ANYWAY.
BUT IF MY MATH IS CORRECT...
...TWO TIMES ZERO IS STILL *ZERO*.
YOU'RE RIGHT! ♪

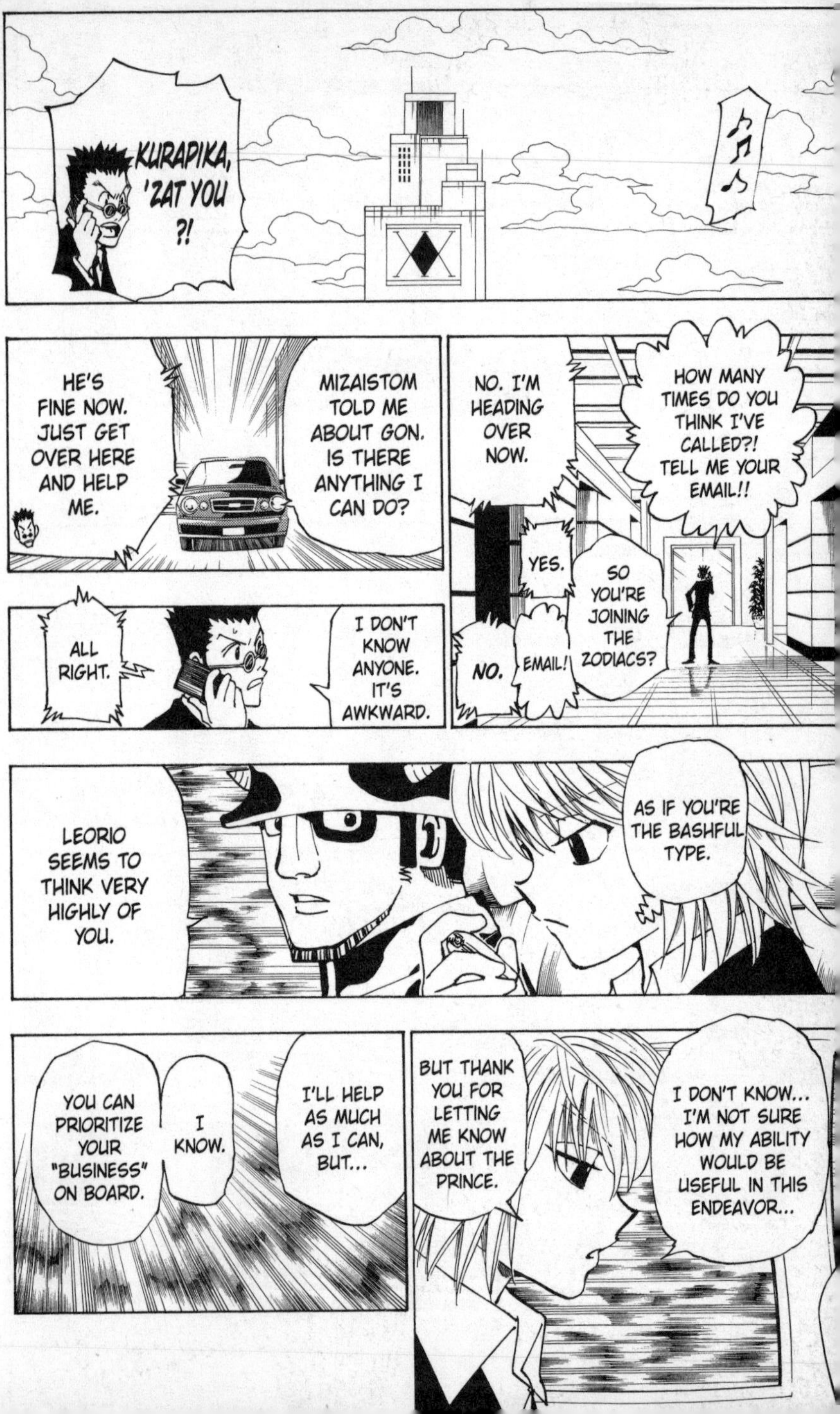
KURAPIKA, 'ZAT YOU?!
HOW MANY TIMES DO YOU THINK I'VE CALLED?! TELL ME YOUR EMAIL!!
NO. I'M HEADING OVER NOW.
SO YOU'RE JOINING THE ZODIACS?
YES.
EMAIL!
NO.
MIZAISTOM TOLD ME ABOUT GON. IS THERE ANYTHING I CAN DO?
HE'S FINE NOW. JUST GET OVER HERE AND HELP ME.
I DON'T KNOW ANYONE. IT'S AWKWARD.
ALL RIGHT.
AS IF YOU'RE THE BASHFUL TYPE.
LEORIO SEEMS TO THINK VERY HIGHLY OF YOU.
I DON'T KNOW... I'M NOT SURE HOW MY ABILITY WOULD BE USEFUL IN THIS ENDEAVOR...
BUT THANK YOU FOR LETTING ME KNOW ABOUT THE PRINCE.
I'LL HELP AS MUCH AS I CAN, BUT...
I KNOW.
YOU CAN PRIORITIZE YOUR "BUSINESS" ON BOARD.

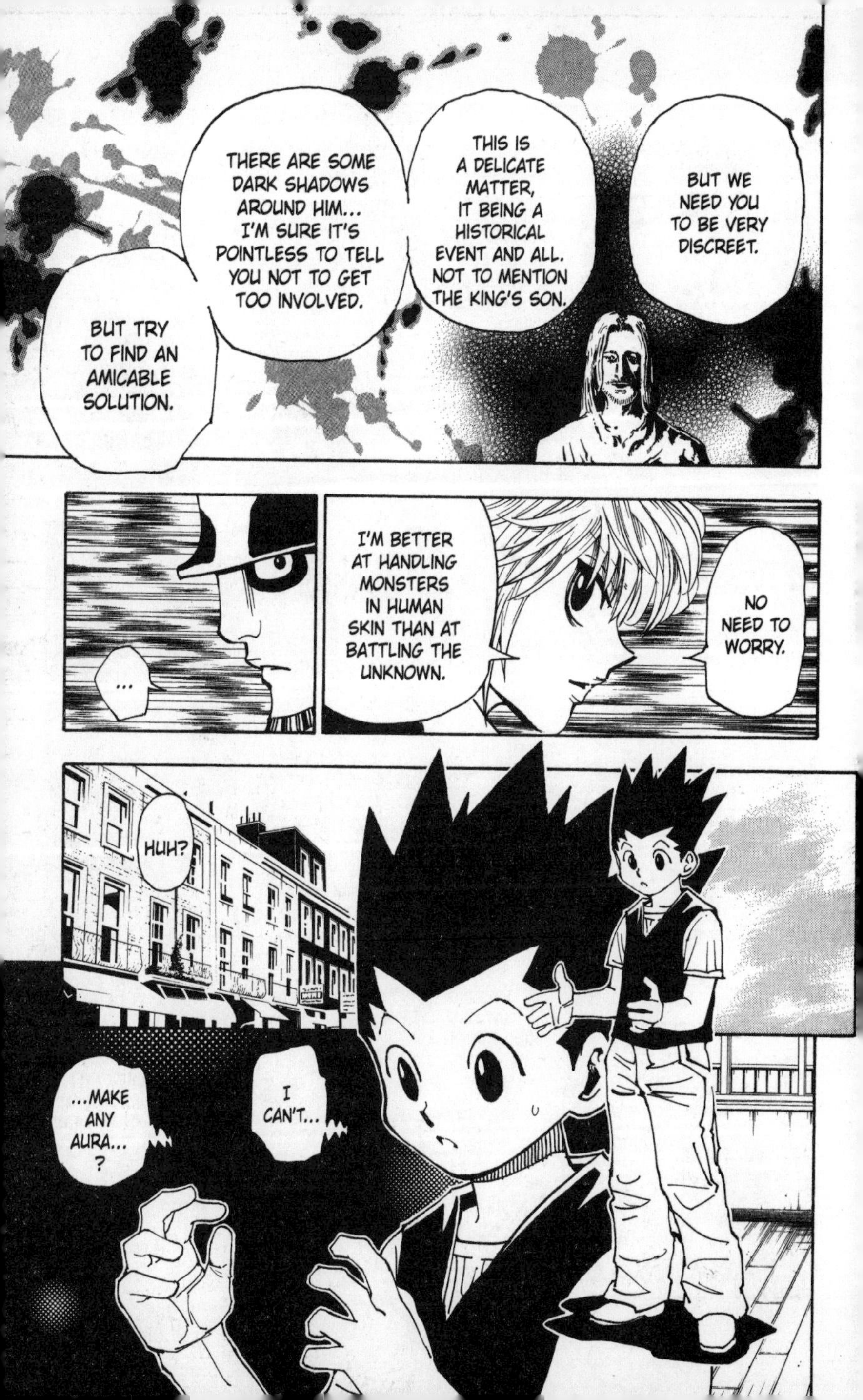

BUT WE NEED YOU TO BE VERY DISCREET.
THIS IS A DELICATE MATTER, IT BEING A HISTORICAL EVENT AND ALL. NOT TO MENTION THE KING'S SON.
THERE ARE SOME DARK SHADOWS AROUND HIM... I'M SURE IT'S POINTLESS TO TELL YOU NOT TO GET TOO INVOLVED.
BUT TRY TO FIND AN AMICABLE SOLUTION.
NO NEED TO WORRY.
I'M BETTER AT HANDLING MONSTERS IN HUMAN SKIN THAN AT BATTLING THE UNKNOWN.
...
HUH?
I CAN'T...
...MAKE ANY AURA...?

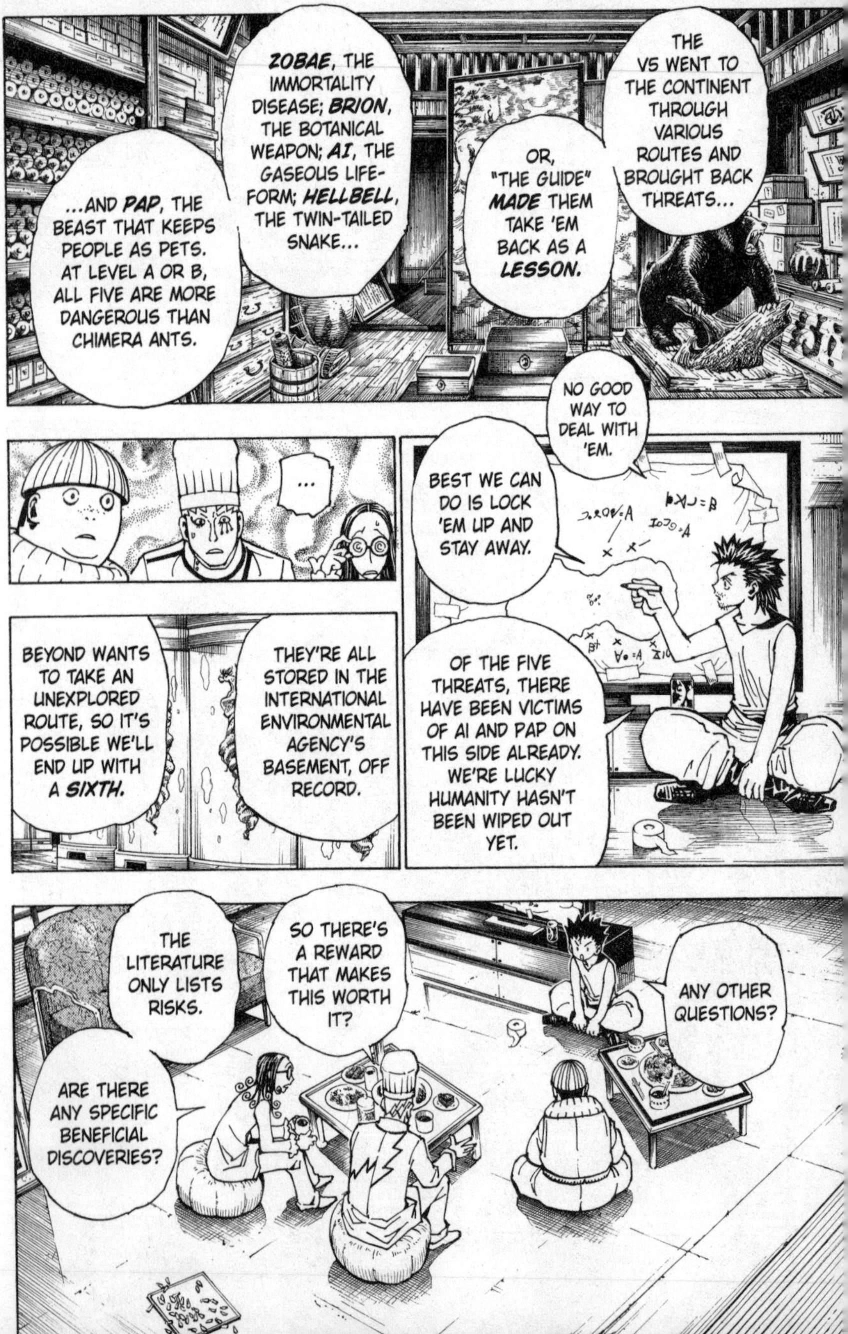
THE V5 WENT TO THE CONTINENT THROUGH VARIOUS ROUTES AND BROUGHT BACK THREATS...
OR, "THE GUIDE" *MADE* THEM TAKE 'EM BACK AS A *LESSON.*
ZOBAE, THE IMMORTALITY DISEASE; *BRION*, THE BOTANICAL WEAPON; *AI*, THE GASEOUS LIFE-FORM; *HELLBELL*, THE TWIN-TAILED SNAKE...
...AND *PAP*, THE BEAST THAT KEEPS PEOPLE AS PETS. AT LEVEL A OR B, ALL FIVE ARE MORE DANGEROUS THAN CHIMERA ANTS.
NO GOOD WAY TO DEAL WITH 'EM.
BEST WE CAN DO IS LOCK 'EM UP AND STAY AWAY.
OF THE FIVE THREATS, THERE HAVE BEEN VICTIMS OF AI AND PAP ON THIS SIDE ALREADY. WE'RE LUCKY HUMANITY HASN'T BEEN WIPED OUT YET.
...
THEY'RE ALL STORED IN THE INTERNATIONAL ENVIRONMENTAL AGENCY'S BASEMENT, OFF RECORD.
BEYOND WANTS TO TAKE AN UNEXPLORED ROUTE, SO IT'S POSSIBLE WE'LL END UP WITH A *SIXTH.*
ANY OTHER QUESTIONS?
SO THERE'S A REWARD THAT MAKES THIS WORTH IT?
THE LITERATURE ONLY LISTS RISKS.
ARE THERE ANY SPECIFIC BENEFICIAL DISCOVERIES?

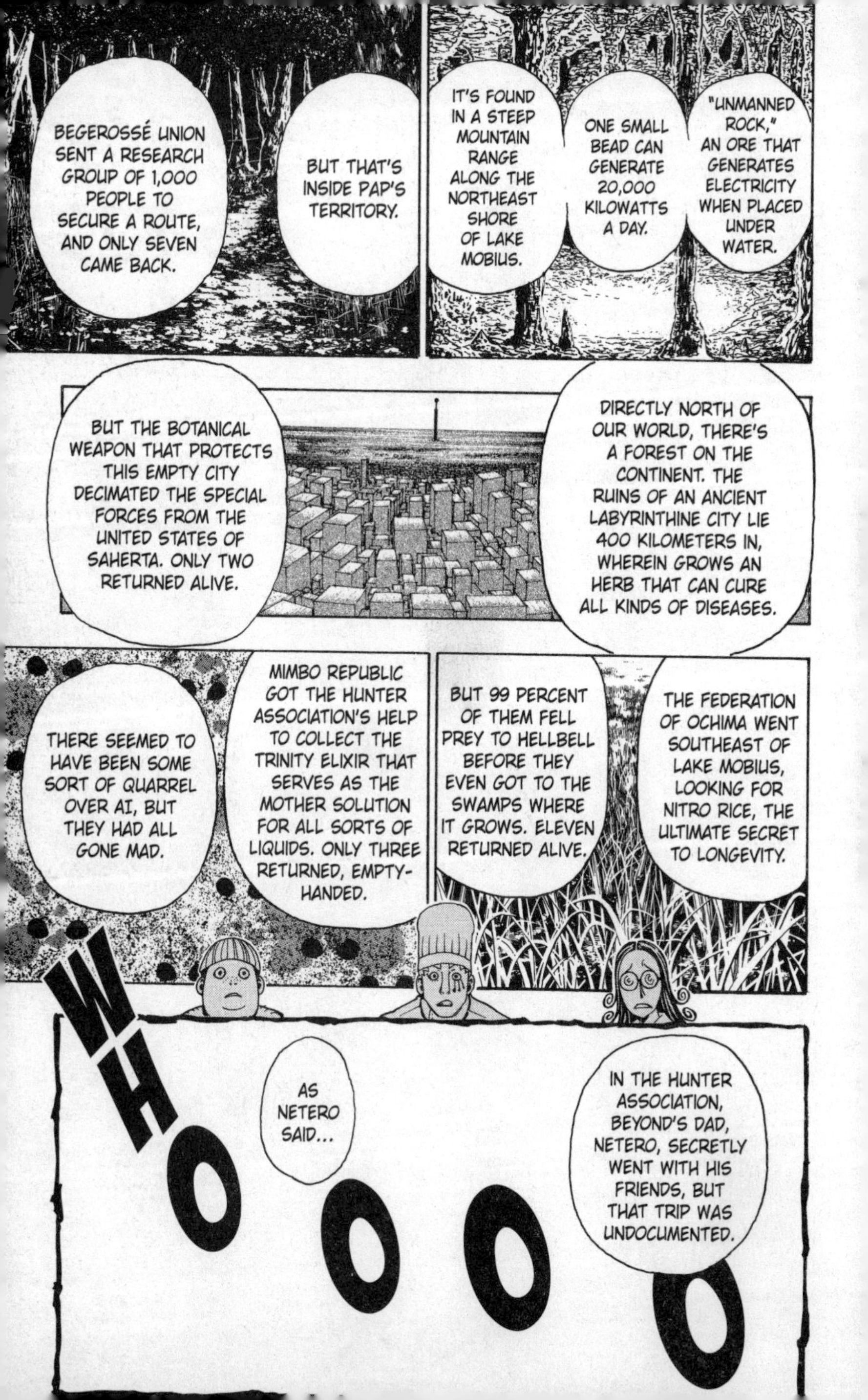
"UNMANNED ROCK," AN ORE THAT GENERATES ELECTRICITY WHEN PLACED UNDER WATER.
ONE SMALL BEAD CAN GENERATE 20,000 KILOWATTS A DAY.
IT'S FOUND IN A STEEP MOUNTAIN RANGE ALONG THE NORTHEAST SHORE OF LAKE MOBIUS.
BUT THAT'S INSIDE PAP'S TERRITORY.
BEGEROSSÉ UNION SENT A RESEARCH GROUP OF 1,000 PEOPLE TO SECURE A ROUTE, AND ONLY SEVEN CAME BACK.
DIRECTLY NORTH OF OUR WORLD, THERE'S A FOREST ON THE CONTINENT. THE RUINS OF AN ANCIENT LABYRINTHINE CITY LIE 400 KILOMETERS IN, WHEREIN GROWS AN HERB THAT CAN CURE ALL KINDS OF DISEASES.
BUT THE BOTANICAL WEAPON THAT PROTECTS THIS EMPTY CITY DECIMATED THE SPECIAL FORCES FROM THE UNITED STATES OF SAHERTA. ONLY TWO RETURNED ALIVE.
THE FEDERATION OF OCHIMA WENT SOUTHEAST OF LAKE MOBIUS, LOOKING FOR NITRO RICE, THE ULTIMATE SECRET TO LONGEVITY.
BUT 99 PERCENT OF THEM FELL PREY TO HELLBELL BEFORE THEY EVEN GOT TO THE SWAMPS WHERE IT GROWS. ELEVEN RETURNED ALIVE.
MIMBO REPUBLIC GOT THE HUNTER ASSOCIATION'S HELP TO COLLECT THE TRINITY ELIXIR THAT SERVES AS THE MOTHER SOLUTION FOR ALL SORTS OF LIQUIDS. ONLY THREE RETURNED, EMPTY-HANDED.
THERE SEEMED TO HAVE BEEN SOME SORT OF QUARREL OVER AI, BUT THEY HAD ALL GONE MAD.
IN THE HUNTER ASSOCIATION, BEYOND'S DAD, NETERO, SECRETLY WENT WITH HIS FRIENDS, BUT THAT TRIP WAS UNDOCUMENTED.
AS NETERO SAID...
WHOOOOO

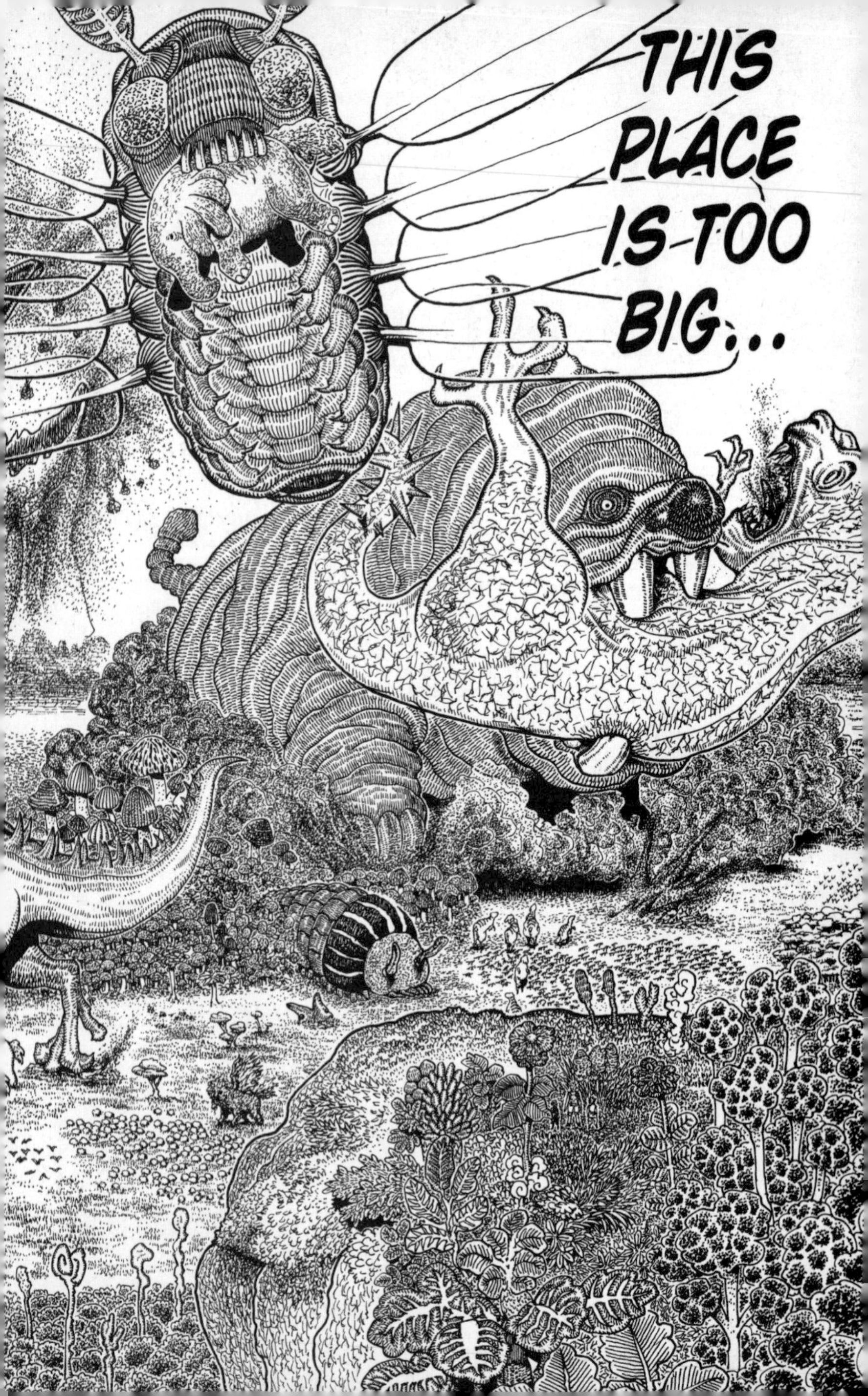
THIS PLACE IS TOO BIG...

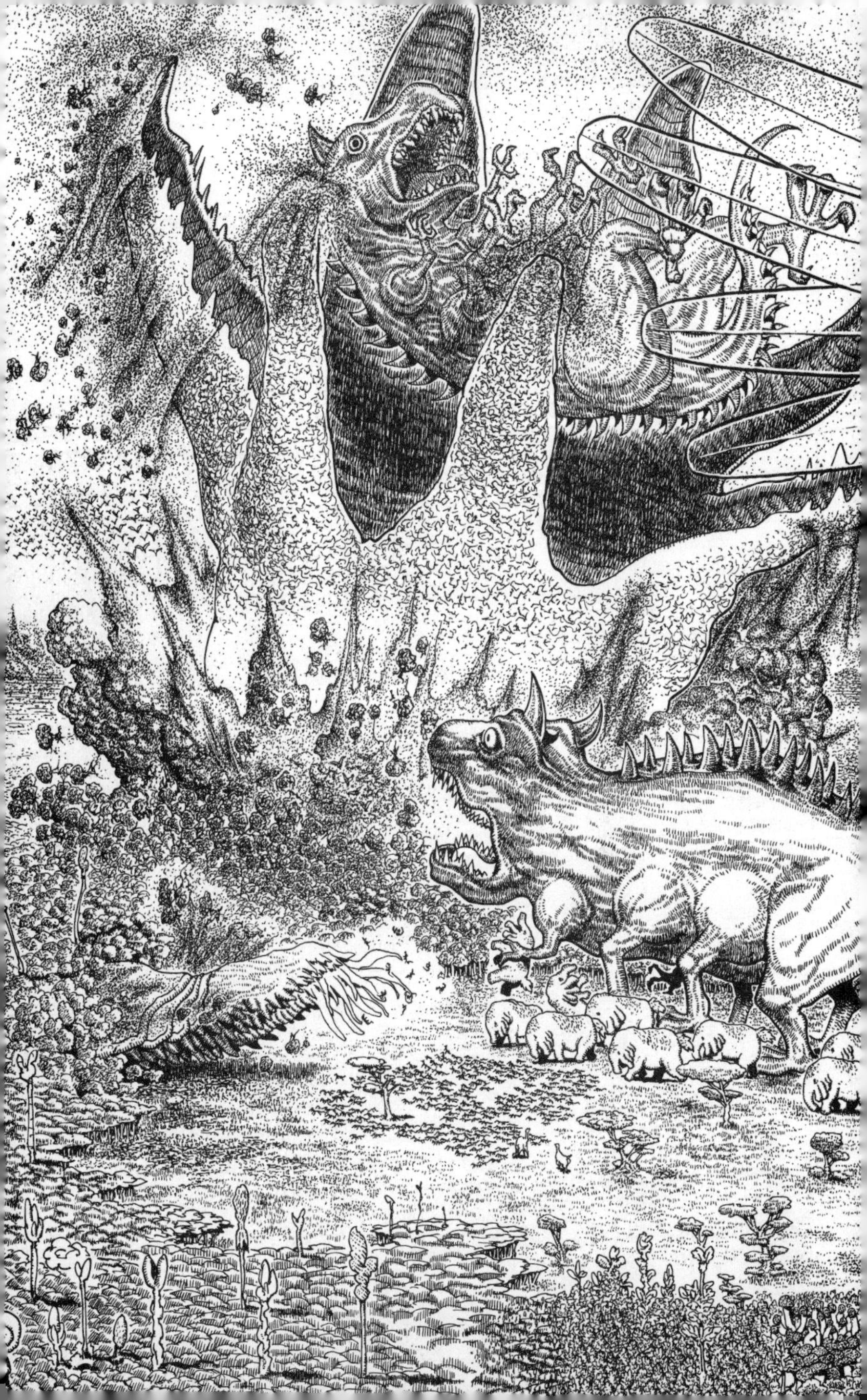

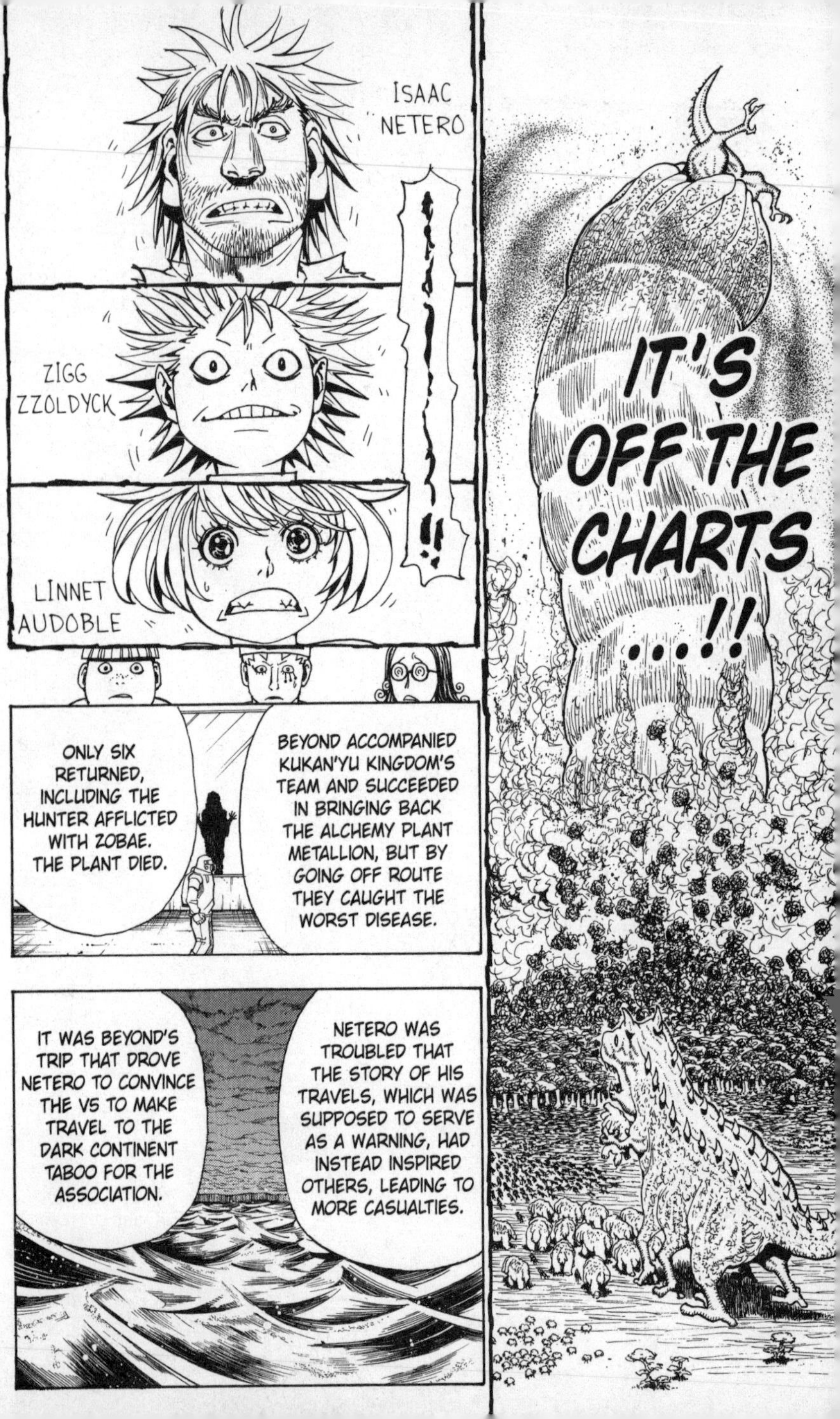
IT'S OFF THE CHARTS...!!
ISAAC NETERO
ZIGG ZZOLDYCK
LINNET AUDOBLE
BEYOND ACCOMPANIED KUKAN'YU KINGDOM'S TEAM AND SUCCEEDED IN BRINGING BACK THE ALCHEMY PLANT METALLION, BUT BY GOING OFF ROUTE THEY CAUGHT THE WORST DISEASE.
ONLY SIX RETURNED, INCLUDING THE HUNTER AFFLICTED WITH ZOBAE. THE PLANT DIED.
NETERO WAS TROUBLED THAT THE STORY OF HIS TRAVELS, WHICH WAS SUPPOSED TO SERVE AS A WARNING, HAD INSTEAD INSPIRED OTHERS, LEADING TO MORE CASUALTIES.
IT WAS BEYOND'S TRIP THAT DROVE NETERO TO CONVINCE THE V5 TO MAKE TRAVEL TO THE DARK CONTINENT TABOO FOR THE ASSOCIATION.

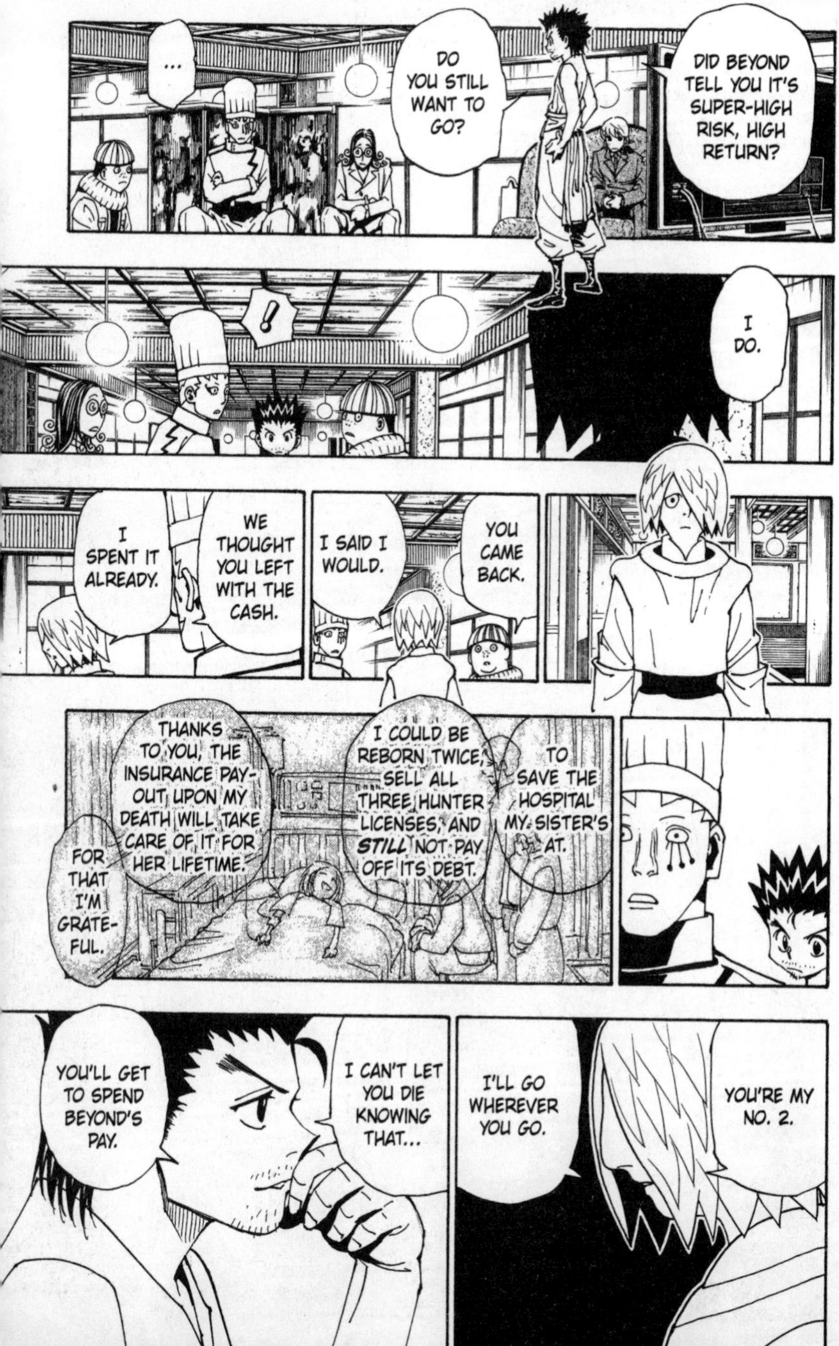
DID BEYOND TELL YOU IT'S SUPER-HIGH RISK, HIGH RETURN?
DO YOU STILL WANT TO GO?
...
I DO.
!
YOU CAME BACK.
I SAID I WOULD.
WE THOUGHT YOU LEFT WITH THE CASH.
I SPENT IT ALREADY.
TO SAVE THE HOSPITAL MY SISTER'S AT.
I COULD BE REBORN TWICE, SELL ALL THREE HUNTER LICENSES, AND *STILL* NOT PAY OFF ITS DEBT.
THANKS TO YOU, THE INSURANCE PAY-OUT UPON MY DEATH WILL TAKE CARE OF IT FOR HER LIFETIME.
FOR THAT I'M GRATE-FUL.
YOU'RE MY NO. 2.
I'LL GO WHEREVER YOU GO.
I CAN'T LET YOU DIE KNOWING THAT...
YOU'LL GET TO SPEND BEYOND'S PAY.

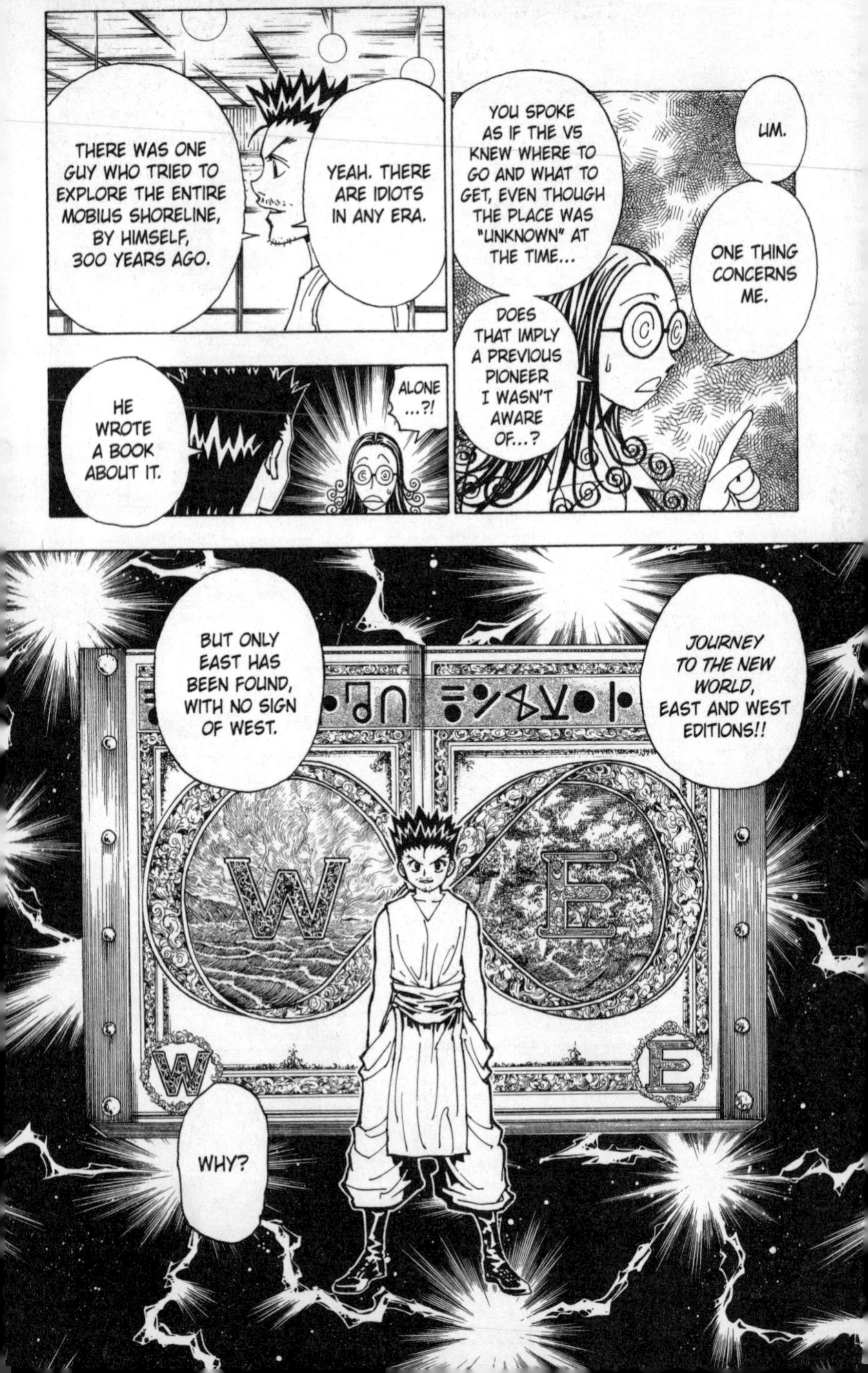
UM.
ONE THING CONCERNS ME.
YOU SPOKE AS IF THE V5 KNEW WHERE TO GO AND WHAT TO GET, EVEN THOUGH THE PLACE WAS "UNKNOWN" AT THE TIME...
DOES THAT IMPLY A PREVIOUS PIONEER I WASN'T AWARE OF...?
YEAH. THERE ARE IDIOTS IN ANY ERA.
THERE WAS ONE GUY WHO TRIED TO EXPLORE THE ENTIRE MOBIUS SHORELINE, BY HIMSELF, 300 YEARS AGO.
ALONE ...?!
HE WROTE A BOOK ABOUT IT.
JOURNEY TO THE NEW WORLD, EAST AND WEST EDITIONS!!
BUT ONLY EAST HAS BEEN FOUND, WITH NO SIGN OF WEST.
WHY?

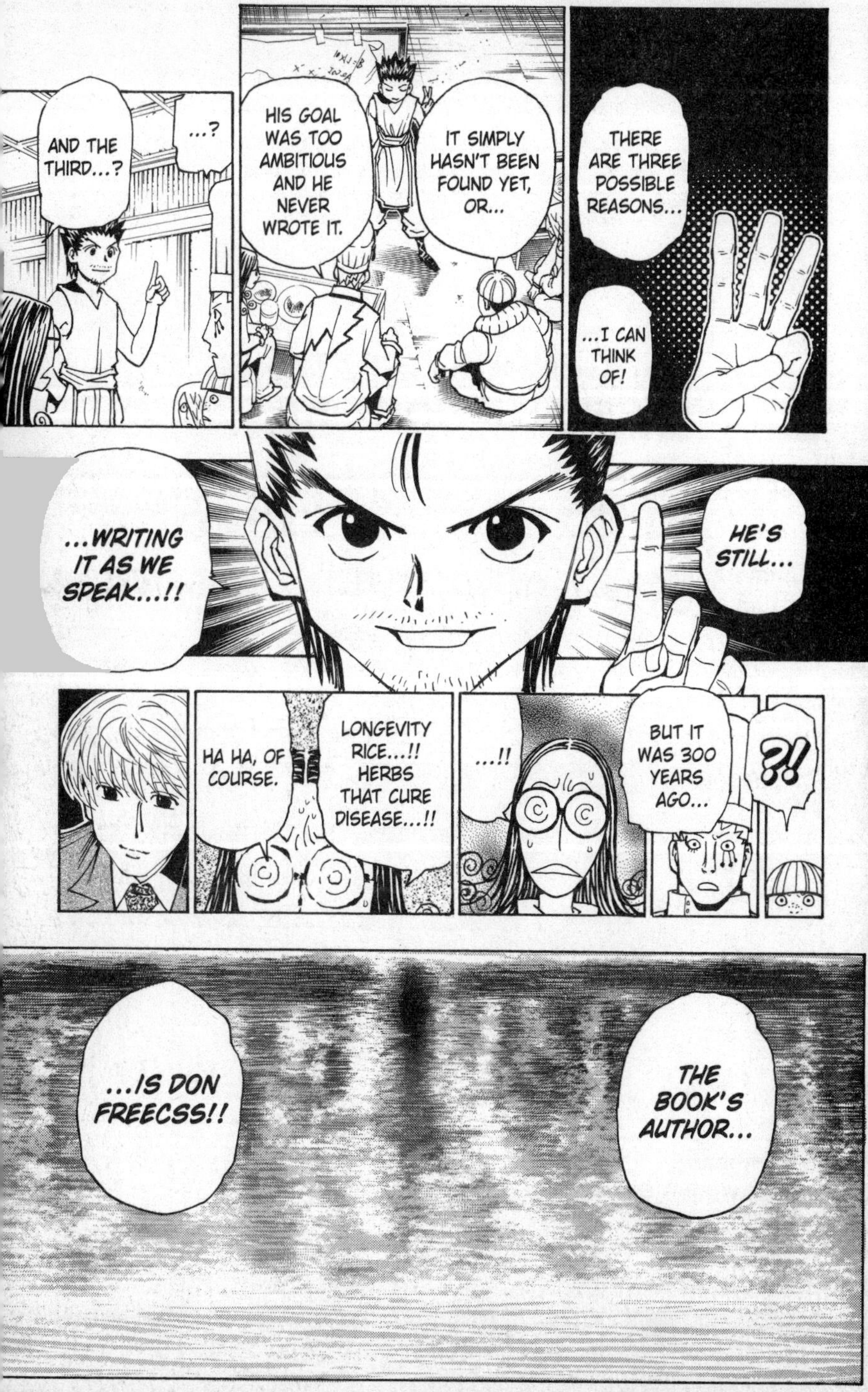
THERE ARE THREE POSSIBLE REASONS...
...I CAN THINK OF!
IT SIMPLY HASN'T BEEN FOUND YET, OR...
HIS GOAL WAS TOO AMBITIOUS AND HE NEVER WROTE IT.
...?
AND THE THIRD...?
HE'S STILL...
...WRITING IT AS WE SPEAK...!!
?!
BUT IT WAS 300 YEARS AGO...
...!!
LONGEVITY RICE...!! HERBS THAT CURE DISEASE...!!
HA HA, OF COURSE.
THE BOOK'S AUTHOR...
...IS DON FREECSS!!

DANGEROUS CREATURES
EVALUATION LIST

	Aggression	Number	Fecundity	Threat of Bodily Harm	Total Score
Chimera Ants (Humanoid)	$B \sim C$ $\left(B \doteqdot {A-1 \atop A-2}\right)$	B	B-1	A	B
Ai	A-2	?	?	$A \sim B$	A
Brion	B $(\doteqdot A-1)$	C	B-2	A-1	B^+
Zobae (Patient)	C-1 $(\doteqdot A-2)$	E	B-2	B-2	B^+
Hellbell	A-1	?	?	A-2	A
Pap	A-2	?	?	B-1	A
Human (Individual)	C	E	C	$B \sim E$	C
Human (Nation)	B $(\doteqdot A-1)$	A	C $(\doteqdot B)$	$A \sim C$	$A^- \sim B^+$

Chapter 345: Signature

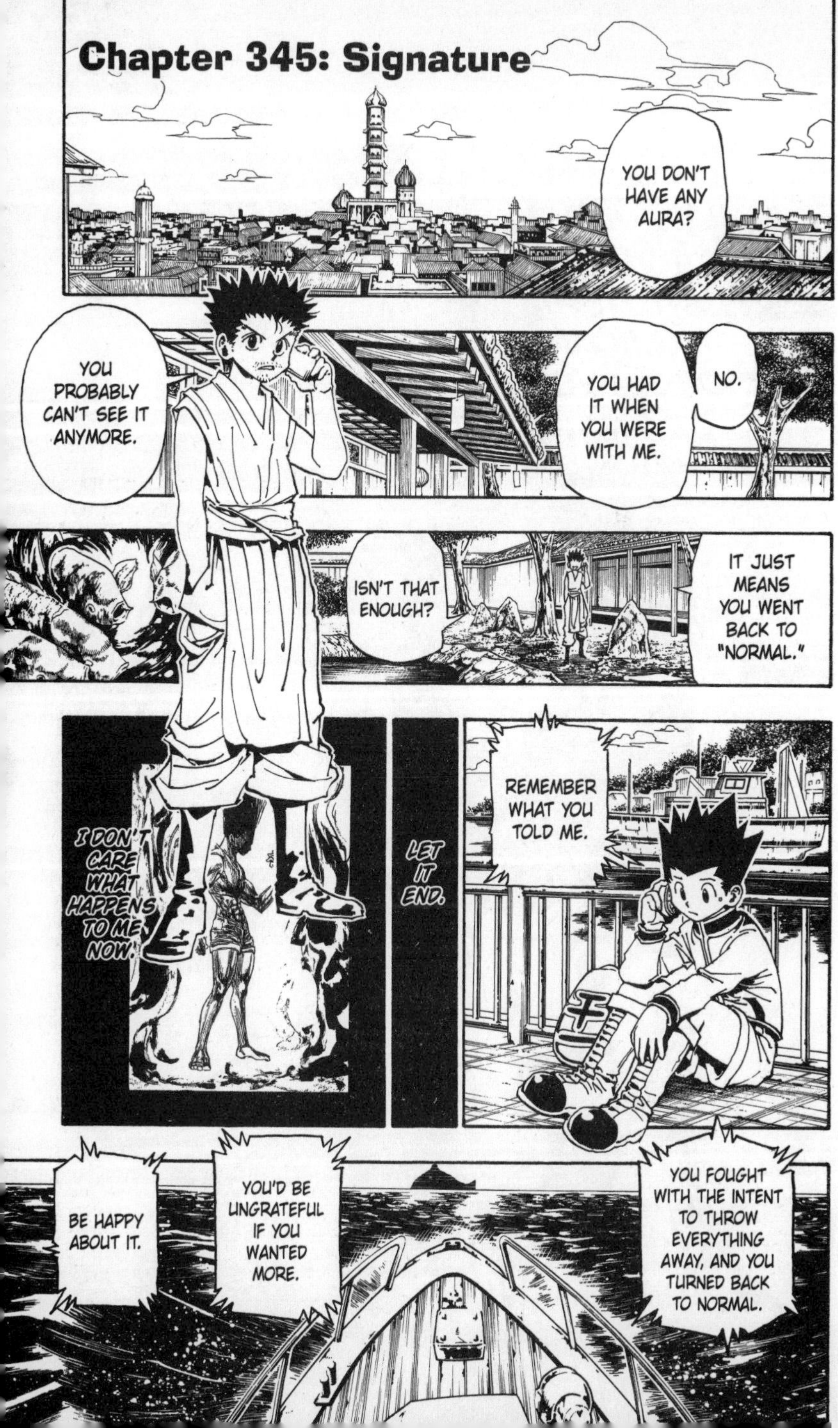
YOU DON'T HAVE ANY AURA?
NO.
YOU HAD IT WHEN YOU WERE WITH ME.
YOU PROBABLY CAN'T SEE IT ANYMORE.
IT JUST MEANS YOU WENT BACK TO "NORMAL."
ISN'T THAT ENOUGH?
REMEMBER WHAT YOU TOLD ME.
LET IT END.
I DON'T CARE WHAT HAPPENS TO ME NOW.
YOU FOUGHT WITH THE INTENT TO THROW EVERYTHING AWAY, AND YOU TURNED BACK TO NORMAL.
YOU'D BE UNGRATEFUL IF YOU WANTED MORE.
BE HAPPY ABOUT IT.

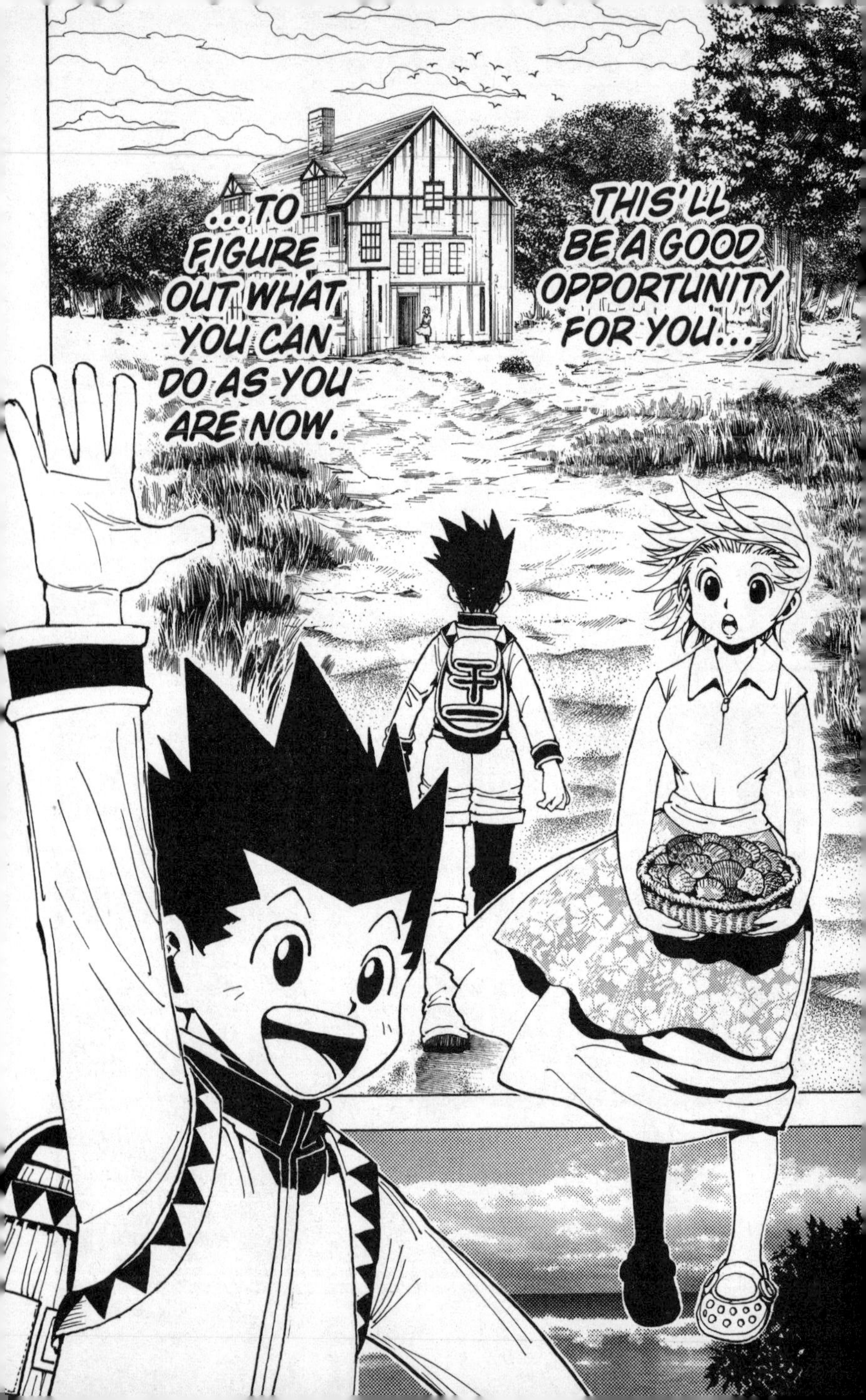
THIS'LL BE A GOOD OPPORTUNITY FOR YOU...
...TO FIGURE OUT WHAT YOU CAN DO AS YOU ARE NOW.

READ THIS WAY

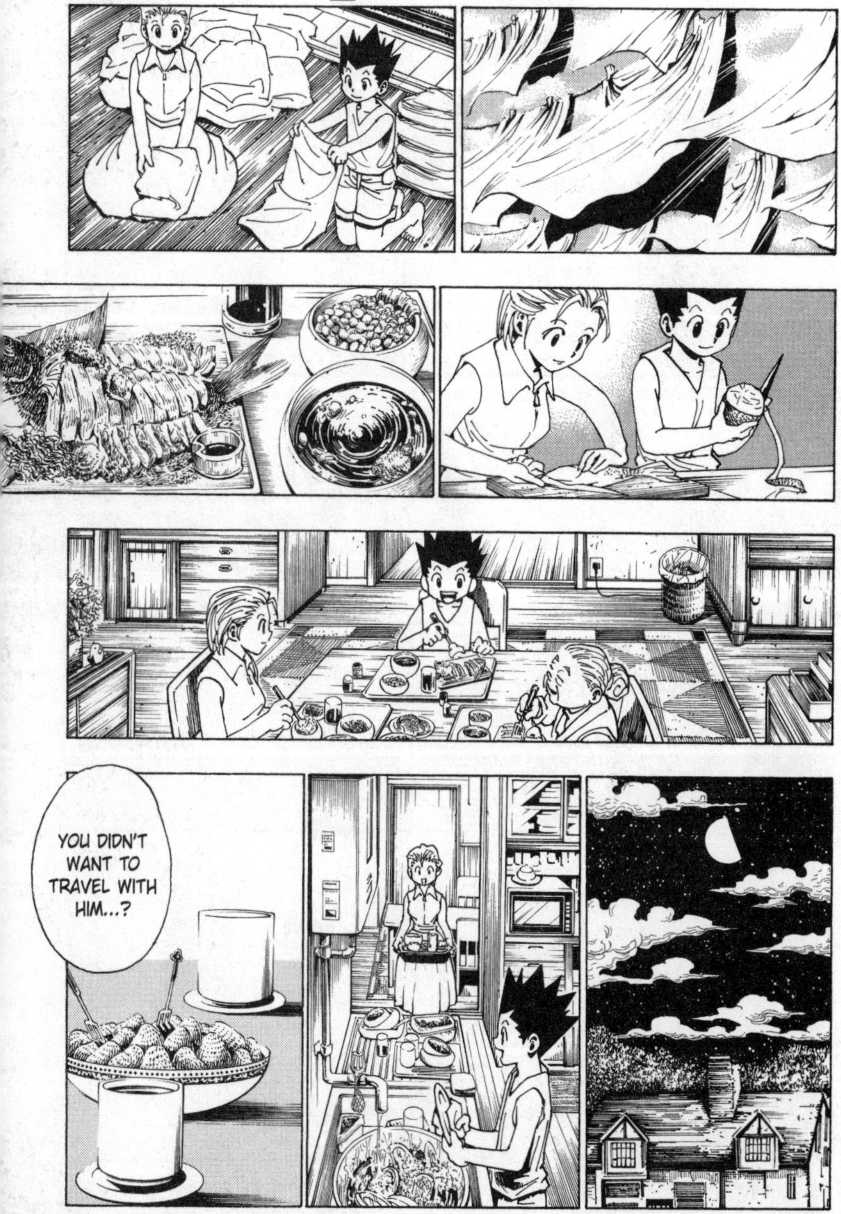
YOU DIDN'T WANT TO TRAVEL WITH HIM...?

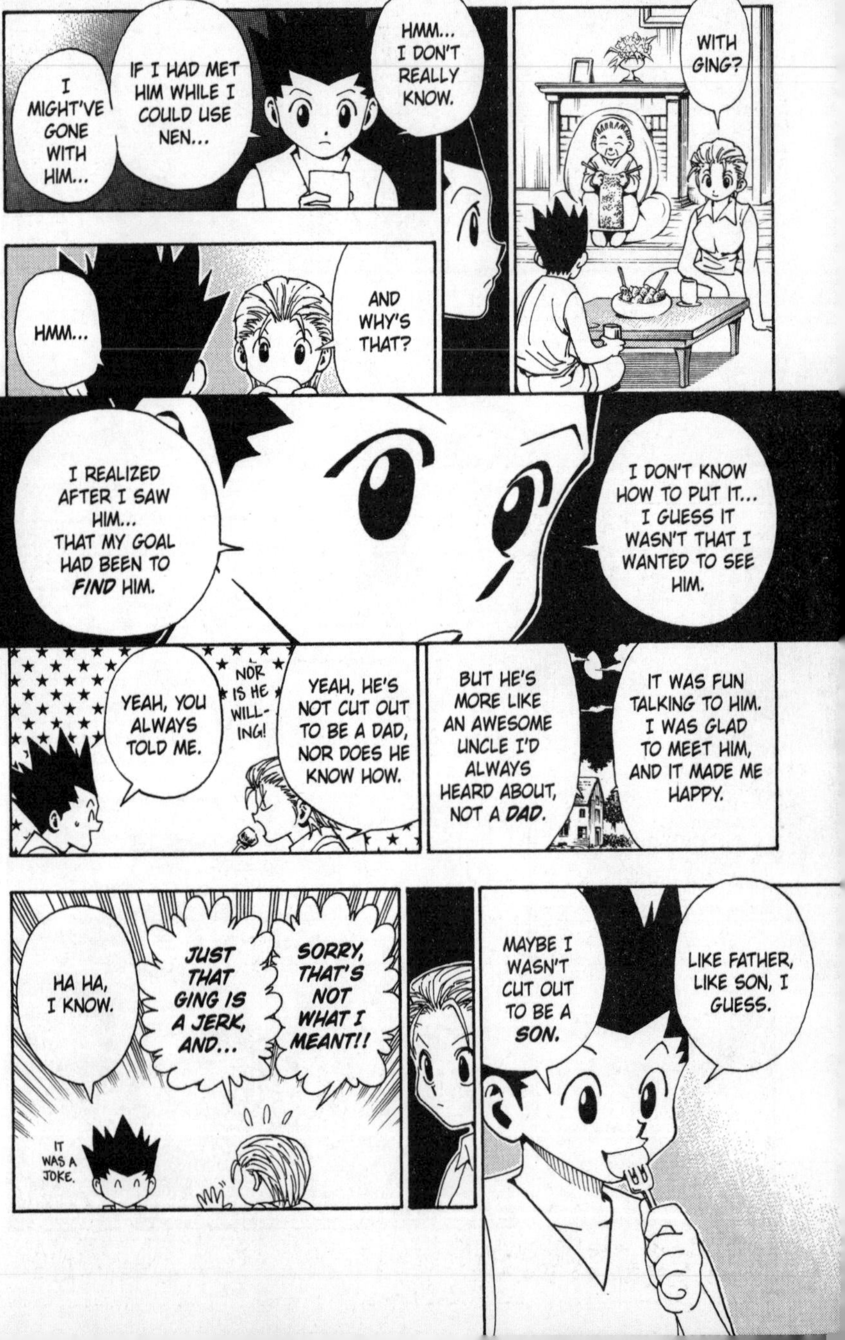
WITH GING?
HMM... I DON'T REALLY KNOW.
IF I HAD MET HIM WHILE I COULD USE NEN...
I MIGHT'VE GONE WITH HIM...
AND WHY'S THAT?
HMM...
I DON'T KNOW HOW TO PUT IT... I GUESS IT WASN'T THAT I WANTED TO SEE HIM.
I REALIZED AFTER I SAW HIM... THAT MY GOAL HAD BEEN TO *FIND* HIM.
IT WAS FUN TALKING TO HIM. I WAS GLAD TO MEET HIM, AND IT MADE ME HAPPY.
BUT HE'S MORE LIKE AN AWESOME UNCLE I'D ALWAYS HEARD ABOUT, NOT A *DAD*.
YEAH, HE'S NOT CUT OUT TO BE A DAD, NOR DOES HE KNOW HOW.
NOR IS HE WILLING!
YEAH, YOU ALWAYS TOLD ME.
LIKE FATHER, LIKE SON, I GUESS.
MAYBE I WASN'T CUT OUT TO BE A **SON.**
SORRY, THAT'S NOT WHAT I MEANT!!
JUST THAT GING IS A JERK, AND...
HA HA, I KNOW.
IT WAS A JOKE.

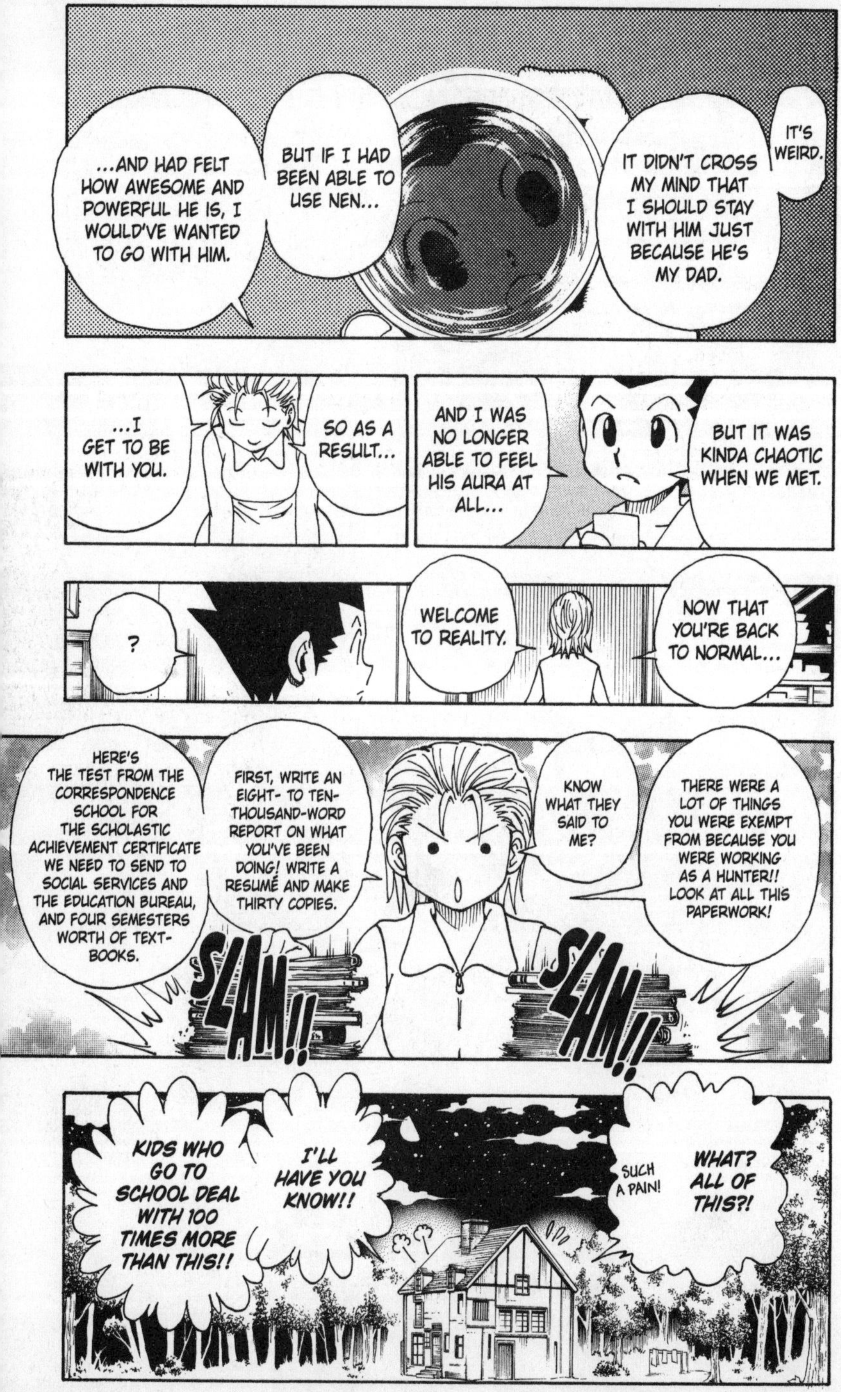
IT'S WEIRD.
IT DIDN'T CROSS MY MIND THAT I SHOULD STAY WITH HIM JUST BECAUSE HE'S MY DAD.
BUT IF I HAD BEEN ABLE TO USE NEN...
...AND HAD FELT HOW AWESOME AND POWERFUL HE IS, I WOULD'VE WANTED TO GO WITH HIM.
BUT IT WAS KINDA CHAOTIC WHEN WE MET.
AND I WAS NO LONGER ABLE TO FEEL HIS AURA AT ALL...
SO AS A RESULT...
...I GET TO BE WITH YOU.
NOW THAT YOU'RE BACK TO NORMAL...
WELCOME TO REALITY.
?
THERE WERE A LOT OF THINGS YOU WERE EXEMPT FROM BECAUSE YOU WERE WORKING AS A HUNTER!! LOOK AT ALL THIS PAPERWORK!
KNOW WHAT THEY SAID TO ME?
FIRST, WRITE AN EIGHT- TO TEN-THOUSAND-WORD REPORT ON WHAT YOU'VE BEEN DOING! WRITE A RESUMÉ AND MAKE THIRTY COPIES.
HERE'S THE TEST FROM THE CORRESPONDENCE SCHOOL FOR THE SCHOLASTIC ACHIEVEMENT CERTIFICATE WE NEED TO SEND TO SOCIAL SERVICES AND THE EDUCATION BUREAU, AND FOUR SEMESTERS WORTH OF TEXT-BOOKS.
SLAM!!
SLAM!!
WHAT? ALL OF THIS?!
SUCH A PAIN!
I'LL HAVE YOU KNOW!!
KIDS WHO GO TO SCHOOL DEAL WITH 100 TIMES MORE THAN THIS!!

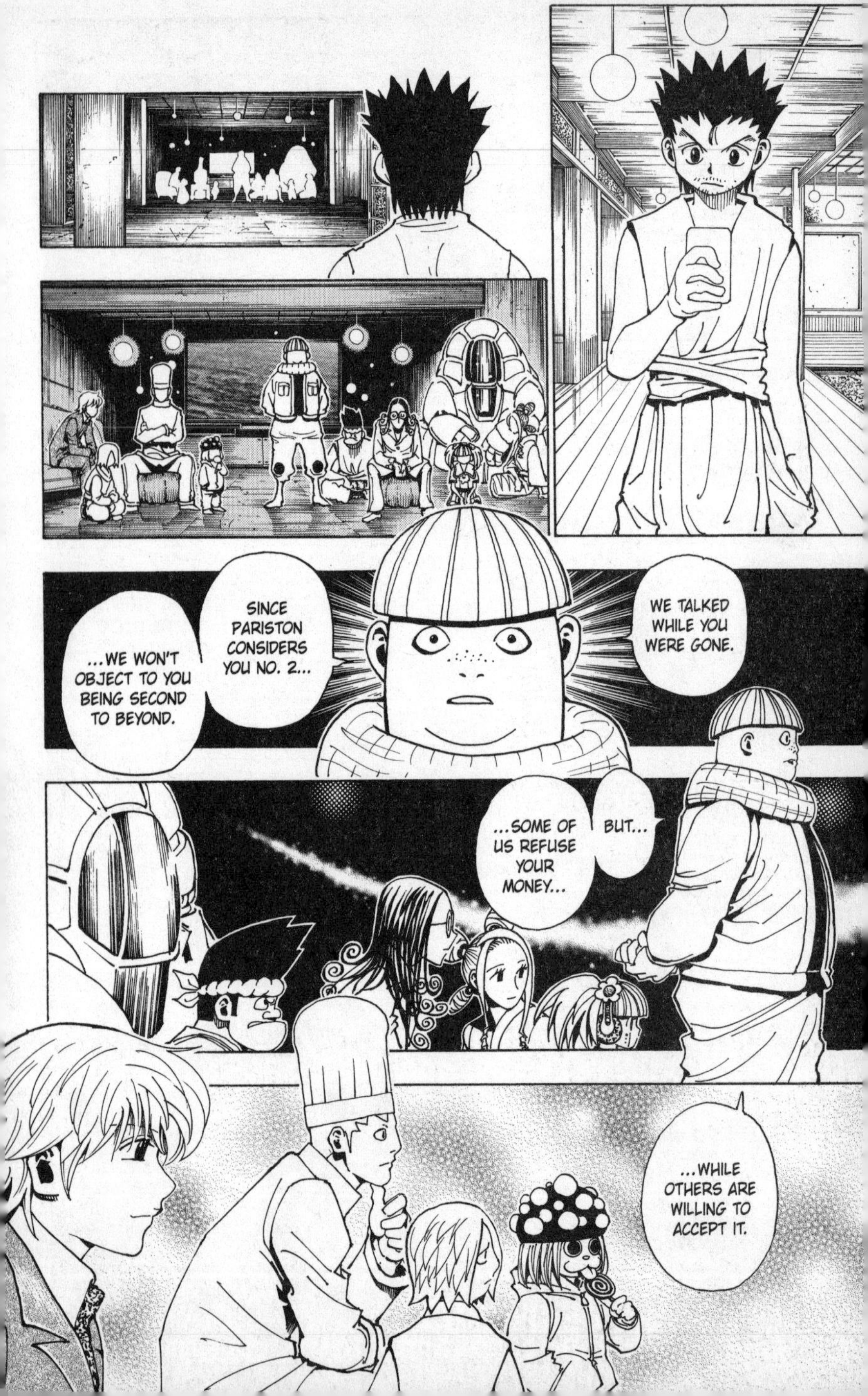
WE TALKED WHILE YOU WERE GONE.
SINCE PARISTON CONSIDERS YOU NO. 2...
...WE WON'T OBJECT TO YOU BEING SECOND TO BEYOND.
BUT...
...SOME OF US REFUSE YOUR MONEY...
...WHILE OTHERS ARE WILLING TO ACCEPT IT.

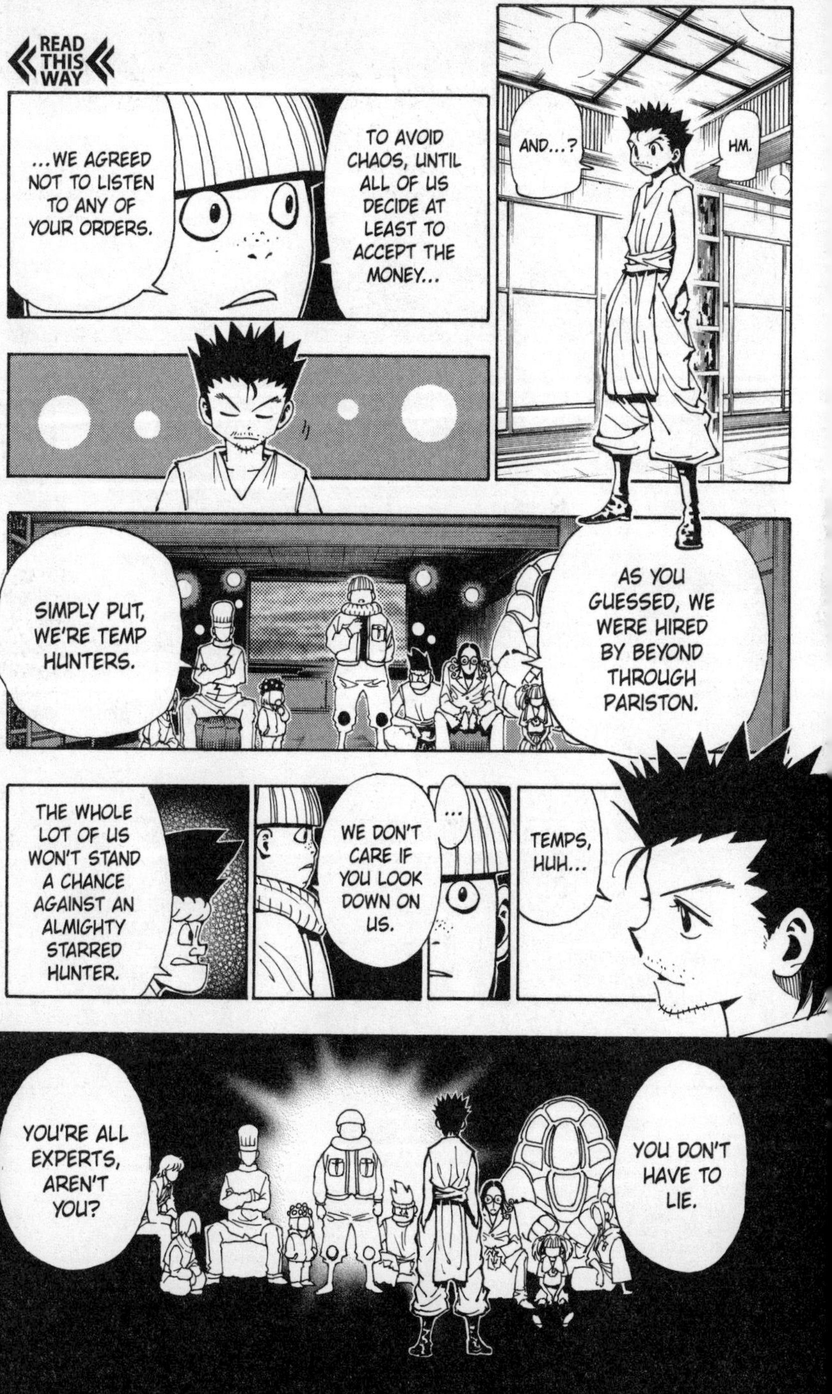
READ THIS WAY
HM.
AND...?
TO AVOID CHAOS, UNTIL ALL OF US DECIDE AT LEAST TO ACCEPT THE MONEY...
...WE AGREED NOT TO LISTEN TO ANY OF YOUR ORDERS.
AS YOU GUESSED, WE WERE HIRED BY BEYOND THROUGH PARISTON.
SIMPLY PUT, WE'RE TEMP HUNTERS.
TEMPS, HUH...
...
WE DON'T CARE IF YOU LOOK DOWN ON US.
THE WHOLE LOT OF US WON'T STAND A CHANCE AGAINST AN ALMIGHTY STARRED HUNTER.
YOU DON'T HAVE TO LIE.
YOU'RE ALL EXPERTS, AREN'T YOU?

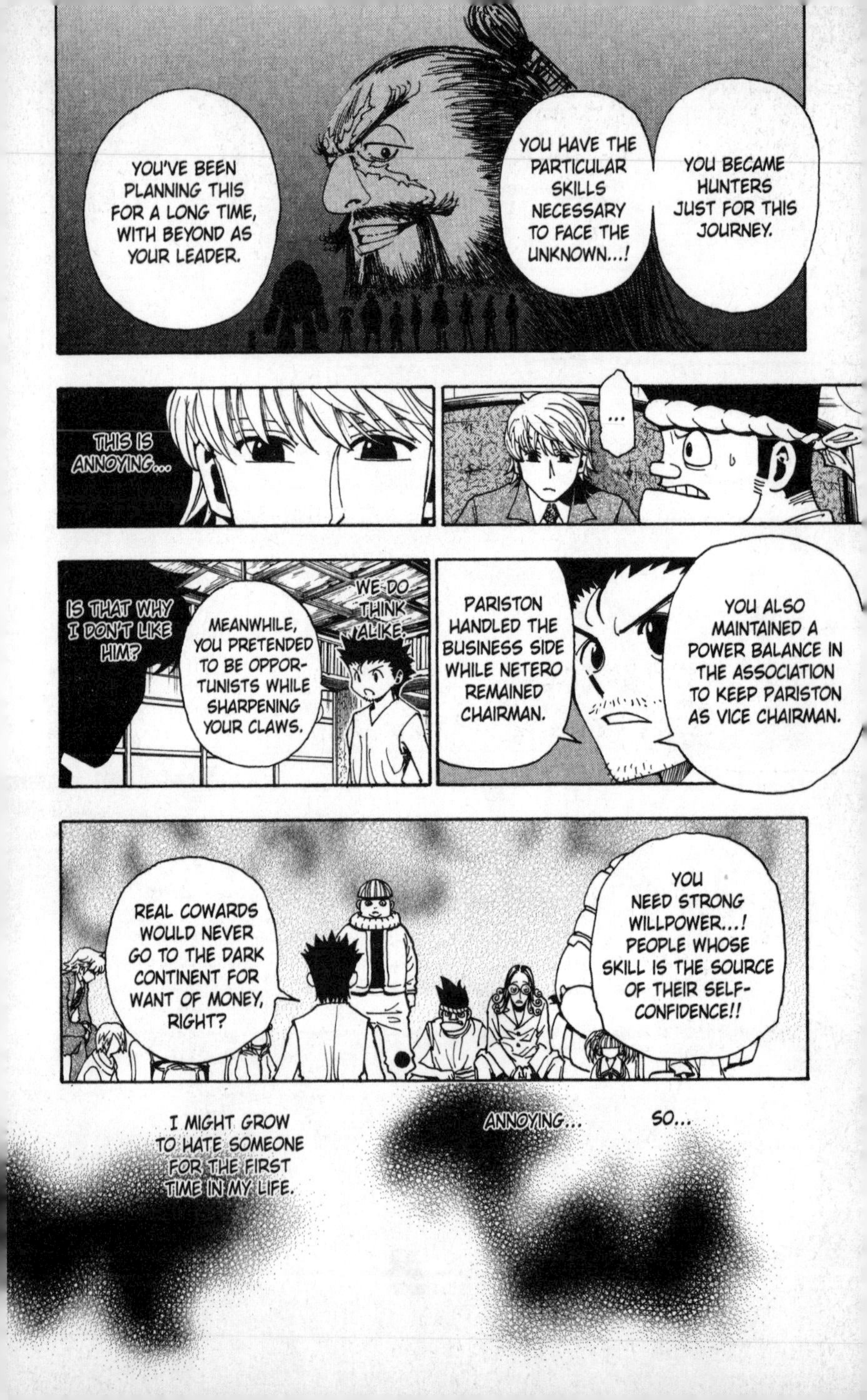
YOU BECAME HUNTERS JUST FOR THIS JOURNEY.
YOU HAVE THE PARTICULAR SKILLS NECESSARY TO FACE THE UNKNOWN...!
YOU'VE BEEN PLANNING THIS FOR A LONG TIME, WITH BEYOND AS YOUR LEADER.
...
THIS IS ANNOYING...
YOU ALSO MAINTAINED A POWER BALANCE IN THE ASSOCIATION TO KEEP PARISTON AS VICE CHAIRMAN.
PARISTON HANDLED THE BUSINESS SIDE WHILE NETERO REMAINED CHAIRMAN.
WE DO THINK ALIKE.
MEANWHILE, YOU PRETENDED TO BE OPPORTUNISTS WHILE SHARPENING YOUR CLAWS.
IS THAT WHY I DON'T LIKE HIM?
YOU NEED STRONG WILLPOWER...! PEOPLE WHOSE SKILL IS THE SOURCE OF THEIR SELF-CONFIDENCE!!
REAL COWARDS WOULD NEVER GO TO THE DARK CONTINENT FOR WANT OF MONEY, RIGHT?
SO...
ANNOYING...
I MIGHT GROW TO HATE SOMEONE FOR THE FIRST TIME IN MY LIFE.

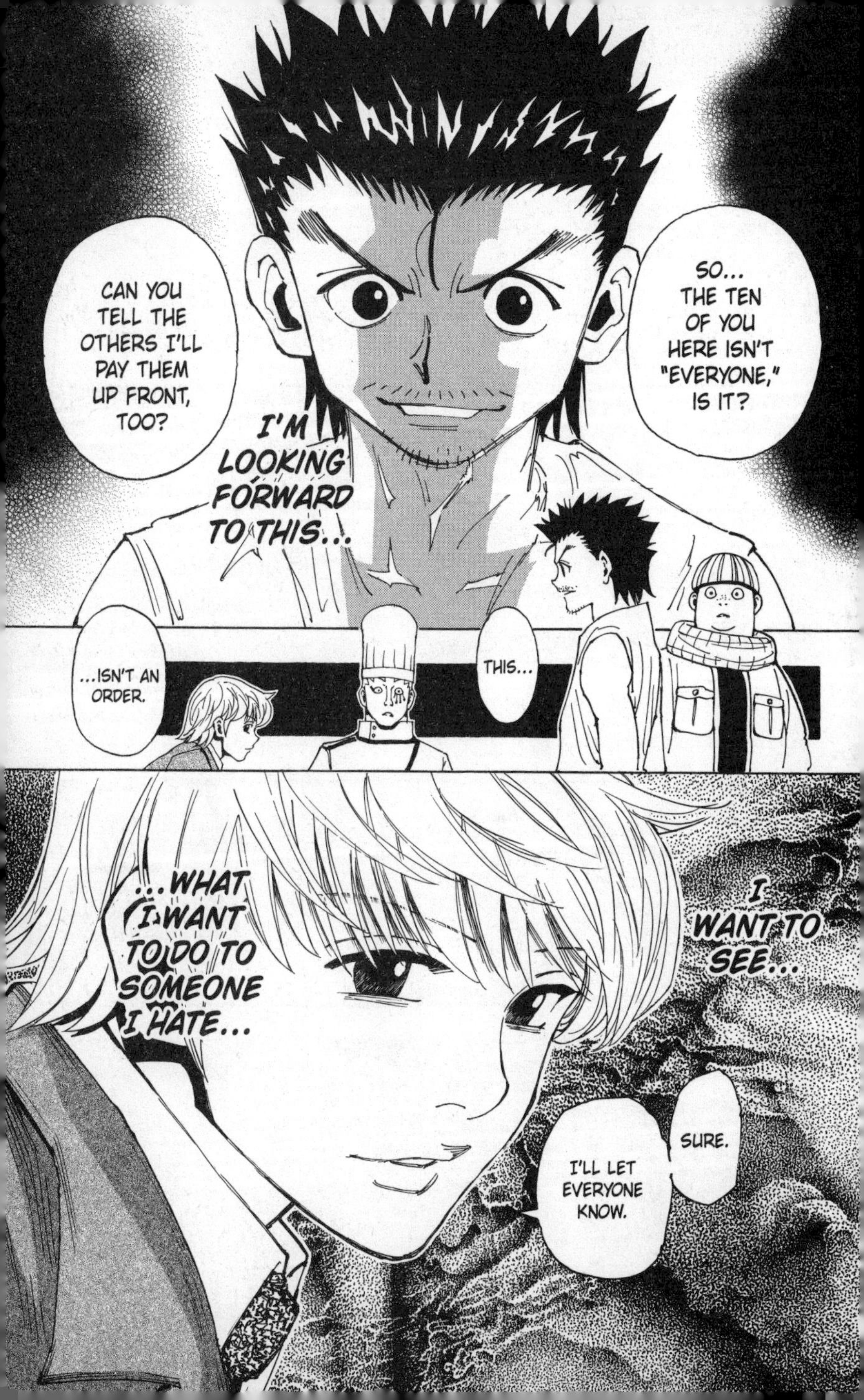
SO... THE TEN OF YOU HERE ISN'T "EVERYONE," IS IT?
CAN YOU TELL THE OTHERS I'LL PAY THEM UP FRONT, TOO?
I'M LOOKING FORWARD TO THIS...
THIS...
...ISN'T AN ORDER.
I WANT TO SEE...
...WHAT I WANT TO DO TO SOMEONE I HATE...
SURE.
I'LL LET EVERYONE KNOW.

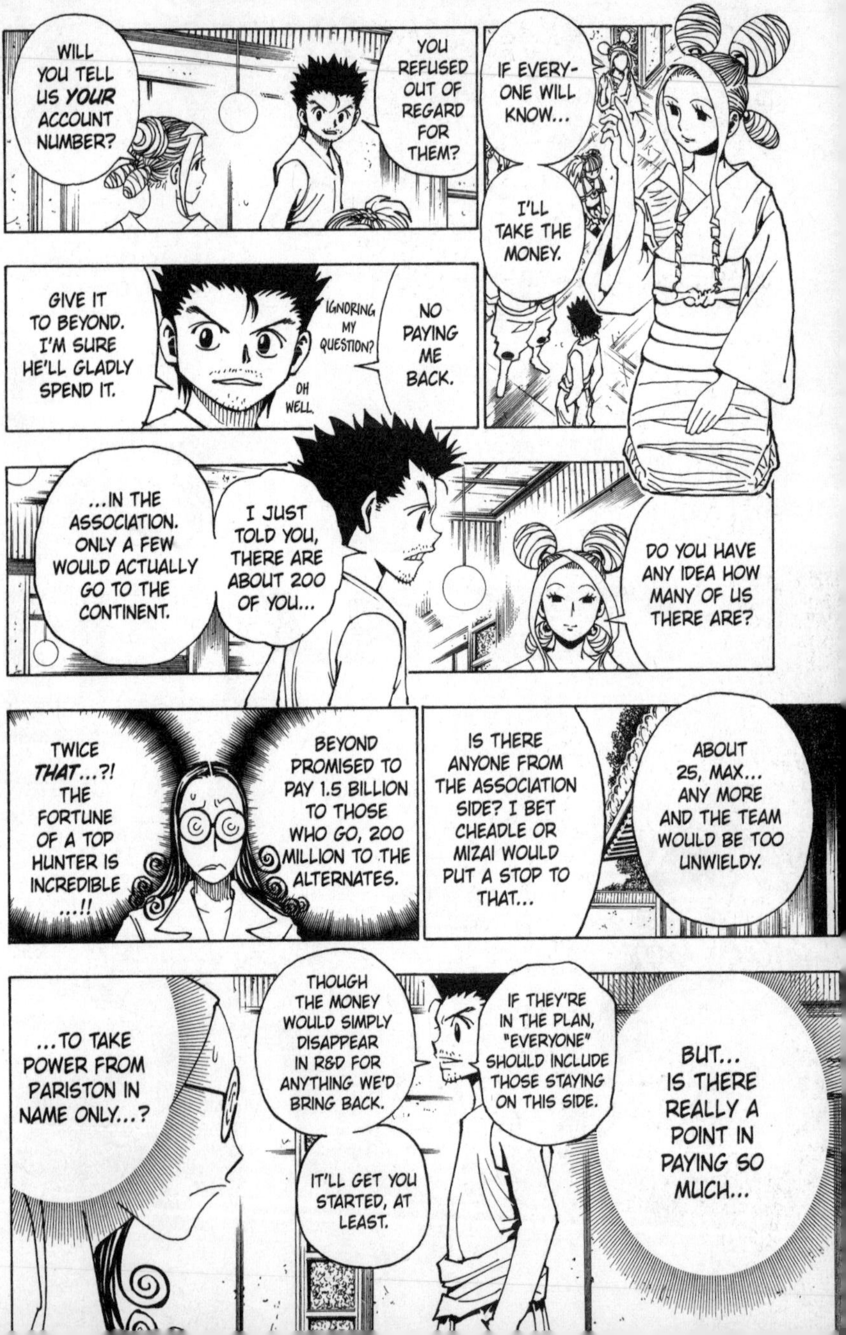
IF EVERYONE WILL KNOW...
I'LL TAKE THE MONEY.
YOU REFUSED OUT OF REGARD FOR THEM?
WILL YOU TELL US *YOUR* ACCOUNT NUMBER?
NO PAYING ME BACK.
IGNORING MY QUESTION?
OH WELL.
GIVE IT TO BEYOND. I'M SURE HE'LL GLADLY SPEND IT.
DO YOU HAVE ANY IDEA HOW MANY OF US THERE ARE?
I JUST TOLD YOU, THERE ARE ABOUT 200 OF YOU...
...IN THE ASSOCIATION. ONLY A FEW WOULD ACTUALLY GO TO THE CONTINENT.
ABOUT 25, MAX... ANY MORE AND THE TEAM WOULD BE TOO UNWIELDY.
IS THERE ANYONE FROM THE ASSOCIATION SIDE? I BET CHEADLE OR MIZAI WOULD PUT A STOP TO THAT...
BEYOND PROMISED TO PAY 1.5 BILLION TO THOSE WHO GO, 200 MILLION TO THE ALTERNATES.
TWICE *THAT*...?! THE FORTUNE OF A TOP HUNTER IS INCREDIBLE ...!!
BUT... IS THERE REALLY A POINT IN PAYING SO MUCH...
IF THEY'RE IN THE PLAN, "EVERYONE" SHOULD INCLUDE THOSE STAYING ON THIS SIDE.
THOUGH THE MONEY WOULD SIMPLY DISAPPEAR IN R&D FOR ANYTHING WE'D BRING BACK.
IT'LL GET YOU STARTED, AT LEAST.
...TO TAKE POWER FROM PARISTON IN NAME ONLY...?

READ THIS WAY

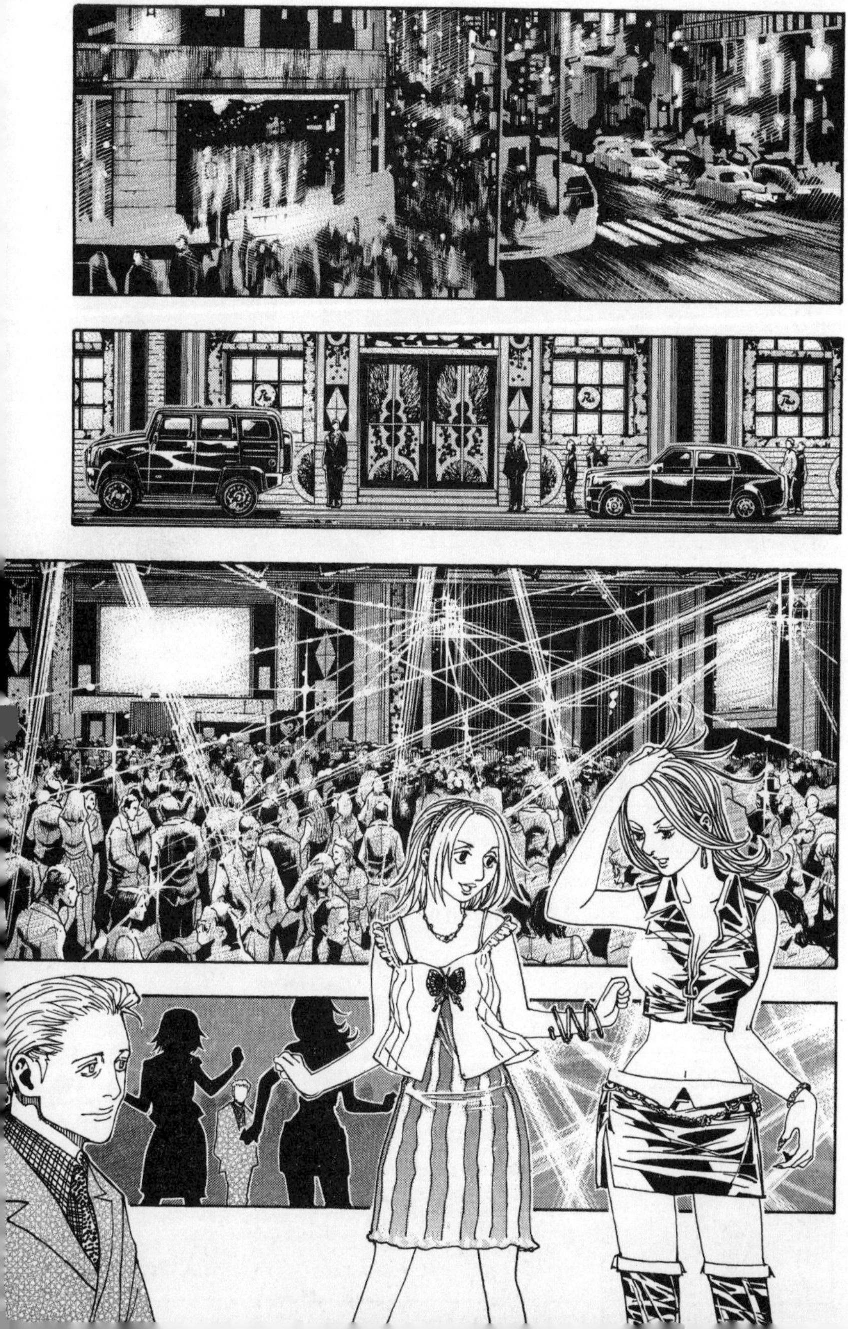

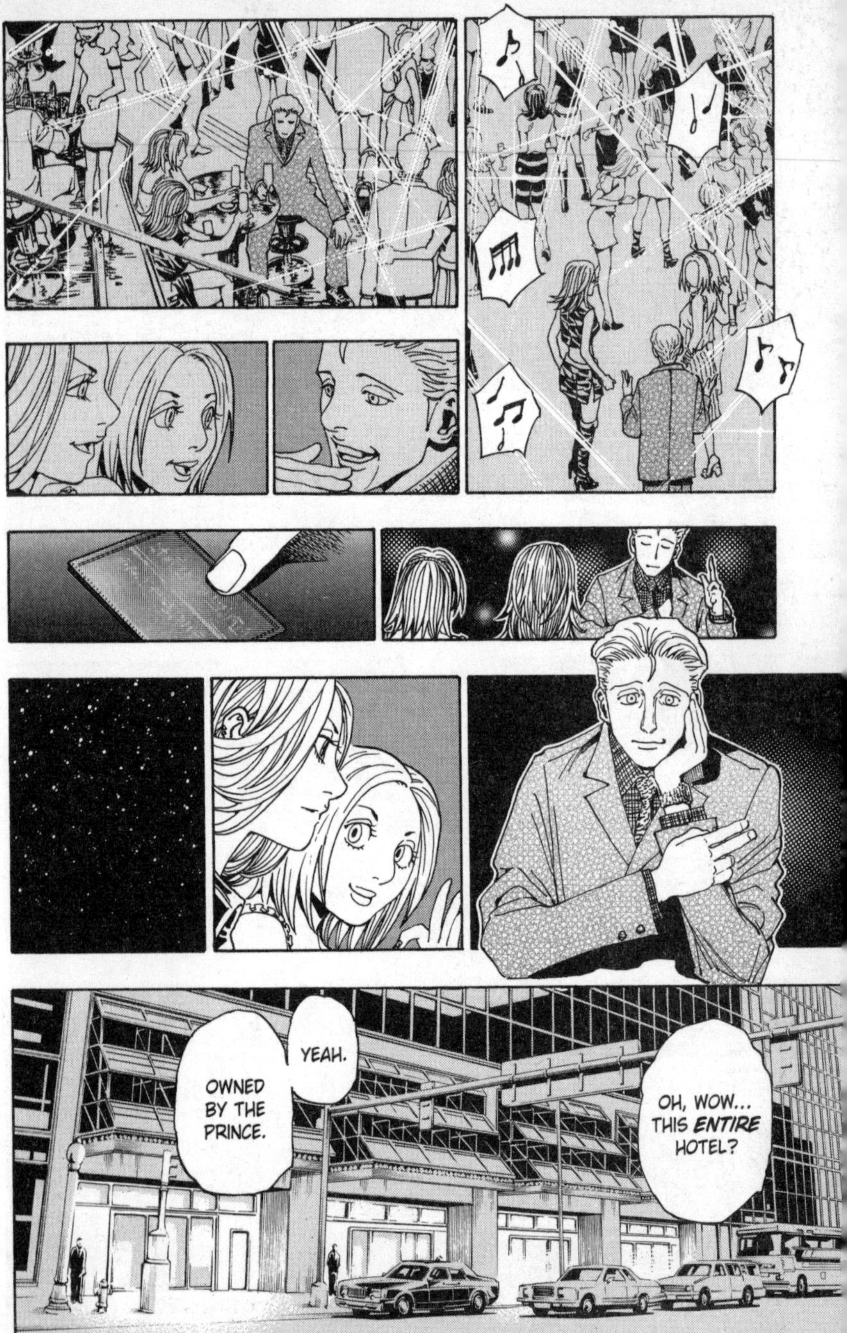
OH, WOW... THIS *ENTIRE* HOTEL?
YEAH.
OWNED BY THE PRINCE.

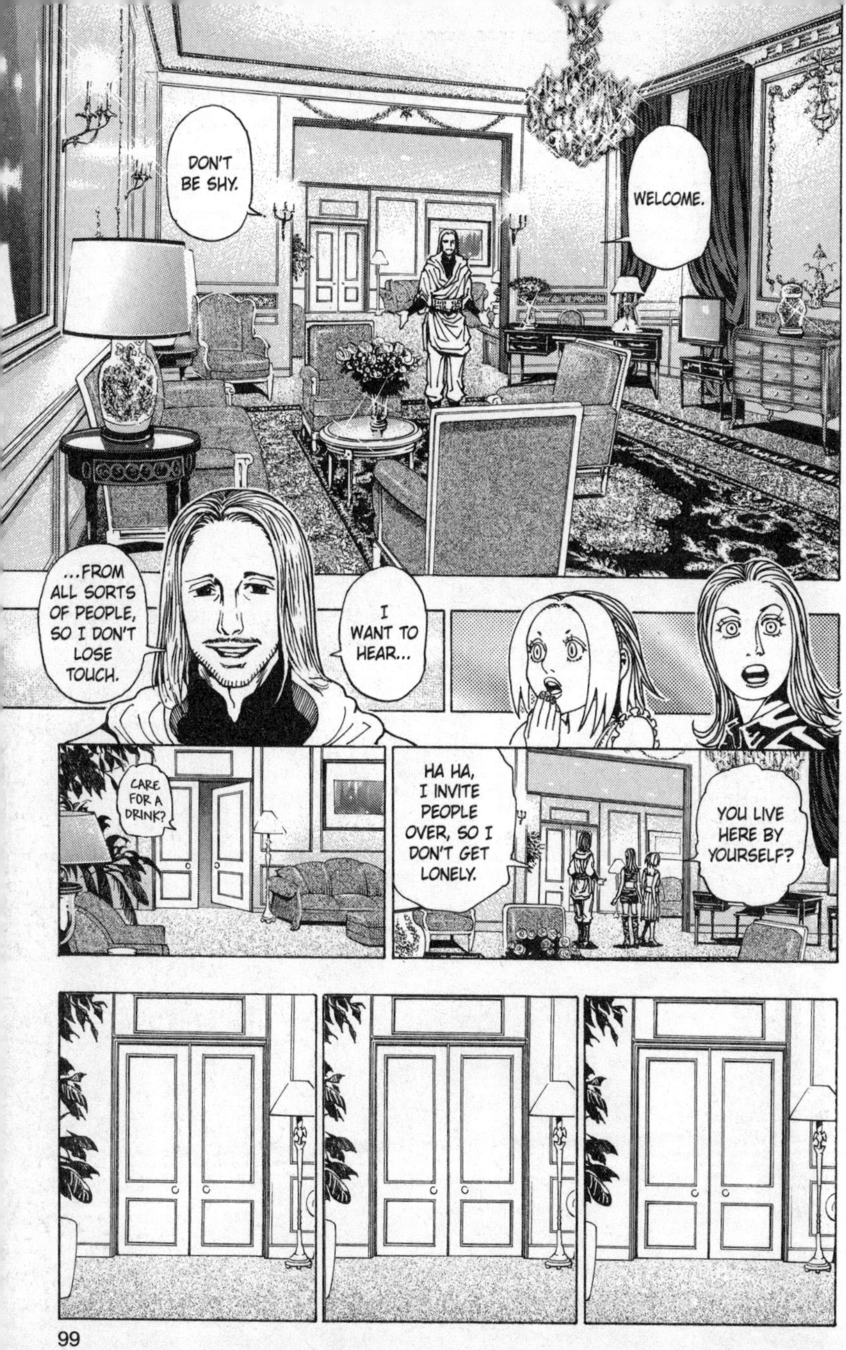
WELCOME.
DON'T BE SHY.
I WANT TO HEAR...
...FROM ALL SORTS OF PEOPLE, SO I DON'T LOSE TOUCH.
YOU LIVE HERE BY YOURSELF?
HA HA, I INVITE PEOPLE OVER, SO I DON'T GET LONELY.
CARE FOR A DRINK?

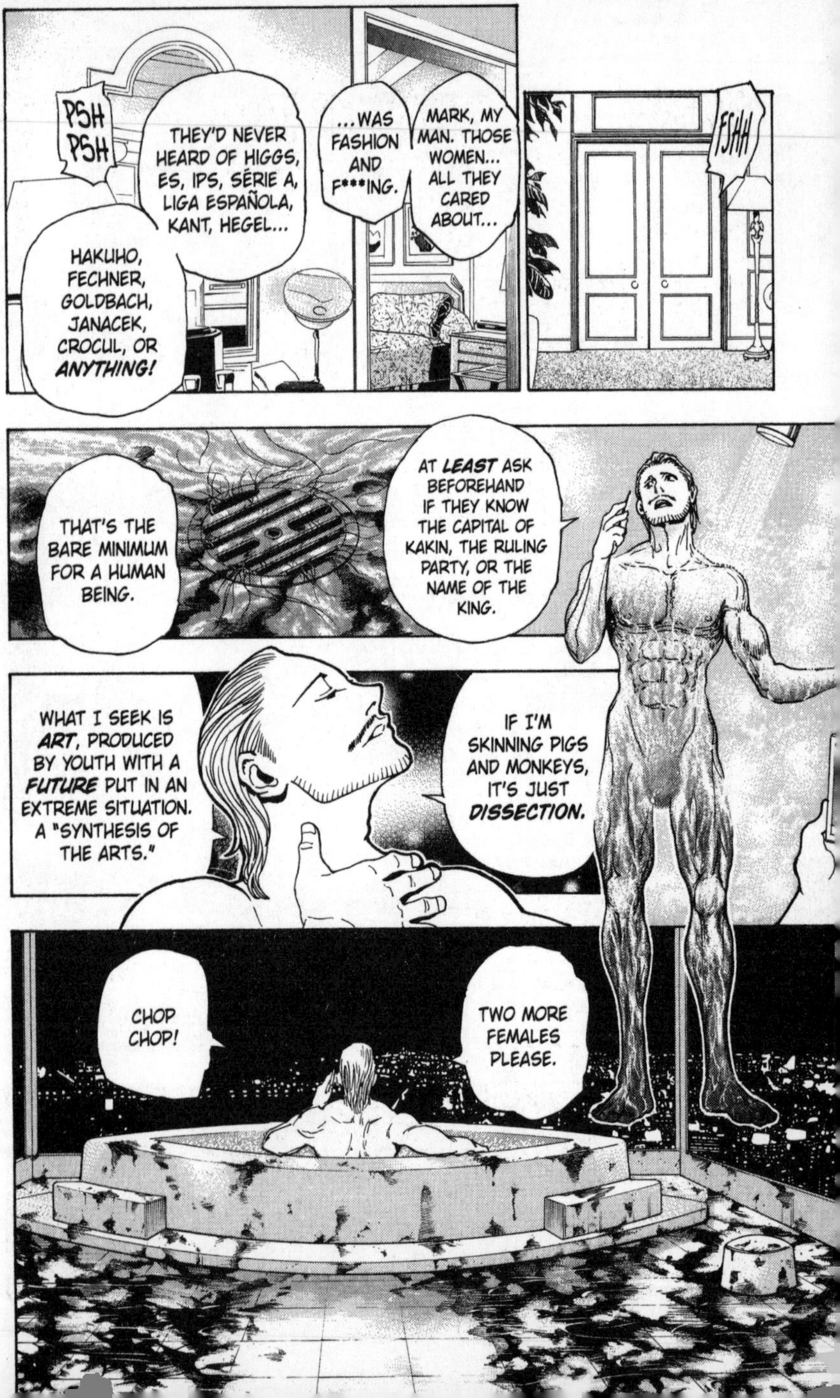
FSHH
MARK, MY MAN. THOSE WOMEN... ALL THEY CARED ABOUT...
...WAS FASHION AND F***ING.
PSH PSH
THEY'D NEVER HEARD OF HIGGS, ES, IPS, SÉRIE A, LIGA ESPAÑOLA, KANT, HEGEL...
HAKUHO, FECHNER, GOLDBACH, JANACEK, CROCUL, OR ANYTHING!
AT LEAST ASK BEFOREHAND IF THEY KNOW THE CAPITAL OF KAKIN, THE RULING PARTY, OR THE NAME OF THE KING.
THAT'S THE BARE MINIMUM FOR A HUMAN BEING.
IF I'M SKINNING PIGS AND MONKEYS, IT'S JUST DISSECTION.
WHAT I SEEK IS ART, PRODUCED BY YOUTH WITH A FUTURE PUT IN AN EXTREME SITUATION. A "SYNTHESIS OF THE ARTS."
TWO MORE FEMALES PLEASE.
CHOP CHOP!

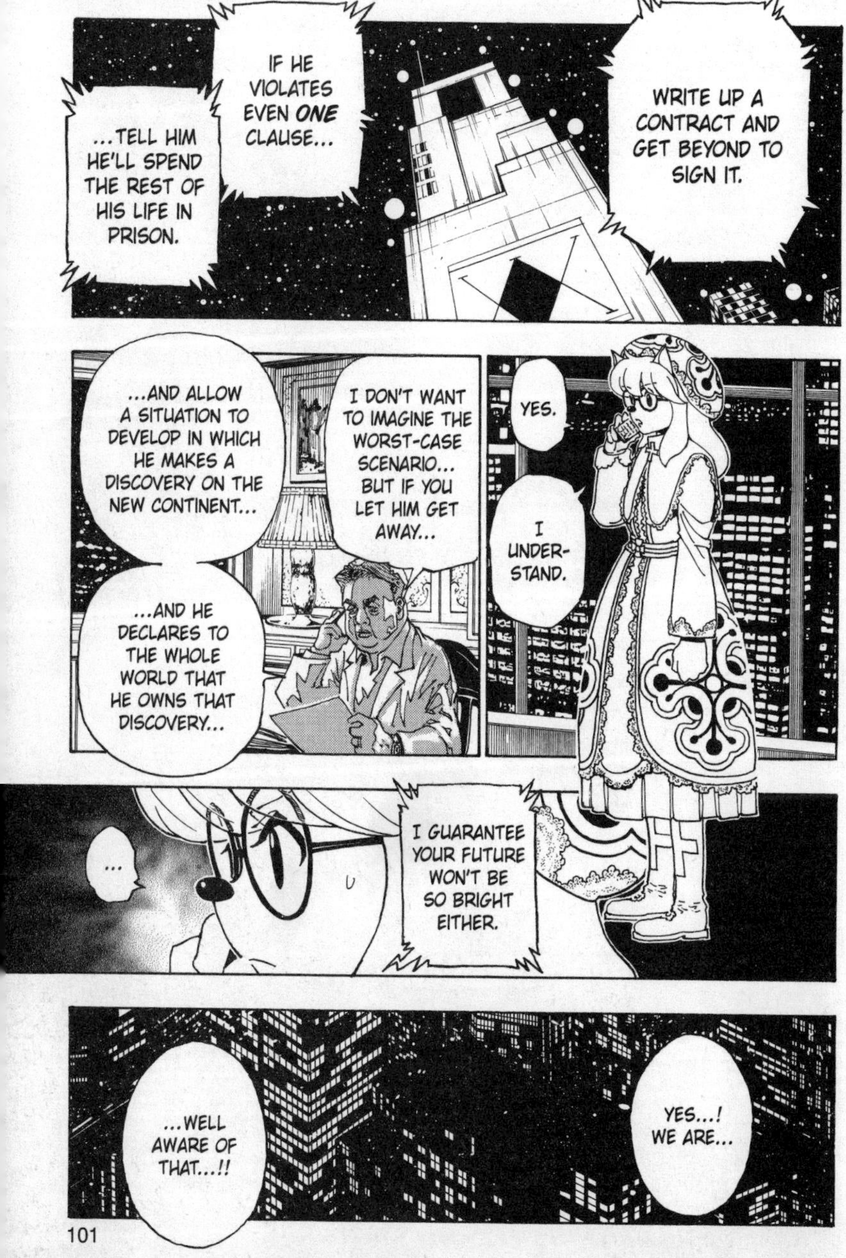
WRITE UP A CONTRACT AND GET BEYOND TO SIGN IT.
IF HE VIOLATES EVEN *ONE* CLAUSE...
...TELL HIM HE'LL SPEND THE REST OF HIS LIFE IN PRISON.
YES.
I UNDERSTAND.
I DON'T WANT TO IMAGINE THE WORST-CASE SCENARIO... BUT IF YOU LET HIM GET AWAY...
...AND ALLOW A SITUATION TO DEVELOP IN WHICH HE MAKES A DISCOVERY ON THE NEW CONTINENT...
...AND HE DECLARES TO THE WHOLE WORLD THAT HE OWNS THAT DISCOVERY...
I GUARANTEE YOUR FUTURE WON'T BE SO BRIGHT EITHER.
...
YES...! WE ARE...
...WELL AWARE OF THAT...!!

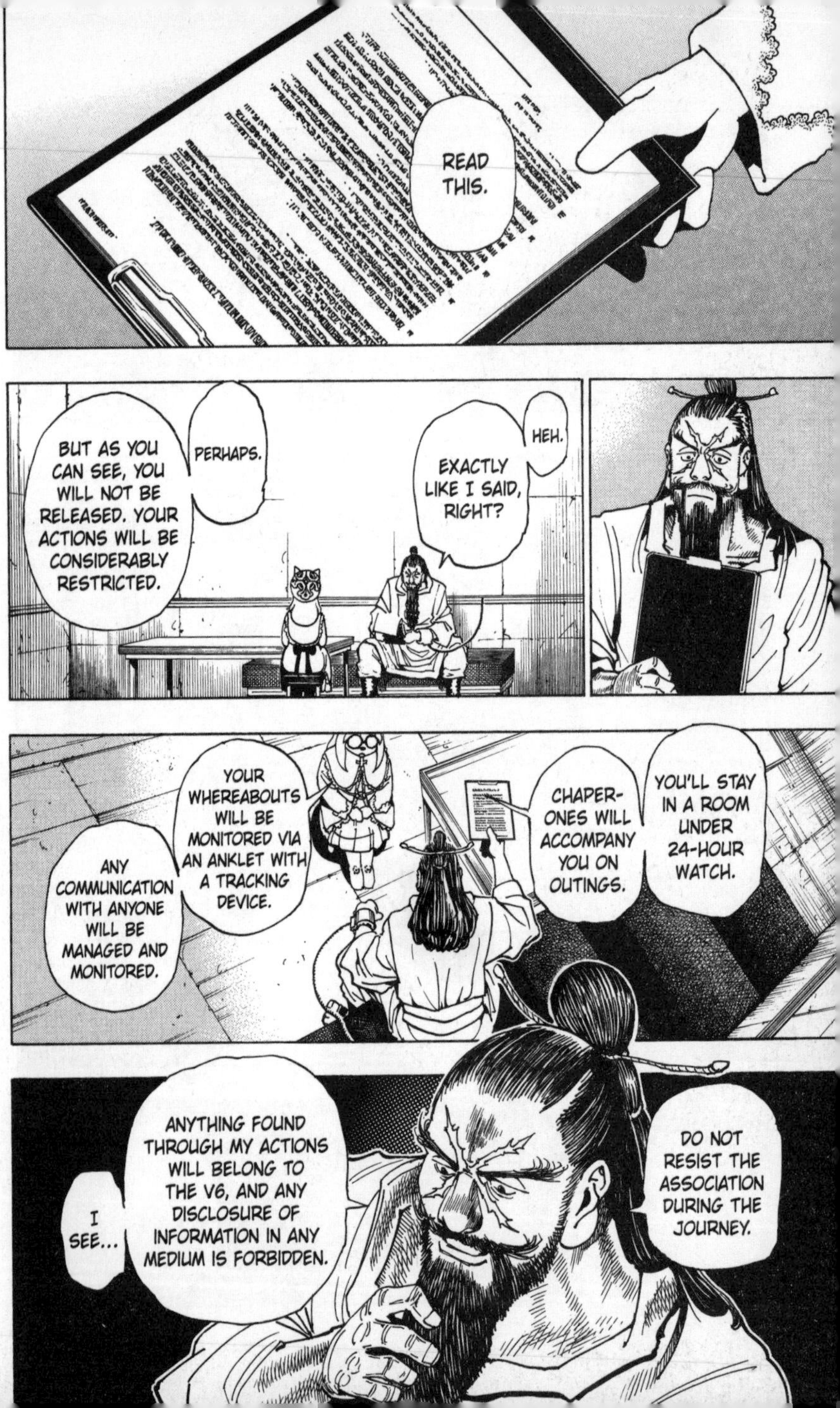
READ THIS.
HEH.
EXACTLY LIKE I SAID, RIGHT?
PERHAPS.
BUT AS YOU CAN SEE, YOU WILL NOT BE RELEASED. YOUR ACTIONS WILL BE CONSIDERABLY RESTRICTED.
YOU'LL STAY IN A ROOM UNDER 24-HOUR WATCH.
CHAPERONES WILL ACCOMPANY YOU ON OUTINGS.
YOUR WHEREABOUTS WILL BE MONITORED VIA AN ANKLET WITH A TRACKING DEVICE.
ANY COMMUNICATION WITH ANYONE WILL BE MANAGED AND MONITORED.
DO NOT RESIST THE ASSOCIATION DURING THE JOURNEY.
ANYTHING FOUND THROUGH MY ACTIONS WILL BELONG TO THE V6, AND ANY DISCLOSURE OF INFORMATION IN ANY MEDIUM IS FORBIDDEN.
I SEE...

READ THIS WAY

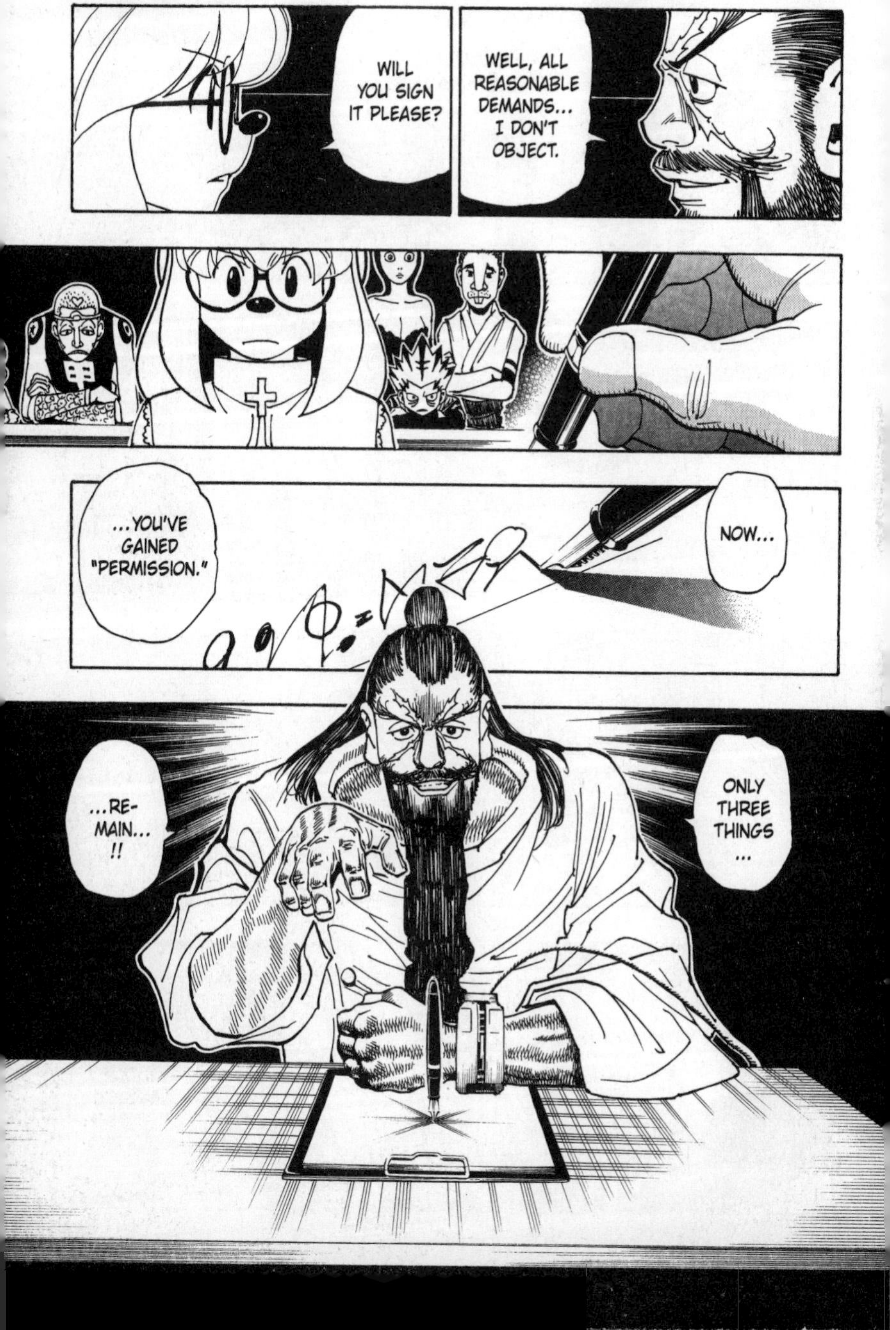
WELL, ALL REASONABLE DEMANDS... I DON'T OBJECT.
WILL YOU SIGN IT PLEASE?
NOW...
...YOU'VE GAINED "PERMISSION."
ONLY THREE THINGS ...
...RE-MAIN... !!

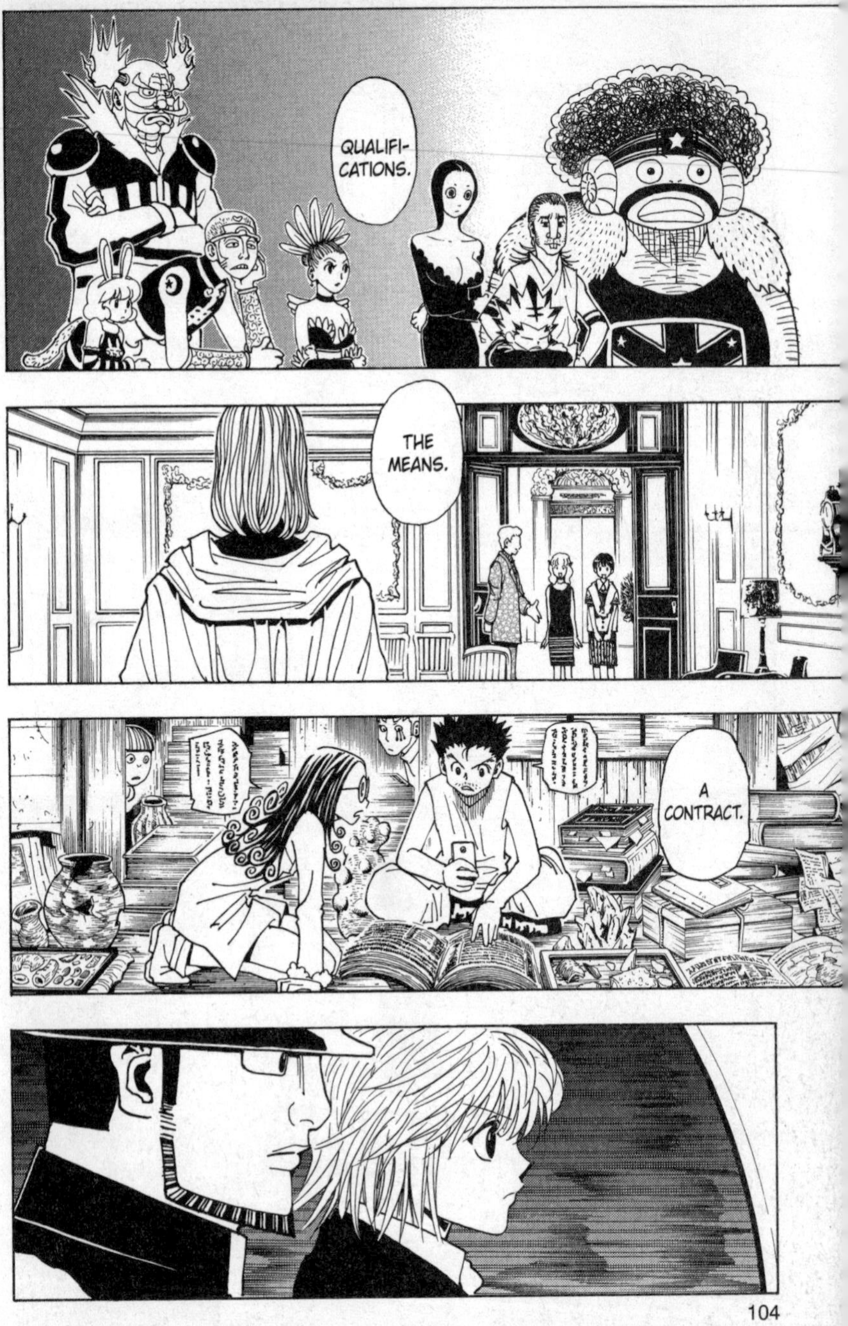
QUALIFI-
CATIONS.
THE
MEANS.
A
CONTRACT.

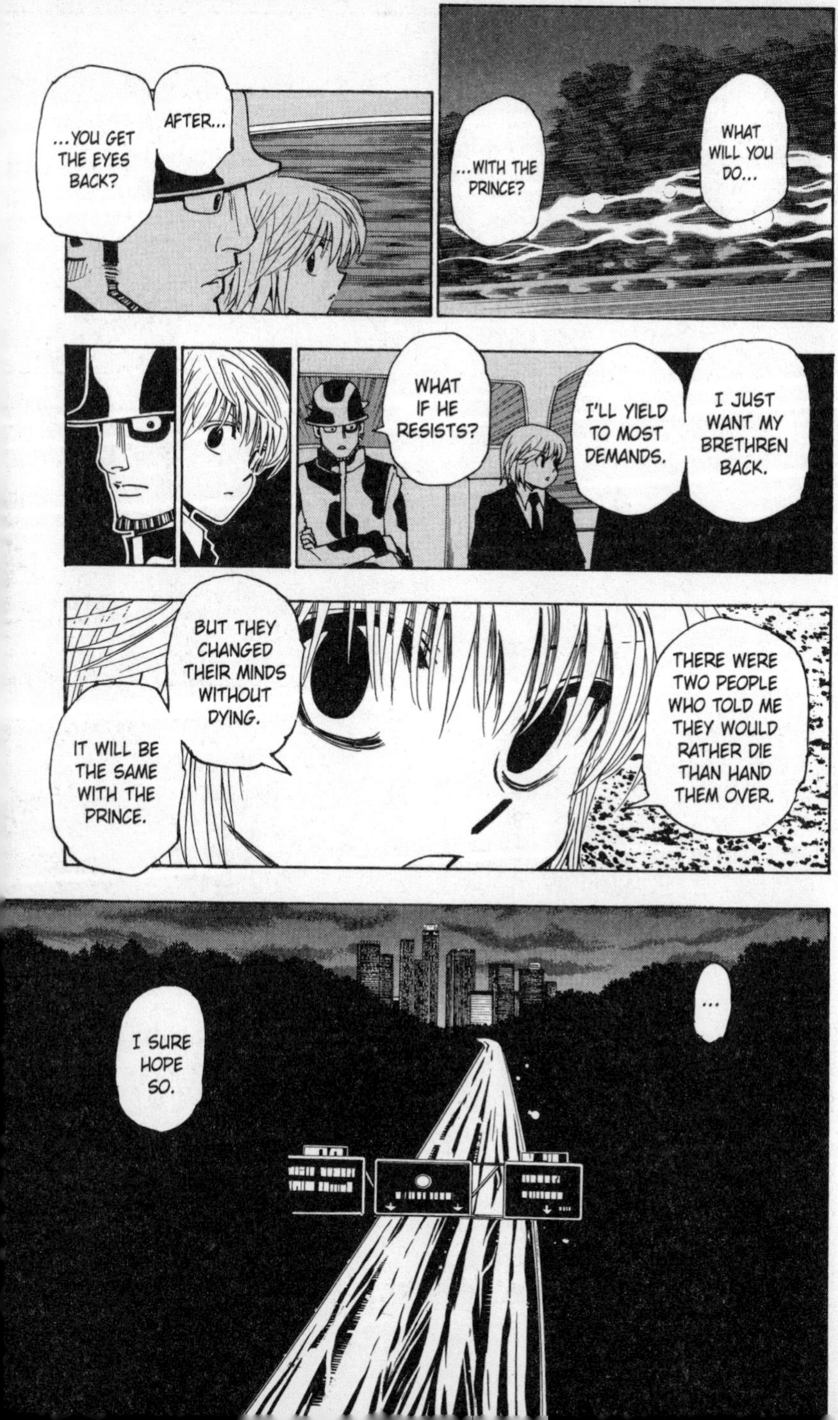
WHAT WILL YOU DO...
...WITH THE PRINCE?
AFTER...
...YOU GET THE EYES BACK?
I JUST WANT MY BRETHREN BACK.
I'LL YIELD TO MOST DEMANDS.
WHAT IF HE RESISTS?
THERE WERE TWO PEOPLE WHO TOLD ME THEY WOULD RATHER DIE THAN HAND THEM OVER.
BUT THEY CHANGED THEIR MINDS WITHOUT DYING.
IT WILL BE THE SAME WITH THE PRINCE.
...
I SURE HOPE SO.

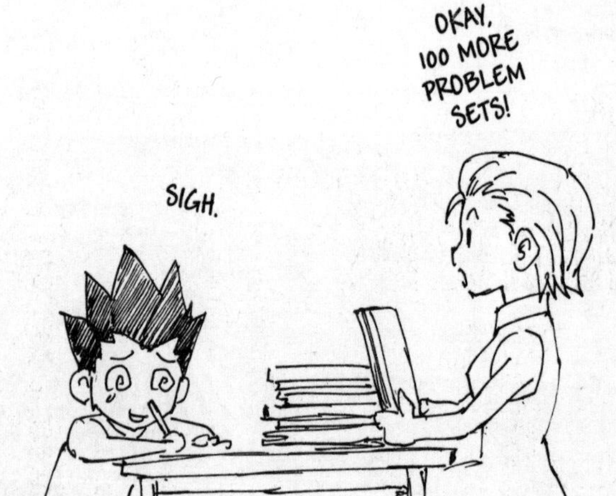
OKAY, 100 MORE PROBLEM SETS!
SIGH.

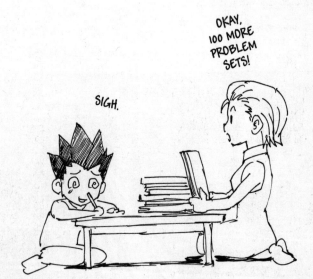

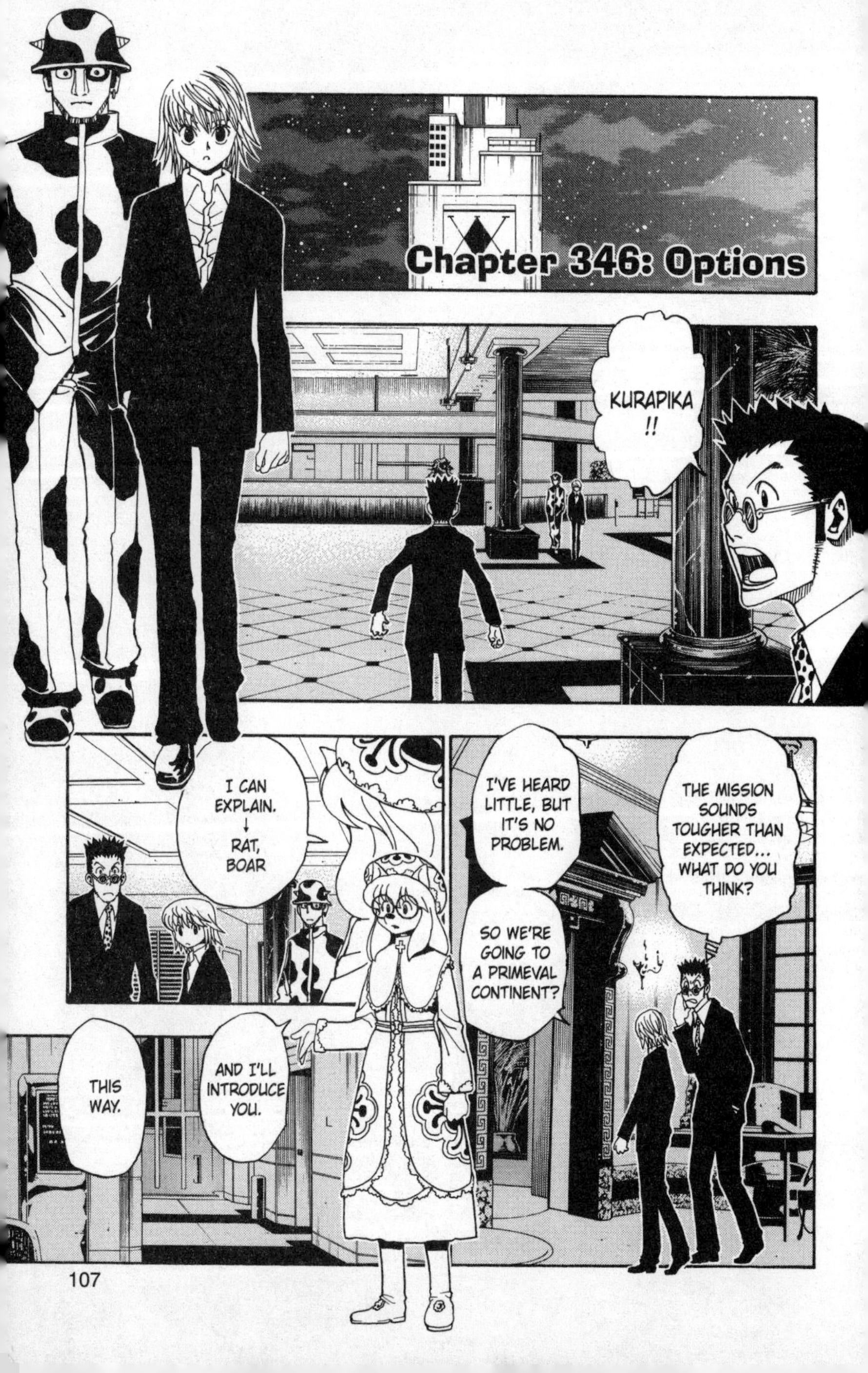
Chapter 346: Options
KURAPIKA !!
THE MISSION SOUNDS TOUGHER THAN EXPECTED... WHAT DO YOU THINK?
I'VE HEARD LITTLE, BUT IT'S NO PROBLEM.
SO WE'RE GOING TO A PRIMEVAL CONTINENT?
I CAN EXPLAIN. ↓ RAT, BOAR
AND I'LL INTRODUCE YOU.
THIS WAY.

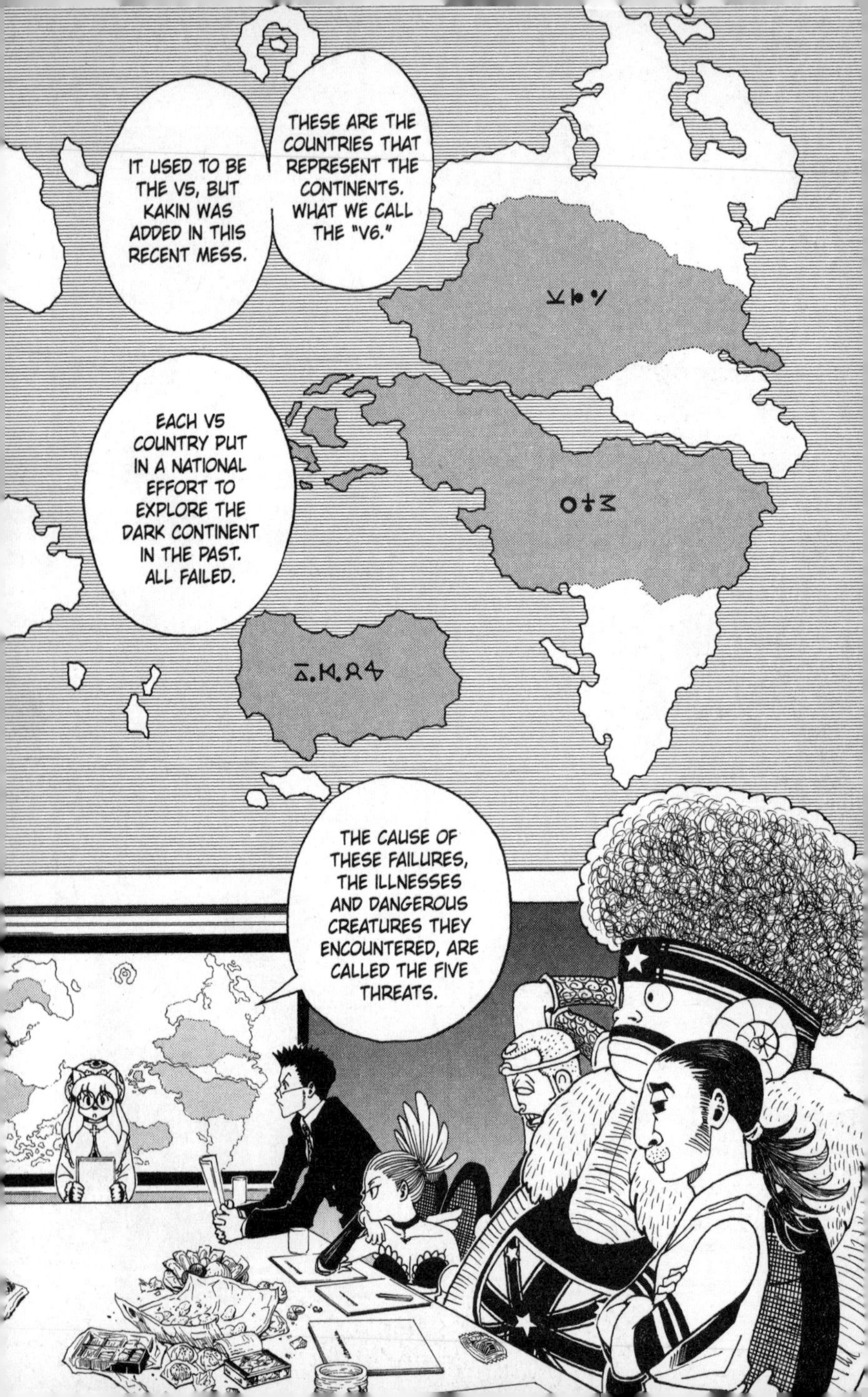
THESE ARE THE COUNTRIES THAT REPRESENT THE CONTINENTS. WHAT WE CALL THE "V6."
IT USED TO BE THE V5, BUT KAKIN WAS ADDED IN THIS RECENT MESS.
EACH V5 COUNTRY PUT IN A NATIONAL EFFORT TO EXPLORE THE DARK CONTINENT IN THE PAST. ALL FAILED.
THE CAUSE OF THESE FAILURES, THE ILLNESSES AND DANGEROUS CREATURES THEY ENCOUNTERED, ARE CALLED THE FIVE THREATS.

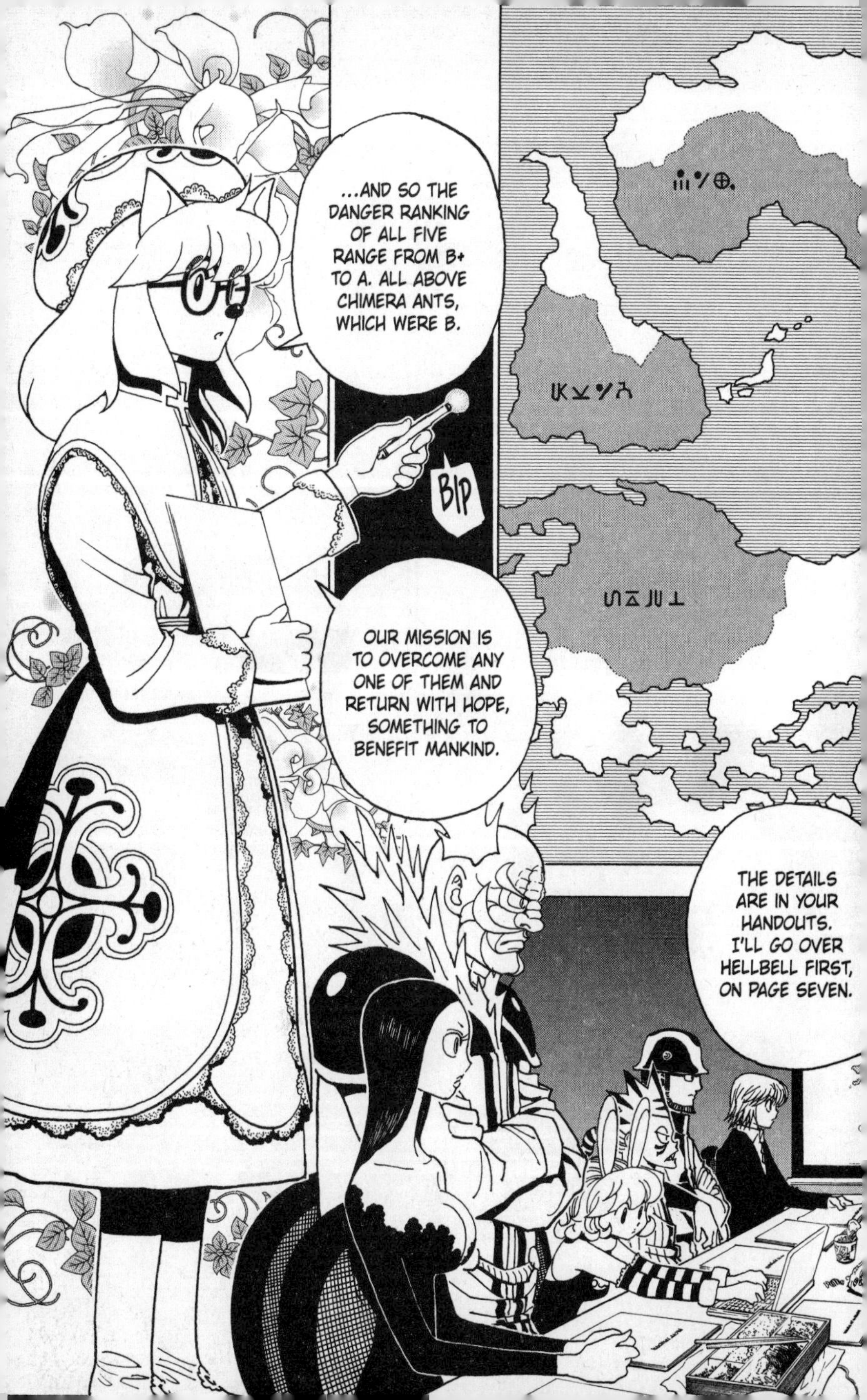
...AND SO THE DANGER RANKING OF ALL FIVE RANGE FROM B+ TO A. ALL ABOVE CHIMERA ANTS, WHICH WERE B.
BIP
OUR MISSION IS TO OVERCOME ANY ONE OF THEM AND RETURN WITH HOPE, SOMETHING TO BENEFIT MANKIND.
THE DETAILS ARE IN YOUR HANDOUTS. I'LL GO OVER HELLBELL FIRST, ON PAGE SEVEN.

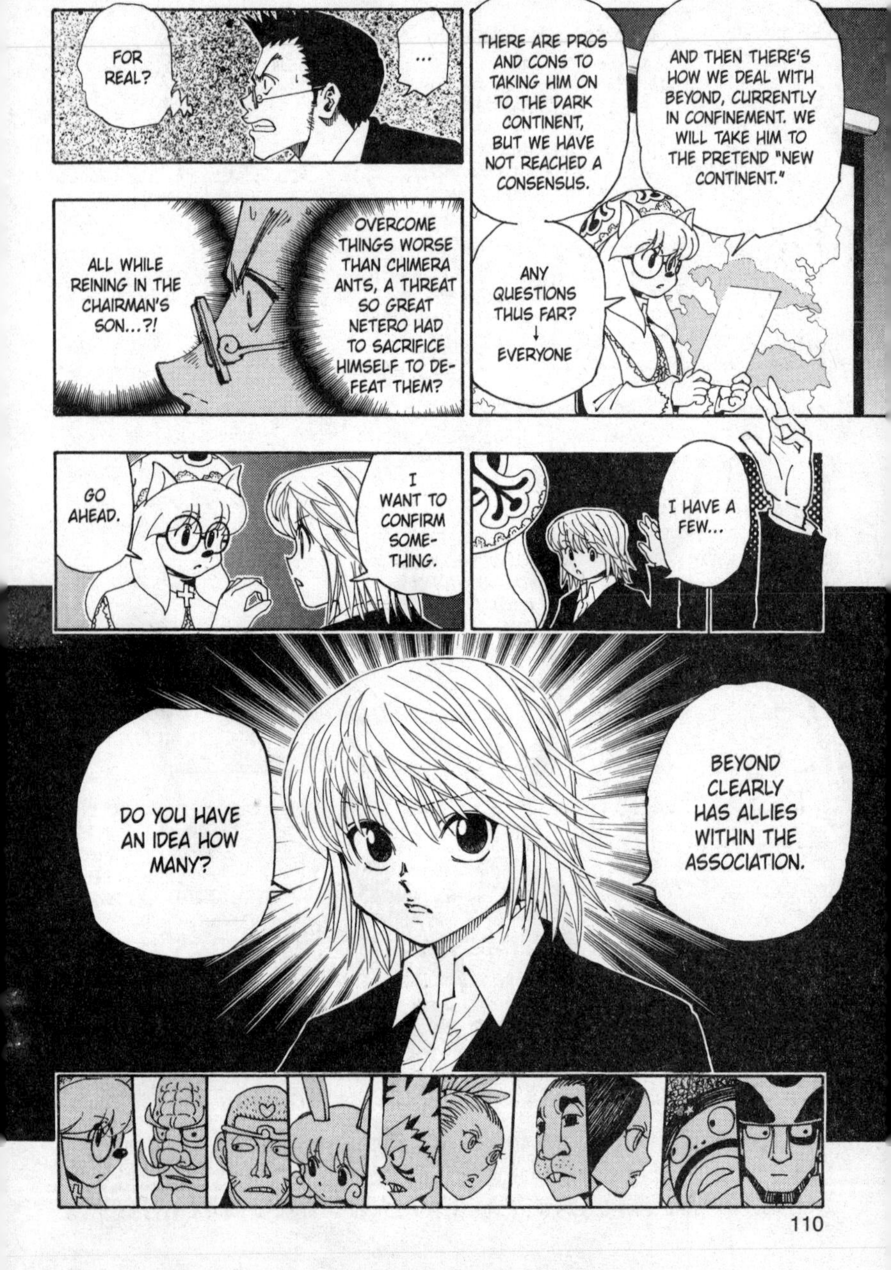
AND THEN THERE'S HOW WE DEAL WITH BEYOND, CURRENTLY IN CONFINEMENT. WE WILL TAKE HIM TO THE PRETEND "NEW CONTINENT."
THERE ARE PROS AND CONS TO TAKING HIM ON TO THE DARK CONTINENT, BUT WE HAVE NOT REACHED A CONSENSUS.
ANY QUESTIONS THUS FAR? ↓ EVERYONE
...
FOR REAL?
OVERCOME THINGS WORSE THAN CHIMERA ANTS, A THREAT SO GREAT NETERO HAD TO SACRIFICE HIMSELF TO DEFEAT THEM?
ALL WHILE REINING IN THE CHAIRMAN'S SON...?!
I HAVE A FEW...
I WANT TO CONFIRM SOMETHING.
GO AHEAD.
BEYOND CLEARLY HAS ALLIES WITHIN THE ASSOCIATION.
DO YOU HAVE AN IDEA HOW MANY?

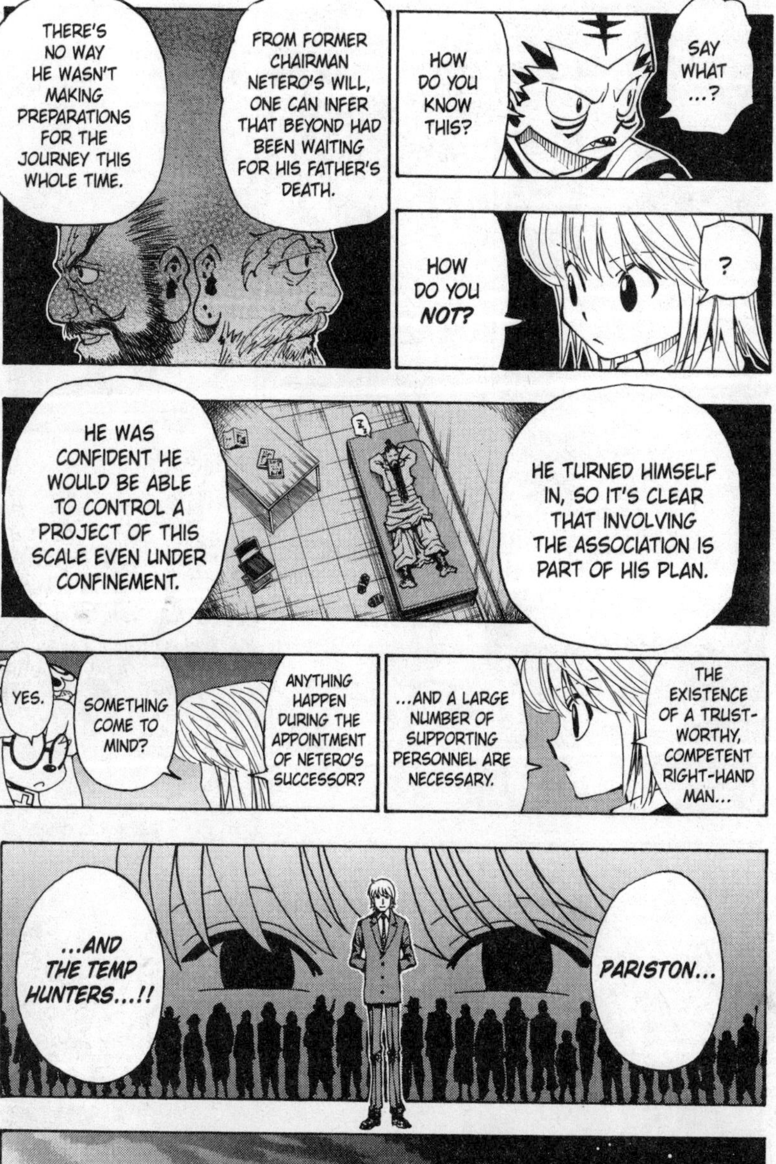
SAY WHAT ...?
HOW DO YOU KNOW THIS?
?
HOW DO YOU *NOT?*
FROM FORMER CHAIRMAN NETERO'S WILL, ONE CAN INFER THAT BEYOND HAD BEEN WAITING FOR HIS FATHER'S DEATH.
THERE'S NO WAY HE WASN'T MAKING PREPARATIONS FOR THE JOURNEY THIS WHOLE TIME.
HE TURNED HIMSELF IN, SO IT'S CLEAR THAT INVOLVING THE ASSOCIATION IS PART OF HIS PLAN.
HE WAS CONFIDENT HE WOULD BE ABLE TO CONTROL A PROJECT OF THIS SCALE EVEN UNDER CONFINEMENT.
THE EXISTENCE OF A TRUST-WORTHY, COMPETENT RIGHT-HAND MAN...
...AND A LARGE NUMBER OF SUPPORTING PERSONNEL ARE NECESSARY.
ANYTHING HAPPEN DURING THE APPOINTMENT OF NETERO'S SUCCESSOR?
SOMETHING COME TO MIND?
YES.
PARISTON...
...AND THE TEMP HUNTERS...!!

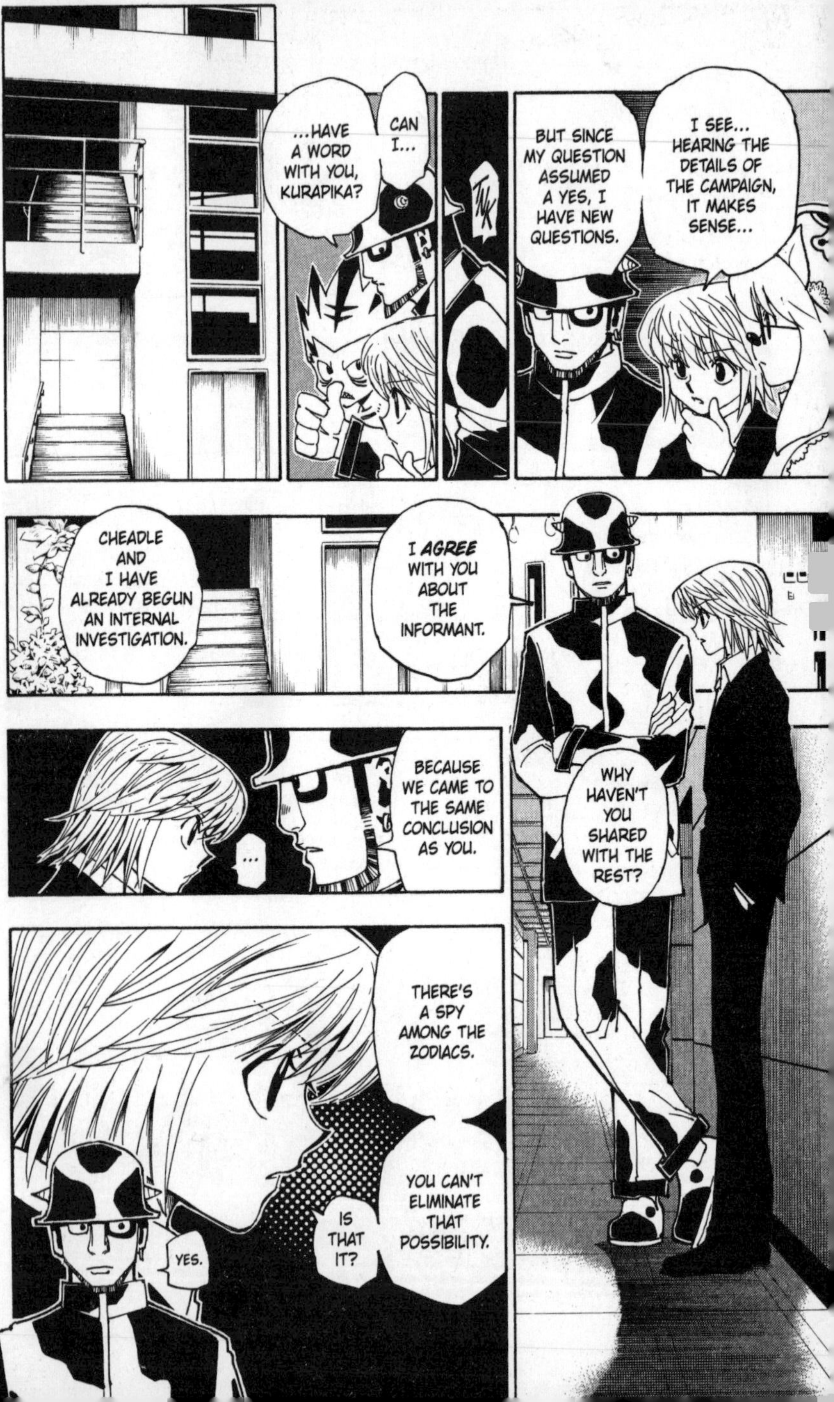
I SEE... HEARING THE DETAILS OF THE CAMPAIGN, IT MAKES SENSE...
BUT SINCE MY QUESTION ASSUMED A YES, I HAVE NEW QUESTIONS.
TNK
CAN I...
...HAVE A WORD WITH YOU, KURAPIKA?
WHY HAVEN'T YOU SHARED WITH THE REST?
I AGREE WITH YOU ABOUT THE INFORMANT.
CHEADLE AND I HAVE ALREADY BEGUN AN INTERNAL INVESTIGATION.
BECAUSE WE CAME TO THE SAME CONCLUSION AS YOU.
...
THERE'S A SPY AMONG THE ZODIACS.
YOU CAN'T ELIMINATE THAT POSSIBILITY.
IS THAT IT?
YES.

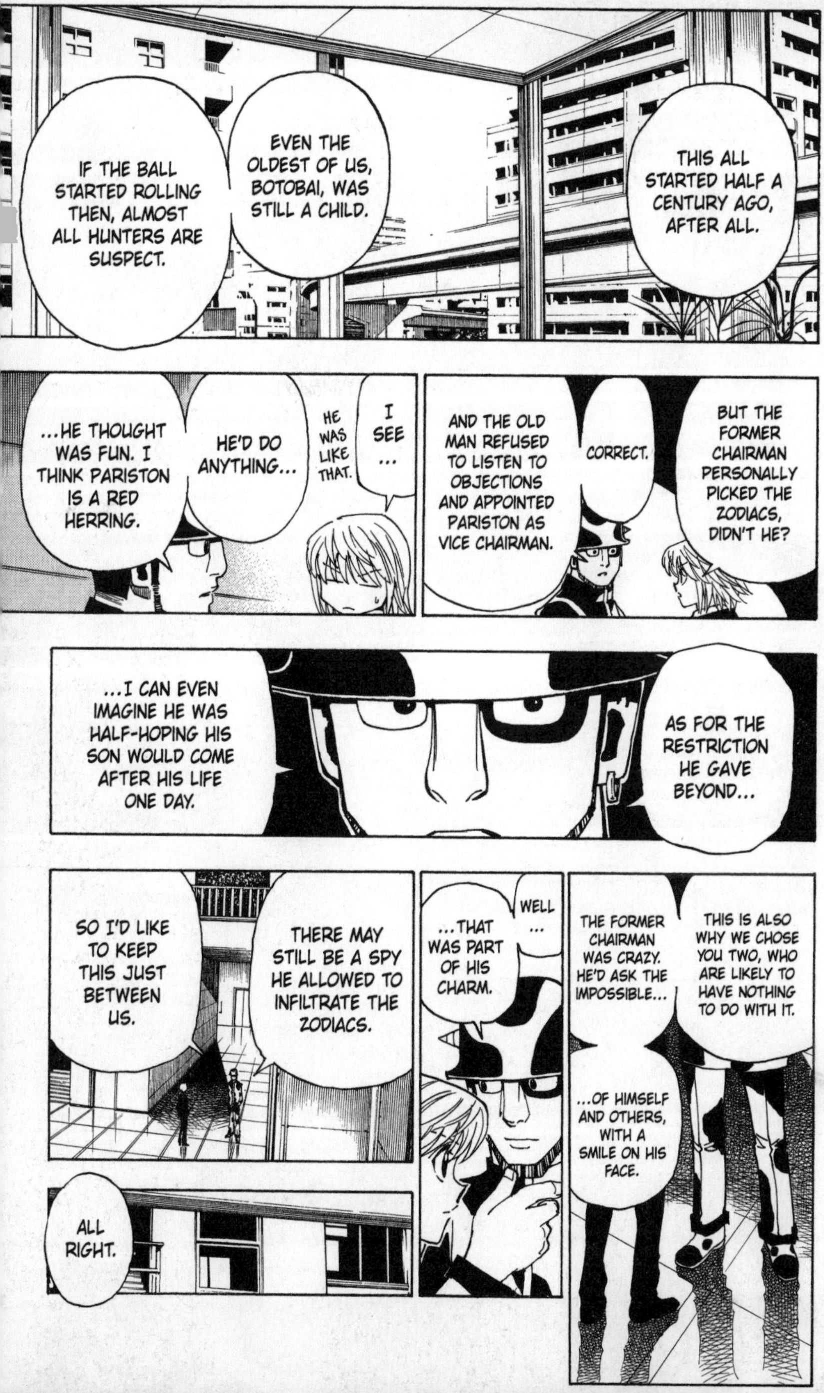
THIS ALL STARTED HALF A CENTURY AGO, AFTER ALL.
EVEN THE OLDEST OF US, BOTOBAI, WAS STILL A CHILD.
IF THE BALL STARTED ROLLING THEN, ALMOST ALL HUNTERS ARE SUSPECT.
BUT THE FORMER CHAIRMAN PERSONALLY PICKED THE ZODIACS, DIDN'T HE?
CORRECT.
AND THE OLD MAN REFUSED TO LISTEN TO OBJECTIONS AND APPOINTED PARISTON AS VICE CHAIRMAN.
I SEE ...
HE WAS LIKE THAT.
HE'D DO ANYTHING...
...HE THOUGHT WAS FUN. I THINK PARISTON IS A RED HERRING.
AS FOR THE RESTRICTION HE GAVE BEYOND...
...I CAN EVEN IMAGINE HE WAS HALF-HOPING HIS SON WOULD COME AFTER HIS LIFE ONE DAY.
THIS IS ALSO WHY WE CHOSE YOU TWO, WHO ARE LIKELY TO HAVE NOTHING TO DO WITH IT.
THE FORMER CHAIRMAN WAS CRAZY. HE'D ASK THE IMPOSSIBLE...
...OF HIMSELF AND OTHERS, WITH A SMILE ON HIS FACE.
WELL ...
...THAT WAS PART OF HIS CHARM.
THERE MAY STILL BE A SPY HE ALLOWED TO INFILTRATE THE ZODIACS.
SO I'D LIKE TO KEEP THIS JUST BETWEEN US.
ALL RIGHT.

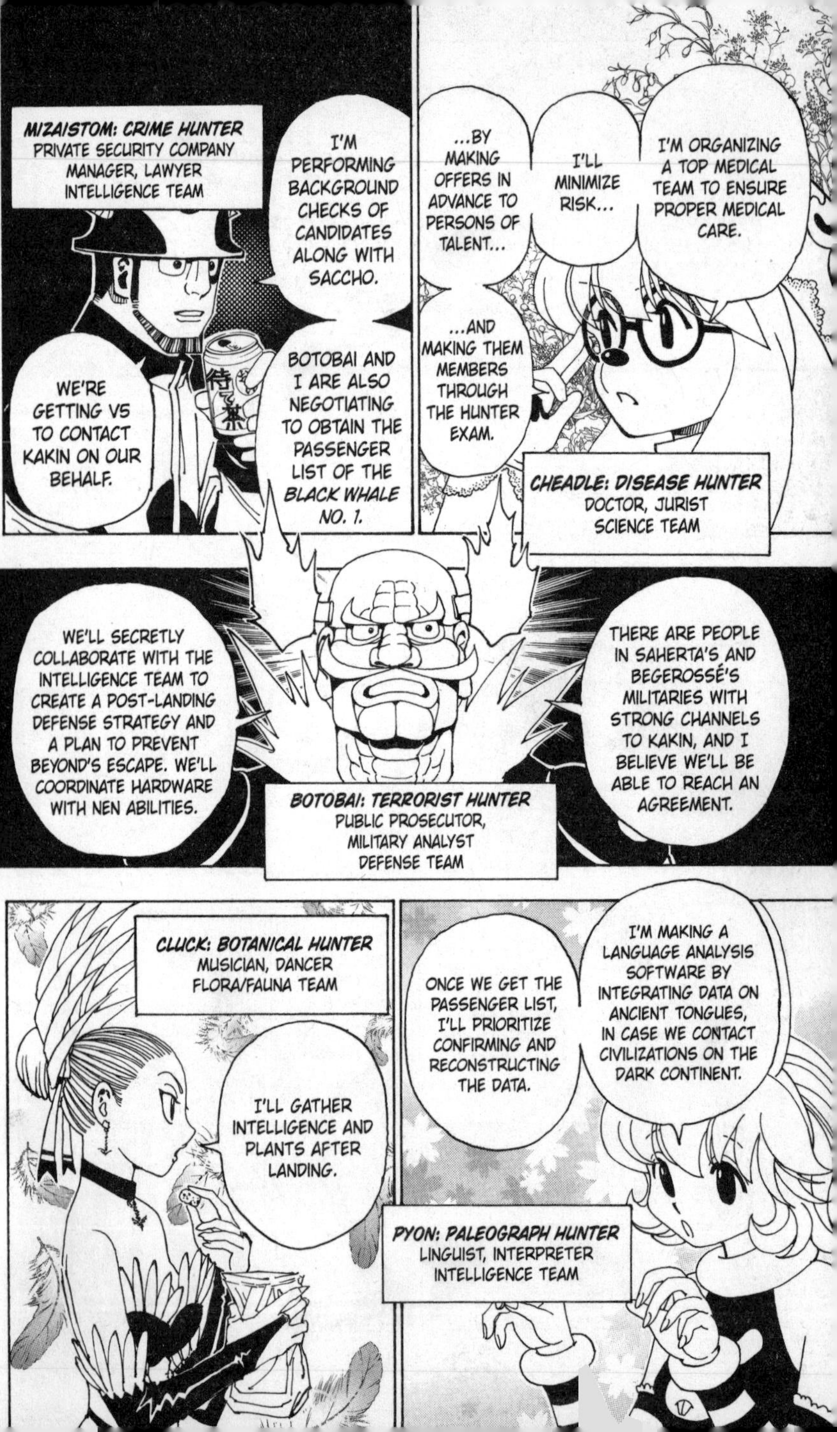
I'M ORGANIZING A TOP MEDICAL TEAM TO ENSURE PROPER MEDICAL CARE.
I'LL MINIMIZE RISK...
...BY MAKING OFFERS IN ADVANCE TO PERSONS OF TALENT...
...AND MAKING THEM MEMBERS THROUGH THE HUNTER EXAM.
CHEADLE: DISEASE HUNTER
DOCTOR, JURIST
SCIENCE TEAM
I'M PERFORMING BACKGROUND CHECKS OF CANDIDATES ALONG WITH SACCHO.
MIZAISTOM: CRIME HUNTER
PRIVATE SECURITY COMPANY MANAGER, LAWYER
INTELLIGENCE TEAM
BOTOBAI AND I ARE ALSO NEGOTIATING TO OBTAIN THE PASSENGER LIST OF THE BLACK WHALE NO. 1.
WE'RE GETTING V5 TO CONTACT KAKIN ON OUR BEHALF.
THERE ARE PEOPLE IN SAHERTA'S AND BEGEROSSÉ'S MILITARIES WITH STRONG CHANNELS TO KAKIN, AND I BELIEVE WE'LL BE ABLE TO REACH AN AGREEMENT.
BOTOBAI: TERRORIST HUNTER
PUBLIC PROSECUTOR, MILITARY ANALYST
DEFENSE TEAM
WE'LL SECRETLY COLLABORATE WITH THE INTELLIGENCE TEAM TO CREATE A POST-LANDING DEFENSE STRATEGY AND A PLAN TO PREVENT BEYOND'S ESCAPE. WE'LL COORDINATE HARDWARE WITH NEN ABILITIES.
I'M MAKING A LANGUAGE ANALYSIS SOFTWARE BY INTEGRATING DATA ON ANCIENT TONGUES, IN CASE WE CONTACT CIVILIZATIONS ON THE DARK CONTINENT.
ONCE WE GET THE PASSENGER LIST, I'LL PRIORITIZE CONFIRMING AND RECONSTRUCTING THE DATA.
PYON: PALEOGRAPH HUNTER
LINGUIST, INTERPRETER
INTELLIGENCE TEAM
CLUCK: BOTANICAL HUNTER
MUSICIAN, DANCER
FLORA/FAUNA TEAM
I'LL GATHER INTELLIGENCE AND PLANTS AFTER LANDING.

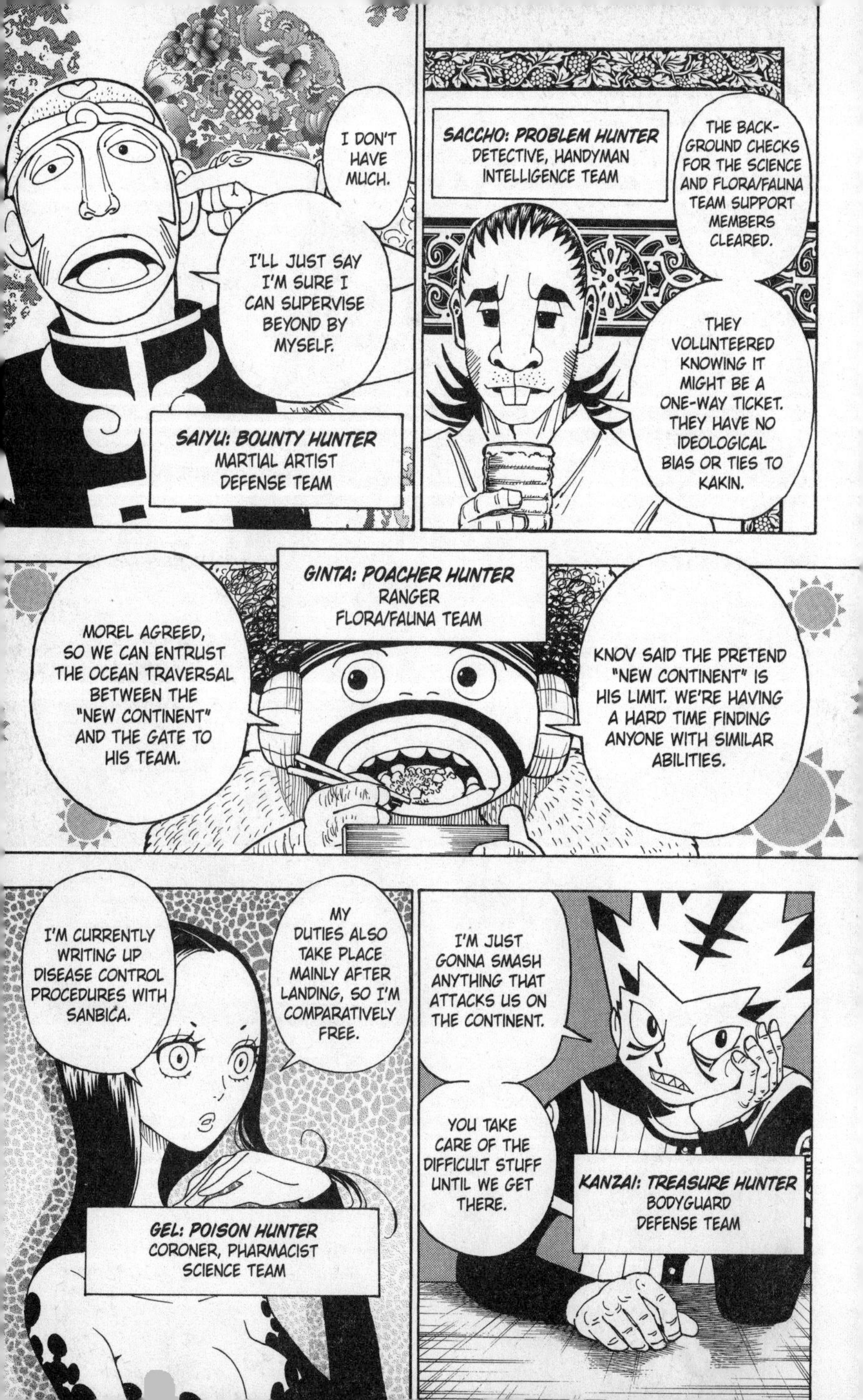
THE BACK-GROUND CHECKS FOR THE SCIENCE AND FLORA/FAUNA TEAM SUPPORT MEMBERS CLEARED.
SACCHO: PROBLEM HUNTER
DETECTIVE, HANDYMAN
INTELLIGENCE TEAM
THEY VOLUNTEERED KNOWING IT MIGHT BE A ONE-WAY TICKET. THEY HAVE NO IDEOLOGICAL BIAS OR TIES TO KAKIN.
I DON'T HAVE MUCH.
I'LL JUST SAY I'M SURE I CAN SUPERVISE BEYOND BY MYSELF.
SAIYU: BOUNTY HUNTER
MARTIAL ARTIST
DEFENSE TEAM
GINTA: POACHER HUNTER
RANGER
FLORA/FAUNA TEAM
KNOV SAID THE PRETEND "NEW CONTINENT" IS HIS LIMIT. WE'RE HAVING A HARD TIME FINDING ANYONE WITH SIMILAR ABILITIES.
MOREL AGREED, SO WE CAN ENTRUST THE OCEAN TRAVERSAL BETWEEN THE "NEW CONTINENT" AND THE GATE TO HIS TEAM.
I'M JUST GONNA SMASH ANYTHING THAT ATTACKS US ON THE CONTINENT.
YOU TAKE CARE OF THE DIFFICULT STUFF UNTIL WE GET THERE.
KANZAI: TREASURE HUNTER
BODYGUARD
DEFENSE TEAM
MY DUTIES ALSO TAKE PLACE MAINLY AFTER LANDING, SO I'M COMPARATIVELY FREE.
I'M CURRENTLY WRITING UP DISEASE CONTROL PROCEDURES WITH SANBICA.
GEL: POISON HUNTER
CORONER, PHARMACIST
SCIENCE TEAM

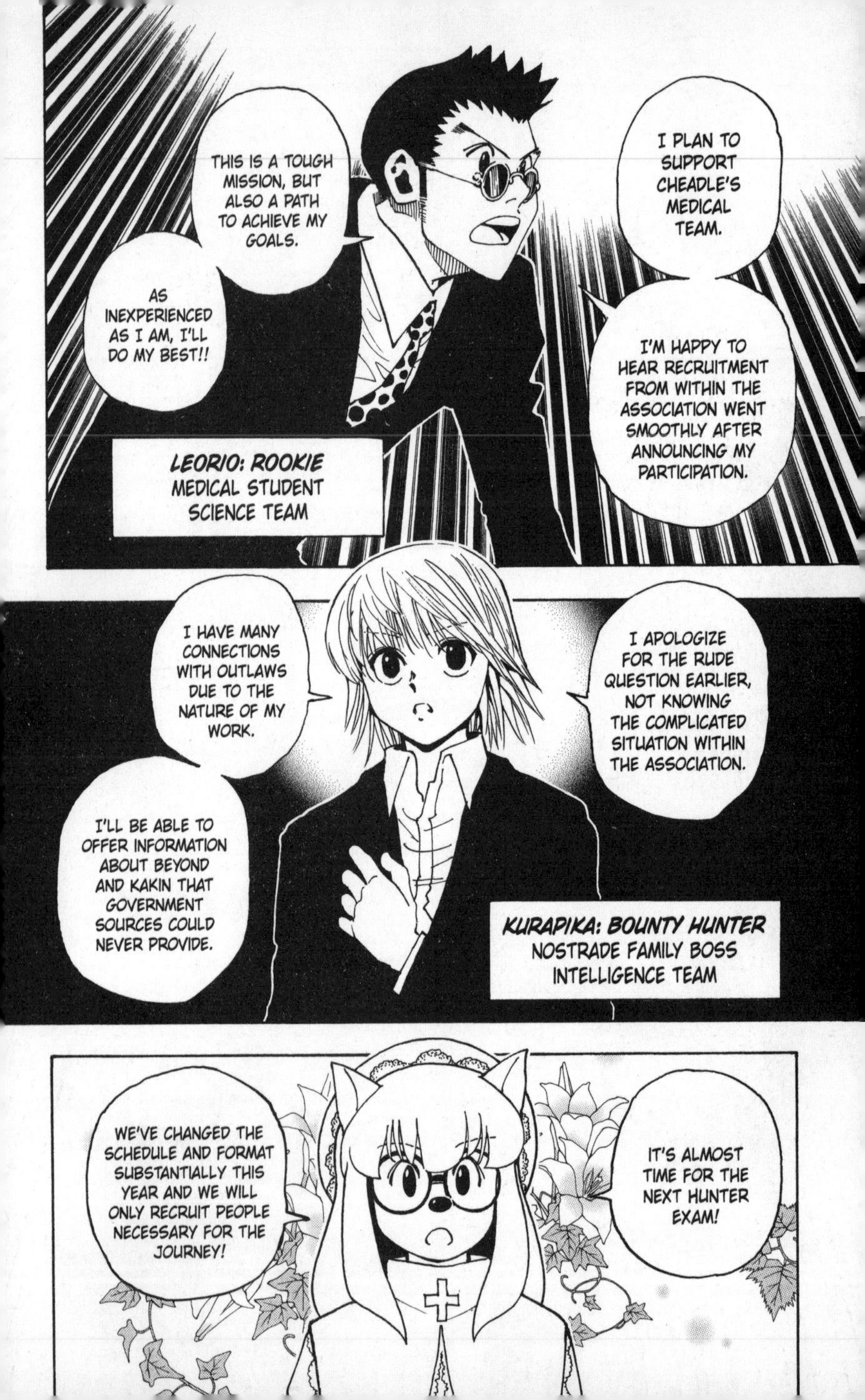
I PLAN TO SUPPORT CHEADLE'S MEDICAL TEAM.
THIS IS A TOUGH MISSION, BUT ALSO A PATH TO ACHIEVE MY GOALS.
AS INEXPERIENCED AS I AM, I'LL DO MY BEST!!
I'M HAPPY TO HEAR RECRUITMENT FROM WITHIN THE ASSOCIATION WENT SMOOTHLY AFTER ANNOUNCING MY PARTICIPATION.
LEORIO: ROOKIE MEDICAL STUDENT SCIENCE TEAM
I APOLOGIZE FOR THE RUDE QUESTION EARLIER, NOT KNOWING THE COMPLICATED SITUATION WITHIN THE ASSOCIATION.
I HAVE MANY CONNECTIONS WITH OUTLAWS DUE TO THE NATURE OF MY WORK.
I'LL BE ABLE TO OFFER INFORMATION ABOUT BEYOND AND KAKIN THAT GOVERNMENT SOURCES COULD NEVER PROVIDE.
KURAPIKA: BOUNTY HUNTER NOSTRADE FAMILY BOSS INTELLIGENCE TEAM
IT'S ALMOST TIME FOR THE NEXT HUNTER EXAM!
WE'VE CHANGED THE SCHEDULE AND FORMAT SUBSTANTIALLY THIS YEAR AND WE WILL ONLY RECRUIT PEOPLE NECESSARY FOR THE JOURNEY!

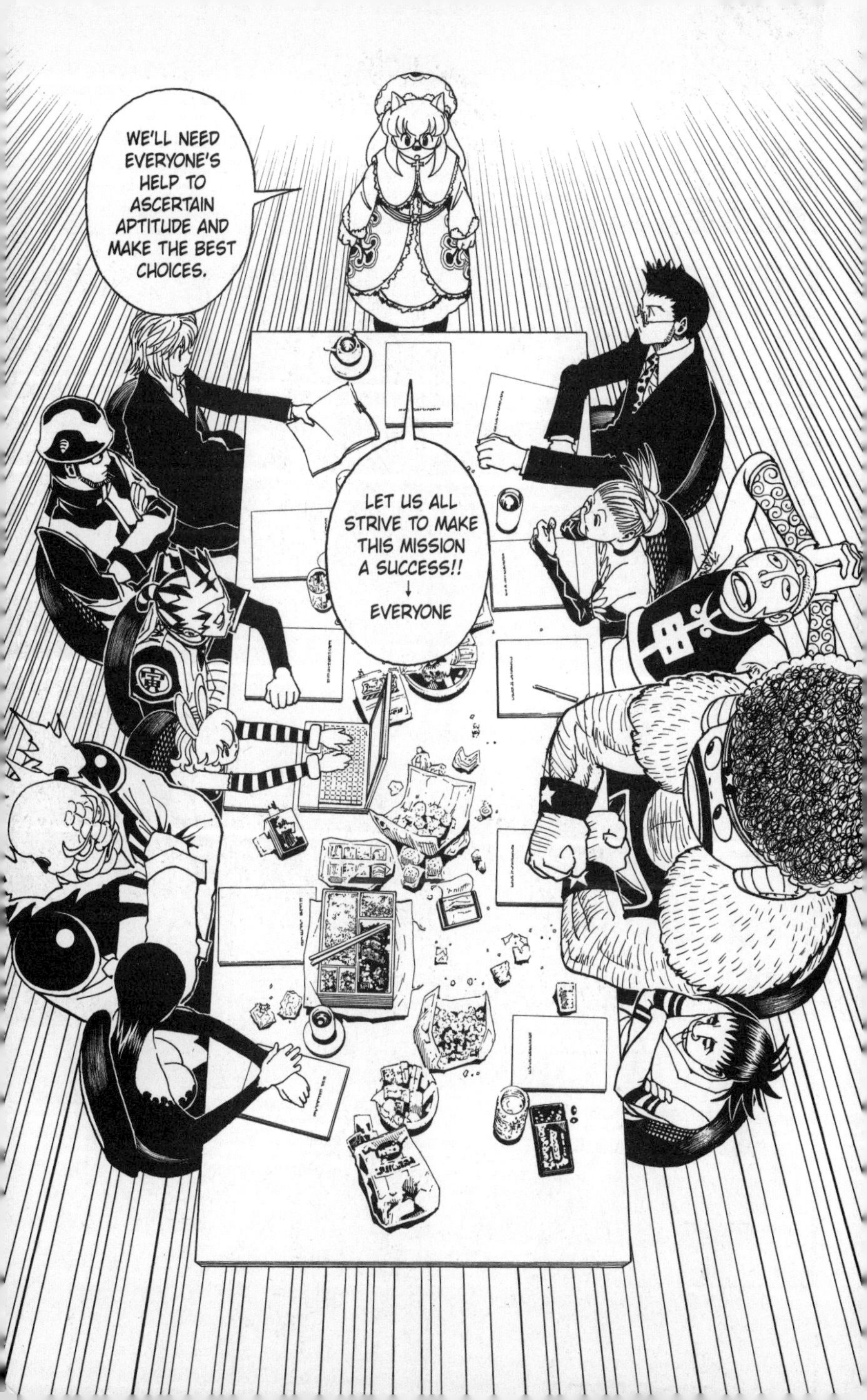
WE'LL NEED EVERYONE'S HELP TO ASCERTAIN APTITUDE AND MAKE THE BEST CHOICES.
LET US ALL STRIVE TO MAKE THIS MISSION A SUCCESS!! ↓ EVERYONE

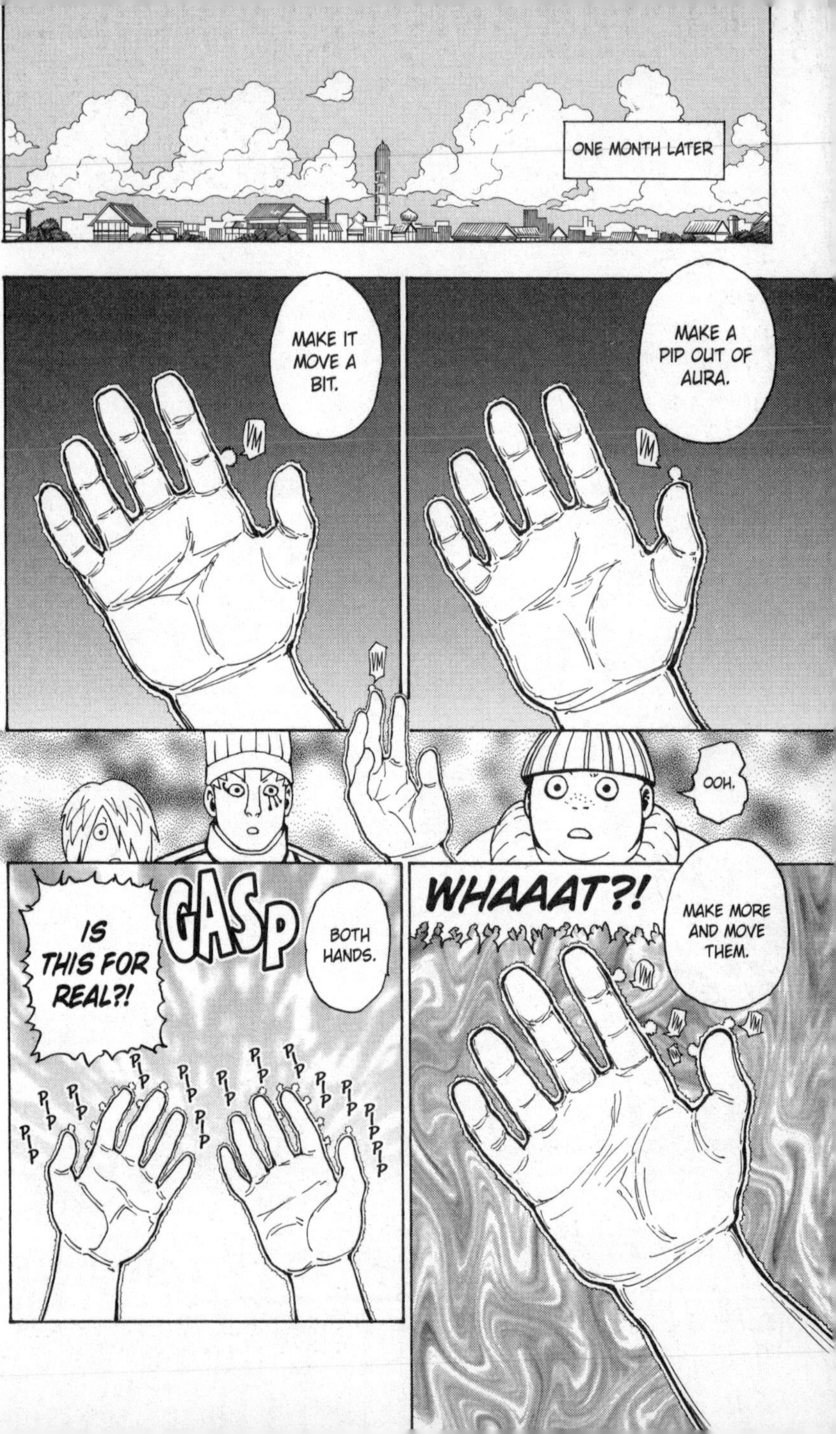
ONE MONTH LATER
MAKE A PIP OUT OF AURA.
VM
MAKE IT MOVE A BIT.
VM
OOH.
VM
MAKE MORE AND MOVE THEM.
WHAAAT?!
VM
VM
VM
VM
BOTH HANDS.
GASP
IS THIS FOR REAL?!
PIP PIP PIP PIP PIP PIP PIP PIP PIP PIP PIP PIP

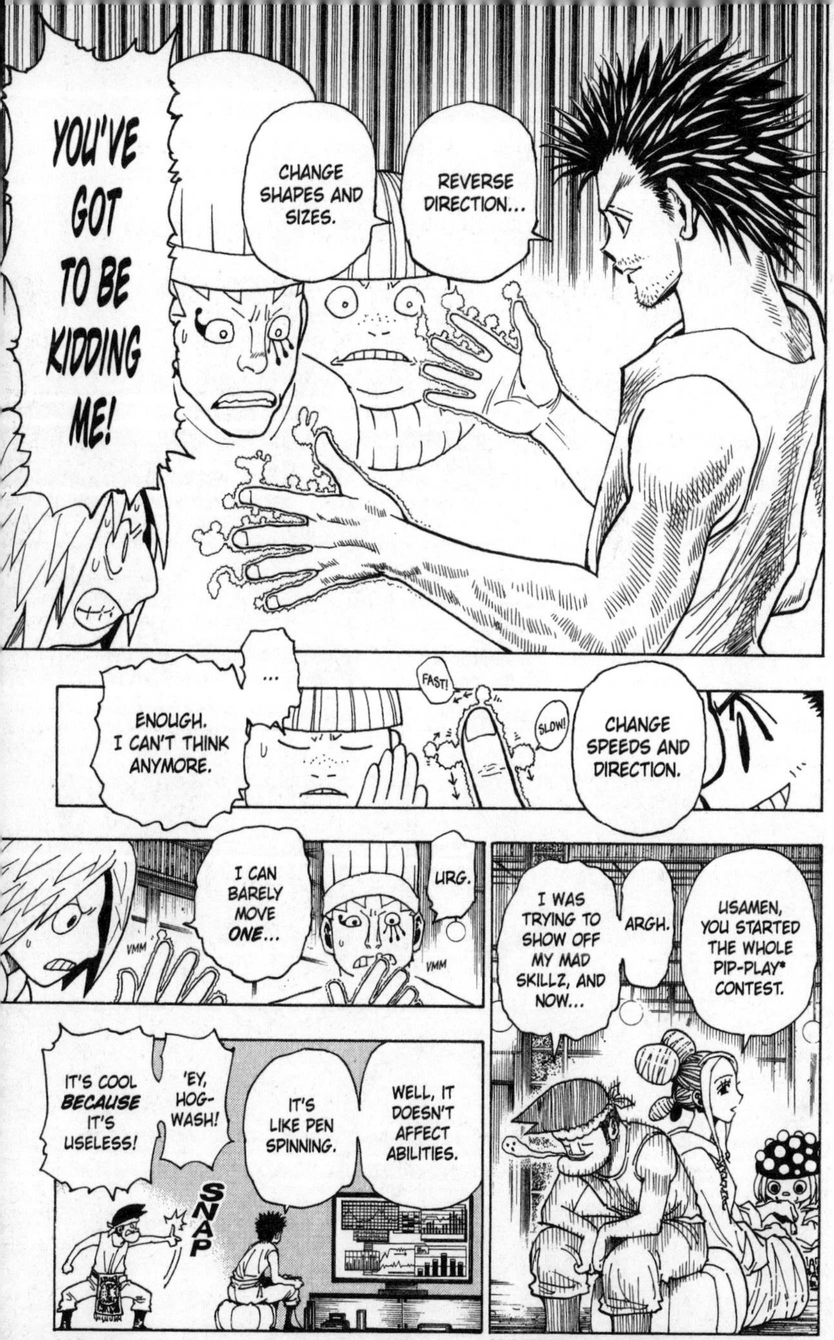

REVERSE DIRECTION...
CHANGE SHAPES AND SIZES.
YOU'VE GOT TO BE KIDDING ME!
CHANGE SPEEDS AND DIRECTION.
SLOW!
FAST!
...
ENOUGH. I CAN'T THINK ANYMORE.
USAMEN, YOU STARTED THE WHOLE PIP-PLAY* CONTEST.
ARGH.
I WAS TRYING TO SHOW OFF MY MAD SKILLZ, AND NOW...
URG.
I CAN BARELY MOVE ONE...
VMM
VMM
WELL, IT DOESN'T AFFECT ABILITIES.
IT'S LIKE PEN SPINNING.
'EY, HOG-WASH!
IT'S COOL BECAUSE IT'S USELESS!
SNAP

*DEXTERITY CHALLENGE USING AURA.

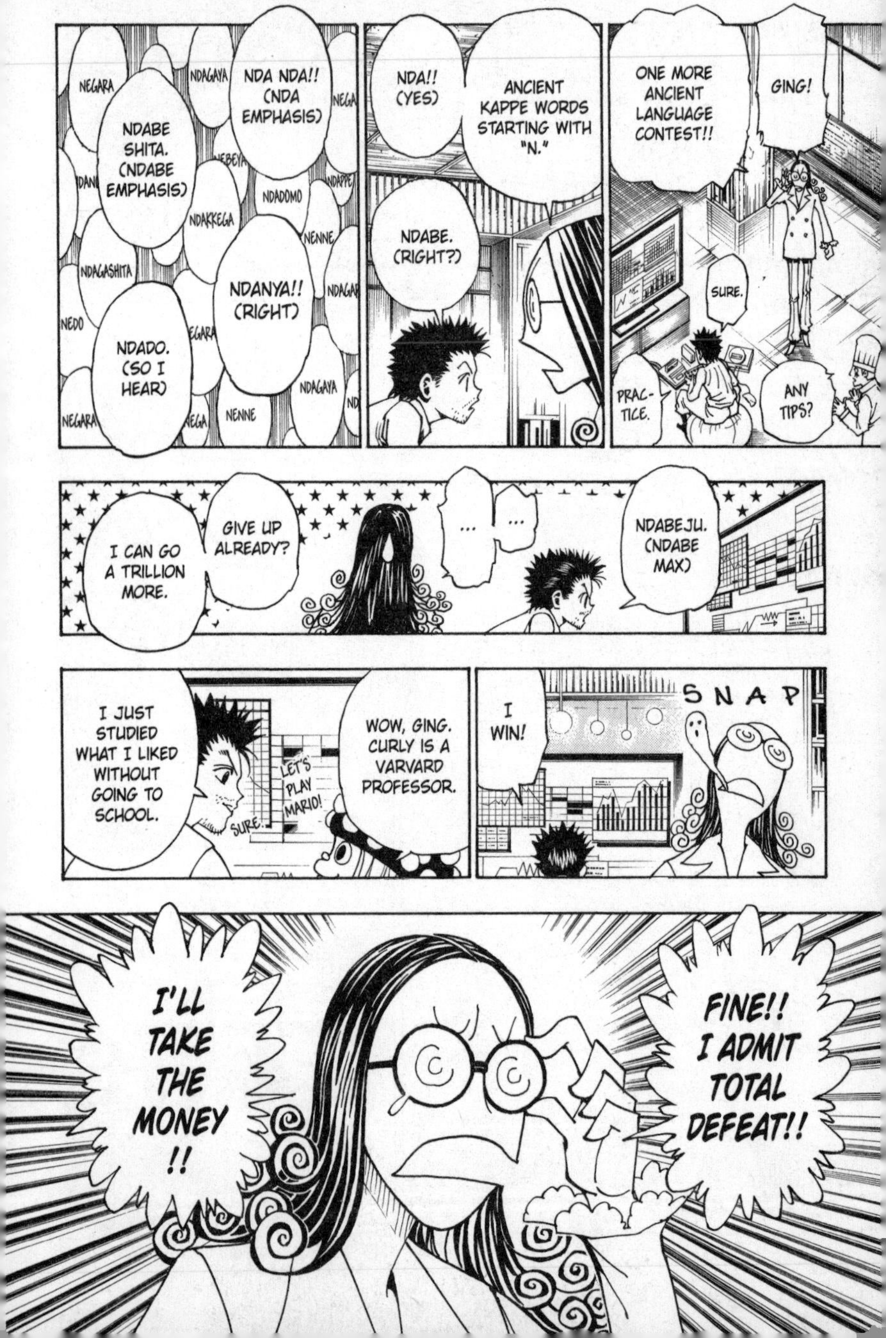
GING!
ONE MORE ANCIENT LANGUAGE CONTEST!!
SURE.
ANY TIPS?
PRAC-TICE.
ANCIENT KAPPE WORDS STARTING WITH "N."
NDA!! (YES)
NDABE. (RIGHT?)
NDA NDA!! (NDA EMPHASIS)
NDAGAYA
NEGARA
NDABE SHITA. (NDABE EMPHASIS)
NEBEYA
NDAPPE
NDADOMO
NDAKKEGA
NENNE
NDAGASHITA
NDANYA!! (RIGHT)
NEDO
NDADO. (SO I HEAR)
NDAGAYA
NENNE
NEGARA
NDABEJU. (NDABE MAX)
...
...
GIVE UP ALREADY?
I CAN GO A TRILLION MORE.
SNAP
I WIN!
WOW, GING. CURLY IS A VARVARD PROFESSOR.
LET'S PLAY MARIO!
SURE.
I JUST STUDIED WHAT I LIKED WITHOUT GOING TO SCHOOL.
FINE!! I ADMIT TOTAL DEFEAT!!
I'LL TAKE THE MONEY!!

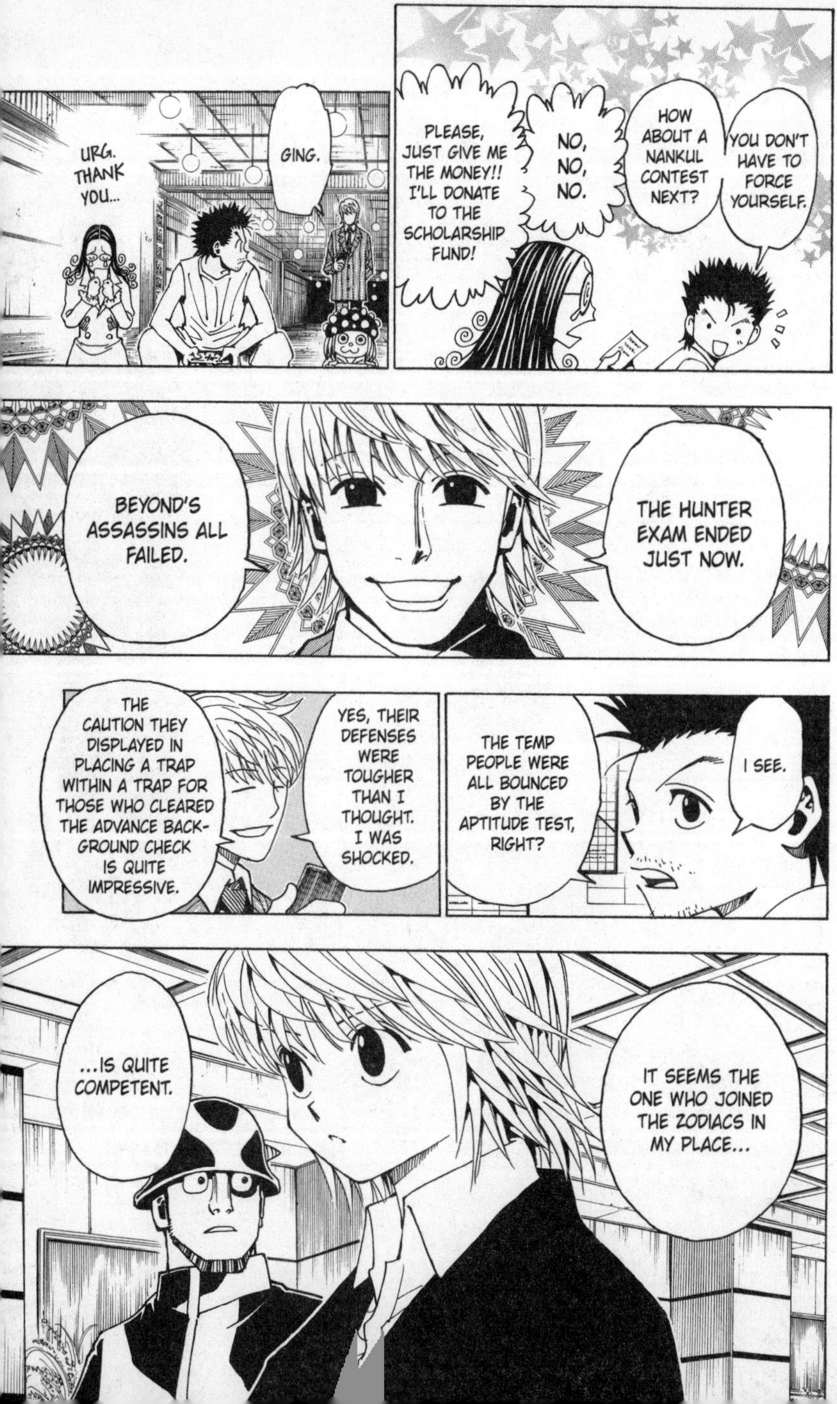
YOU DON'T HAVE TO FORCE YOURSELF.
HOW ABOUT A NANKUL CONTEST NEXT?
NO, NO, NO.
PLEASE, JUST GIVE ME THE MONEY!! I'LL DONATE TO THE SCHOLARSHIP FUND!
GING.
URG. THANK YOU...
THE HUNTER EXAM ENDED JUST NOW.
BEYOND'S ASSASSINS ALL FAILED.
I SEE.
THE TEMP PEOPLE WERE ALL BOUNCED BY THE APTITUDE TEST, RIGHT?
YES, THEIR DEFENSES WERE TOUGHER THAN I THOUGHT. I WAS SHOCKED.
THE CAUTION THEY DISPLAYED IN PLACING A TRAP WITHIN A TRAP FOR THOSE WHO CLEARED THE ADVANCE BACK-GROUND CHECK IS QUITE IMPRESSIVE.
IT SEEMS THE ONE WHO JOINED THE ZODIACS IN MY PLACE...
...IS QUITE COMPETENT.

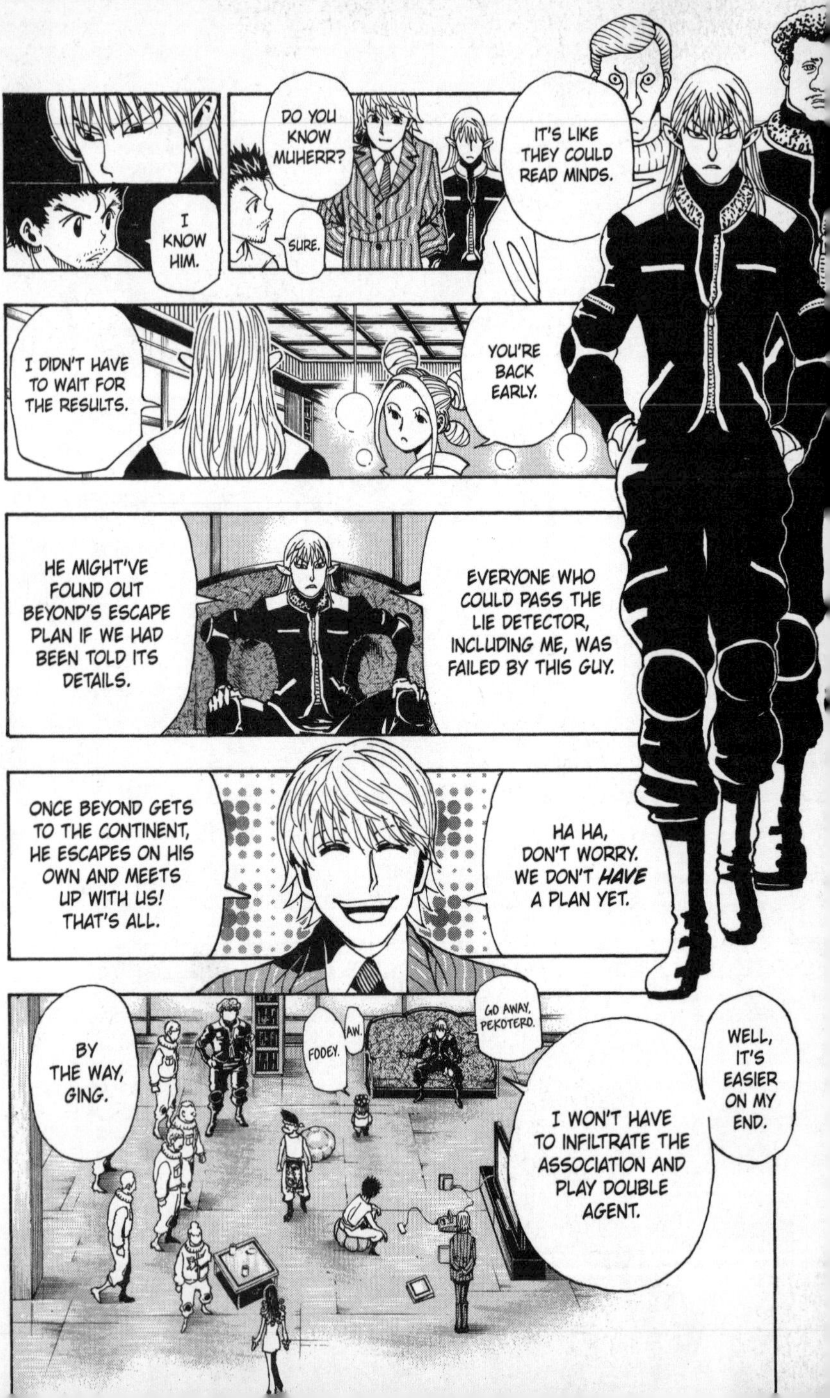
IT'S LIKE THEY COULD READ MINDS.
DO YOU KNOW MUHERR?
SURE.
I KNOW HIM.
YOU'RE BACK EARLY.
I DIDN'T HAVE TO WAIT FOR THE RESULTS.
EVERYONE WHO COULD PASS THE LIE DETECTOR, INCLUDING ME, WAS FAILED BY THIS GUY.
HE MIGHT'VE FOUND OUT BEYOND'S ESCAPE PLAN IF WE HAD BEEN TOLD ITS DETAILS.
HA HA, DON'T WORRY. WE DON'T *HAVE* A PLAN YET.
ONCE BEYOND GETS TO THE CONTINENT, HE ESCAPES ON HIS OWN AND MEETS UP WITH US! THAT'S ALL.
WELL, IT'S EASIER ON MY END.
I WON'T HAVE TO INFILTRATE THE ASSOCIATION AND PLAY DOUBLE AGENT.
GO AWAY, PEKOTERO.
AW.
FOOEY.
BY THE WAY, GING.

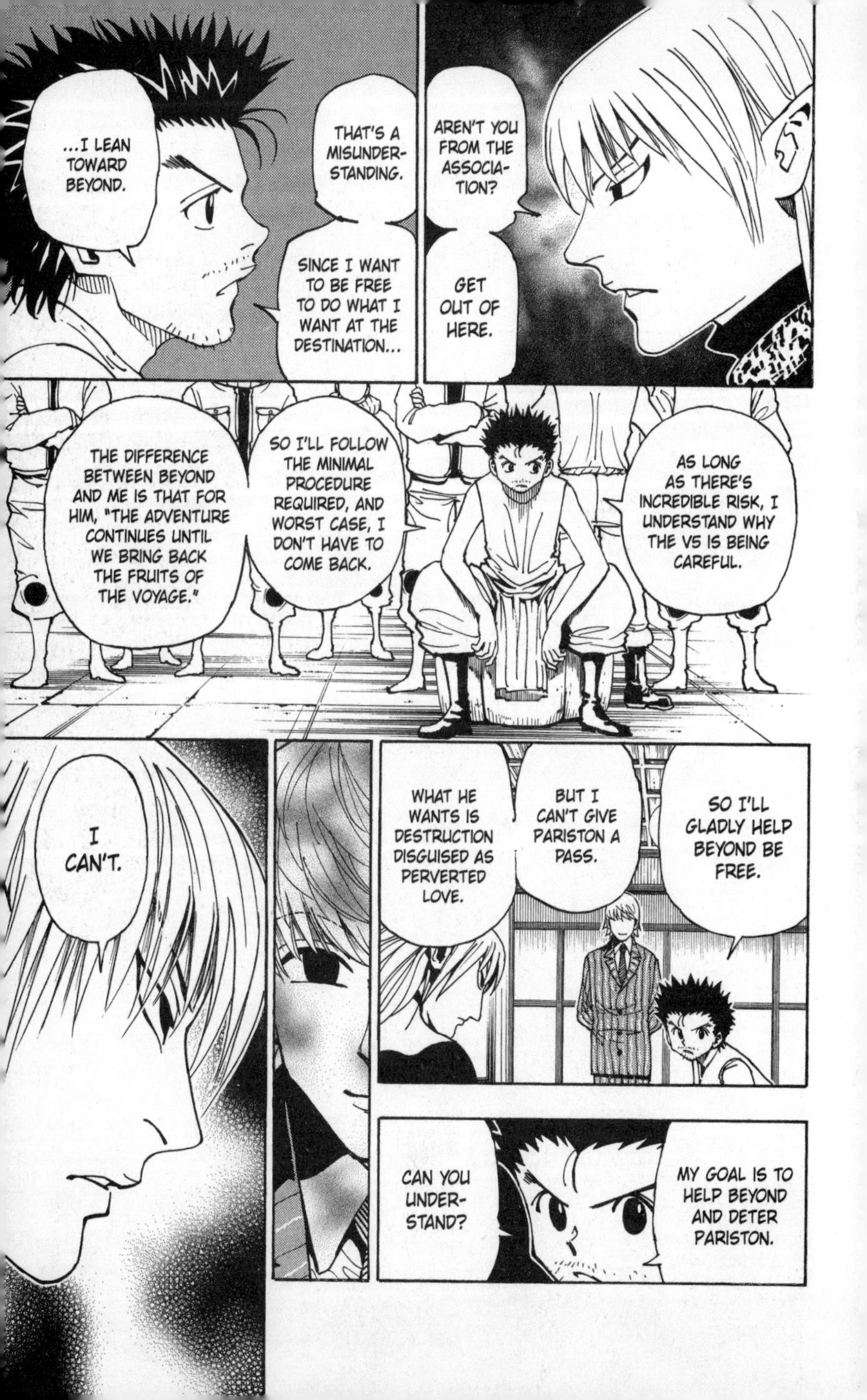
AREN'T YOU FROM THE ASSOCIATION?
GET OUT OF HERE.
THAT'S A MISUNDER-STANDING.
SINCE I WANT TO BE FREE TO DO WHAT I WANT AT THE DESTINATION...
...I LEAN TOWARD BEYOND.
AS LONG AS THERE'S INCREDIBLE RISK, I UNDERSTAND WHY THE V5 IS BEING CAREFUL.
SO I'LL FOLLOW THE MINIMAL PROCEDURE REQUIRED, AND WORST CASE, I DON'T HAVE TO COME BACK.
THE DIFFERENCE BETWEEN BEYOND AND ME IS THAT FOR HIM, "THE ADVENTURE CONTINUES UNTIL WE BRING BACK THE FRUITS OF THE VOYAGE."
SO I'LL GLADLY HELP BEYOND BE FREE.
BUT I CAN'T GIVE PARISTON A PASS.
WHAT HE WANTS IS DESTRUCTION DISGUISED AS PERVERTED LOVE.
MY GOAL IS TO HELP BEYOND AND DETER PARISTON.
CAN YOU UNDER-STAND?
I CAN'T.

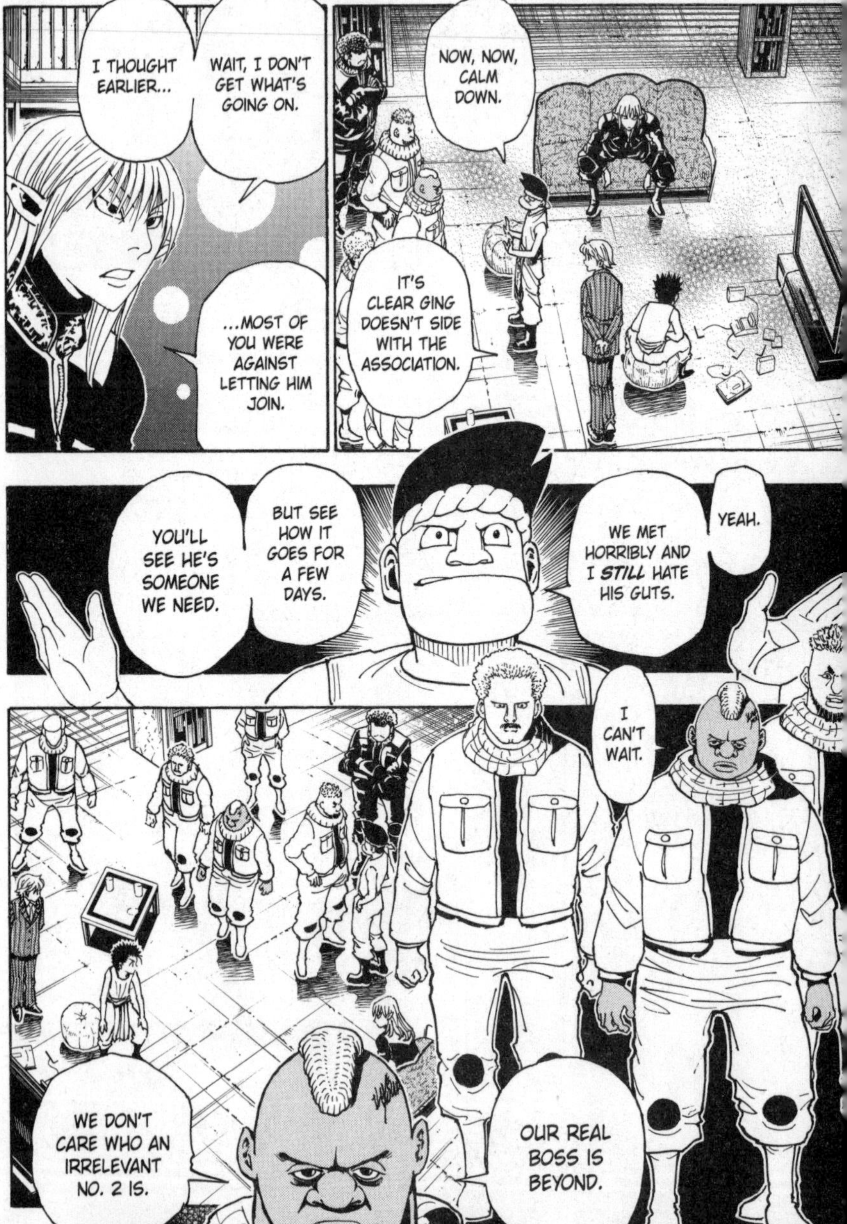
NOW, NOW, CALM DOWN.
IT'S CLEAR GING DOESN'T SIDE WITH THE ASSOCIATION.
WAIT, I DON'T GET WHAT'S GOING ON.
I THOUGHT EARLIER...
...MOST OF YOU WERE AGAINST LETTING HIM JOIN.
YEAH.
WE MET HORRIBLY AND I *STILL* HATE HIS GUTS.
BUT SEE HOW IT GOES FOR A FEW DAYS.
YOU'LL SEE HE'S SOMEONE WE NEED.
I CAN'T WAIT.
OUR REAL BOSS IS BEYOND.
WE DON'T CARE WHO AN IRRELEVANT NO. 2 IS.

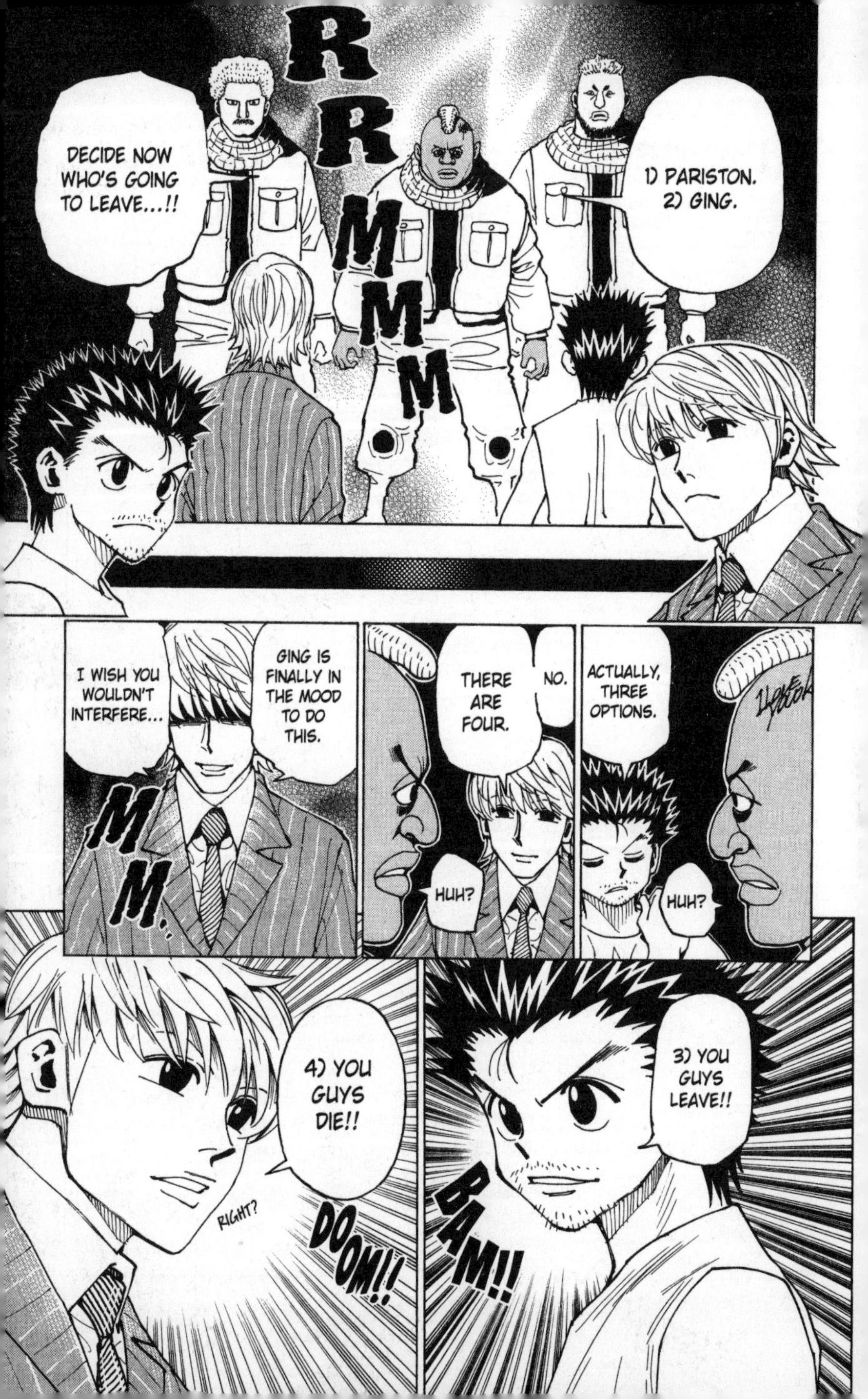
RRRMMMM
1) PARISTON. 2) GING.
DECIDE NOW WHO'S GOING TO LEAVE...!!
ACTUALLY, THREE OPTIONS.
HUH?
NO.
THERE ARE FOUR.
HUH?
GING IS FINALLY IN THE MOOD TO DO THIS.
I WISH YOU WOULDN'T INTERFERE...
MM.
3) YOU GUYS LEAVE!!
BAM!!
4) YOU GUYS DIE!!
RIGHT?
DOOM!!

DANGEROUS CREATURES RANKING

HIGH ————————————→ LOW

	A	B	C	D	E
Aggression Towards Human	1) Attacks without provocation 2) Ecology or behavior endangers many lives	Species ranks A under certain conditions (climate, food source, exposure to chemicals)	1) Individual differences 2) Individuals can rank A under certain conditions (smell of blood, under threat, breeding season, defending young)	Passive: sudden encounters may provoke a defensive or evasive attack (emission of gas, liquid, needles, body slam)	None
Number	One nest, host or herd numbers in 10,000 or more	100s-1,000s	<100	<10	Individuals
Fecundity	Explosive growth once breeding begins	1) Breeds several times a year, with >10 young. 2) Conditions can put the species closer to A	Comparable to that of humans	Long intervals between matings, with few young	Does not reproduce, or at low enough frequency to be negligible
Threat of Bodily Harm	1) High probability of death 2) Injuries affect daily life, complete recovery difficult, lifelong aftereffects	1) How to avoid them is known, but failure leads to serious injuries or death 2) Complete recovery difficult, lifelong aftereffects	1) Long-term rest and treatment is necessary. Death is also possible. 2) Indirectly affects many lives (damage to crops, livestock)	1) Does not affect daily life, but mild aftereffects or scars remain 2) Recovery is possible with a few weeks of treatment	1) Recovery in days with drugs or treatment. 2) Limited indirect adverse effects (limited contamination, temporary evacuation)
Total	Immediate eradication is necessary but method is uncertain; global cooperation is essential	Immediate eradication is necessary at high cost and high risk; international response is necessary	Immediate measures are necessary, but local response suffices	Response to individual cases necessary but not urgent or dangerous	A warning to civilians is necessary, but situation is not serious

Chapter 347: Inauguration

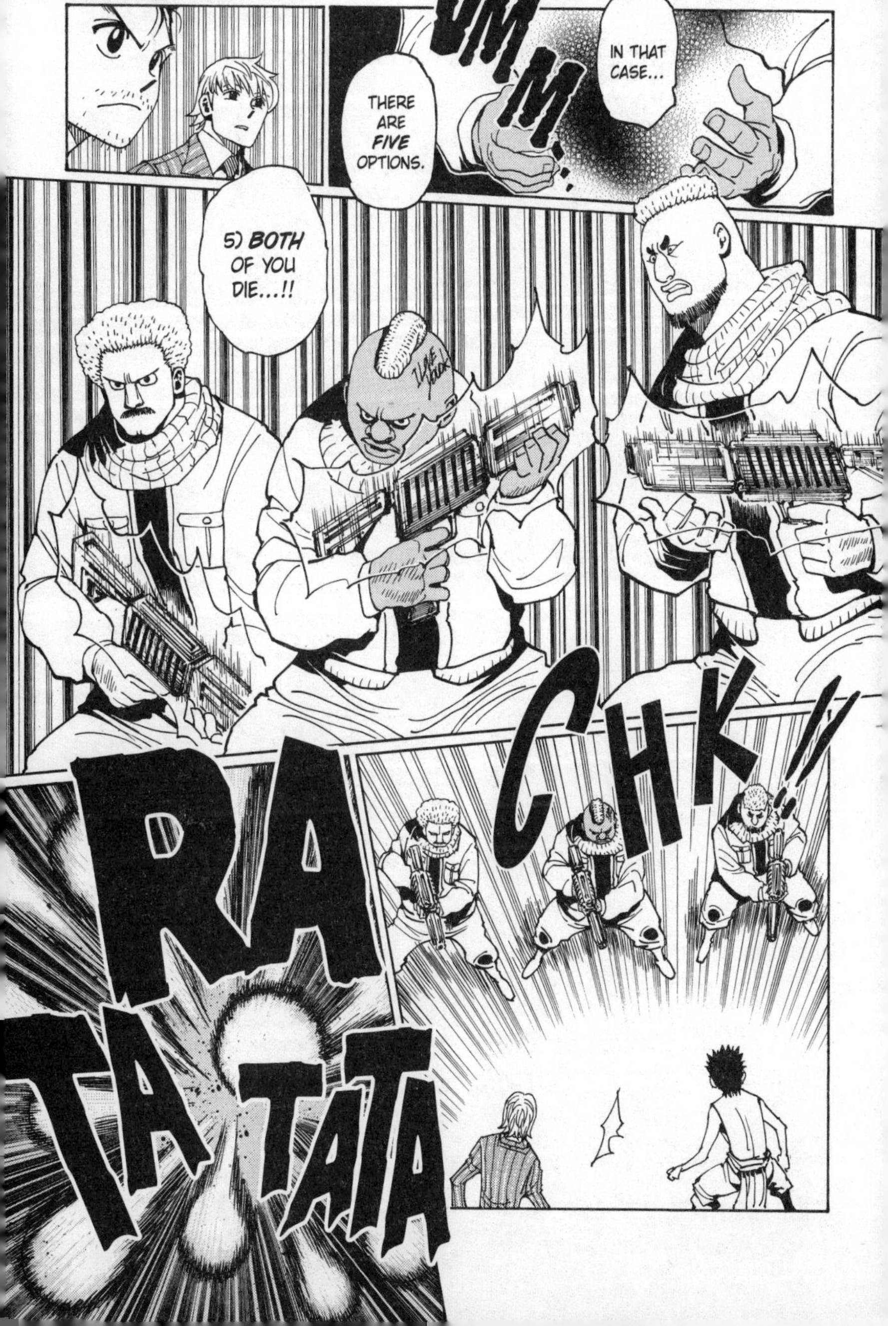
UMMM..
IN THAT CASE...
THERE ARE *FIVE* OPTIONS.
5) *BOTH* OF YOU DIE...!!
CHK!!
RATATATA

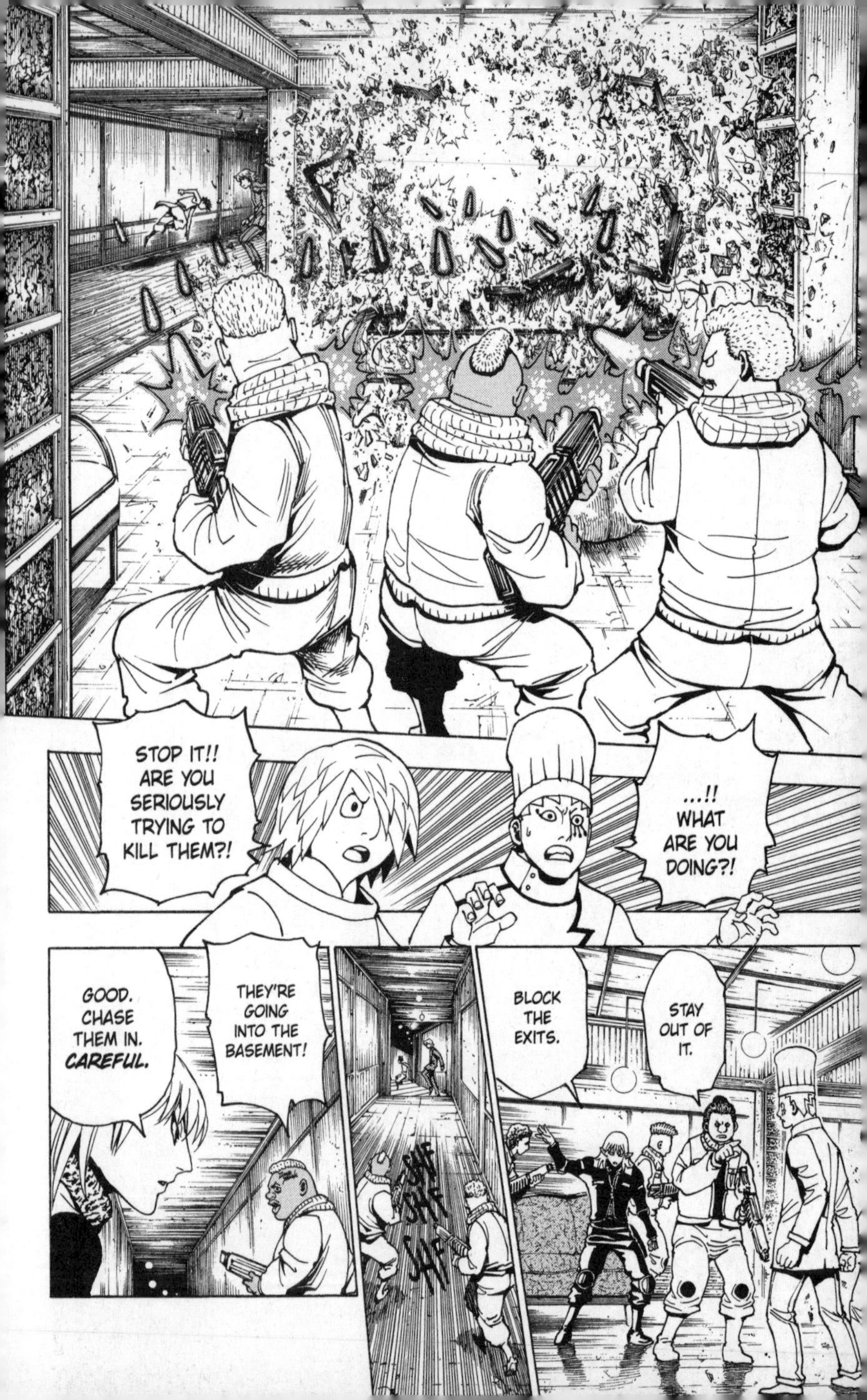
...!! WHAT ARE YOU DOING?!
STOP IT!! ARE YOU SERIOUSLY TRYING TO KILL THEM?!
STAY OUT OF IT.
BLOCK THE EXITS.
SHF SHF SHF
THEY'RE GOING INTO THE BASEMENT!
GOOD. CHASE THEM IN. *CAREFUL.*

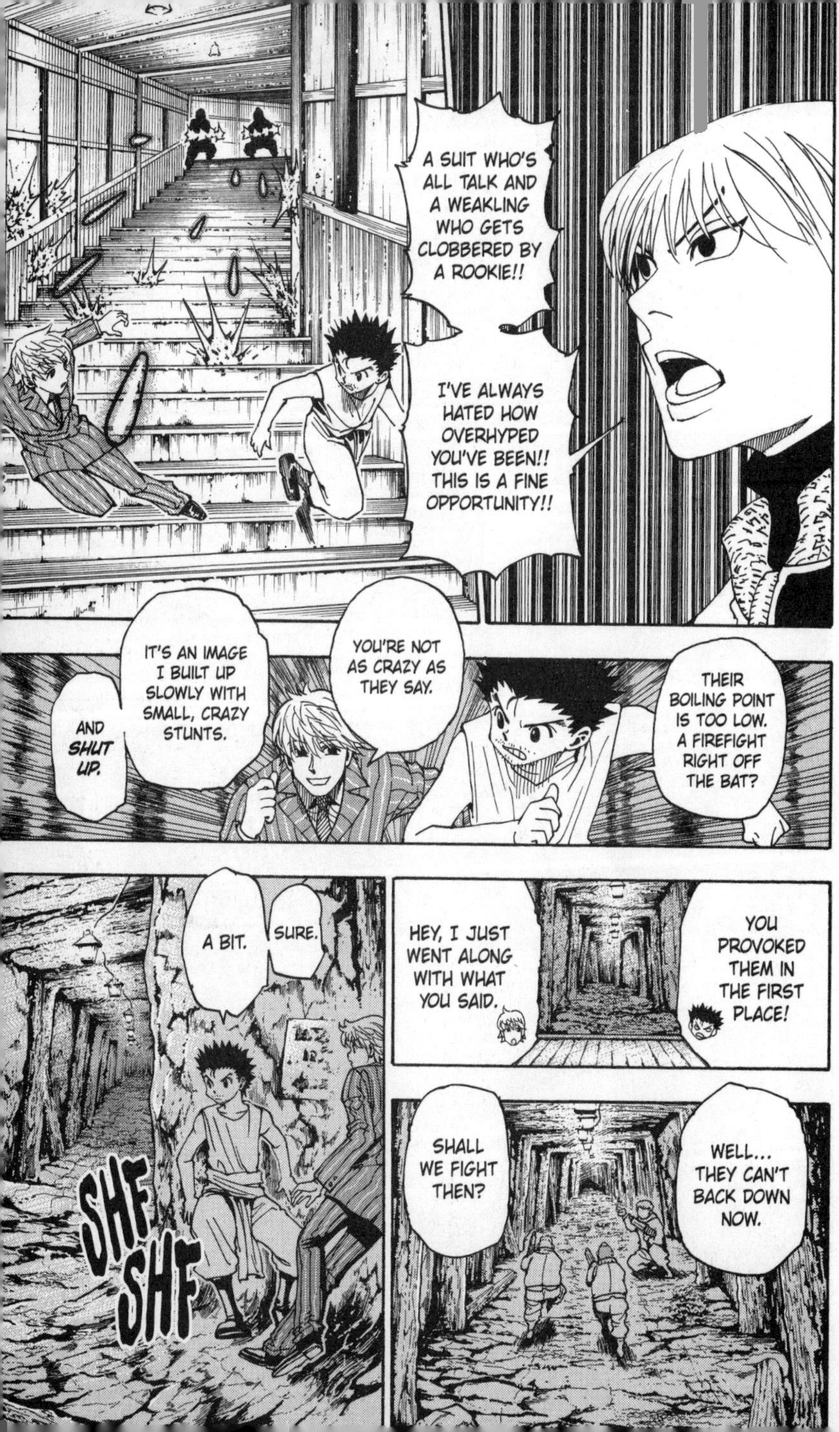
A SUIT WHO'S ALL TALK AND A WEAKLING WHO GETS CLOBBERED BY A ROOKIE!!
I'VE ALWAYS HATED HOW OVERHYPED YOU'VE BEEN!! THIS IS A FINE OPPORTUNITY!!
THEIR BOILING POINT IS TOO LOW. A FIREFIGHT RIGHT OFF THE BAT?
YOU'RE NOT AS CRAZY AS THEY SAY.
IT'S AN IMAGE I BUILT UP SLOWLY WITH SMALL, CRAZY STUNTS.
AND SHUT UP.
YOU PROVOKED THEM IN THE FIRST PLACE!
HEY, I JUST WENT ALONG WITH WHAT YOU SAID.
WELL... THEY CAN'T BACK DOWN NOW.
SHALL WE FIGHT THEN?
SURE.
A BIT.
SHF SHF

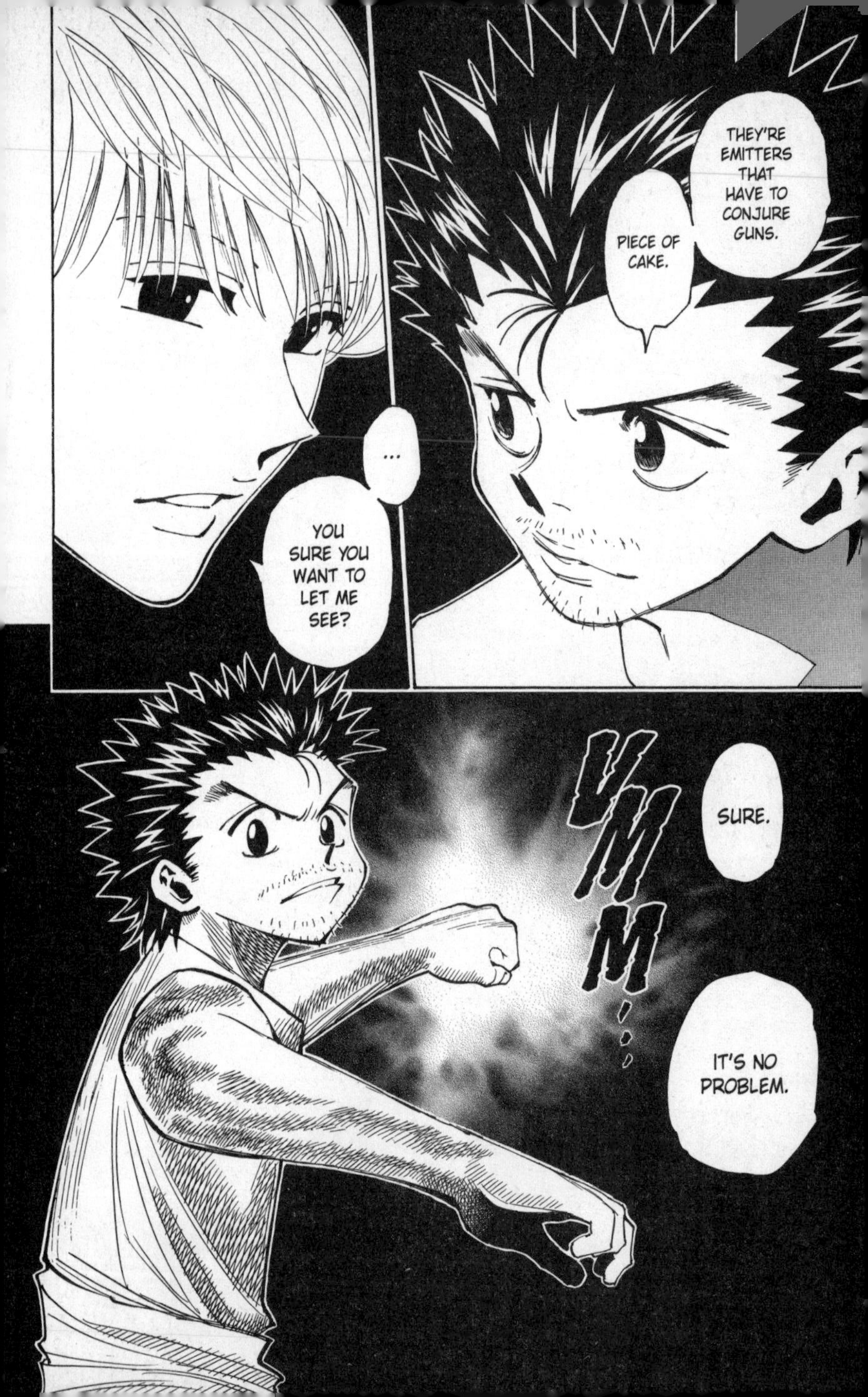
THEY'RE EMITTERS THAT HAVE TO CONJURE GUNS.
PIECE OF CAKE.
...
YOU SURE YOU WANT TO LET ME SEE?
SURE.
VMM...
IT'S NO PROBLEM.

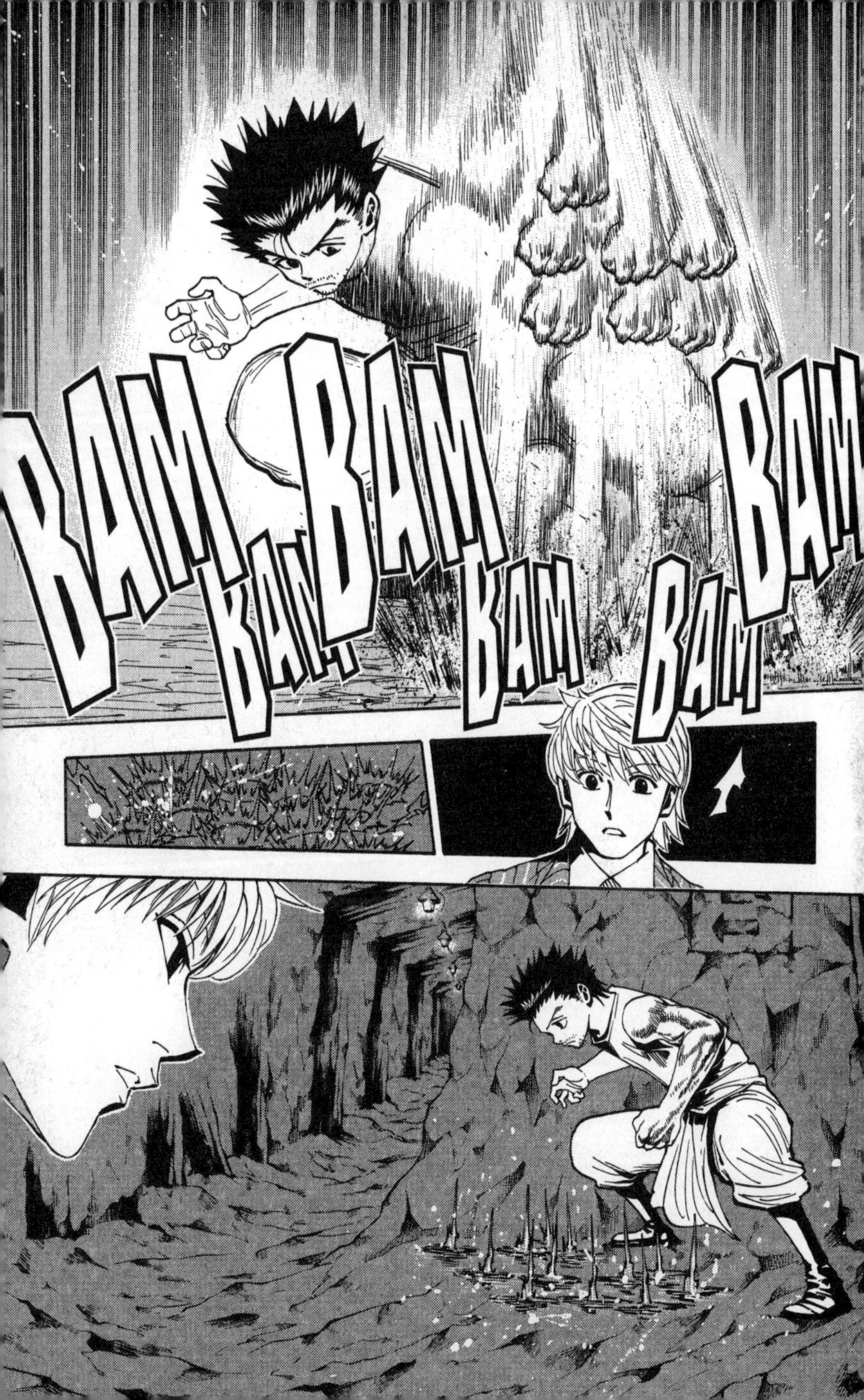
BAM
BAM
BAM
BAM
BAM
BAM

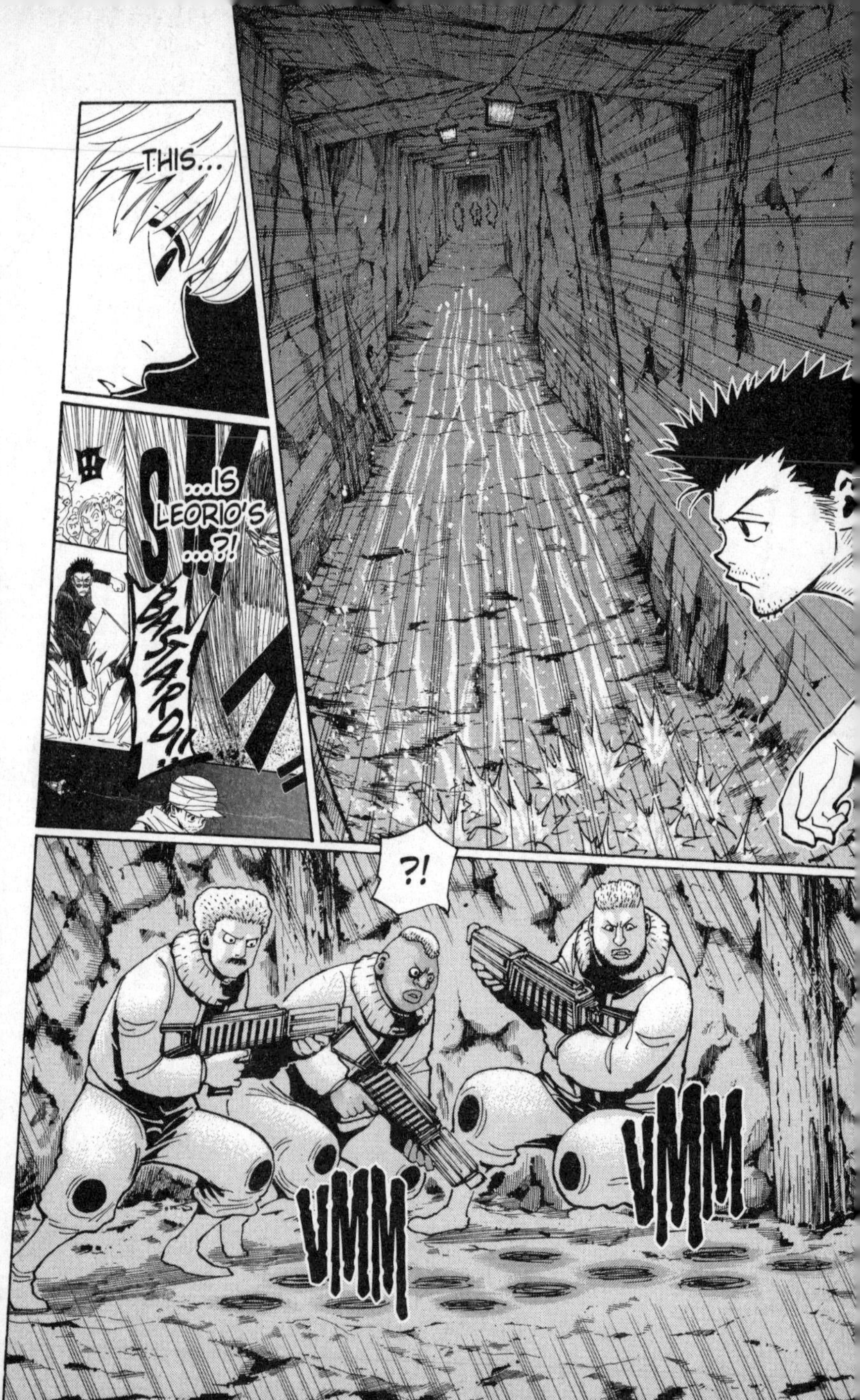
THIS...
...IS LEORIO'S ...?!
!!
BASTARD!!
?!
VMM
VMM

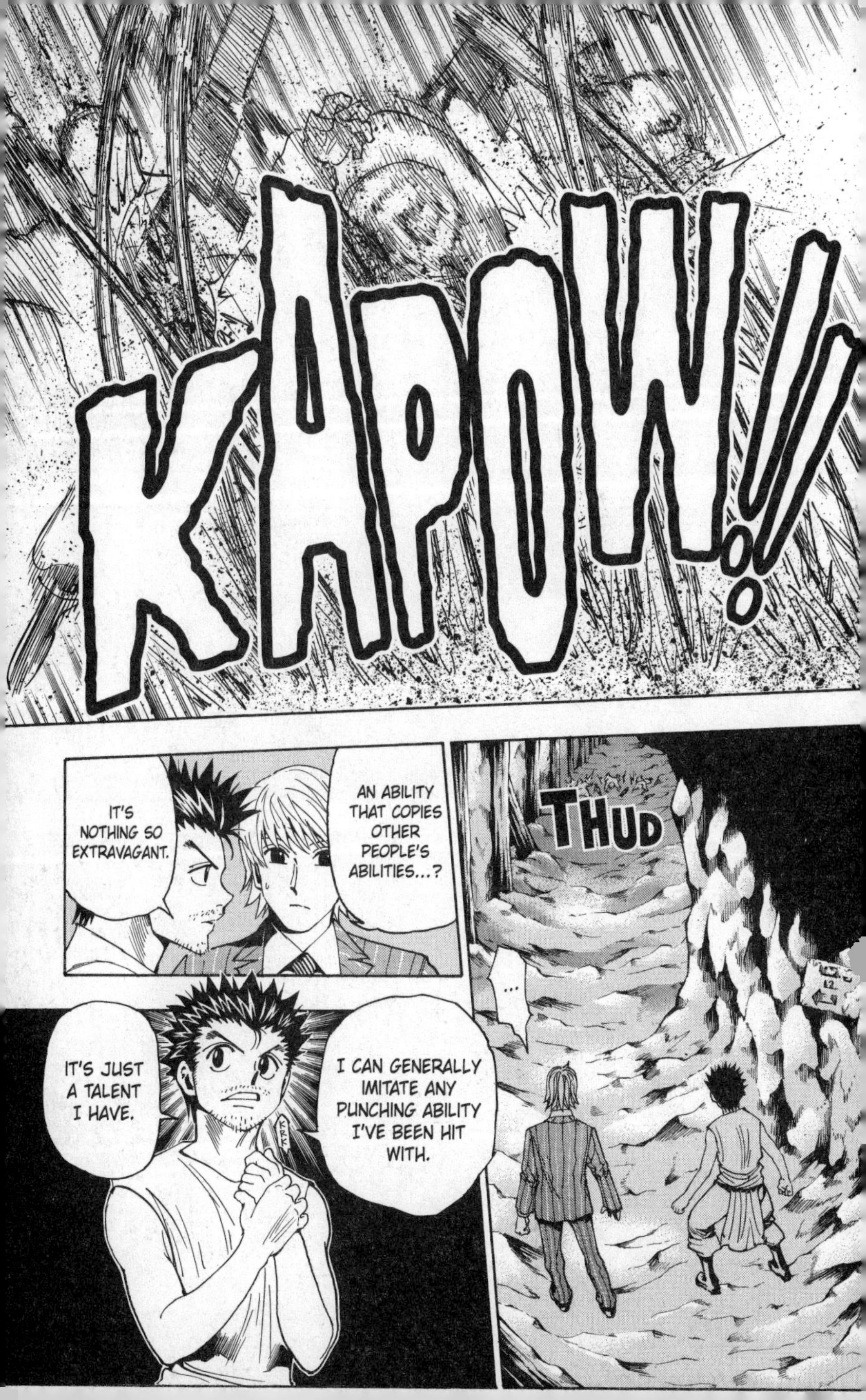
KAPOW!!
THUD
...
AN ABILITY THAT COPIES OTHER PEOPLE'S ABILITIES...?
IT'S NOTHING SO EXTRAVAGANT.
I CAN GENERALLY IMITATE ANY PUNCHING ABILITY I'VE BEEN HIT WITH.
IT'S JUST A TALENT I HAVE.

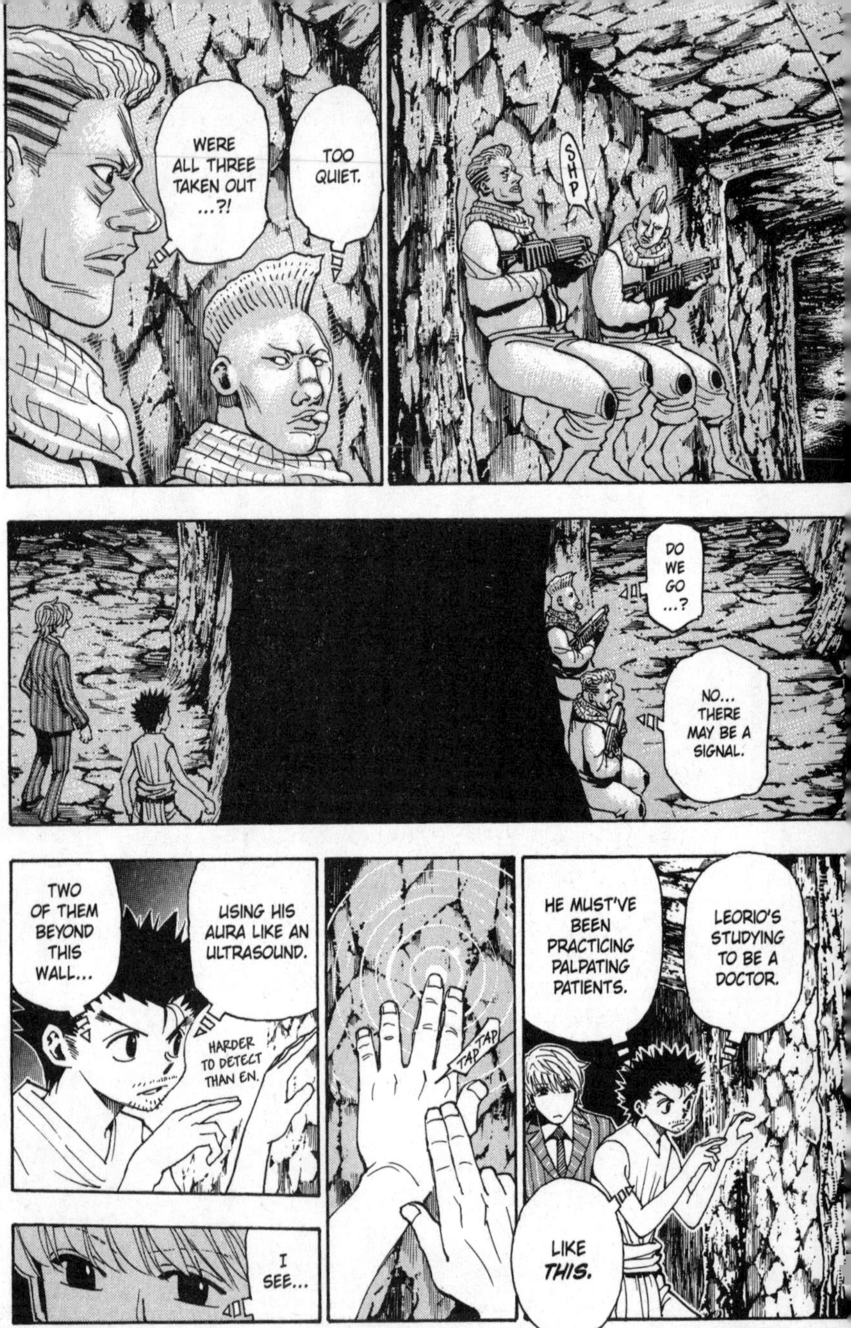
SHP
TOO QUIET.
WERE ALL THREE TAKEN OUT ...?!
DO WE GO ...?
NO... THERE MAY BE A SIGNAL.
LEORIO'S STUDYING TO BE A DOCTOR.
HE MUST'VE BEEN PRACTICING PALPATING PATIENTS.
LIKE THIS.
TAP TAP
USING HIS AURA LIKE AN ULTRASOUND.
TWO OF THEM BEYOND THIS WALL...
HARDER TO DETECT THAN EN.
I SEE...

READ THIS WAY

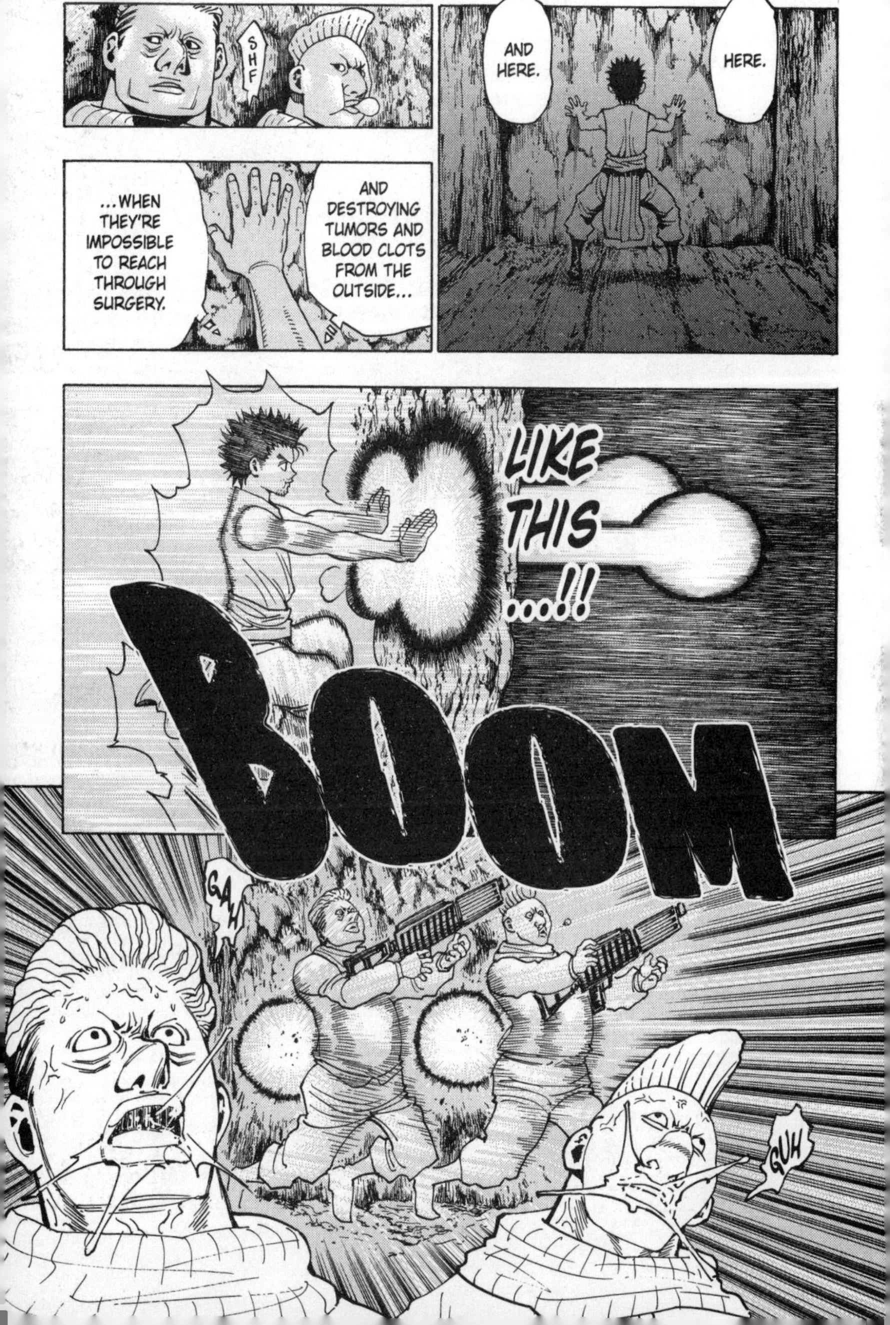
HERE.
AND HERE.
SHF
AND DESTROYING TUMORS AND BLOOD CLOTS FROM THE OUTSIDE...
...WHEN THEY'RE IMPOSSIBLE TO REACH THROUGH SURGERY.
LIKE THIS...!!
BOOM
GUH
GAH

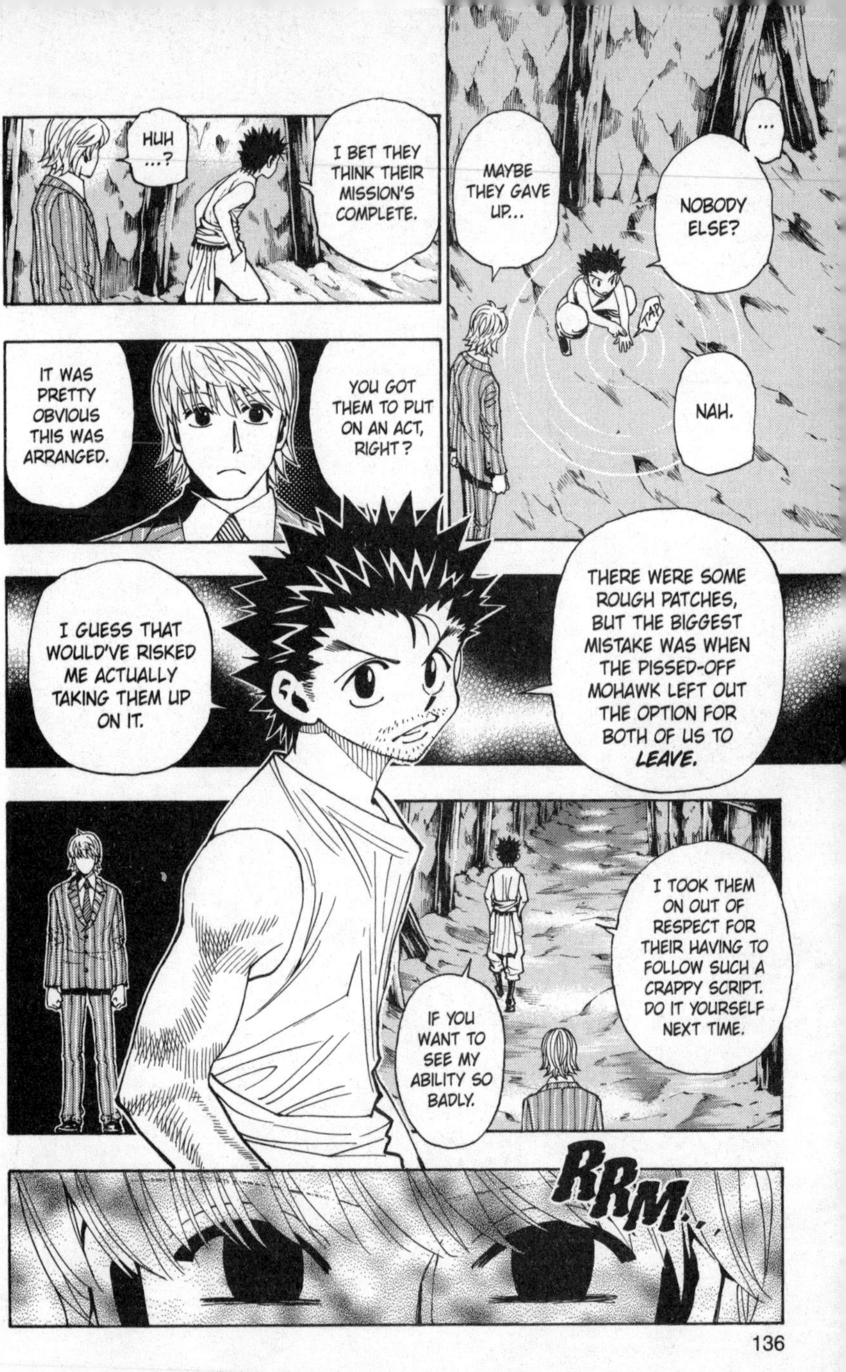
...
NOBODY ELSE?
TAP
NAH.
MAYBE THEY GAVE UP...
I BET THEY THINK THEIR MISSION'S COMPLETE.
HUH ...?
YOU GOT THEM TO PUT ON AN ACT, RIGHT?
IT WAS PRETTY OBVIOUS THIS WAS ARRANGED.
THERE WERE SOME ROUGH PATCHES, BUT THE BIGGEST MISTAKE WAS WHEN THE PISSED-OFF MOHAWK LEFT OUT THE OPTION FOR BOTH OF US TO *LEAVE.*
I GUESS THAT WOULD'VE RISKED ME ACTUALLY TAKING THEM UP ON IT.
I TOOK THEM ON OUT OF RESPECT FOR THEIR HAVING TO FOLLOW SUCH A CRAPPY SCRIPT. DO IT YOURSELF NEXT TIME.
IF YOU WANT TO SEE MY ABILITY SO BADLY.
RRM.

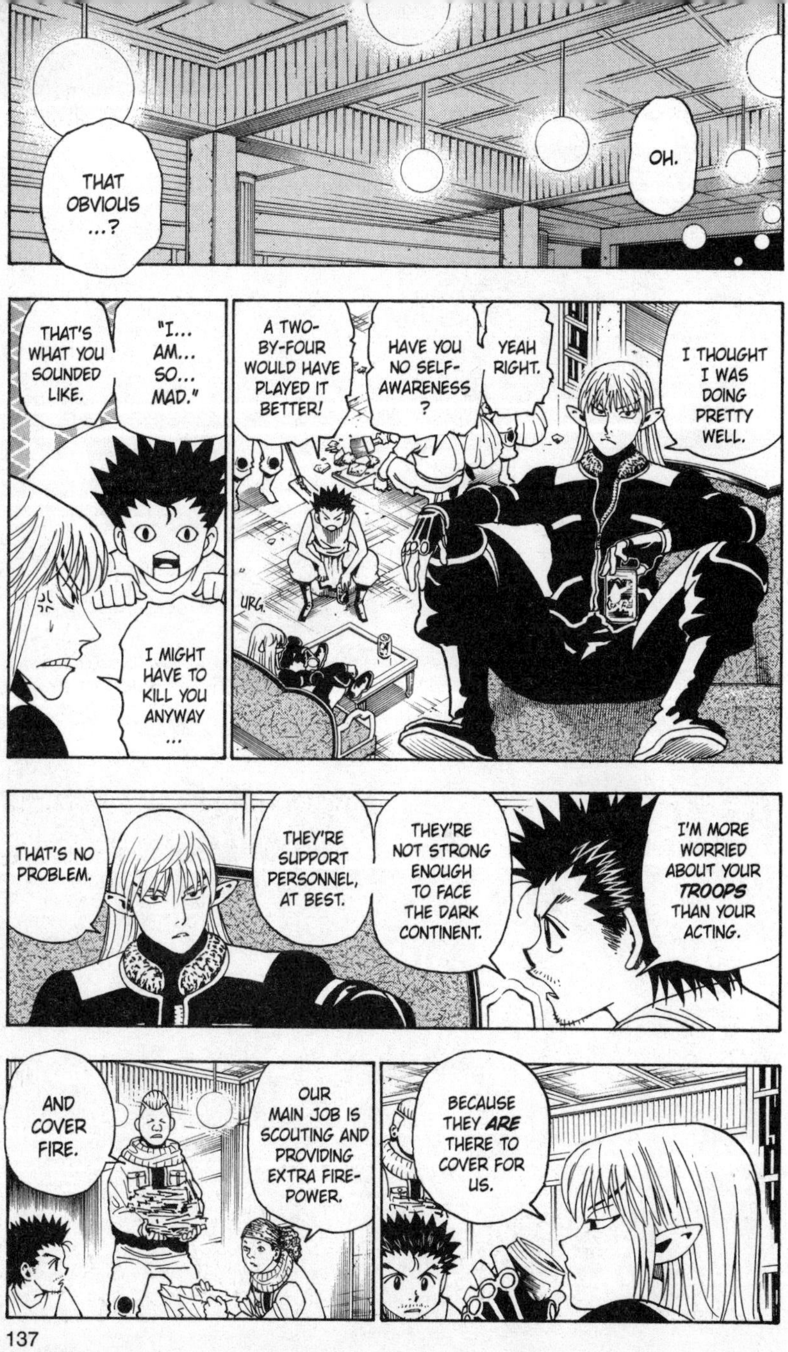
OH.
THAT OBVIOUS ...?
I THOUGHT I WAS DOING PRETTY WELL.
YEAH RIGHT.
HAVE YOU NO SELF-AWARENESS?
A TWO-BY-FOUR WOULD HAVE PLAYED IT BETTER!
URG.
"I... AM... SO... MAD."
THAT'S WHAT YOU SOUNDED LIKE.
I MIGHT HAVE TO KILL YOU ANYWAY ...
I'M MORE WORRIED ABOUT YOUR *TROOPS* THAN YOUR ACTING.
THEY'RE NOT STRONG ENOUGH TO FACE THE DARK CONTINENT.
THEY'RE SUPPORT PERSONNEL, AT BEST.
THAT'S NO PROBLEM.
BECAUSE THEY *ARE* THERE TO COVER FOR US.
OUR MAIN JOB IS SCOUTING AND PROVIDING EXTRA FIRE-POWER.
AND COVER FIRE.

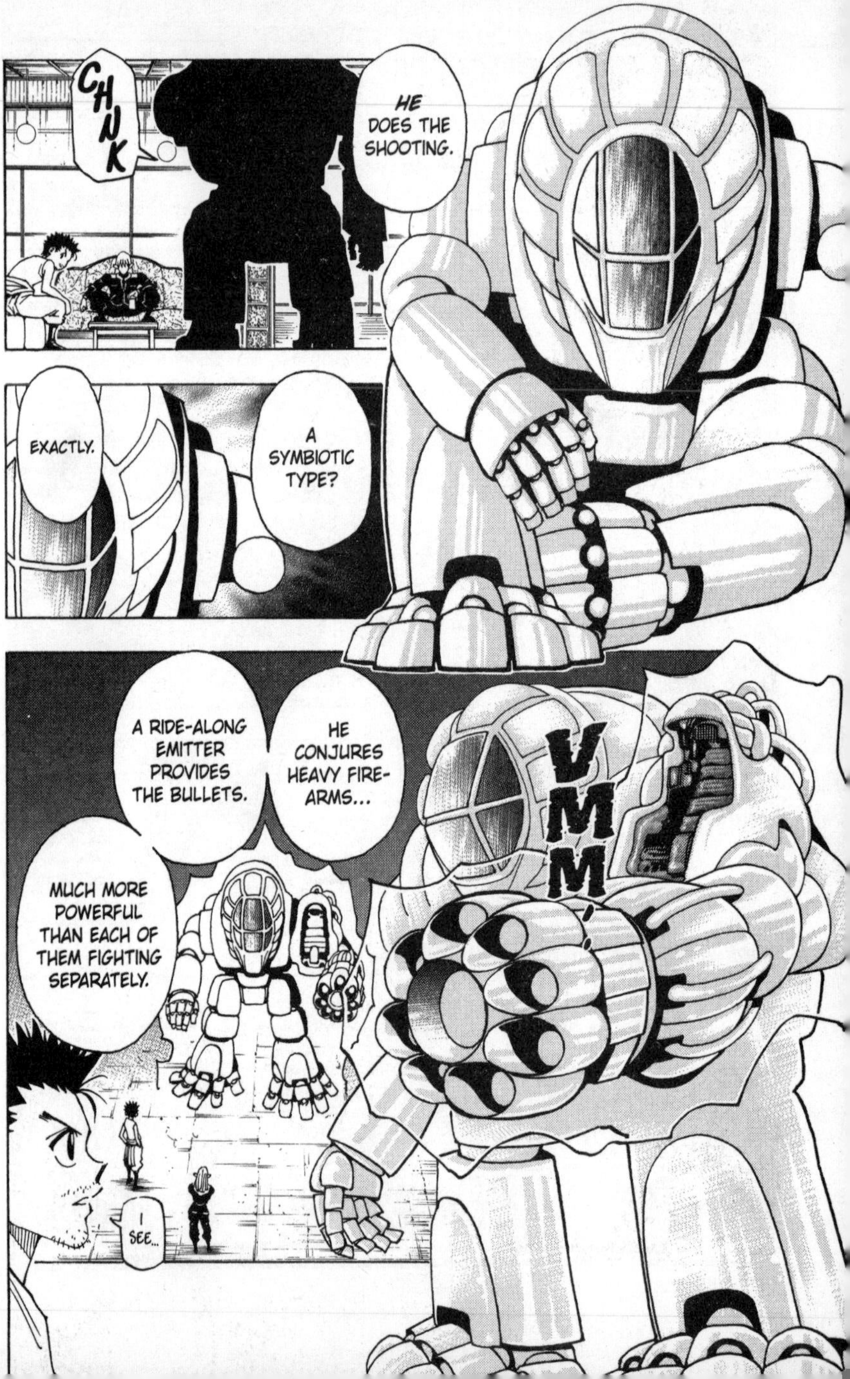
HE DOES THE SHOOTING.
CHNK
A SYMBIOTIC TYPE?
EXACTLY.
VMM
HE CONJURES HEAVY FIRE-ARMS...
A RIDE-ALONG EMITTER PROVIDES THE BULLETS.
MUCH MORE POWERFUL THAN EACH OF THEM FIGHTING SEPARATELY.
I SEE...

READ THIS WAY

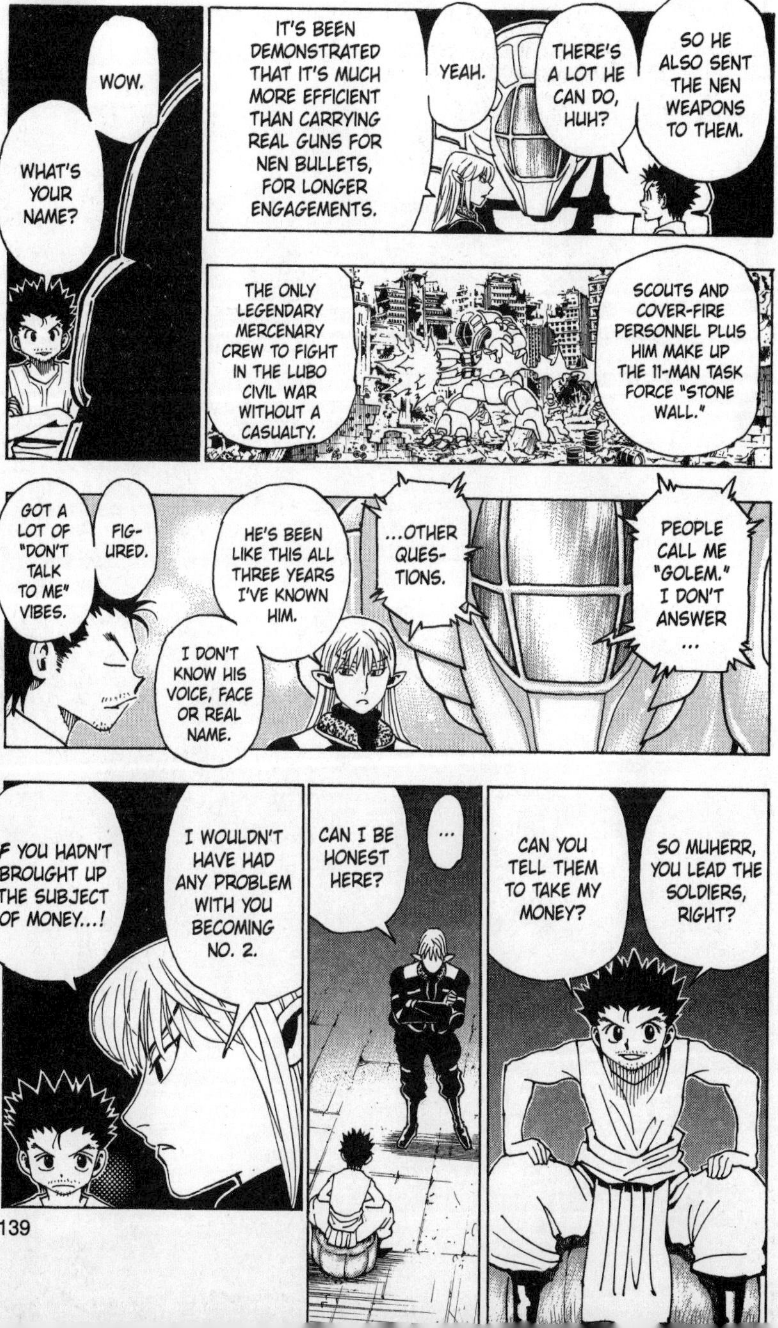
SO HE ALSO SENT THE NEN WEAPONS TO THEM.
THERE'S A LOT HE CAN DO, HUH?
YEAH.
IT'S BEEN DEMONSTRATED THAT IT'S MUCH MORE EFFICIENT THAN CARRYING REAL GUNS FOR NEN BULLETS, FOR LONGER ENGAGEMENTS.
SCOUTS AND COVER-FIRE PERSONNEL PLUS HIM MAKE UP THE 11-MAN TASK FORCE "STONE WALL."
THE ONLY LEGENDARY MERCENARY CREW TO FIGHT IN THE LUBO CIVIL WAR WITHOUT A CASUALTY.
WOW.
WHAT'S YOUR NAME?
PEOPLE CALL ME "GOLEM." I DON'T ANSWER ...
...OTHER QUES-TIONS.
HE'S BEEN LIKE THIS ALL THREE YEARS I'VE KNOWN HIM.
I DON'T KNOW HIS VOICE, FACE OR REAL NAME.
FIG-URED.
GOT A LOT OF "DON'T TALK TO ME" VIBES.
SO MUHERR, YOU LEAD THE SOLDIERS, RIGHT?
CAN YOU TELL THEM TO TAKE MY MONEY?
...
CAN I BE HONEST HERE?
I WOULDN'T HAVE HAD ANY PROBLEM WITH YOU BECOMING NO. 2.
IF YOU HADN'T BROUGHT UP THE SUBJECT OF MONEY...!

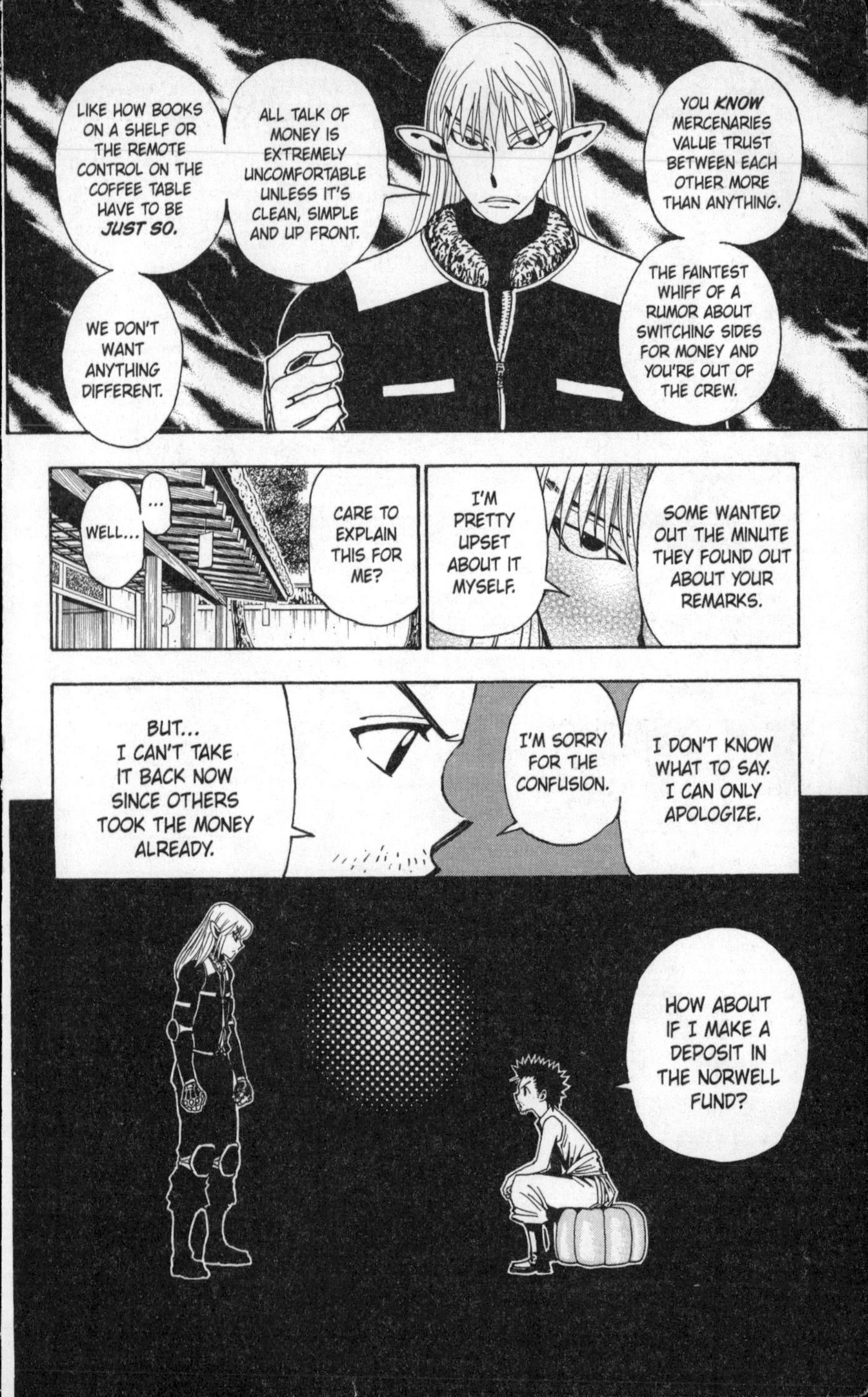
YOU KNOW MERCENARIES VALUE TRUST BETWEEN EACH OTHER MORE THAN ANYTHING.
THE FAINTEST WHIFF OF A RUMOR ABOUT SWITCHING SIDES FOR MONEY AND YOU'RE OUT OF THE CREW.
ALL TALK OF MONEY IS EXTREMELY UNCOMFORTABLE UNLESS IT'S CLEAN, SIMPLE AND UP FRONT.
LIKE HOW BOOKS ON A SHELF OR THE REMOTE CONTROL ON THE COFFEE TABLE HAVE TO BE JUST SO.
WE DON'T WANT ANYTHING DIFFERENT.
SOME WANTED OUT THE MINUTE THEY FOUND OUT ABOUT YOUR REMARKS.
I'M PRETTY UPSET ABOUT IT MYSELF.
CARE TO EXPLAIN THIS FOR ME?
...
WELL...
I DON'T KNOW WHAT TO SAY. I CAN ONLY APOLOGIZE.
I'M SORRY FOR THE CONFUSION.
BUT... I CAN'T TAKE IT BACK NOW SINCE OTHERS TOOK THE MONEY ALREADY.
HOW ABOUT IF I MAKE A DEPOSIT IN THE NORWELL FUND?

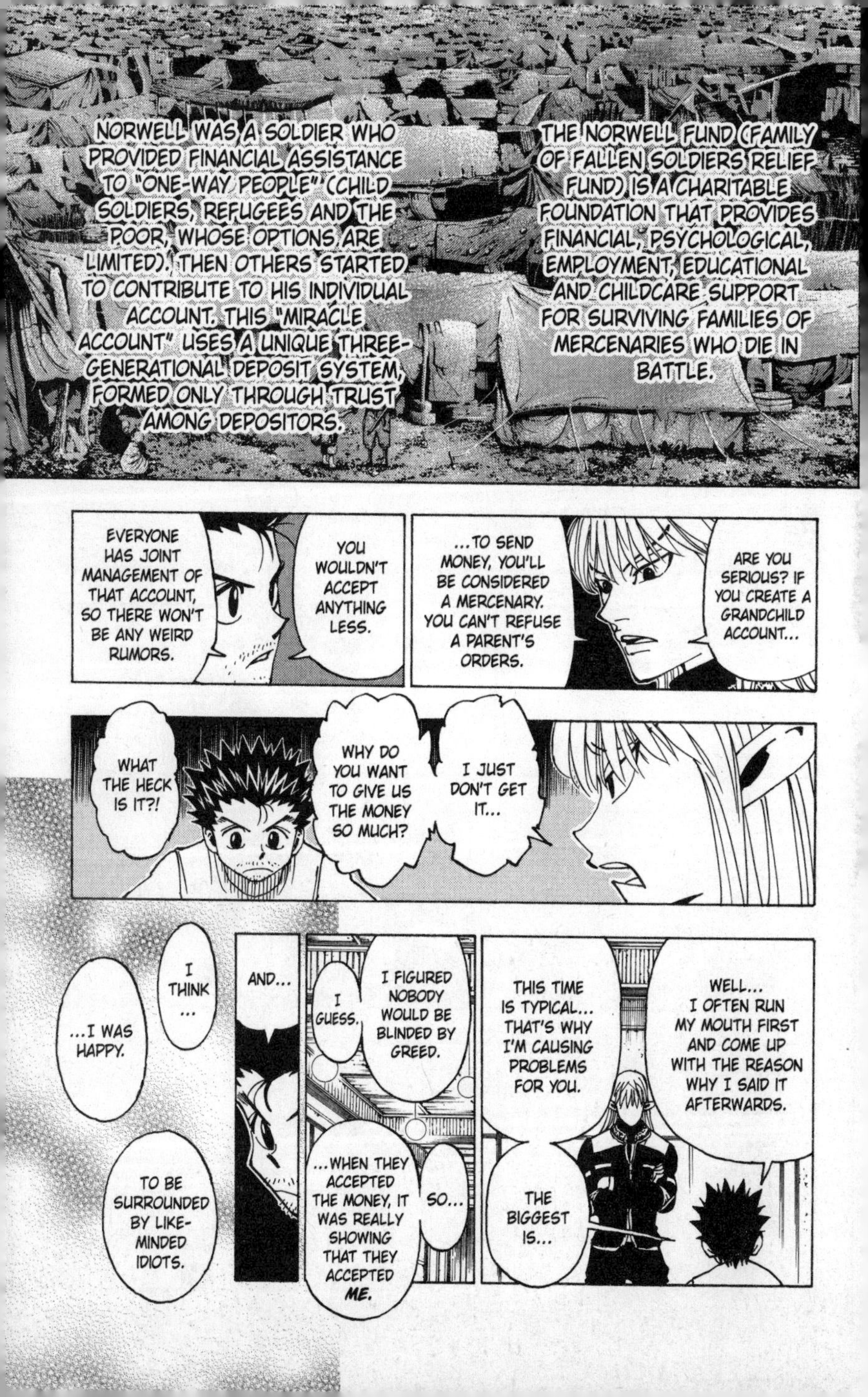
THE NORWELL FUND (FAMILY OF FALLEN SOLDIERS RELIEF FUND) IS A CHARITABLE FOUNDATION THAT PROVIDES FINANCIAL, PSYCHOLOGICAL, EMPLOYMENT, EDUCATIONAL AND CHILDCARE SUPPORT FOR SURVIVING FAMILIES OF MERCENARIES WHO DIE IN BATTLE.
NORWELL WAS A SOLDIER WHO PROVIDED FINANCIAL ASSISTANCE TO "ONE-WAY PEOPLE" (CHILD SOLDIERS, REFUGEES AND THE POOR, WHOSE OPTIONS ARE LIMITED). THEN OTHERS STARTED TO CONTRIBUTE TO HIS INDIVIDUAL ACCOUNT. THIS "MIRACLE ACCOUNT" USES A UNIQUE THREE-GENERATIONAL DEPOSIT SYSTEM, FORMED ONLY THROUGH TRUST AMONG DEPOSITORS.
ARE YOU SERIOUS? IF YOU CREATE A GRANDCHILD ACCOUNT...
...TO SEND MONEY, YOU'LL BE CONSIDERED A MERCENARY. YOU CAN'T REFUSE A PARENT'S ORDERS.
YOU WOULDN'T ACCEPT ANYTHING LESS.
EVERYONE HAS JOINT MANAGEMENT OF THAT ACCOUNT, SO THERE WON'T BE ANY WEIRD RUMORS.
I JUST DON'T GET IT...
WHY DO YOU WANT TO GIVE US THE MONEY SO MUCH?
WHAT THE HECK IS IT?!
WELL... I OFTEN RUN MY MOUTH FIRST AND COME UP WITH THE REASON WHY I SAID IT AFTERWARDS.
THIS TIME IS TYPICAL... THAT'S WHY I'M CAUSING PROBLEMS FOR YOU.
THE BIGGEST IS...
I FIGURED NOBODY WOULD BE BLINDED BY GREED.
I GUESS.
SO...
...WHEN THEY ACCEPTED THE MONEY, IT WAS REALLY SHOWING THAT THEY ACCEPTED ME.
AND...
I THINK...
...I WAS HAPPY.
TO BE SURROUNDED BY LIKE-MINDED IDIOTS.

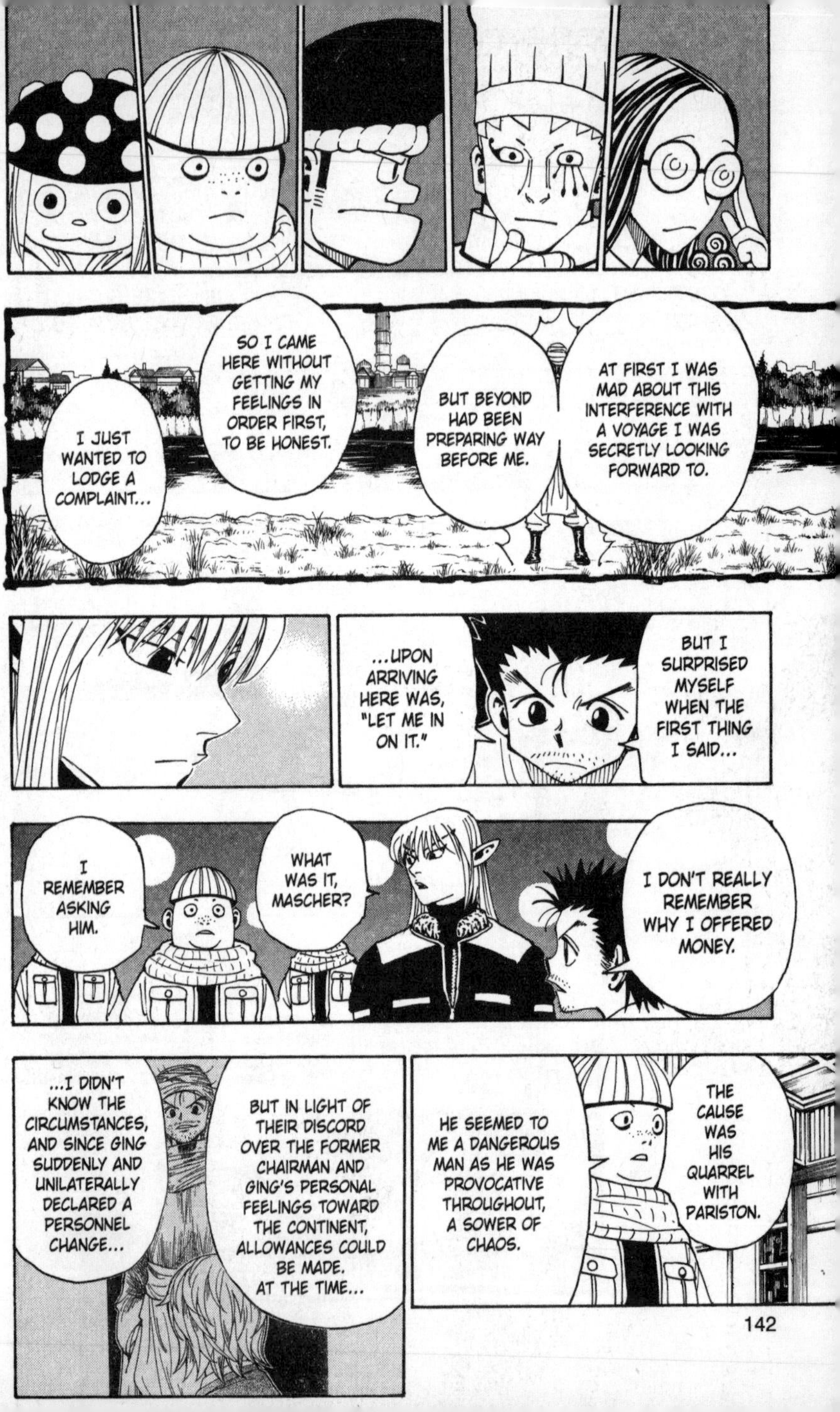
AT FIRST I WAS MAD ABOUT THIS INTERFERENCE WITH A VOYAGE I WAS SECRETLY LOOKING FORWARD TO.
BUT BEYOND HAD BEEN PREPARING WAY BEFORE ME.
SO I CAME HERE WITHOUT GETTING MY FEELINGS IN ORDER FIRST, TO BE HONEST.
I JUST WANTED TO LODGE A COMPLAINT...
BUT I SURPRISED MYSELF WHEN THE FIRST THING I SAID...
...UPON ARRIVING HERE WAS, "LET ME IN ON IT."
I DON'T REALLY REMEMBER WHY I OFFERED MONEY.
WHAT WAS IT, MASCHER?
I REMEMBER ASKING HIM.
THE CAUSE WAS HIS QUARREL WITH PARISTON.
HE SEEMED TO ME A DANGEROUS MAN AS HE WAS PROVOCATIVE THROUGHOUT, A SOWER OF CHAOS.
BUT IN LIGHT OF THEIR DISCORD OVER THE FORMER CHAIRMAN AND GING'S PERSONAL FEELINGS TOWARD THE CONTINENT, ALLOWANCES COULD BE MADE. AT THE TIME...
...I DIDN'T KNOW THE CIRCUMSTANCES, AND SINCE GING SUDDENLY AND UNILATERALLY DECLARED A PERSONNEL CHANGE...

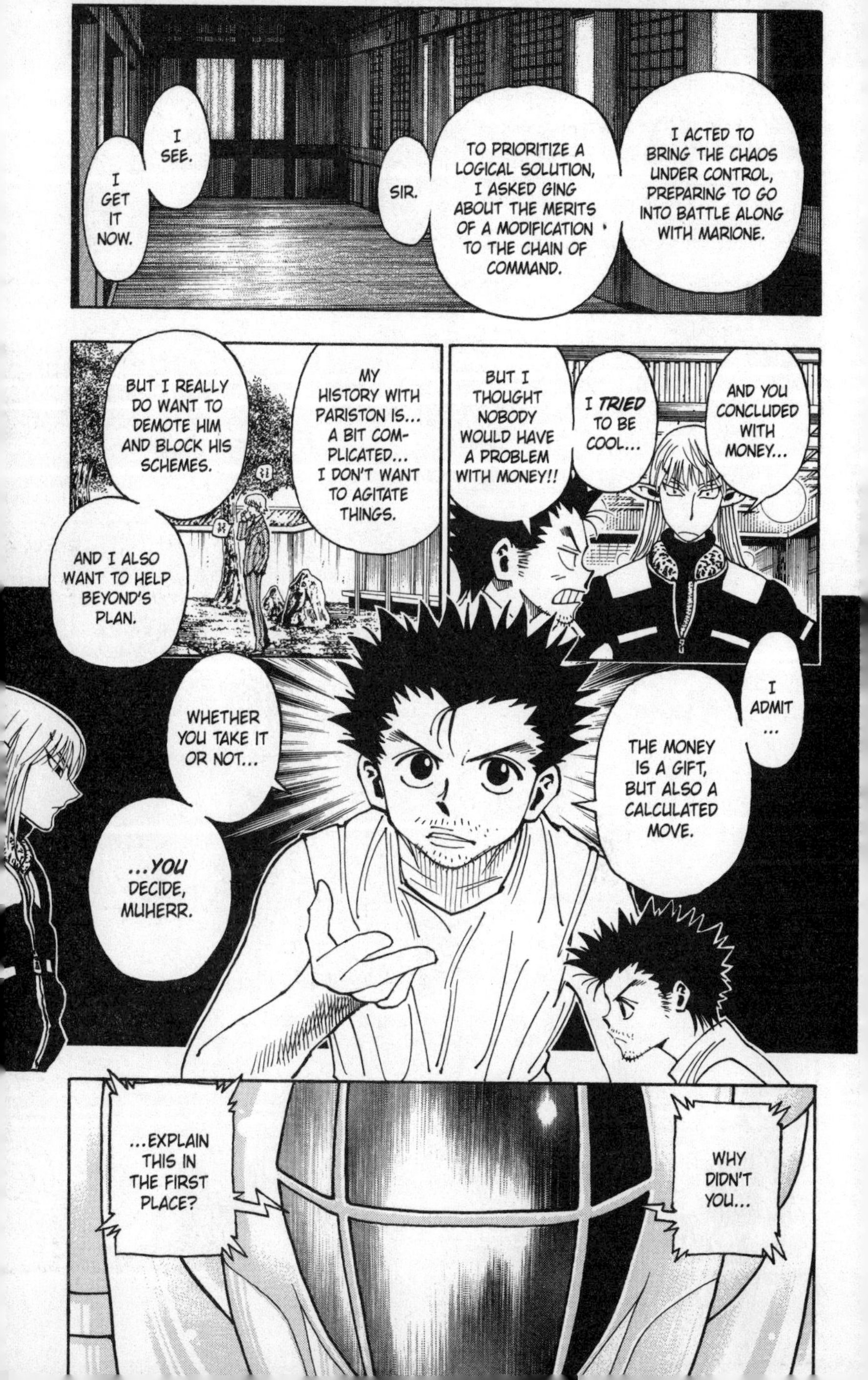
I ACTED TO BRING THE CHAOS UNDER CONTROL, PREPARING TO GO INTO BATTLE ALONG WITH MARIONE.
TO PRIORITIZE A LOGICAL SOLUTION, I ASKED GING ABOUT THE MERITS OF A MODIFICATION TO THE CHAIN OF COMMAND.
SIR.
I SEE.
I GET IT NOW.
AND YOU CONCLUDED WITH MONEY...
I *TRIED* TO BE COOL...
BUT I THOUGHT NOBODY WOULD HAVE A PROBLEM WITH MONEY!!
MY HISTORY WITH PARISTON IS... A BIT COMPLICATED... I DON'T WANT TO AGITATE THINGS.
BUT I REALLY DO WANT TO DEMOTE HIM AND BLOCK HIS SCHEMES.
AND I ALSO WANT TO HELP BEYOND'S PLAN.
I ADMIT...
THE MONEY IS A GIFT, BUT ALSO A CALCULATED MOVE.
WHETHER YOU TAKE IT OR NOT...
...*YOU* DECIDE, MUHERR.
WHY DIDN'T YOU...
...EXPLAIN THIS IN THE FIRST PLACE?

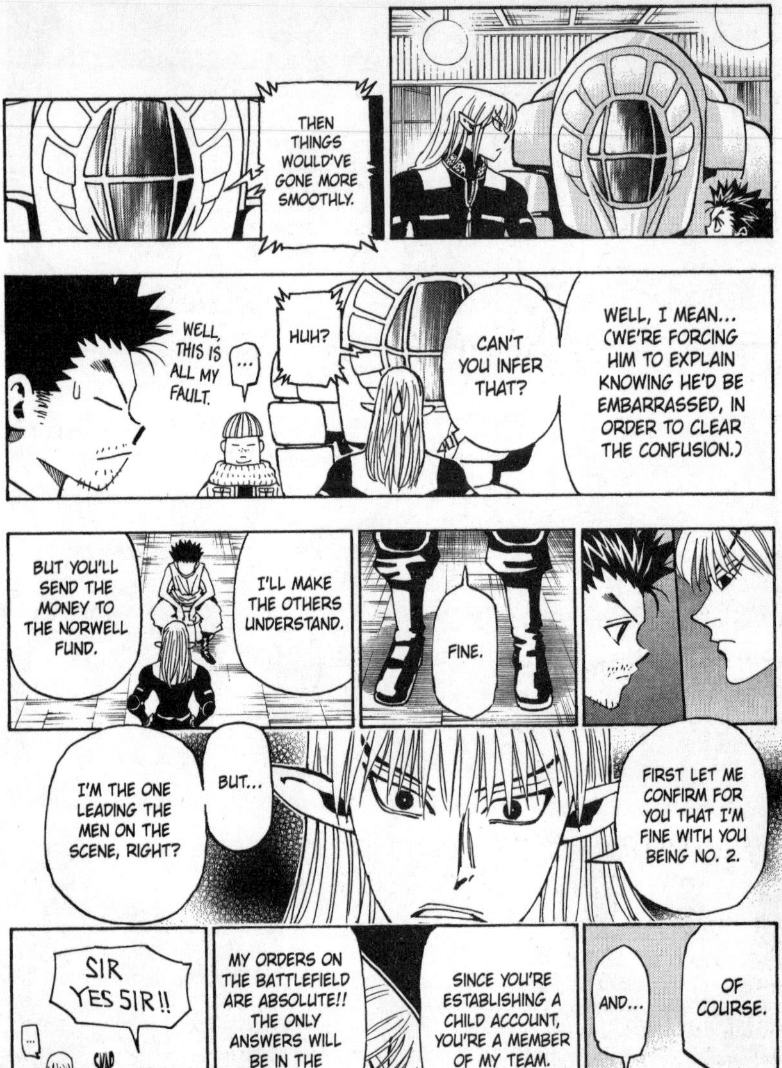
THEN THINGS WOULD'VE GONE MORE SMOOTHLY.
WELL, I MEAN... (WE'RE FORCING HIM TO EXPLAIN KNOWING HE'D BE EMBARRASSED, IN ORDER TO CLEAR THE CONFUSION.)
CAN'T YOU INFER THAT?
HUH?
...
WELL, THIS IS ALL MY FAULT.
FINE.
I'LL MAKE THE OTHERS UNDERSTAND.
BUT YOU'LL SEND THE MONEY TO THE NORWELL FUND.
FIRST LET ME CONFIRM FOR YOU THAT I'M FINE WITH YOU BEING NO. 2.
BUT...
I'M THE ONE LEADING THE MEN ON THE SCENE, RIGHT?
OF COURSE.
AND...
SINCE YOU'RE ESTABLISHING A CHILD ACCOUNT, YOU'RE A MEMBER OF MY TEAM.
MY ORDERS ON THE BATTLEFIELD ARE ABSOLUTE!! THE ONLY ANSWERS WILL BE IN THE AFFIRMATIVE.
GOT IT, NO. 2...?!
SIR YES SIR!!
...
SNAP
SNAP

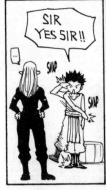

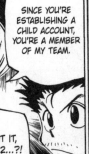

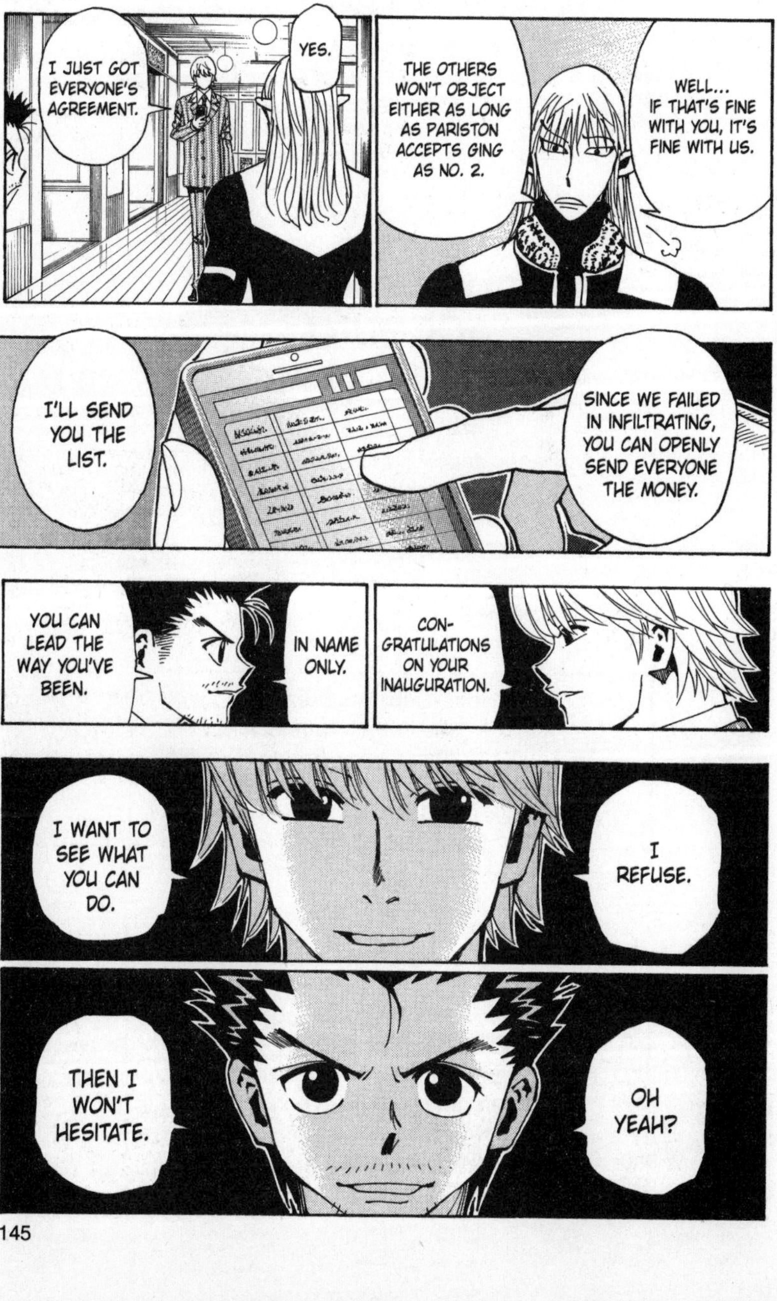
WELL... IF THAT'S FINE WITH YOU, IT'S FINE WITH US.
THE OTHERS WON'T OBJECT EITHER AS LONG AS PARISTON ACCEPTS GING AS NO. 2.
YES.
I JUST GOT EVERYONE'S AGREEMENT.
SINCE WE FAILED IN INFILTRATING, YOU CAN OPENLY SEND EVERYONE THE MONEY.
I'LL SEND YOU THE LIST.
CON-GRATULATIONS ON YOUR INAUGURATION.
IN NAME ONLY.
YOU CAN LEAD THE WAY YOU'VE BEEN.
I REFUSE.
I WANT TO SEE WHAT YOU CAN DO.
OH YEAH?
THEN I WON'T HESITATE.

THREE-GENERATIONAL ACCOUNT

Parent Account
Manages deposits from sub accounts.
All members can share and mutually
manage information on withdrawals and
purchases by all accounts.

Child (Sub) Account
Manages one or more grandchild
accounts. A grandchild cannot refuse
a child's dispatch orders. Operational
procedures are the same as a
grandchild account.

Grandchild (Sub) Account
A deposit-only account, which all goes
to the parent account. Has a designated
credit card that can make purchases
from associated stores (including
online). No usage limit.

Chapter 348: Resolve

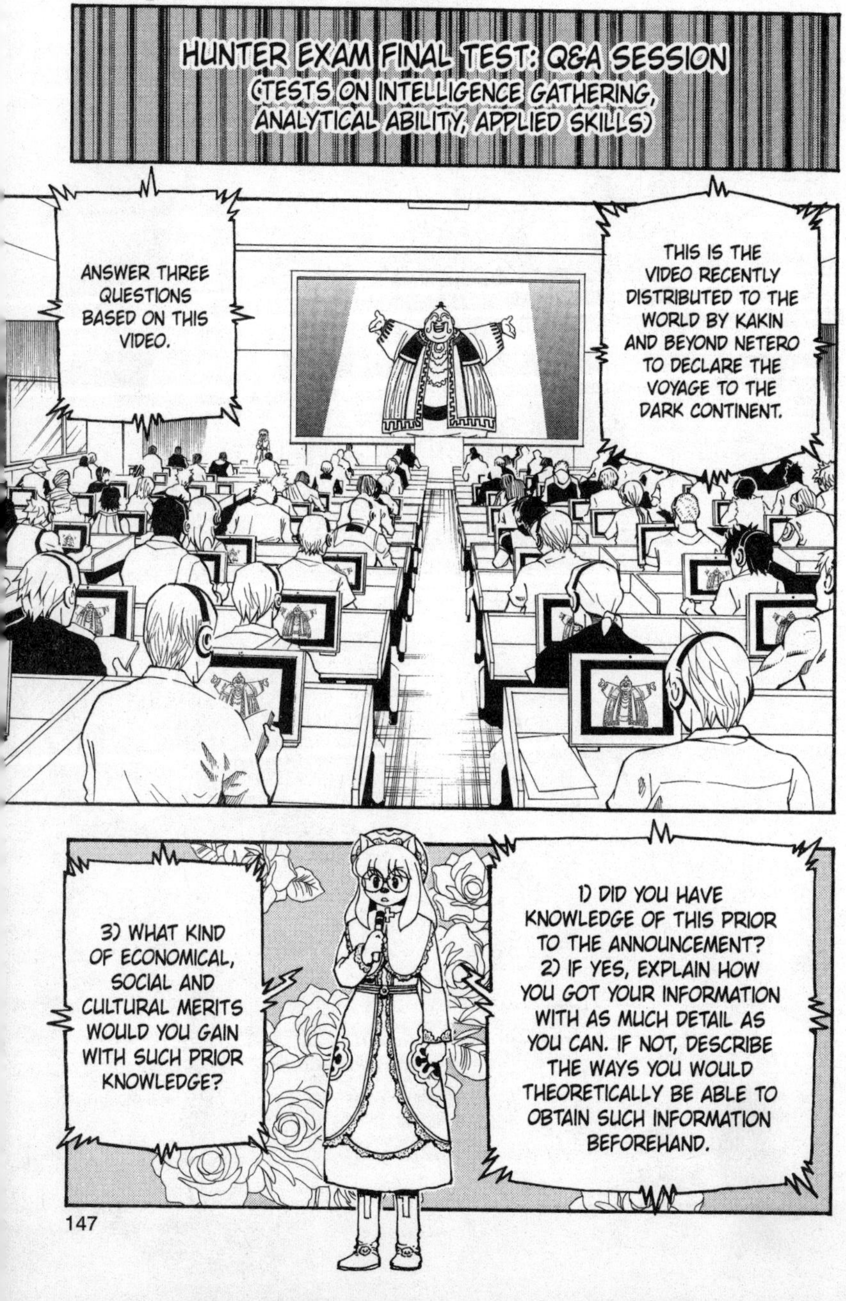
HUNTER EXAM FINAL TEST: Q&A SESSION
(TESTS ON INTELLIGENCE GATHERING, ANALYTICAL ABILITY, APPLIED SKILLS)
THIS IS THE VIDEO RECENTLY DISTRIBUTED TO THE WORLD BY KAKIN AND BEYOND NETERO TO DECLARE THE VOYAGE TO THE DARK CONTINENT.
ANSWER THREE QUESTIONS BASED ON THIS VIDEO.
1) DID YOU HAVE KNOWLEDGE OF THIS PRIOR TO THE ANNOUNCEMENT? 2) IF YES, EXPLAIN HOW YOU GOT YOUR INFORMATION WITH AS MUCH DETAIL AS YOU CAN. IF NOT, DESCRIBE THE WAYS YOU WOULD THEORETICALLY BE ABLE TO OBTAIN SUCH INFORMATION BEFOREHAND.
3) WHAT KIND OF ECONOMICAL, SOCIAL AND CULTURAL MERITS WOULD YOU GAIN WITH SUCH PRIOR KNOWLEDGE?

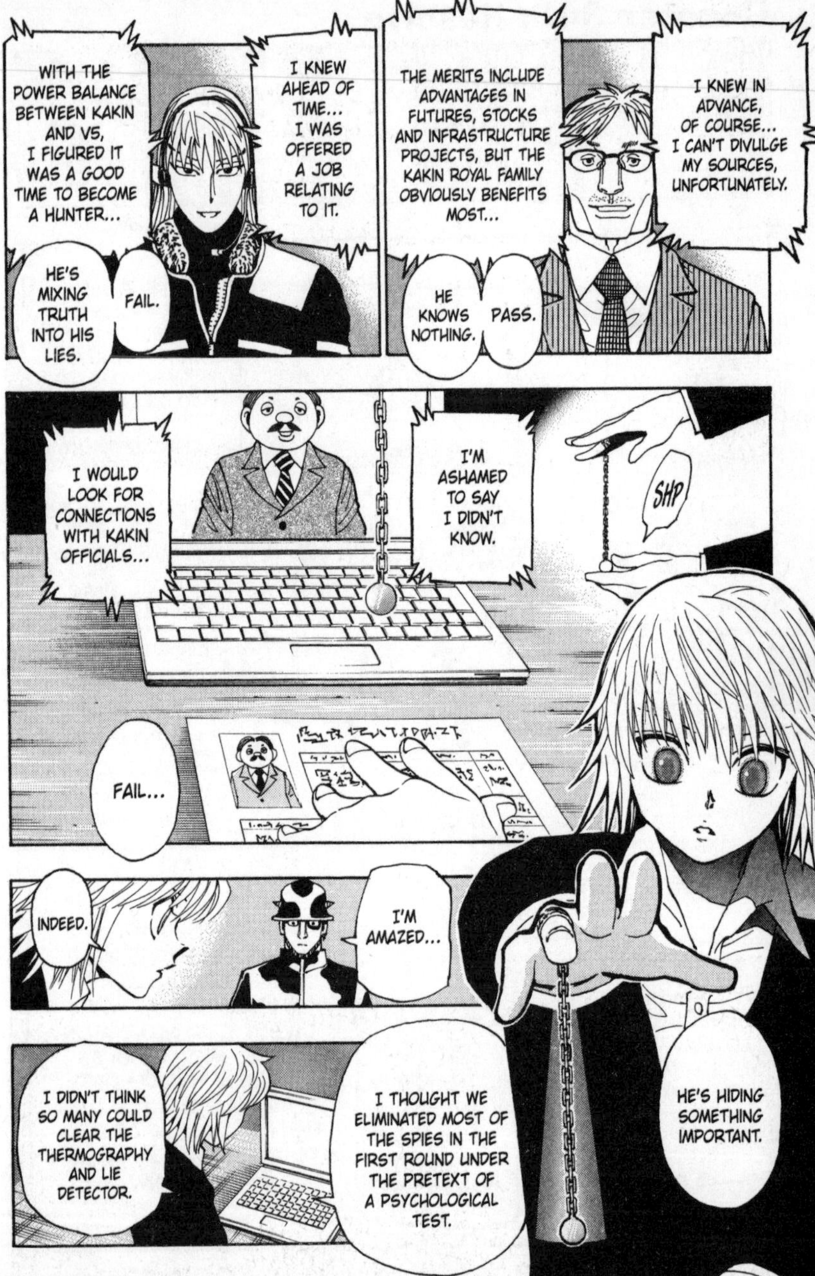
I KNEW IN ADVANCE, OF COURSE... I CAN'T DIVULGE MY SOURCES, UNFORTUNATELY.
THE MERITS INCLUDE ADVANTAGES IN FUTURES, STOCKS AND INFRASTRUCTURE PROJECTS, BUT THE KAKIN ROYAL FAMILY OBVIOUSLY BENEFITS MOST...
PASS.
HE KNOWS NOTHING.
I KNEW AHEAD OF TIME... I WAS OFFERED A JOB RELATING TO IT.
WITH THE POWER BALANCE BETWEEN KAKIN AND V5, I FIGURED IT WAS A GOOD TIME TO BECOME A HUNTER...
FAIL.
HE'S MIXING TRUTH INTO HIS LIES.
SHP
I'M ASHAMED TO SAY I DIDN'T KNOW.
I WOULD LOOK FOR CONNECTIONS WITH KAKIN OFFICIALS...
FAIL...
I'M AMAZED...
INDEED.
HE'S HIDING SOMETHING IMPORTANT.
I THOUGHT WE ELIMINATED MOST OF THE SPIES IN THE FIRST ROUND UNDER THE PRETEXT OF A PSYCHOLOGICAL TEST.
I DIDN'T THINK SO MANY COULD CLEAR THE THERMOGRAPHY AND LIE DETECTOR.

READ THIS WAY

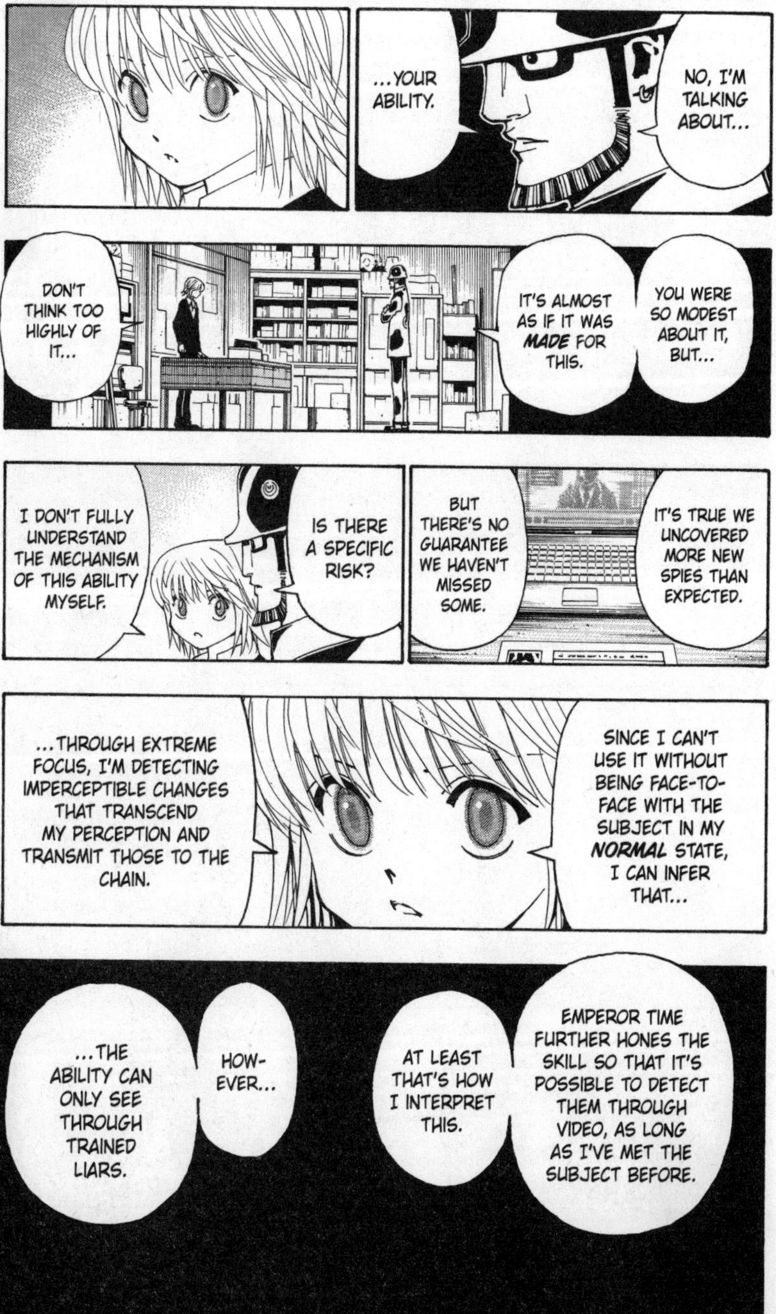
NO, I'M TALKING ABOUT...
...YOUR ABILITY.
YOU WERE SO MODEST ABOUT IT, BUT...
IT'S ALMOST AS IF IT WAS *MADE* FOR THIS.
DON'T THINK TOO HIGHLY OF IT...
IT'S TRUE WE UNCOVERED MORE NEW SPIES THAN EXPECTED.
BUT THERE'S NO GUARANTEE WE HAVEN'T MISSED SOME.
IS THERE A SPECIFIC RISK?
I DON'T FULLY UNDERSTAND THE MECHANISM OF THIS ABILITY MYSELF.
SINCE I CAN'T USE IT WITHOUT BEING FACE-TO-FACE WITH THE SUBJECT IN MY *NORMAL* STATE, I CAN INFER THAT...
...THROUGH EXTREME FOCUS, I'M DETECTING IMPERCEPTIBLE CHANGES THAT TRANSCEND MY PERCEPTION AND TRANSMIT THOSE TO THE CHAIN.
EMPEROR TIME FURTHER HONES THE SKILL SO THAT IT'S POSSIBLE TO DETECT THEM THROUGH VIDEO, AS LONG AS I'VE MET THE SUBJECT BEFORE.
AT LEAST THAT'S HOW I INTERPRET THIS.
HOW-EVER...
...THE ABILITY CAN ONLY SEE THROUGH TRAINED LIARS.

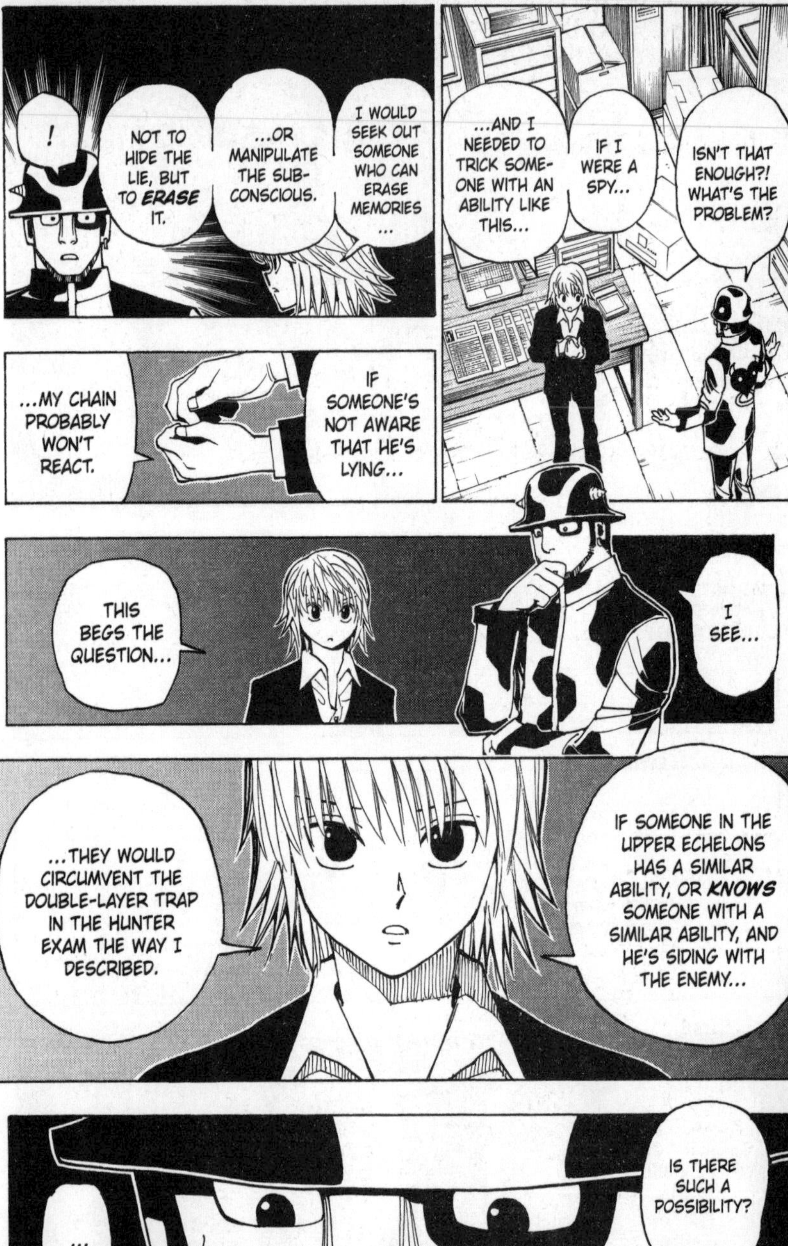
ISN'T THAT ENOUGH?! WHAT'S THE PROBLEM?
IF I WERE A SPY...
...AND I NEEDED TO TRICK SOME-ONE WITH AN ABILITY LIKE THIS...
I WOULD SEEK OUT SOMEONE WHO CAN ERASE MEMORIES ...
...OR MANIPULATE THE SUB-CONSCIOUS.
NOT TO HIDE THE LIE, BUT TO *ERASE* IT.
!
IF SOMEONE'S NOT AWARE THAT HE'S LYING...
...MY CHAIN PROBABLY WON'T REACT.
I SEE...
THIS BEGS THE QUESTION...
IF SOMEONE IN THE UPPER ECHELONS HAS A SIMILAR ABILITY, OR *KNOWS* SOMEONE WITH A SIMILAR ABILITY, AND HE'S SIDING WITH THE ENEMY...
...THEY WOULD CIRCUMVENT THE DOUBLE-LAYER TRAP IN THE HUNTER EXAM THE WAY I DESCRIBED.
IS THERE SUCH A POSSIBILITY?
...

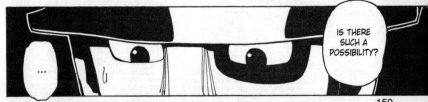

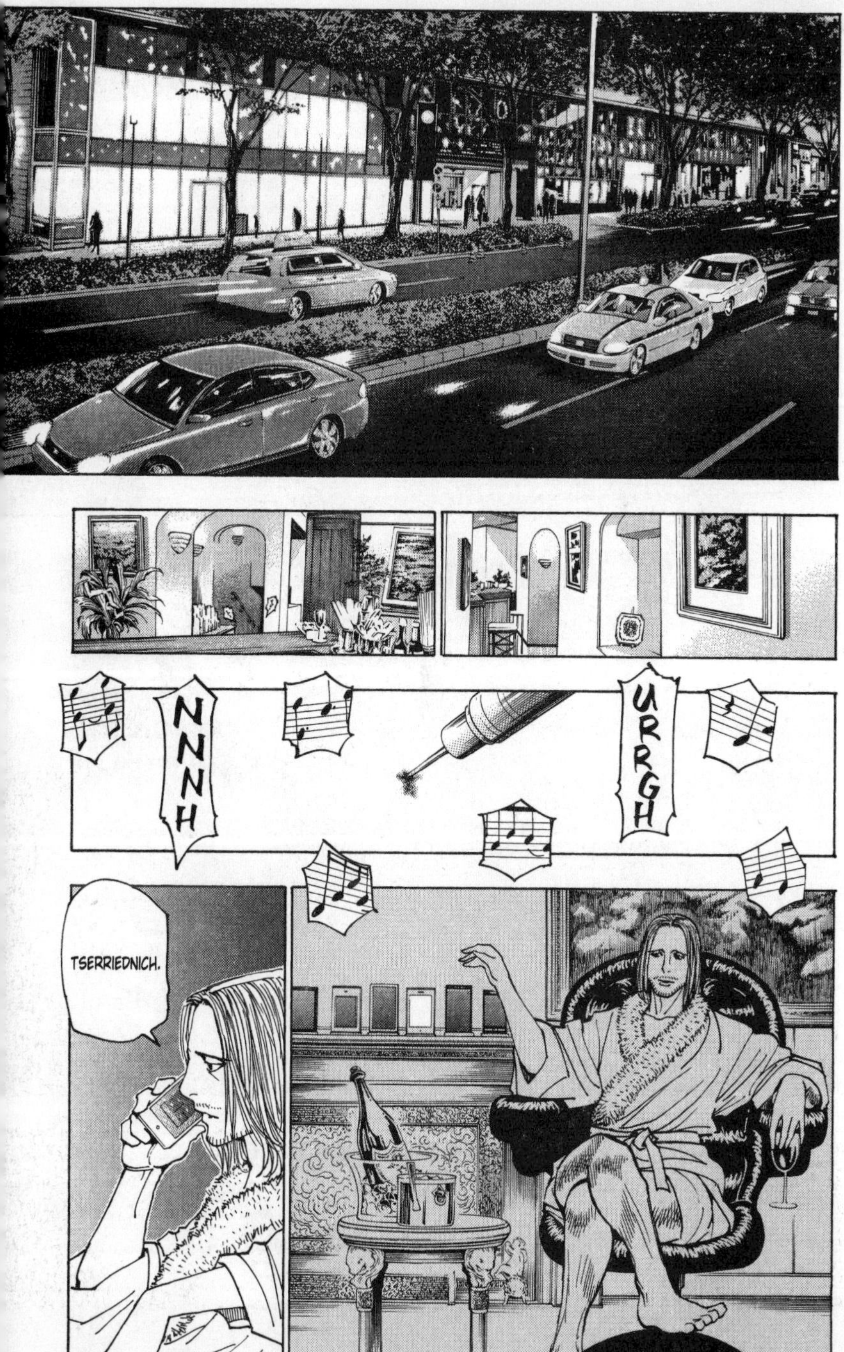
URRGH
NNNH
TSERRIEDNICH.

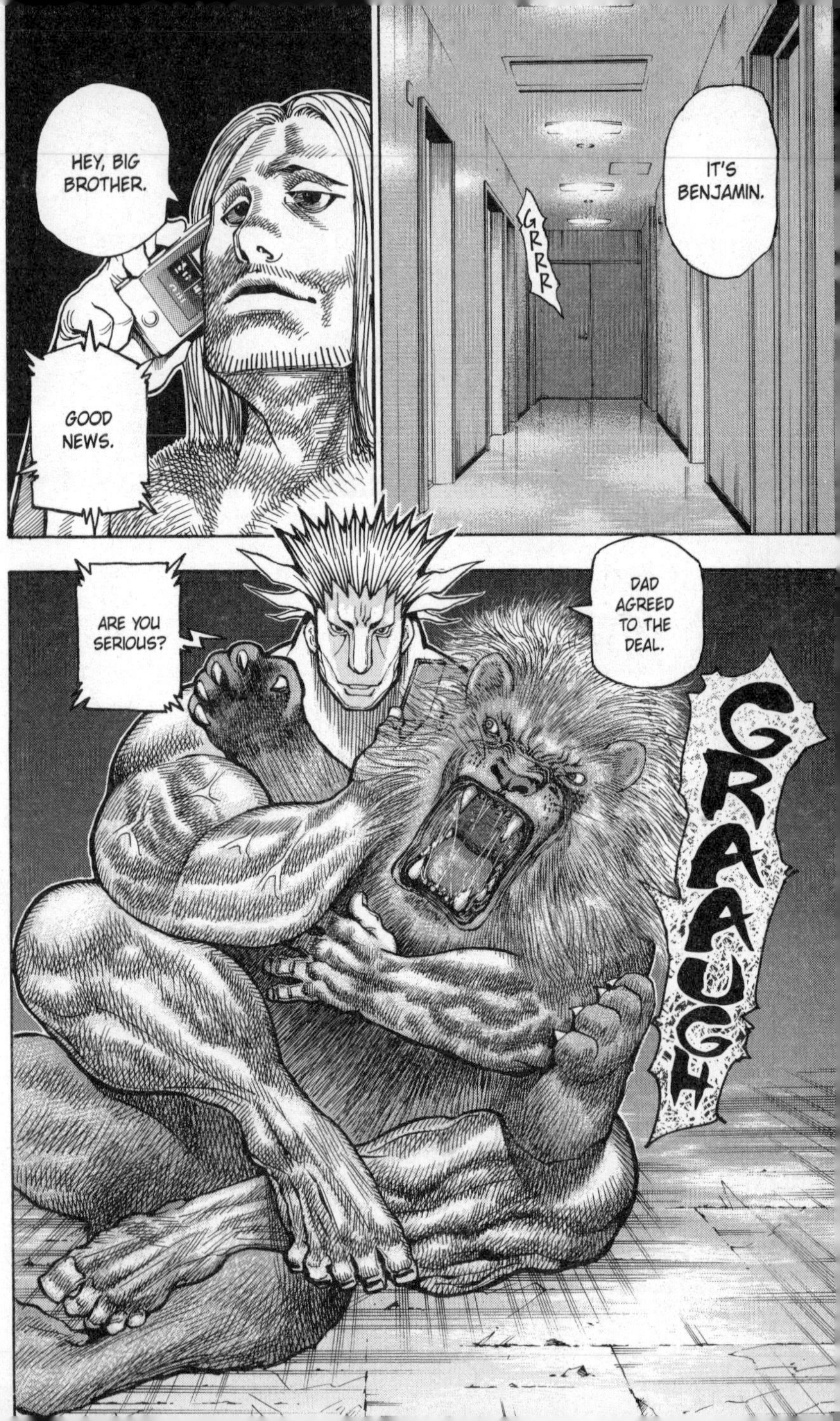
IT'S BENJAMIN.
GRRR
HEY, BIG BROTHER.
GOOD NEWS.
DAD AGREED TO THE DEAL.
GRAAUGH
ARE YOU SERIOUS?

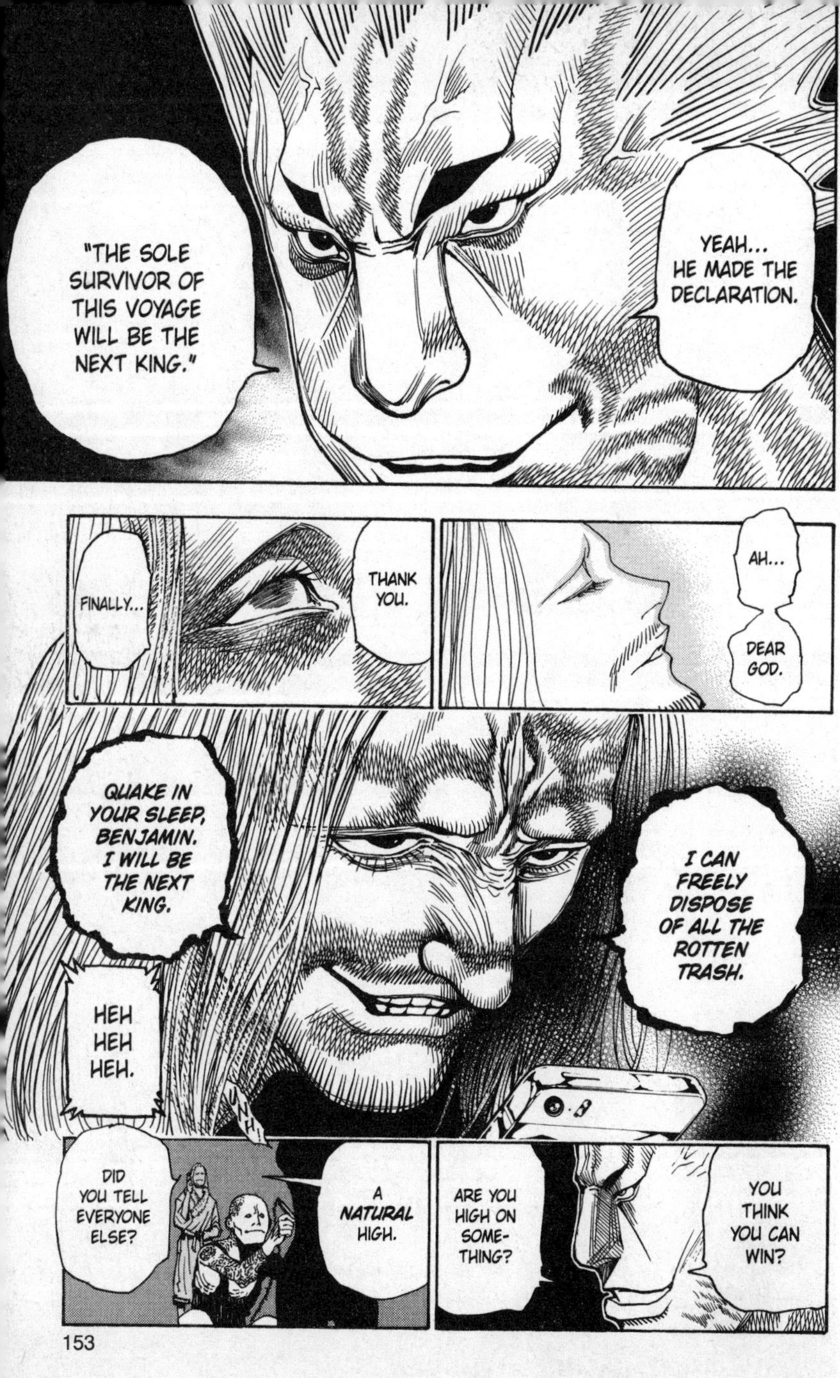
YEAH... HE MADE THE DECLARATION.
"THE SOLE SURVIVOR OF THIS VOYAGE WILL BE THE NEXT KING."
AH...
DEAR GOD.
THANK YOU.
FINALLY...
I CAN FREELY DISPOSE OF ALL THE ROTTEN TRASH.
QUAKE IN YOUR SLEEP, BENJAMIN. I WILL BE THE NEXT KING.
HEH HEH HEH.
UNH!
YOU THINK YOU CAN WIN?
ARE YOU HIGH ON SOMETHING?
A NATURAL HIGH.
DID YOU TELL EVERYONE ELSE?

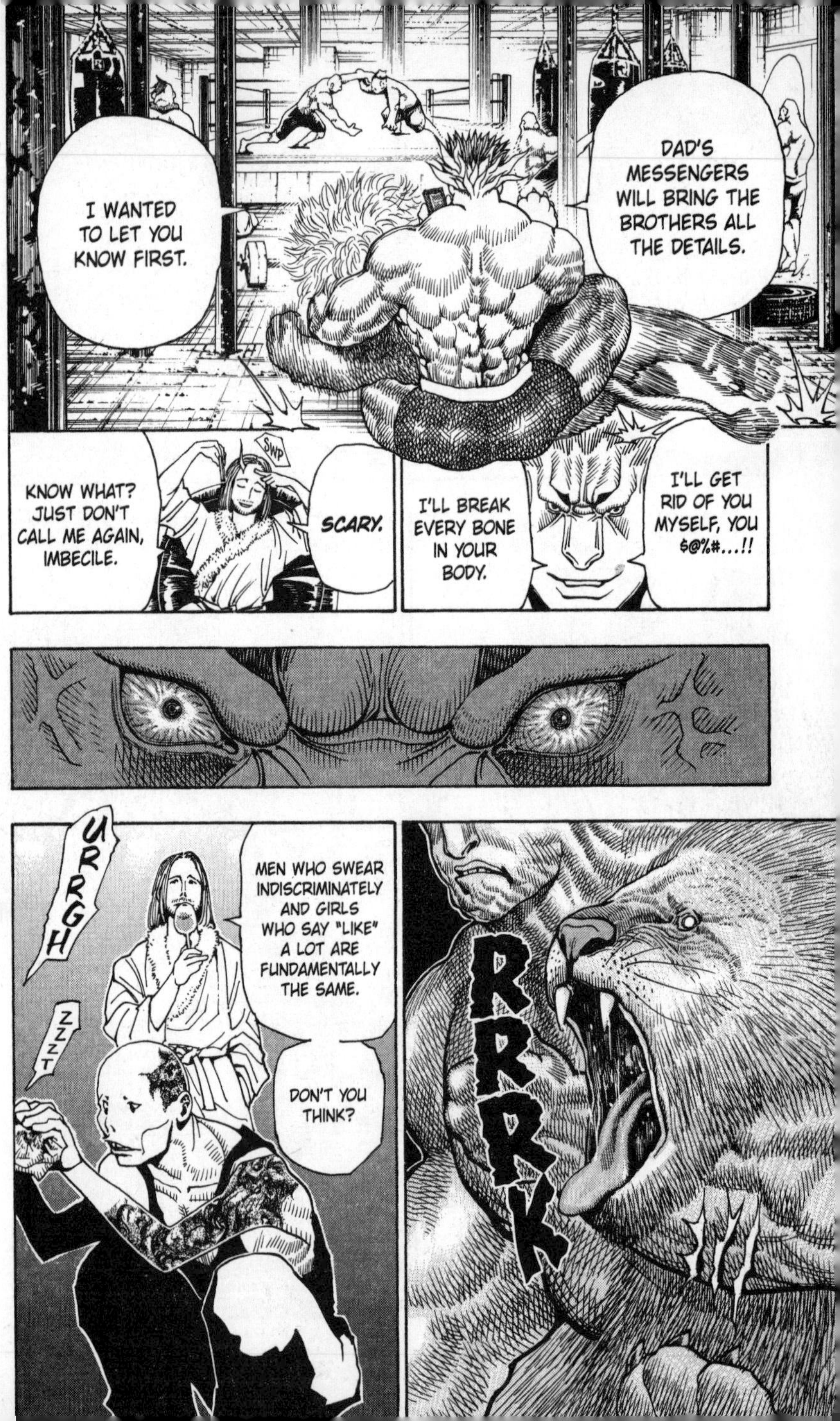
DAD'S MESSENGERS WILL BRING THE BROTHERS ALL THE DETAILS.
I WANTED TO LET YOU KNOW FIRST.
I'LL GET RID OF YOU MYSELF, YOU $@%#...!!
I'LL BREAK EVERY BONE IN YOUR BODY.
SWP
SCARY.
KNOW WHAT? JUST DON'T CALL ME AGAIN, IMBECILE.
RRRK
URRGH
MEN WHO SWEAR INDISCRIMINATELY AND GIRLS WHO SAY "LIKE" A LOT ARE FUNDAMENTALLY THE SAME.
DON'T YOU THINK?
ZZZT

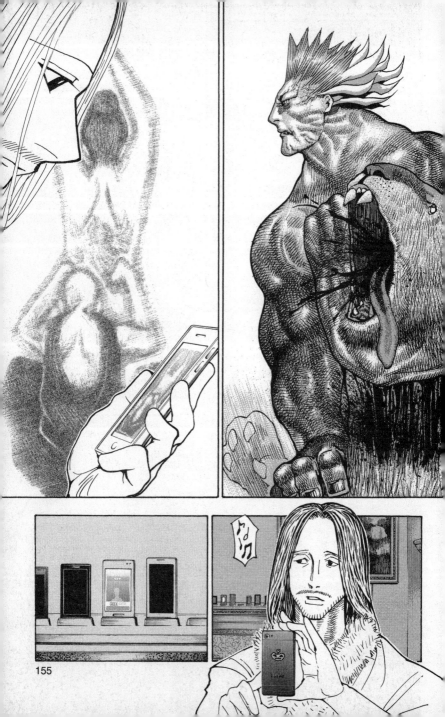

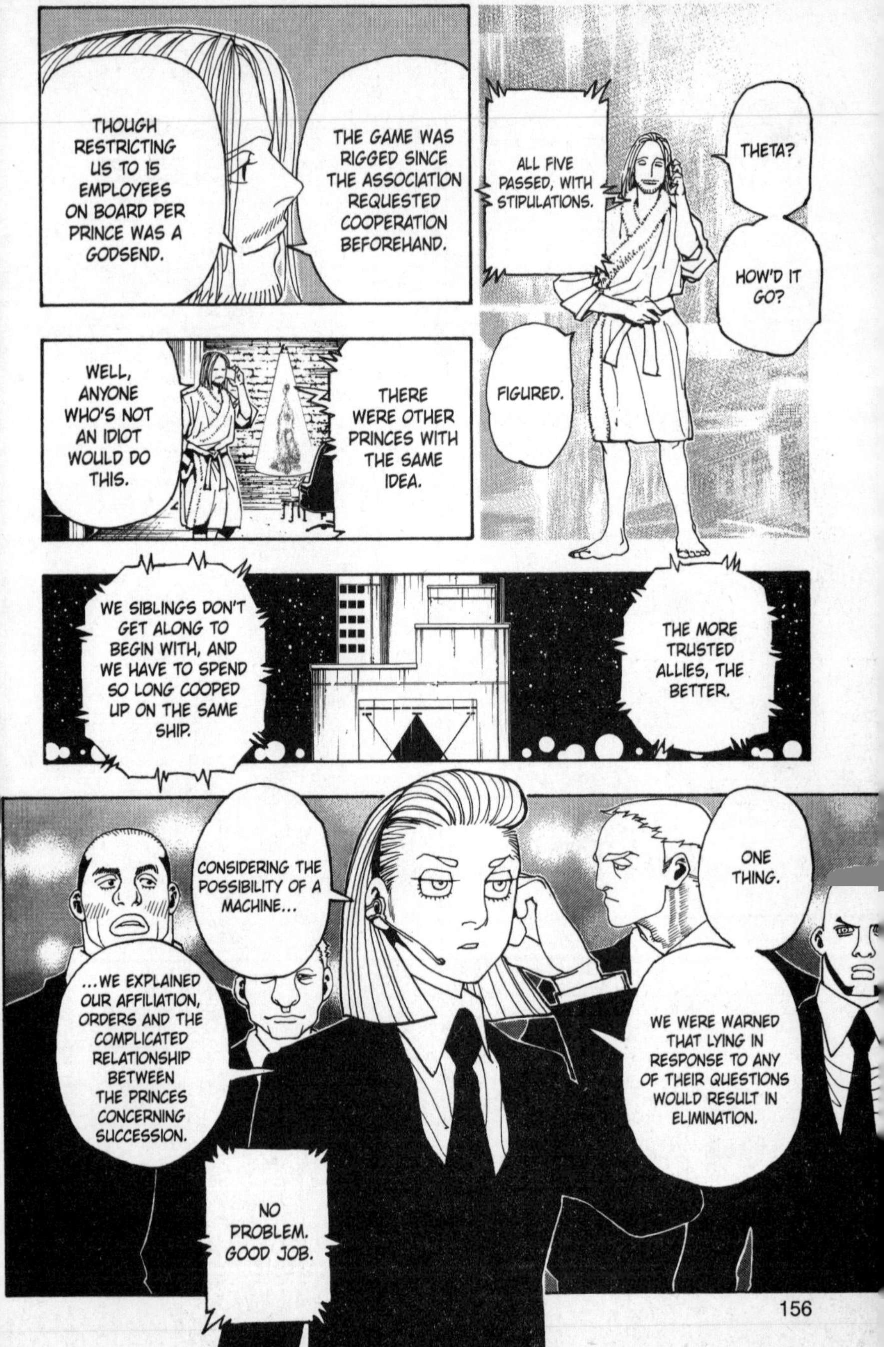
THETA?
HOW'D IT GO?
ALL FIVE PASSED, WITH STIPULATIONS.
THE GAME WAS RIGGED SINCE THE ASSOCIATION REQUESTED COOPERATION BEFOREHAND.
THOUGH RESTRICTING US TO 15 EMPLOYEES ON BOARD PER PRINCE WAS A GODSEND.
FIGURED.
THERE WERE OTHER PRINCES WITH THE SAME IDEA.
WELL, ANYONE WHO'S NOT AN IDIOT WOULD DO THIS.
WE SIBLINGS DON'T GET ALONG TO BEGIN WITH, AND WE HAVE TO SPEND SO LONG COOPED UP ON THE SAME SHIP.
THE MORE TRUSTED ALLIES, THE BETTER.
ONE THING.
WE WERE WARNED THAT LYING IN RESPONSE TO ANY OF THEIR QUESTIONS WOULD RESULT IN ELIMINATION.
CONSIDERING THE POSSIBILITY OF A MACHINE...
...WE EXPLAINED OUR AFFILIATION, ORDERS AND THE COMPLICATED RELATIONSHIP BETWEEN THE PRINCES CONCERNING SUCCESSION.
NO PROBLEM. GOOD JOB.

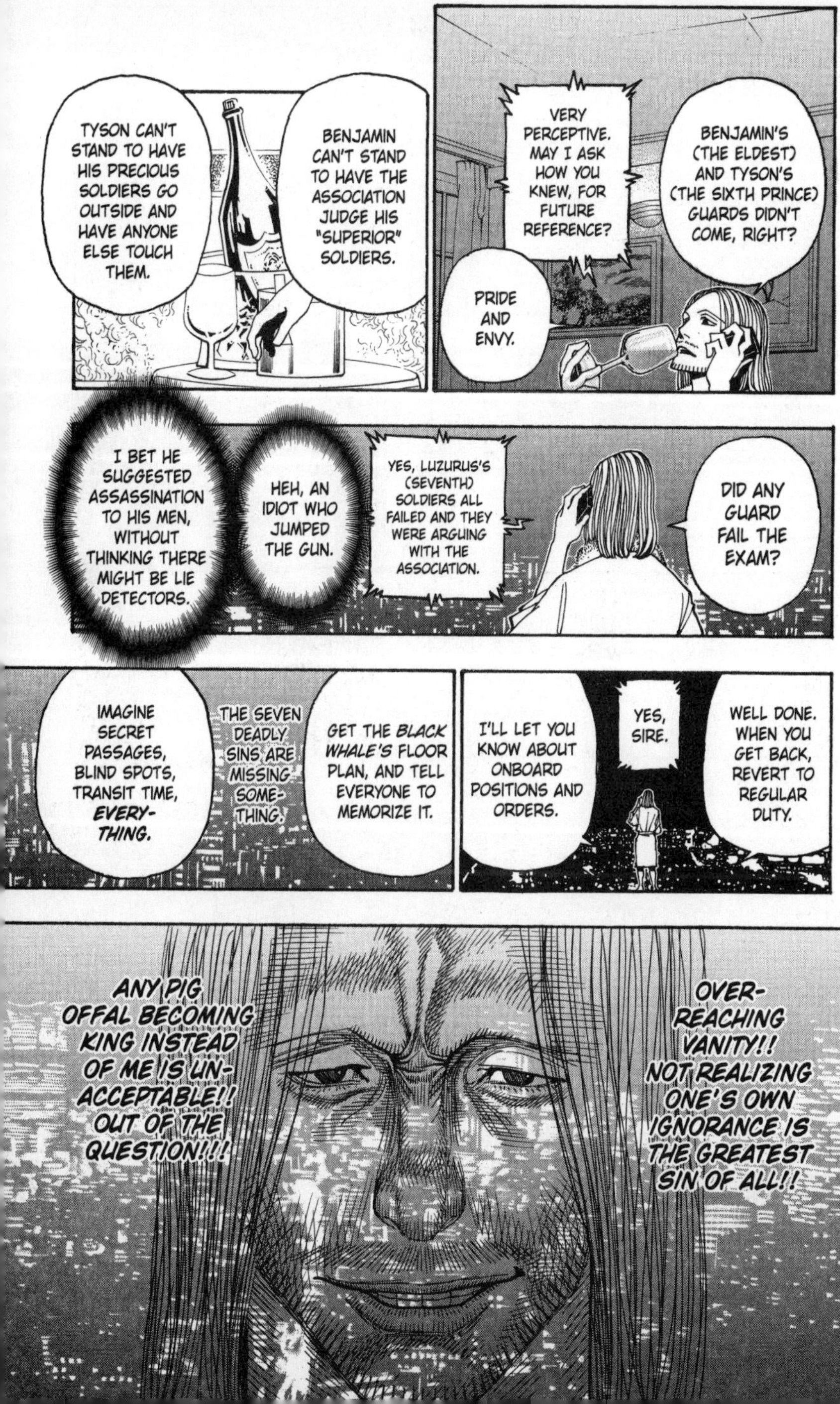
BENJAMIN'S (THE ELDEST) AND TYSON'S (THE SIXTH PRINCE) GUARDS DIDN'T COME, RIGHT?
VERY PERCEPTIVE. MAY I ASK HOW YOU KNEW, FOR FUTURE REFERENCE?
PRIDE AND ENVY.
BENJAMIN CAN'T STAND TO HAVE THE ASSOCIATION JUDGE HIS "SUPERIOR" SOLDIERS.
TYSON CAN'T STAND TO HAVE HIS PRECIOUS SOLDIERS GO OUTSIDE AND HAVE ANYONE ELSE TOUCH THEM.
DID ANY GUARD FAIL THE EXAM?
YES, LUZURUS'S (SEVENTH) SOLDIERS ALL FAILED AND THEY WERE ARGUING WITH THE ASSOCIATION.
HEH, AN IDIOT WHO JUMPED THE GUN.
I BET HE SUGGESTED ASSASSINATION TO HIS MEN, WITHOUT THINKING THERE MIGHT BE LIE DETECTORS.
WELL DONE. WHEN YOU GET BACK, REVERT TO REGULAR DUTY.
YES, SIRE.
I'LL LET YOU KNOW ABOUT ONBOARD POSITIONS AND ORDERS.
GET THE *BLACK WHALE'S* FLOOR PLAN, AND TELL EVERYONE TO MEMORIZE IT.
THE SEVEN DEADLY SINS ARE MISSING SOME-THING.
IMAGINE SECRET PASSAGES, BLIND SPOTS, TRANSIT TIME, *EVERY-THING.*
OVER-REACHING VANITY!! NOT REALIZING ONE'S OWN IGNORANCE IS THE GREATEST SIN OF ALL!!
ANY PIG OFFAL BECOMING KING INSTEAD OF ME IS UN-ACCEPTABLE!! OUT OF THE QUESTION!!!

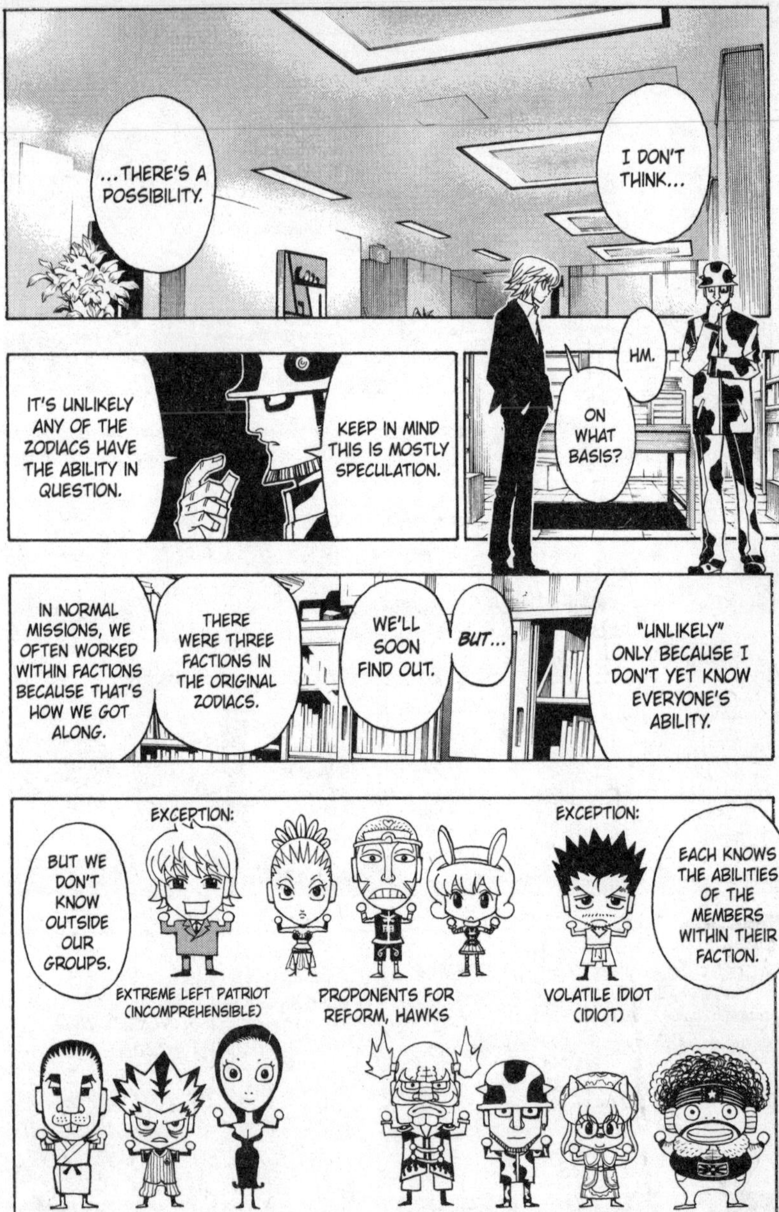
I DON'T THINK...
...THERE'S A POSSIBILITY.
HM.
ON WHAT BASIS?
KEEP IN MIND THIS IS MOSTLY SPECULATION.
IT'S UNLIKELY ANY OF THE ZODIACS HAVE THE ABILITY IN QUESTION.
"UNLIKELY" ONLY BECAUSE I DON'T YET KNOW EVERYONE'S ABILITY.
BUT...
WE'LL SOON FIND OUT.
THERE WERE THREE FACTIONS IN THE ORIGINAL ZODIACS.
IN NORMAL MISSIONS, WE OFTEN WORKED WITHIN FACTIONS BECAUSE THAT'S HOW WE GOT ALONG.
EACH KNOWS THE ABILITIES OF THE MEMBERS WITHIN THEIR FACTION.
EXCEPTION:
VOLATILE IDIOT (IDIOT)
PROPONENTS FOR REFORM, HAWKS
EXCEPTION:
EXTREME LEFT PATRIOT (INCOMPREHENSIBLE)
BUT WE DON'T KNOW OUTSIDE OUR GROUPS.
PRIORITIZE BALANCE, MODERATE CONSERVATIVE
LIBERAL/APOLITICAL

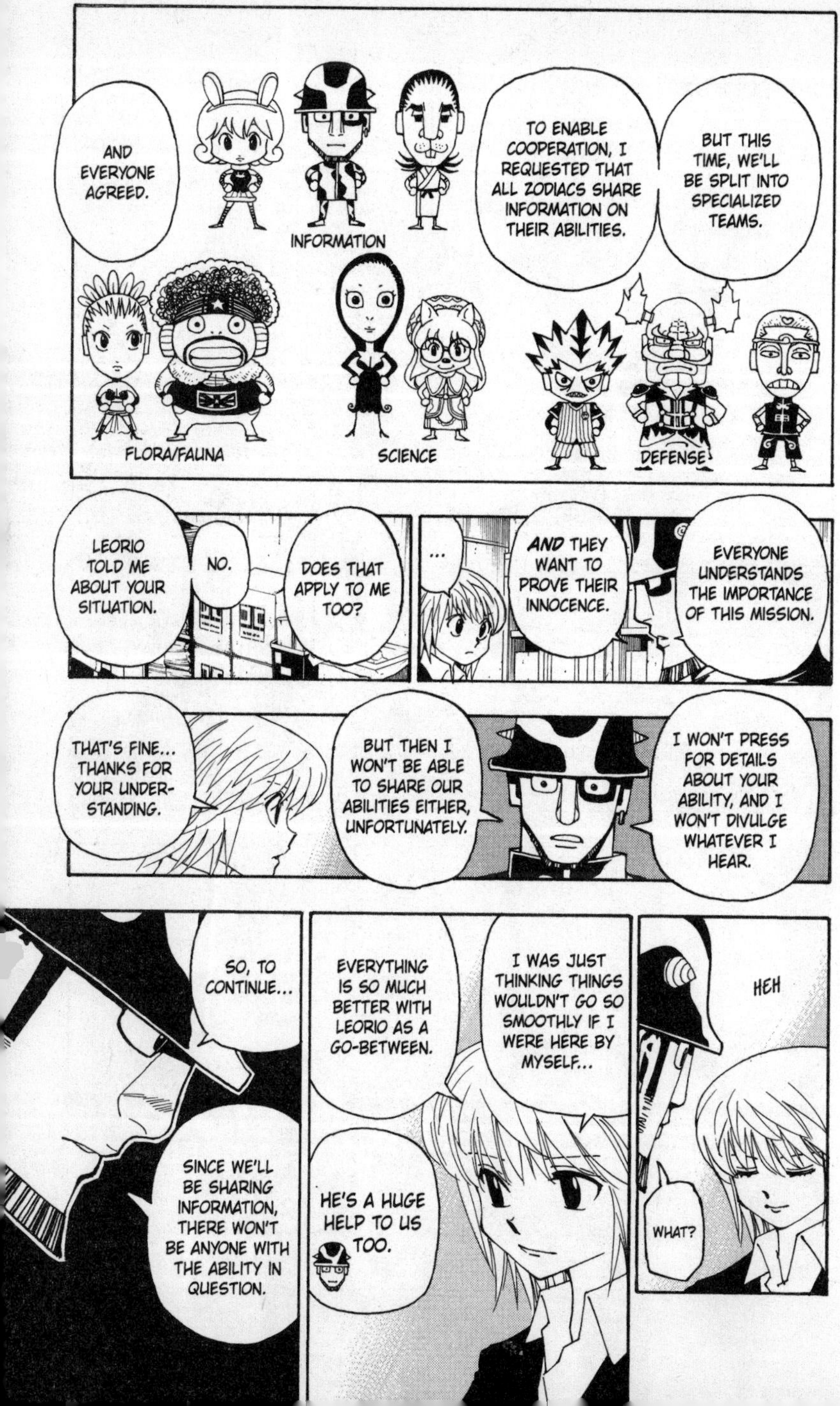
BUT THIS TIME, WE'LL BE SPLIT INTO SPECIALIZED TEAMS.
TO ENABLE COOPERATION, I REQUESTED THAT ALL ZODIACS SHARE INFORMATION ON THEIR ABILITIES.
INFORMATION
AND EVERYONE AGREED.
DEFENSE
SCIENCE
FLORA/FAUNA
EVERYONE UNDERSTANDS THE IMPORTANCE OF THIS MISSION.
AND THEY WANT TO PROVE THEIR INNOCENCE.
...
DOES THAT APPLY TO ME TOO?
NO.
LEORIO TOLD ME ABOUT YOUR SITUATION.
I WON'T PRESS FOR DETAILS ABOUT YOUR ABILITY, AND I WON'T DIVULGE WHATEVER I HEAR.
BUT THEN I WON'T BE ABLE TO SHARE OUR ABILITIES EITHER, UNFORTUNATELY.
THAT'S FINE... THANKS FOR YOUR UNDER-STANDING.
HEH
WHAT?
I WAS JUST THINKING THINGS WOULDN'T GO SO SMOOTHLY IF I WERE HERE BY MYSELF...
EVERYTHING IS SO MUCH BETTER WITH LEORIO AS A GO-BETWEEN.
HE'S A HUGE HELP TO US TOO.
SO, TO CONTINUE...
SINCE WE'LL BE SHARING INFORMATION, THERE WON'T BE ANYONE WITH THE ABILITY IN QUESTION.

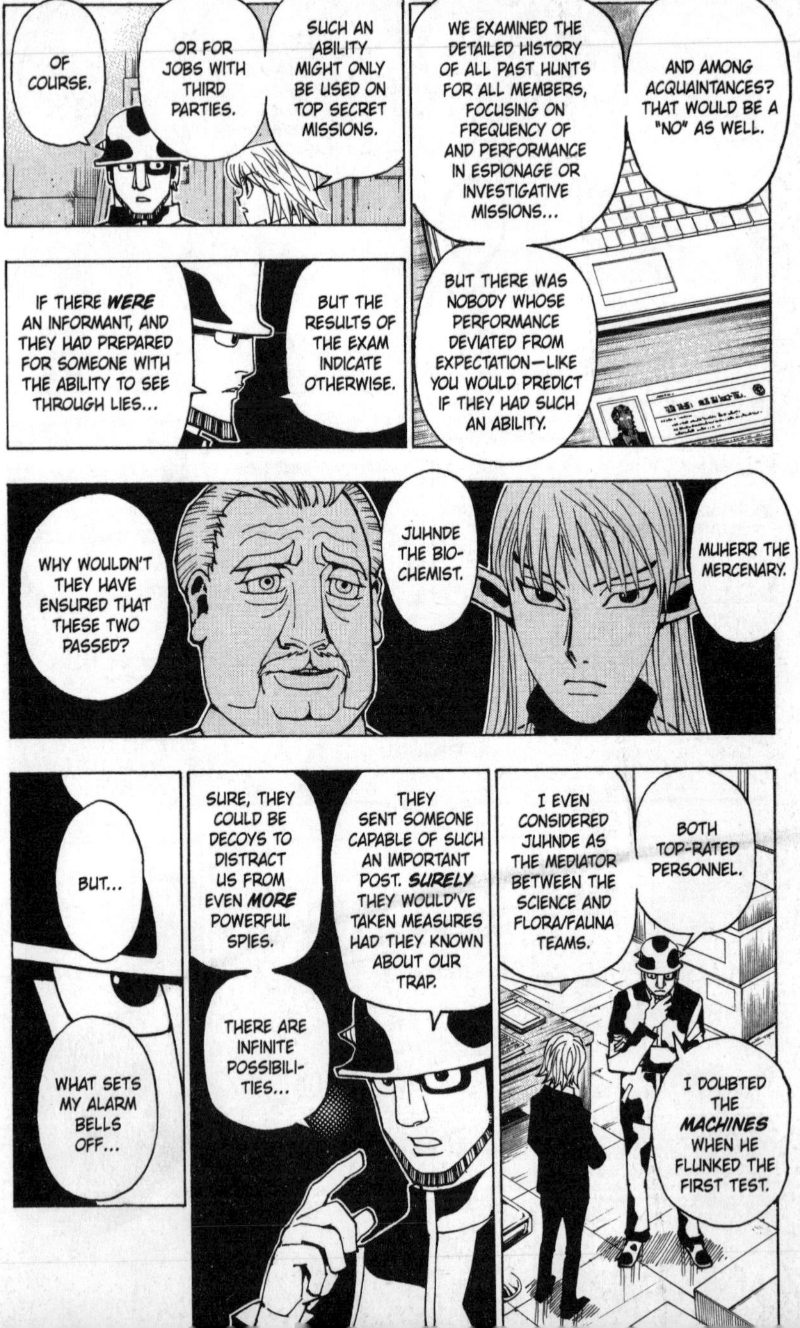
AND AMONG ACQUAINTANCES? THAT WOULD BE A "NO" AS WELL.
WE EXAMINED THE DETAILED HISTORY OF ALL PAST HUNTS FOR ALL MEMBERS, FOCUSING ON FREQUENCY OF AND PERFORMANCE IN ESPIONAGE OR INVESTIGATIVE MISSIONS...
BUT THERE WAS NOBODY WHOSE PERFORMANCE DEVIATED FROM EXPECTATION—LIKE YOU WOULD PREDICT IF THEY HAD SUCH AN ABILITY.
SUCH AN ABILITY MIGHT ONLY BE USED ON TOP SECRET MISSIONS.
OR FOR JOBS WITH THIRD PARTIES.
OF COURSE.
BUT THE RESULTS OF THE EXAM INDICATE OTHERWISE.
IF THERE WERE AN INFORMANT, AND THEY HAD PREPARED FOR SOMEONE WITH THE ABILITY TO SEE THROUGH LIES...
MUHERR THE MERCENARY.
JUHNDE THE BIO-CHEMIST.
WHY WOULDN'T THEY HAVE ENSURED THAT THESE TWO PASSED?
BOTH TOP-RATED PERSONNEL.
I EVEN CONSIDERED JUHNDE AS THE MEDIATOR BETWEEN THE SCIENCE AND FLORA/FAUNA TEAMS.
I DOUBTED THE MACHINES WHEN HE FLUNKED THE FIRST TEST.
THEY SENT SOMEONE CAPABLE OF SUCH AN IMPORTANT POST. SURELY THEY WOULD'VE TAKEN MEASURES HAD THEY KNOWN ABOUT OUR TRAP.
SURE, THEY COULD BE DECOYS TO DISTRACT US FROM EVEN MORE POWERFUL SPIES.
THERE ARE INFINITE POSSIBILI-TIES...
BUT...
WHAT SETS MY ALARM BELLS OFF...

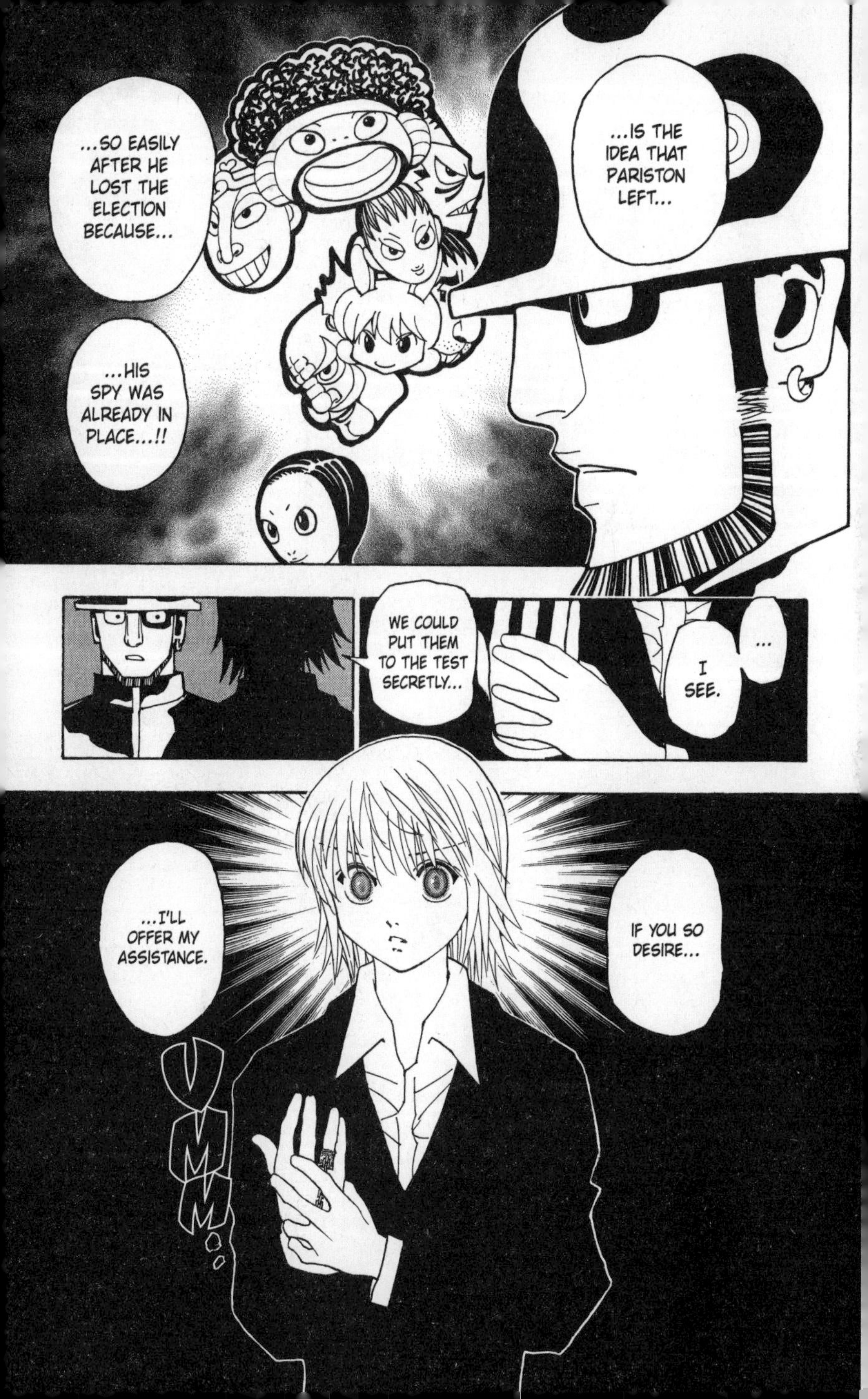
...IS THE IDEA THAT PARISTON LEFT...
...SO EASILY AFTER HE LOST THE ELECTION BECAUSE...
...HIS SPY WAS ALREADY IN PLACE...!!
... I SEE.
WE COULD PUT THEM TO THE TEST SECRETLY...
IF YOU SO DESIRE...
...I'LL OFFER MY ASSISTANCE.
UMMM

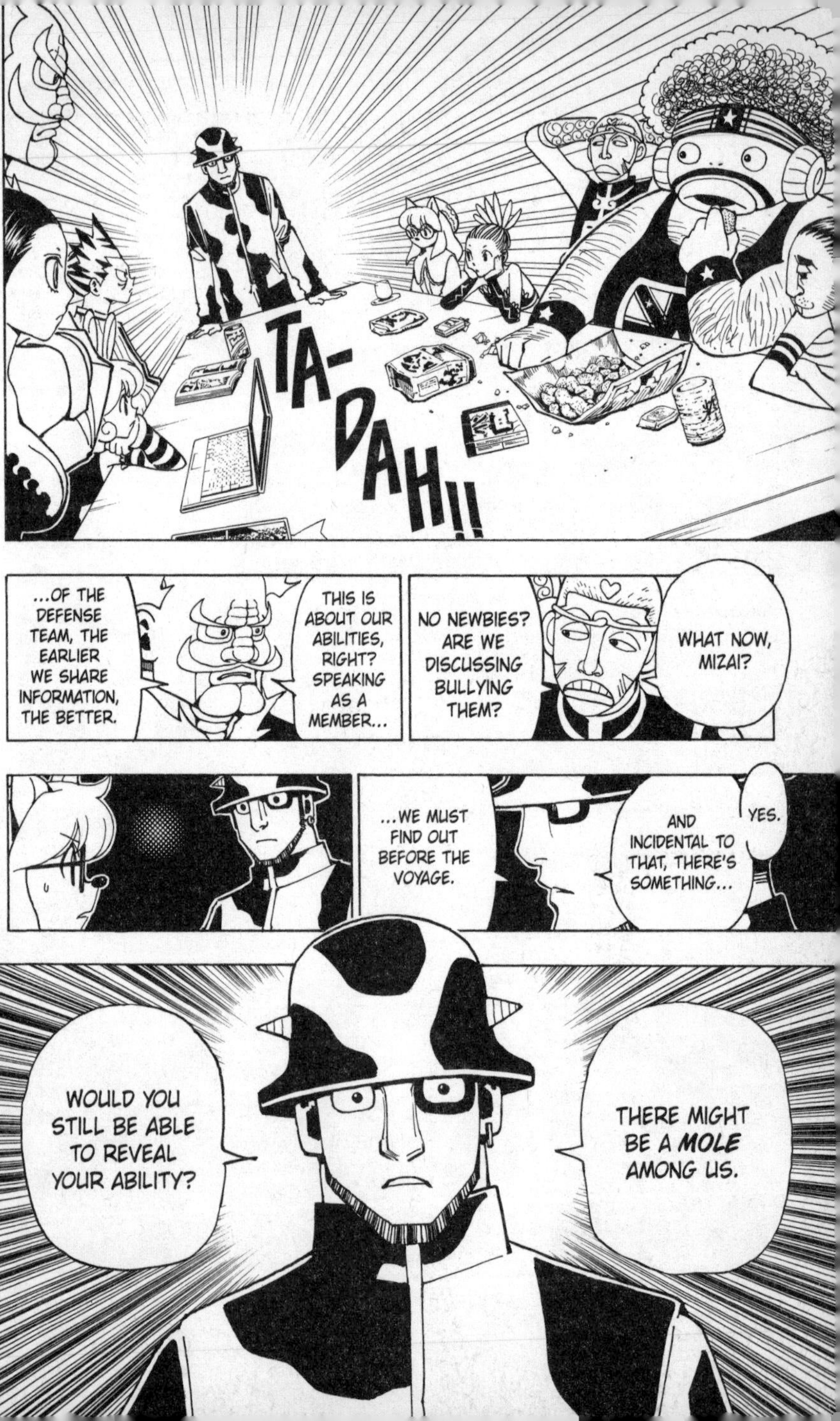
TA-DAH!!
WHAT NOW, MIZAI?
NO NEWBIES? ARE WE DISCUSSING BULLYING THEM?
THIS IS ABOUT OUR ABILITIES, RIGHT? SPEAKING AS A MEMBER...
...OF THE DEFENSE TEAM, THE EARLIER WE SHARE INFORMATION, THE BETTER.
YES.
AND INCIDENTAL TO THAT, THERE'S SOMETHING...
...WE MUST FIND OUT BEFORE THE VOYAGE.
THERE MIGHT BE A *MOLE* AMONG US.
WOULD YOU STILL BE ABLE TO REVEAL YOUR ABILITY?

READ THIS WAY

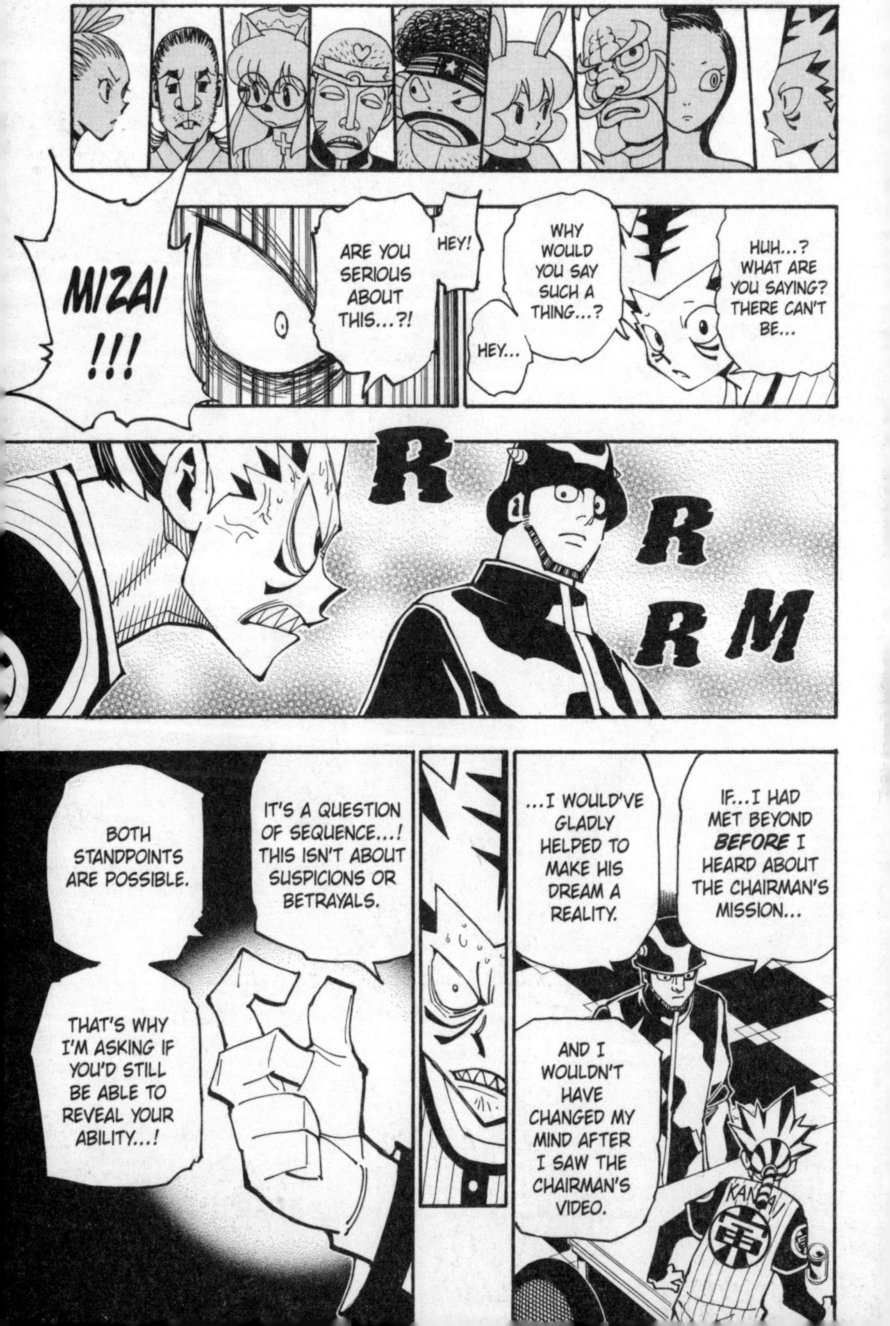
HUH...? WHAT ARE YOU SAYING? THERE CAN'T BE...
WHY WOULD YOU SAY SUCH A THING...?
HEY...
HEY!
ARE YOU SERIOUS ABOUT THIS...?!
MIZAI !!!
RRRM
IF...I HAD MET BEYOND *BEFORE* I HEARD ABOUT THE CHAIRMAN'S MISSION...
...I WOULD'VE GLADLY HELPED TO MAKE HIS DREAM A REALITY.
AND I WOULDN'T HAVE CHANGED MY MIND AFTER I SAW THE CHAIRMAN'S VIDEO.
IT'S A QUESTION OF SEQUENCE...! THIS ISN'T ABOUT SUSPICIONS OR BETRAYALS.
BOTH STANDPOINTS ARE POSSIBLE.
THAT'S WHY I'M ASKING IF YOU'D STILL BE ABLE TO REVEAL YOUR ABILITY...!

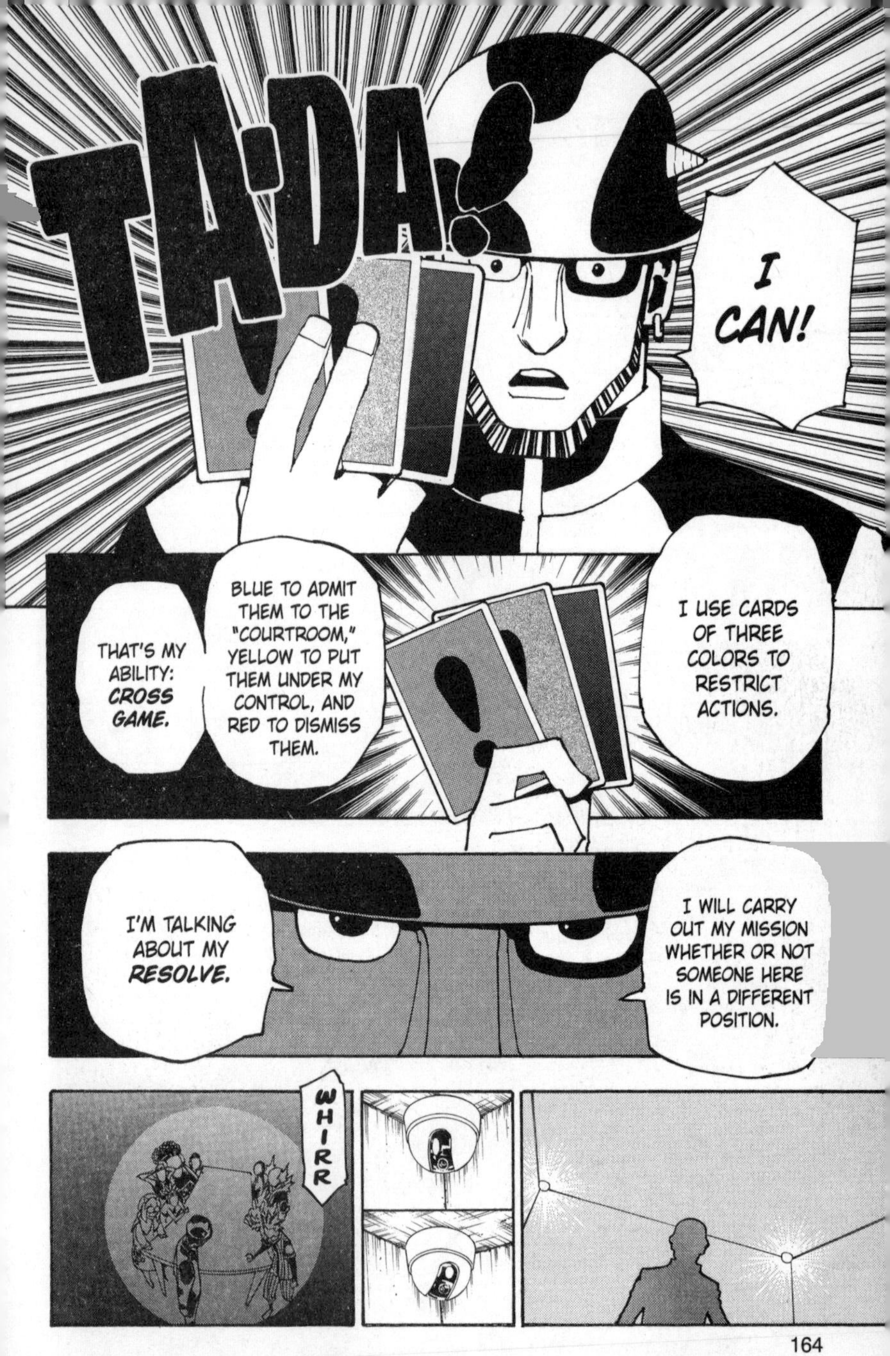
TA-DA!
I CAN!
I USE CARDS OF THREE COLORS TO RESTRICT ACTIONS.
BLUE TO ADMIT THEM TO THE "COURTROOM," YELLOW TO PUT THEM UNDER MY CONTROL, AND RED TO DISMISS THEM.
THAT'S MY ABILITY: *CROSS GAME.*
I WILL CARRY OUT MY MISSION WHETHER OR NOT SOMEONE HERE IS IN A DIFFERENT POSITION.
I'M TALKING ABOUT MY *RESOLVE.*
WHIRR

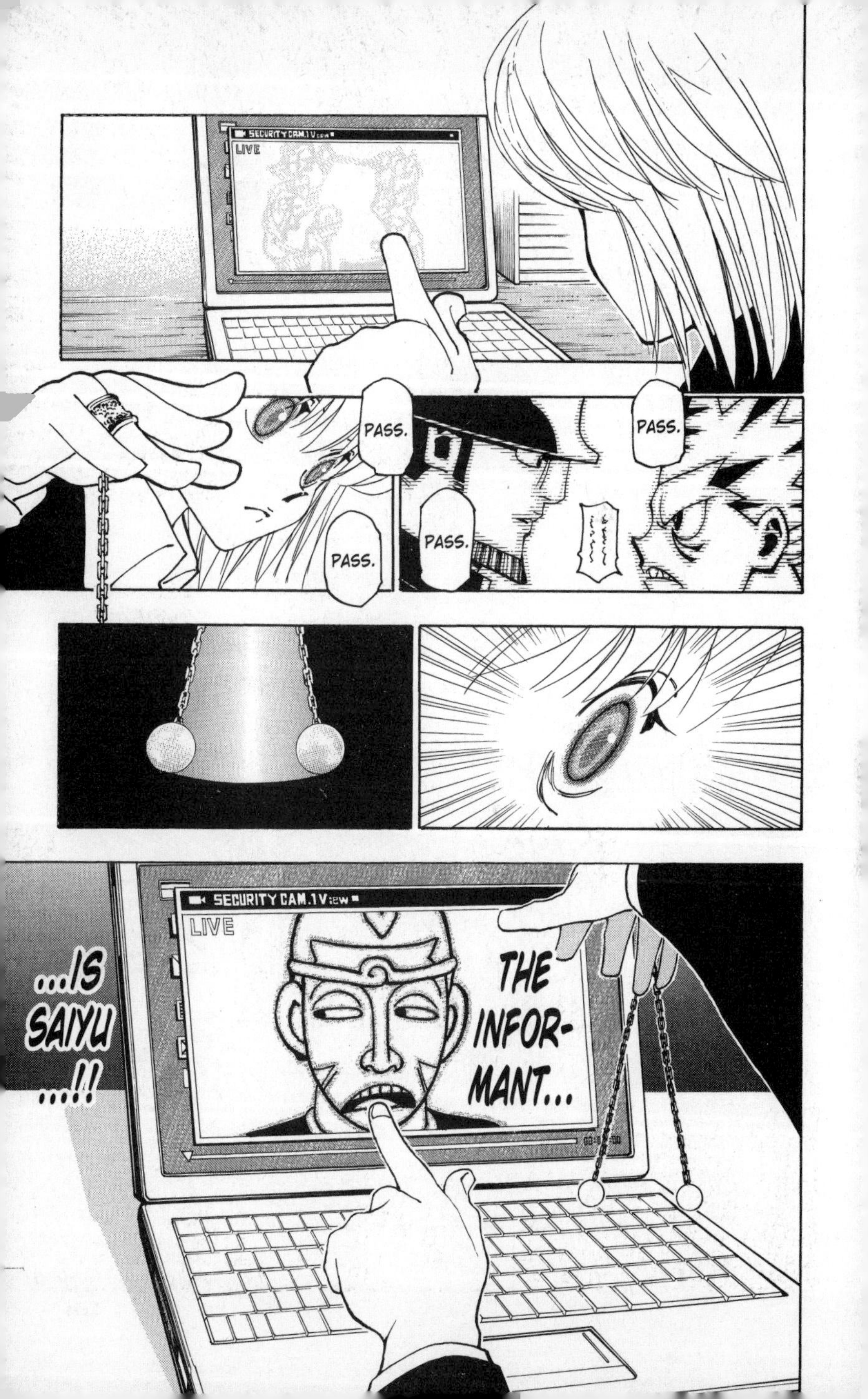
SECURITY CAM.1V
LIVE
PASS.
PASS.
PASS.
PASS.
SECURITY CAM.1V
LIVE
THE INFORMANT...
...IS SAIYU ...!!

NOT
RECKLESS?

NOT THAT
KIND OF
"CRAZY."

THE AWESOME
KIND OF CRAZY.

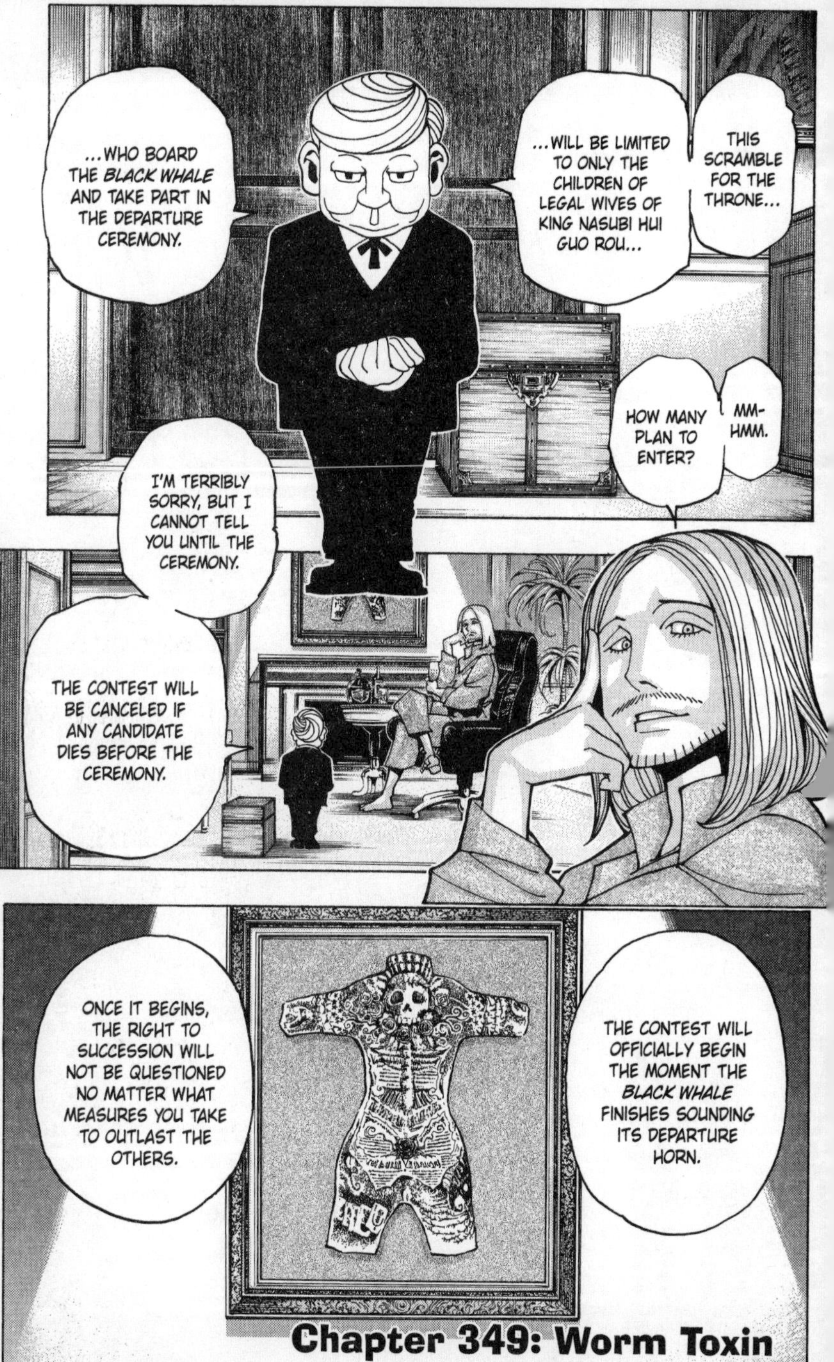
THIS SCRAMBLE FOR THE THRONE...
...WILL BE LIMITED TO ONLY THE CHILDREN OF LEGAL WIVES OF KING NASUBI HUI GUO ROU...
...WHO BOARD THE *BLACK WHALE* AND TAKE PART IN THE DEPARTURE CEREMONY.
MM-HMM.
HOW MANY PLAN TO ENTER?
I'M TERRIBLY SORRY, BUT I CANNOT TELL YOU UNTIL THE CEREMONY.
THE CONTEST WILL BE CANCELED IF ANY CANDIDATE DIES BEFORE THE CEREMONY.
THE CONTEST WILL OFFICIALLY BEGIN THE MOMENT THE *BLACK WHALE* FINISHES SOUNDING ITS DEPARTURE HORN.
ONCE IT BEGINS, THE RIGHT TO SUCCESSION WILL NOT BE QUESTIONED NO MATTER WHAT MEASURES YOU TAKE TO OUTLAST THE OTHERS.
Chapter 349: Worm Toxin

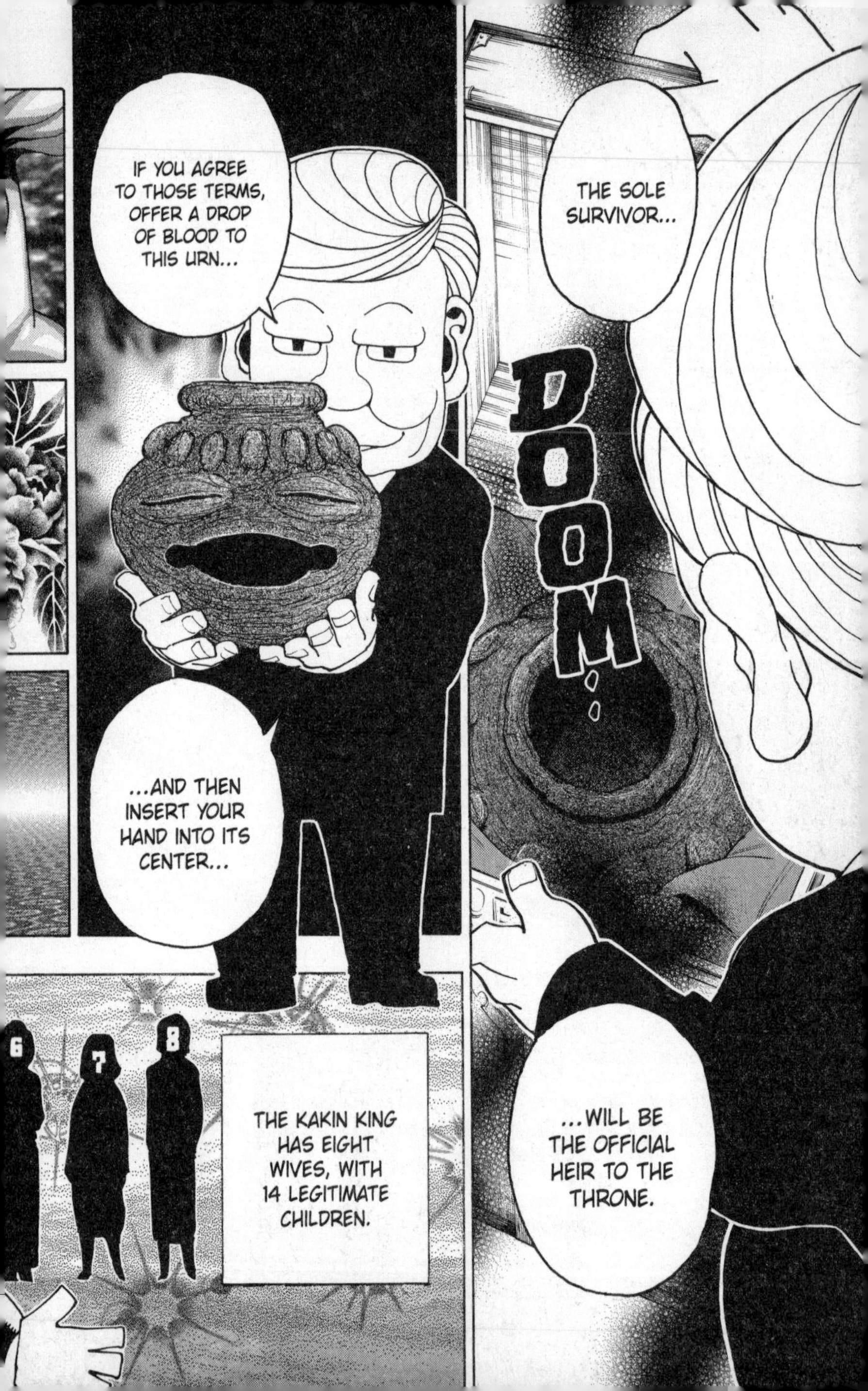
THE SOLE SURVIVOR...
DOOM
...WILL BE THE OFFICIAL HEIR TO THE THRONE.
IF YOU AGREE TO THOSE TERMS, OFFER A DROP OF BLOOD TO THIS URN...
...AND THEN INSERT YOUR HAND INTO ITS CENTER...
THE KAKIN KING HAS EIGHT WIVES, WITH 14 LEGITIMATE CHILDREN.
8
7
6

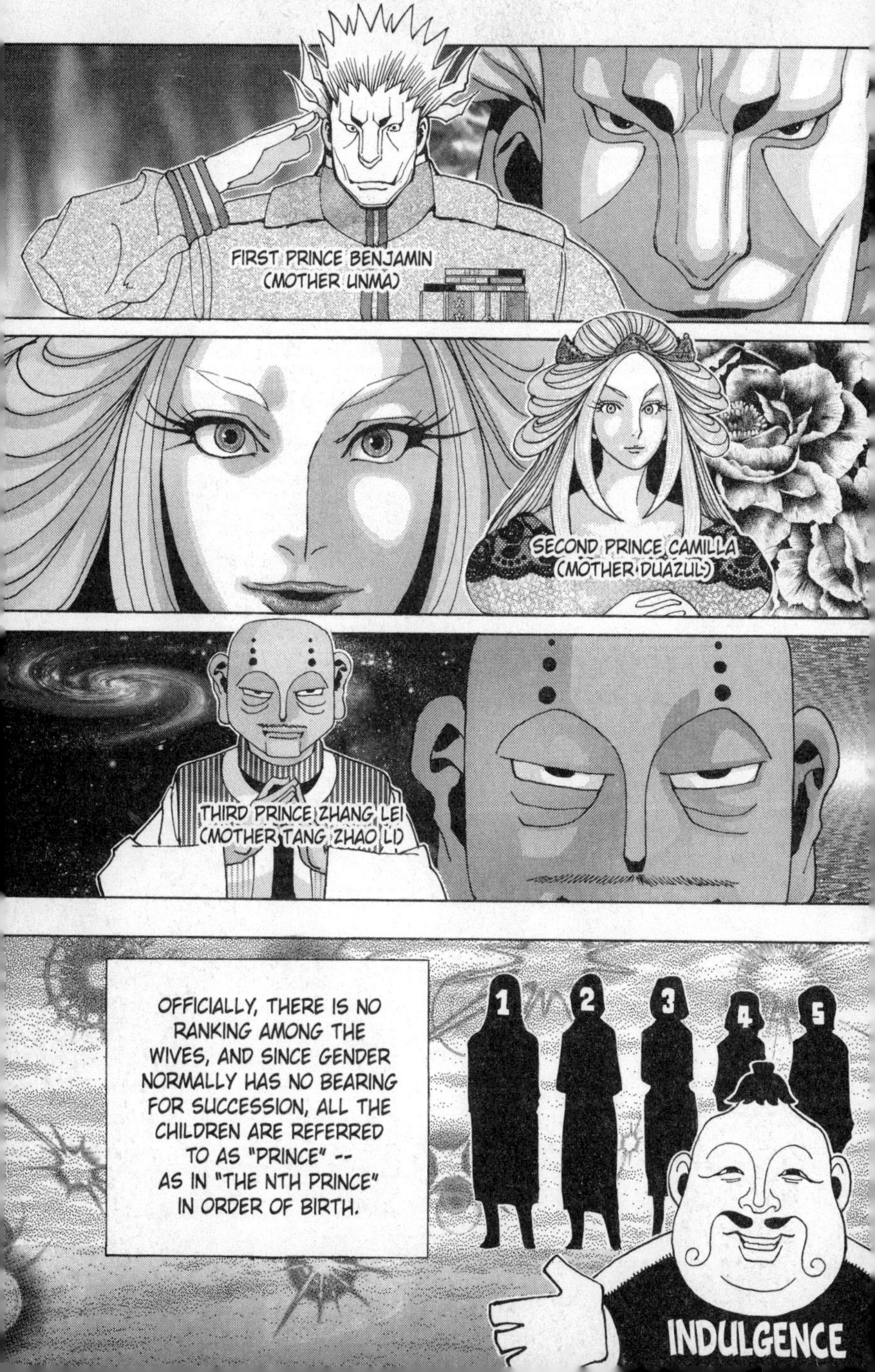
FIRST PRINCE BENJAMIN (MOTHER UNMA)
SECOND PRINCE CAMILLA (MOTHER DUAZUL)
THIRD PRINCE ZHANG LEI (MOTHER TANG ZHAO LI)
OFFICIALLY, THERE IS NO RANKING AMONG THE WIVES, AND SINCE GENDER NORMALLY HAS NO BEARING FOR SUCCESSION, ALL THE CHILDREN ARE REFERRED TO AS "PRINCE" -- AS IN "THE NTH PRINCE" IN ORDER OF BIRTH.
1
2
3
4
5
INDULGENCE

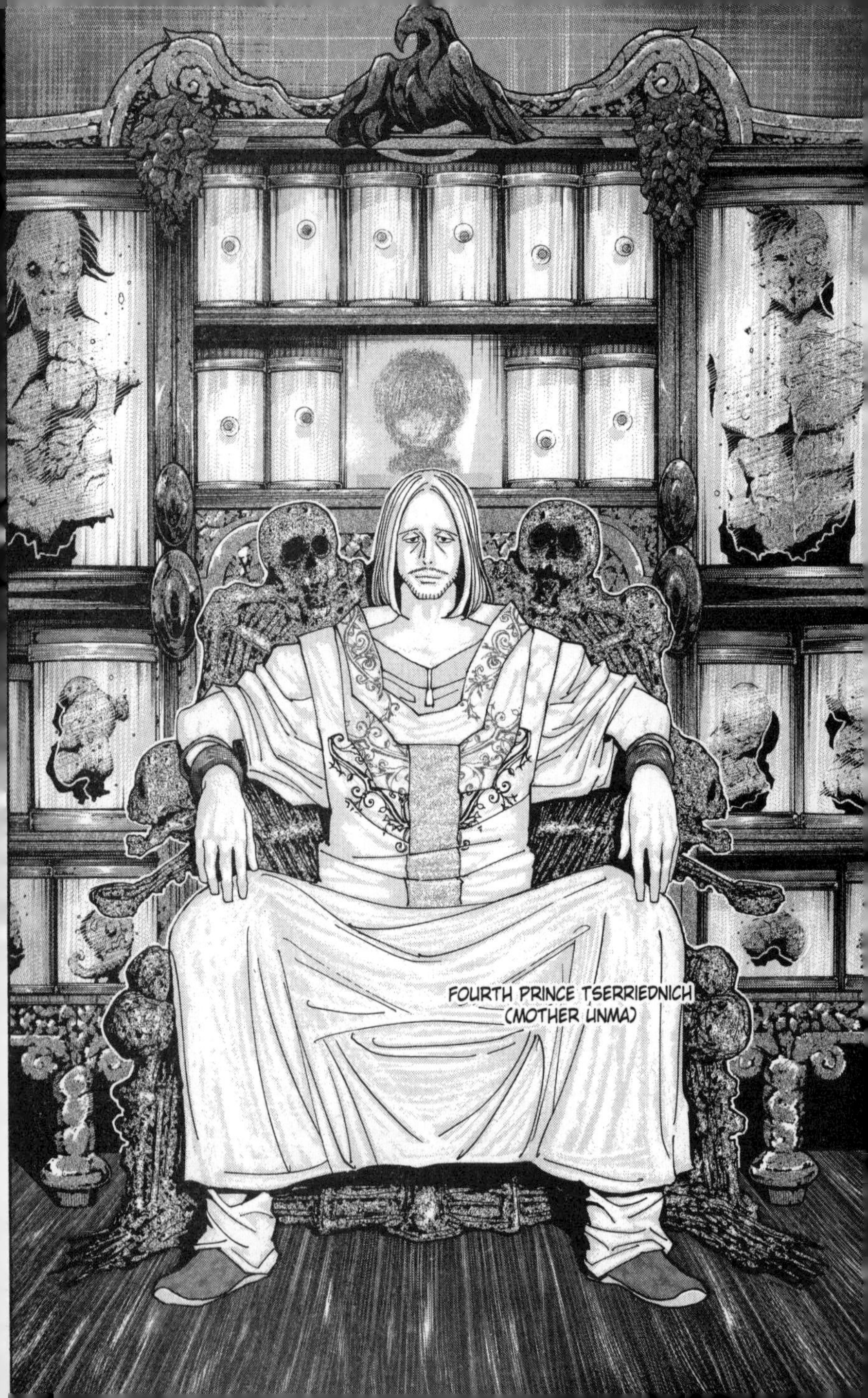
FOURTH PRINCE TSERRIEDNICH
(MOTHER UNMA)

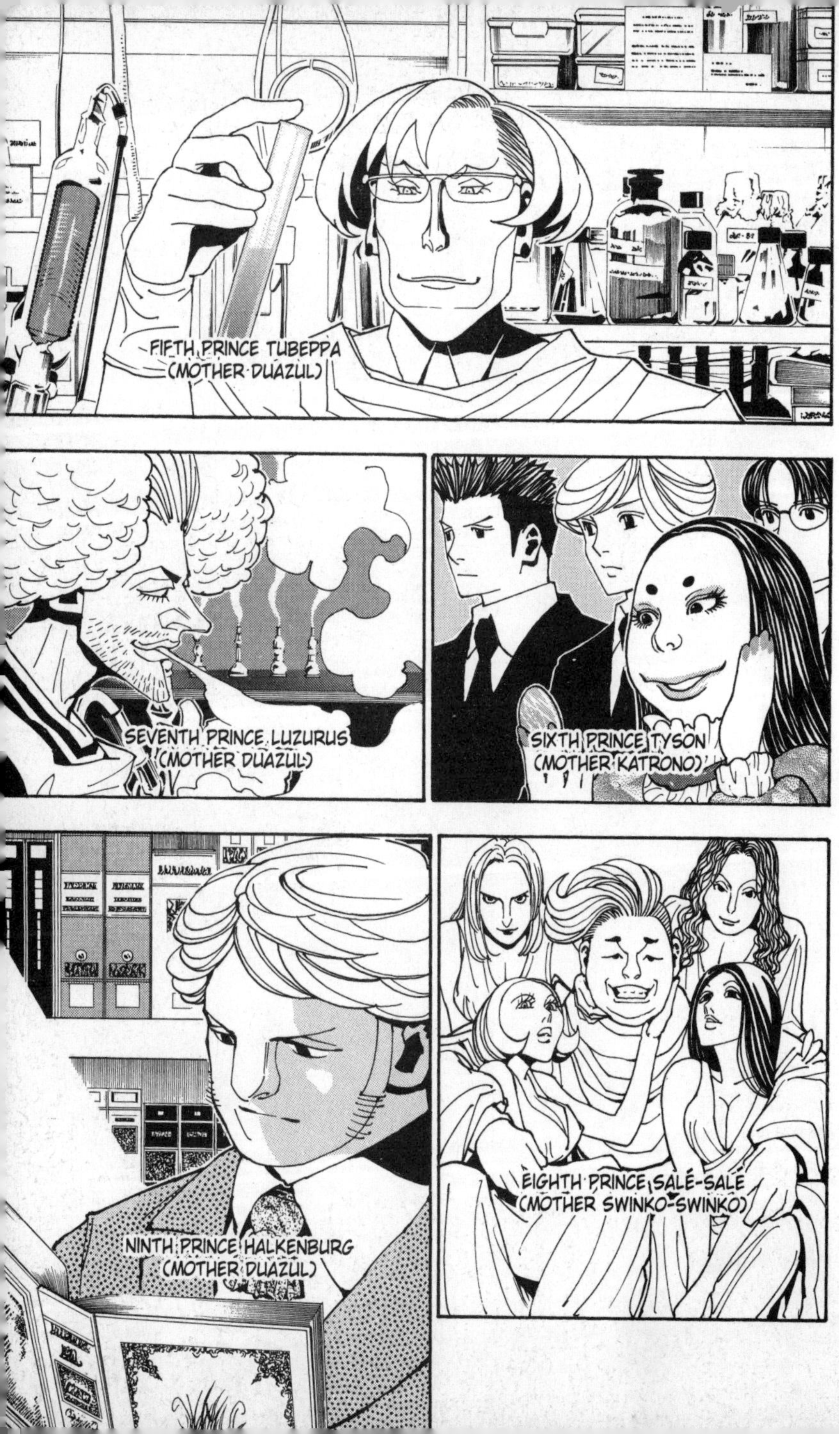
FIFTH PRINCE TUBEPPA
(MOTHER DUAZUL)
SIXTH PRINCE TYSON
(MOTHER KATRONO)
SEVENTH PRINCE LUZURUS
(MOTHER DUAZUL)
EIGHTH PRINCE SALÉ-SALÉ
(MOTHER SWINKO-SWINKO)
NINTH PRINCE HALKENBURG
(MOTHER DUAZUL)

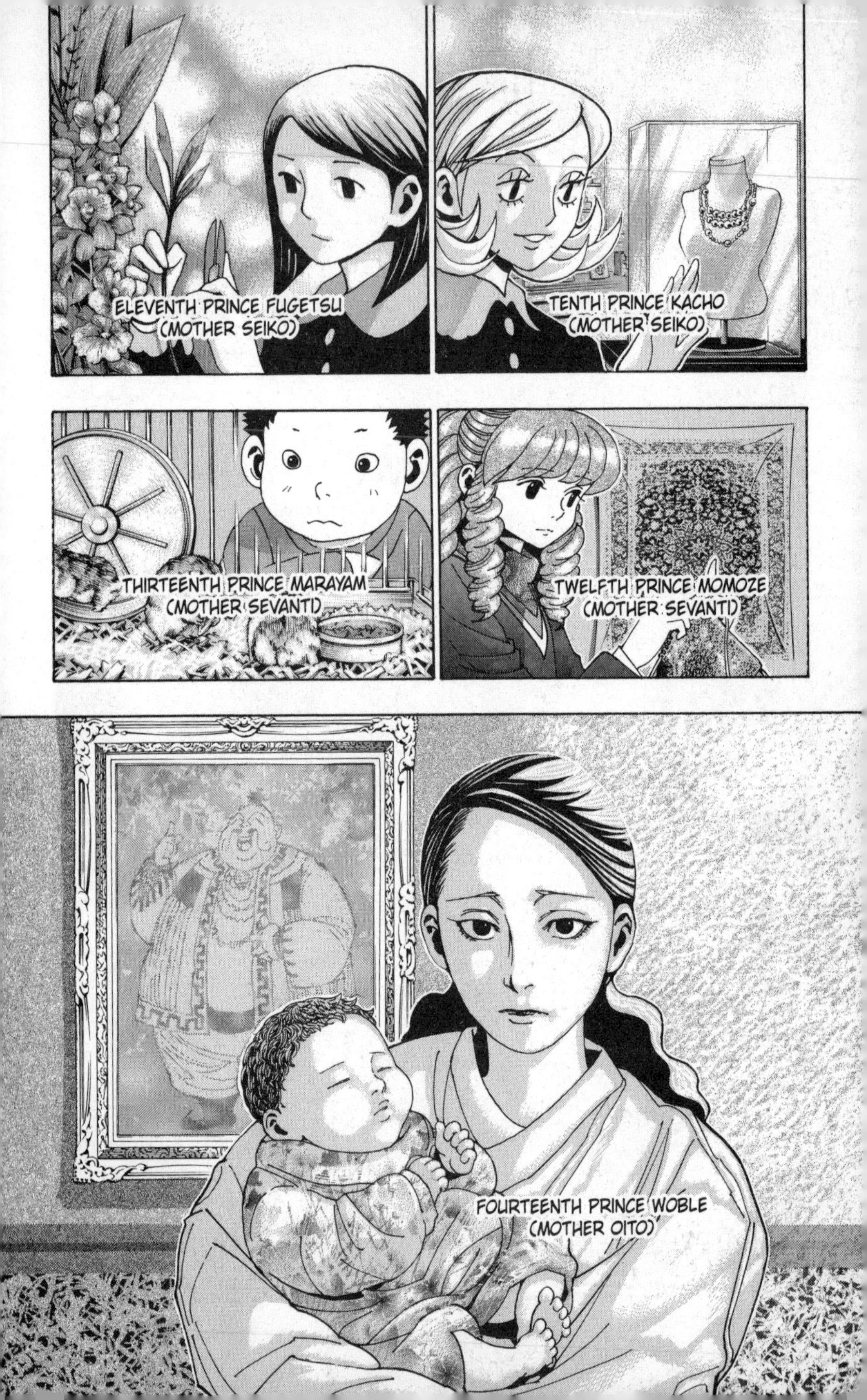
TENTH PRINCE KACHO
(MOTHER SEIKO)
ELEVENTH PRINCE FUGETSU
(MOTHER SEIKO)
TWELFTH PRINCE MOMOZE
(MOTHER SEVANTI)
THIRTEENTH PRINCE MARAYAM
(MOTHER SEVANTI)
FOURTEENTH PRINCE WOBLE
(MOTHER OITO)

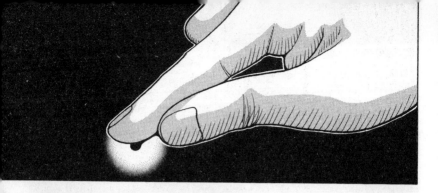

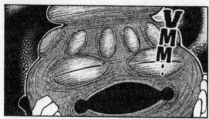

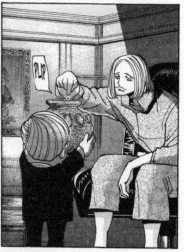

PLIP
VMM...
NOW PLEASE INSERT YOUR HAND...
...INTO THE CENTER OF THE URN.
IT'S NOT GOING TO BITE ME, IS IT?
NOT TO WORRY.
VMMM

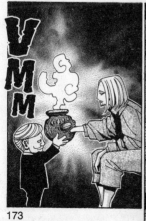

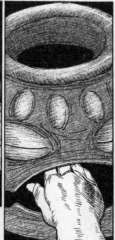

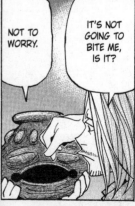

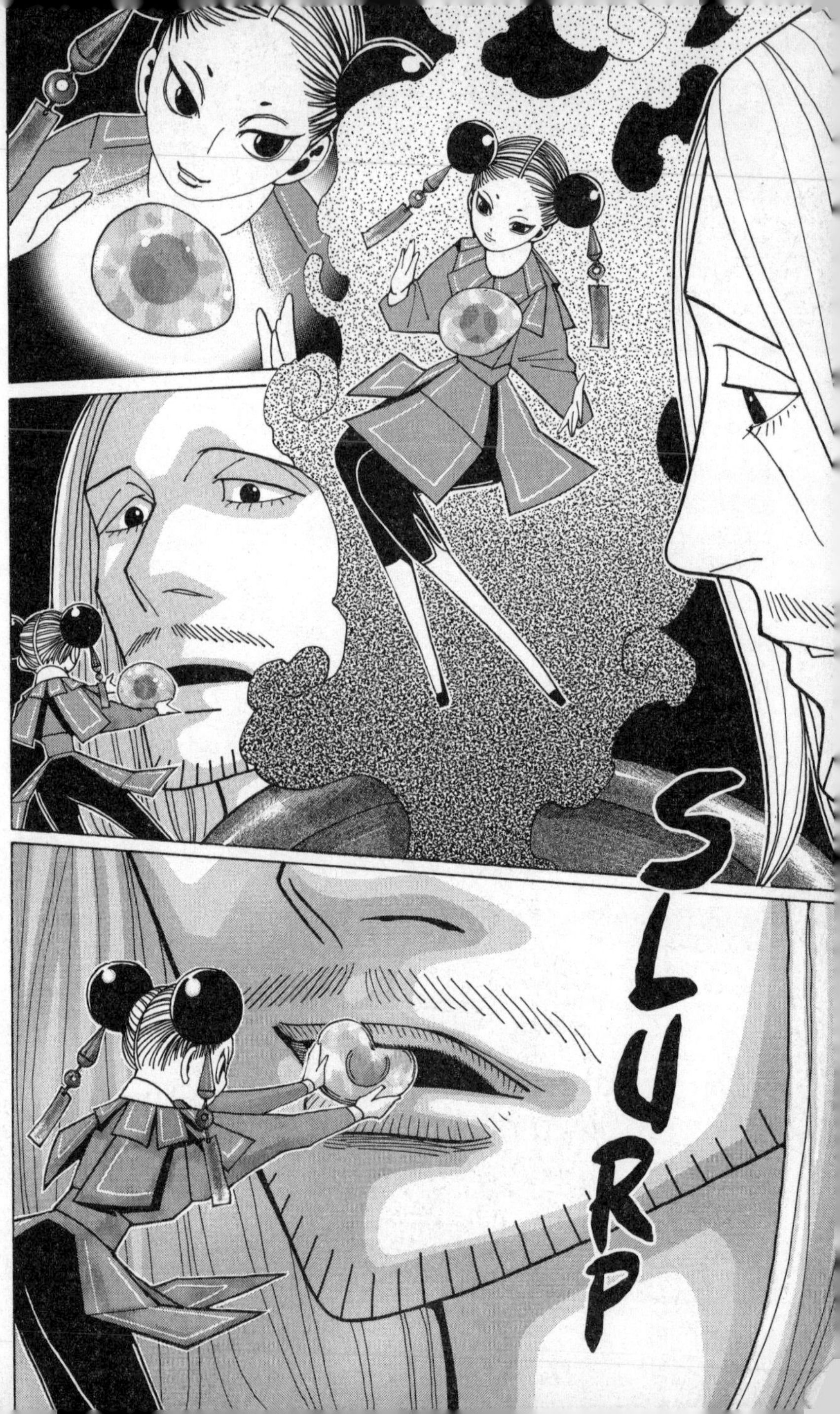
SLURP

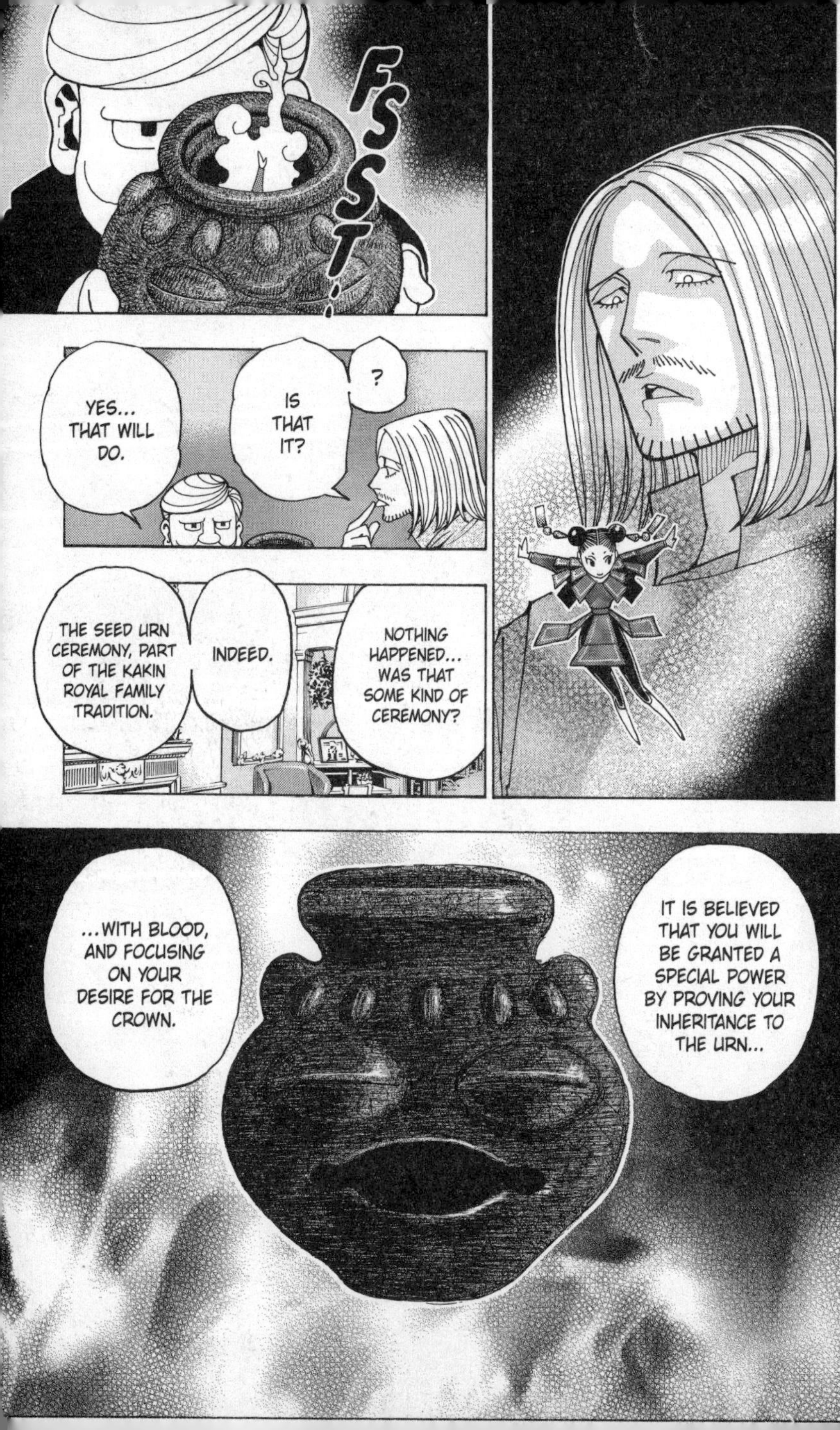
FSST...
?
IS THAT IT?
YES... THAT WILL DO.
NOTHING HAPPENED... WAS THAT SOME KIND OF CEREMONY?
INDEED.
THE SEED URN CEREMONY, PART OF THE KAKIN ROYAL FAMILY TRADITION.
IT IS BELIEVED THAT YOU WILL BE GRANTED A SPECIAL POWER BY PROVING YOUR INHERITANCE TO THE URN...
...WITH BLOOD, AND FOCUSING ON YOUR DESIRE FOR THE CROWN.

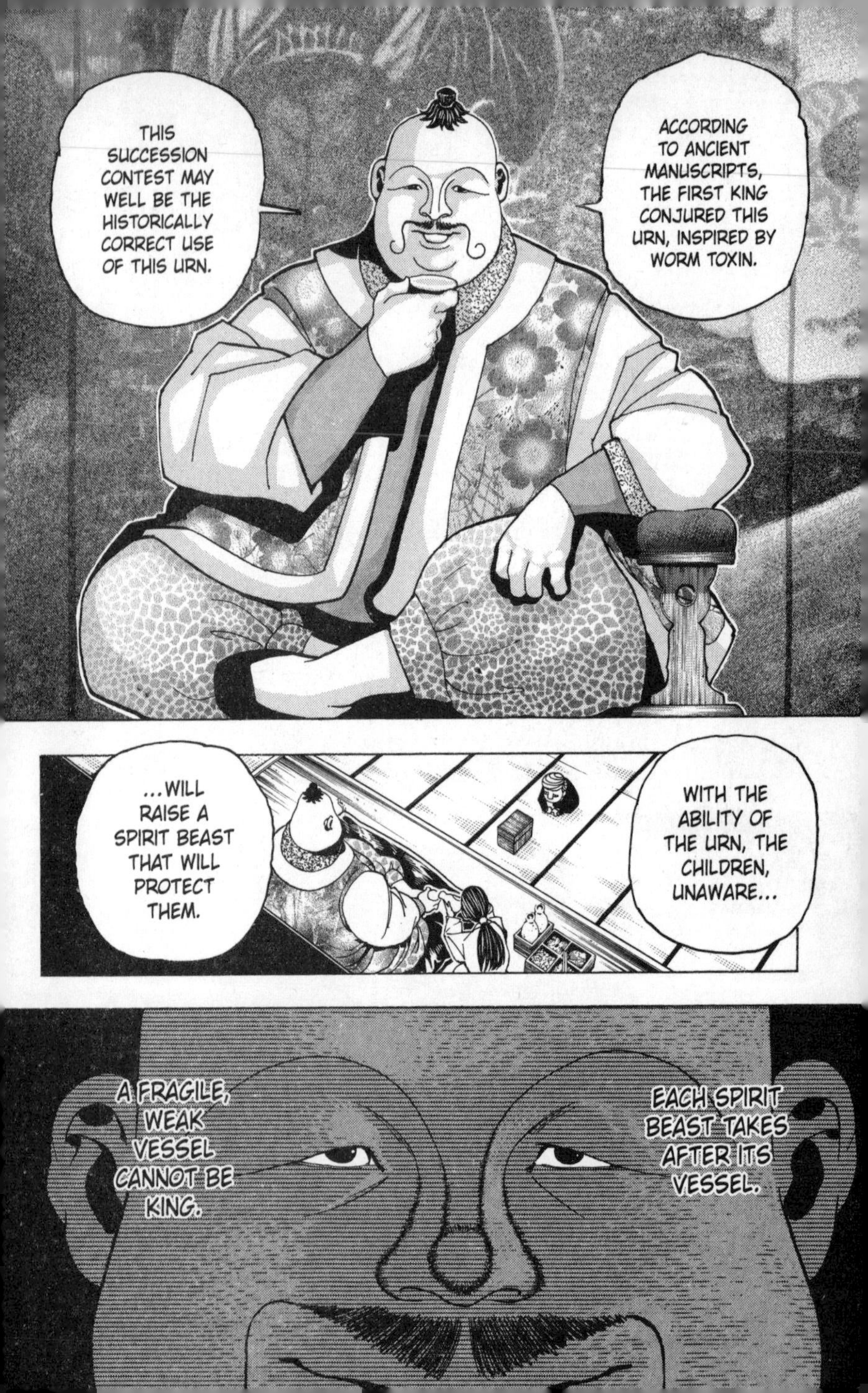
ACCORDING TO ANCIENT MANUSCRIPTS, THE FIRST KING CONJURED THIS URN, INSPIRED BY WORM TOXIN.
THIS SUCCESSION CONTEST MAY WELL BE THE HISTORICALLY CORRECT USE OF THIS URN.
WITH THE ABILITY OF THE URN, THE CHILDREN, UNAWARE...
...WILL RAISE A SPIRIT BEAST THAT WILL PROTECT THEM.
EACH SPIRIT BEAST TAKES AFTER ITS VESSEL.
A FRAGILE, WEAK VESSEL CANNOT BE KING.

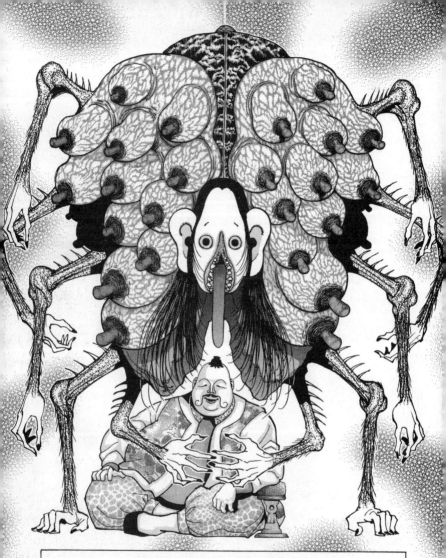

GUARDIAN SPIRIT BEAST

A NEN BEAST CREATED AT THE TIME OF DEATH BY THE POWERFUL DESIRE FOR THE PERPETUATION OF ONE'S DESCENDANTS. POSSESSES SOMEONE CLOSELY RELATED TO THE DEAD, FEEDS ON HIS AURA, AND METAMORPHOSES INTO A FORM AND ABILITY INFLUENCED BY HIS DISPOSITION. HOWEVER, SINCE IT WAS NOT HIS DIRECT CREATION, IT CANNOT BE MANIPULATED AT WILL.

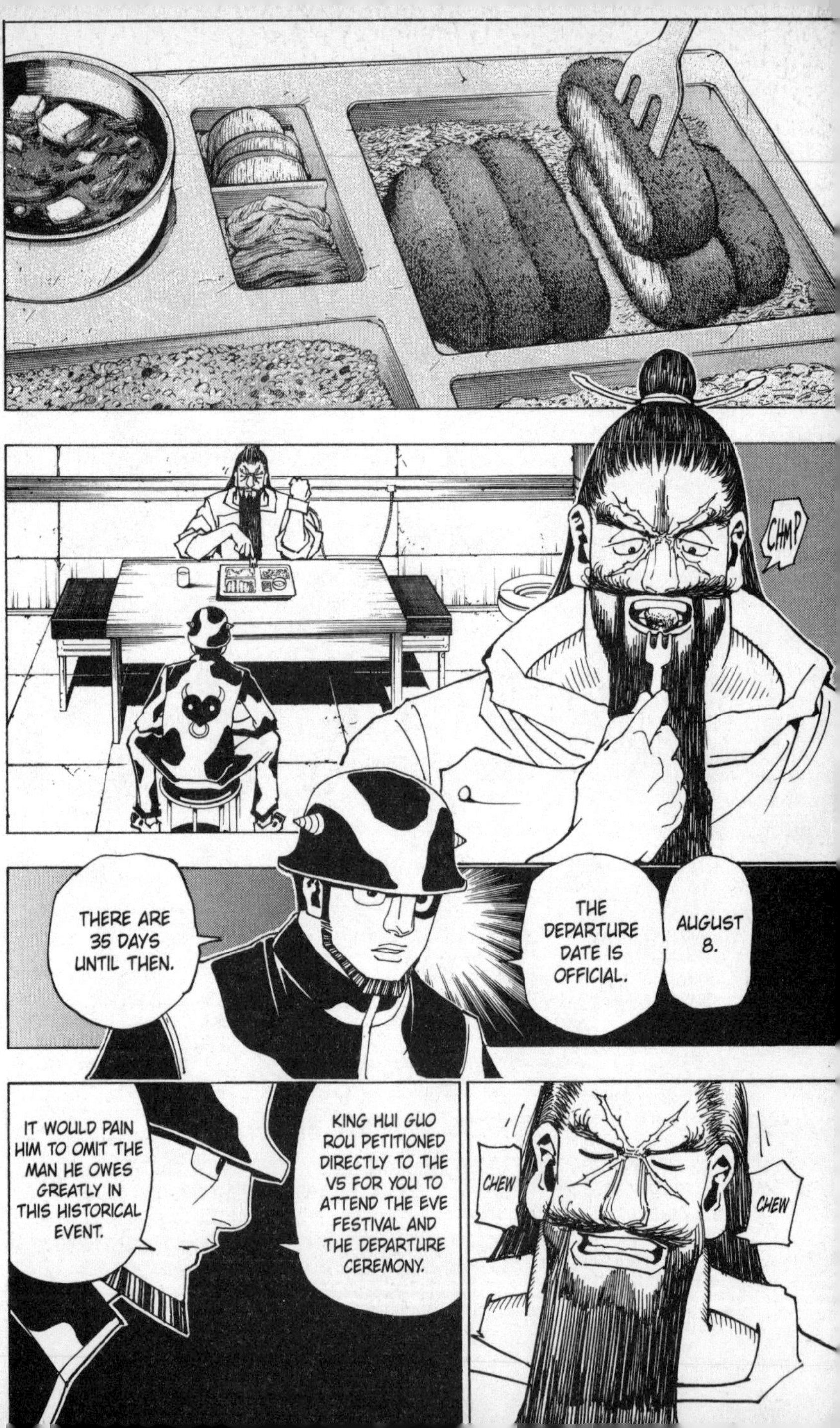
CHMP
AUGUST 8.
THE DEPARTURE DATE IS OFFICIAL.
THERE ARE 35 DAYS UNTIL THEN.
CHEW
CHEW
KING HUI GUO ROU PETITIONED DIRECTLY TO THE V5 FOR YOU TO ATTEND THE EVE FESTIVAL AND THE DEPARTURE CEREMONY.
IT WOULD PAIN HIM TO OMIT THE MAN HE OWES GREATLY IN THIS HISTORICAL EVENT.

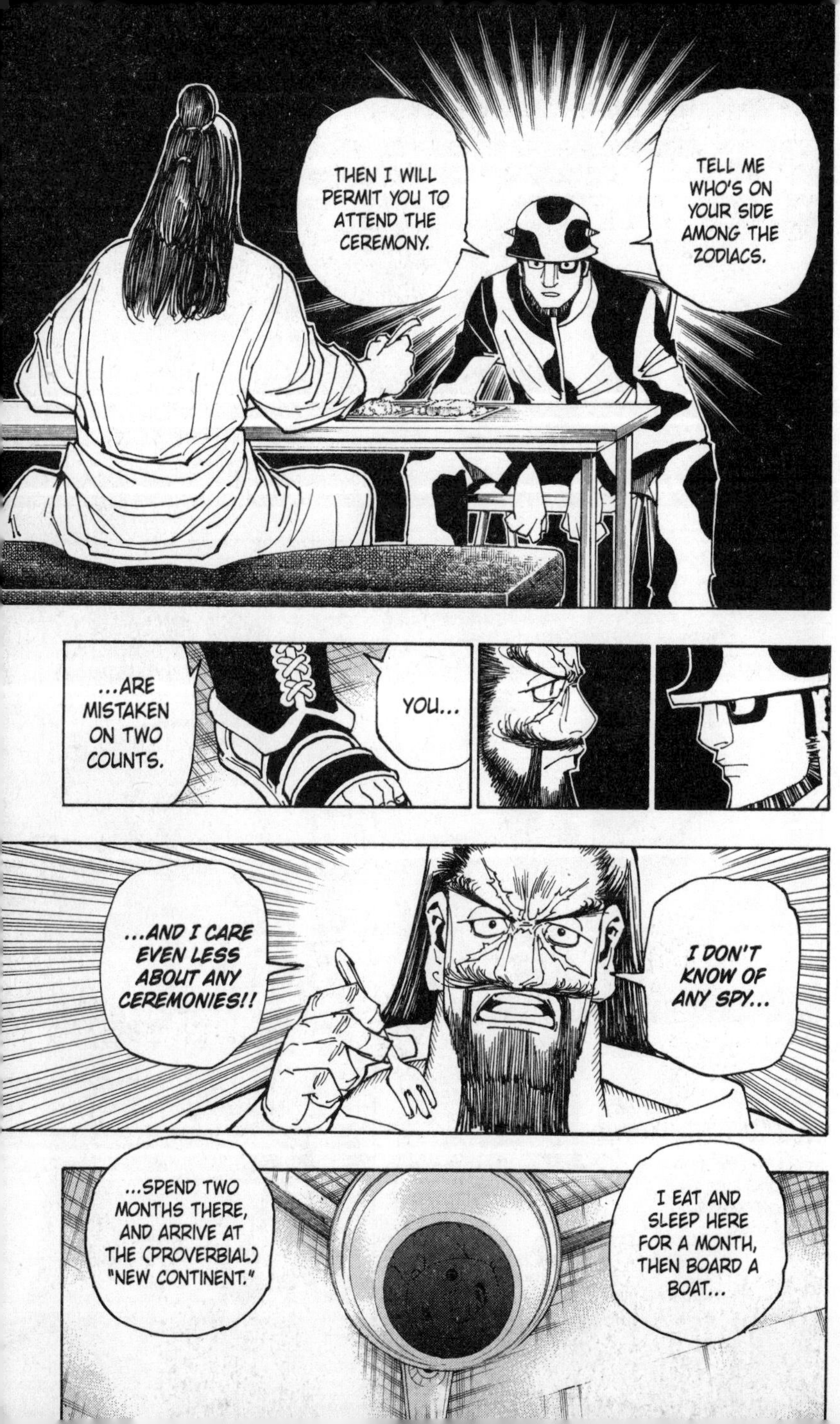
TELL ME WHO'S ON YOUR SIDE AMONG THE ZODIACS.
THEN I WILL PERMIT YOU TO ATTEND THE CEREMONY.
YOU...
...ARE MISTAKEN ON TWO COUNTS.
I DON'T KNOW OF ANY SPY...
...AND I CARE EVEN LESS ABOUT ANY CEREMONIES!!
I EAT AND SLEEP HERE FOR A MONTH, THEN BOARD A BOAT...
...SPEND TWO MONTHS THERE, AND ARRIVE AT THE (PROVERBIAL) "NEW CONTINENT."

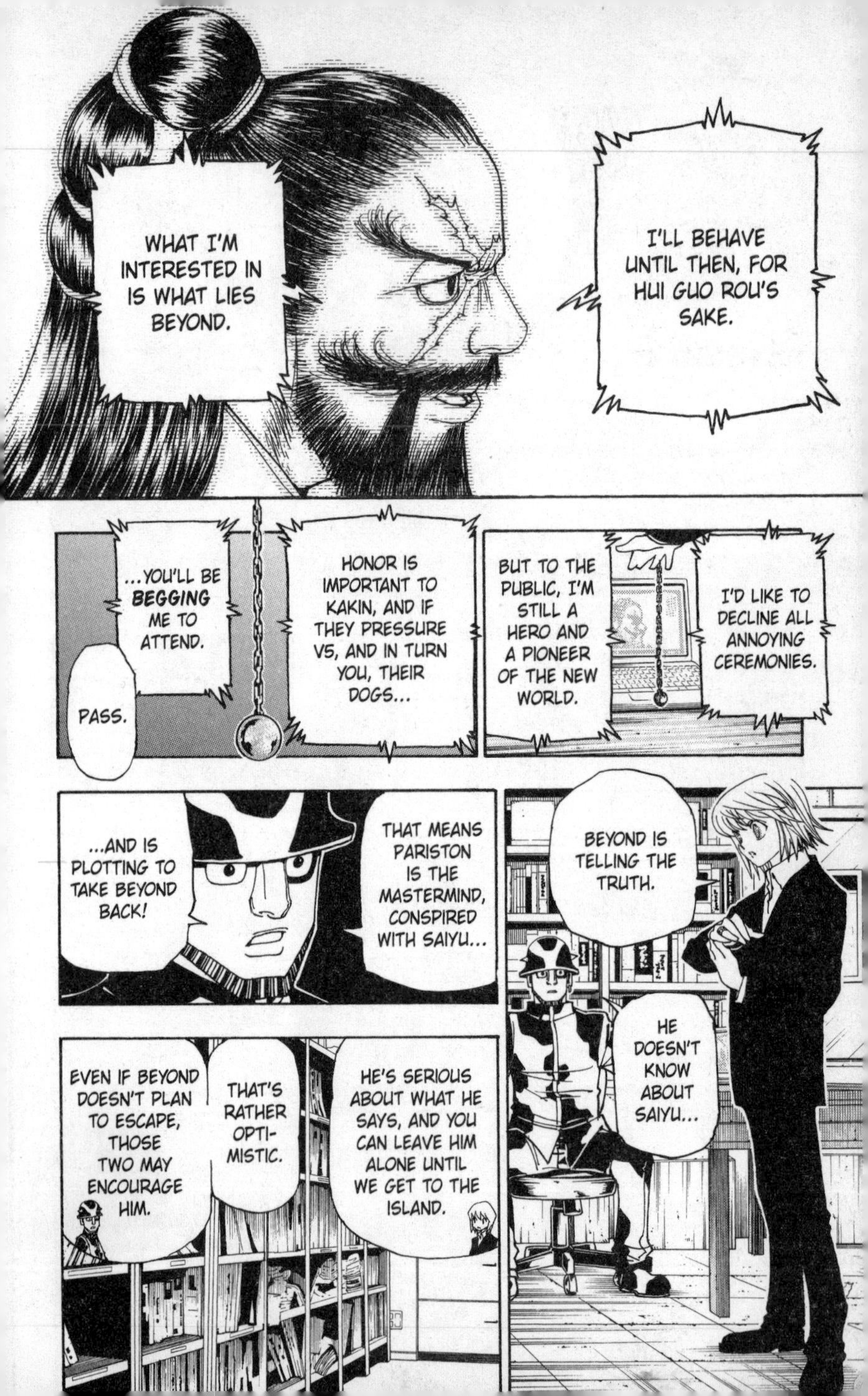
I'LL BEHAVE UNTIL THEN, FOR HUI GUO ROU'S SAKE.
WHAT I'M INTERESTED IN IS WHAT LIES BEYOND.
I'D LIKE TO DECLINE ALL ANNOYING CEREMONIES.
BUT TO THE PUBLIC, I'M STILL A HERO AND A PIONEER OF THE NEW WORLD.
HONOR IS IMPORTANT TO KAKIN, AND IF THEY PRESSURE V5, AND IN TURN YOU, THEIR DOGS...
...YOU'LL BE **BEGGING** ME TO ATTEND.
PASS.
BEYOND IS TELLING THE TRUTH.
HE DOESN'T KNOW ABOUT SAIYU...
THAT MEANS PARISTON IS THE MASTERMIND, CONSPIRED WITH SAIYU...
...AND IS PLOTTING TO TAKE BEYOND BACK!
HE'S SERIOUS ABOUT WHAT HE SAYS, AND YOU CAN LEAVE HIM ALONE UNTIL WE GET TO THE ISLAND.
THAT'S RATHER OPTI-MISTIC.
EVEN IF BEYOND DOESN'T PLAN TO ESCAPE, THOSE TWO MAY ENCOURAGE HIM.

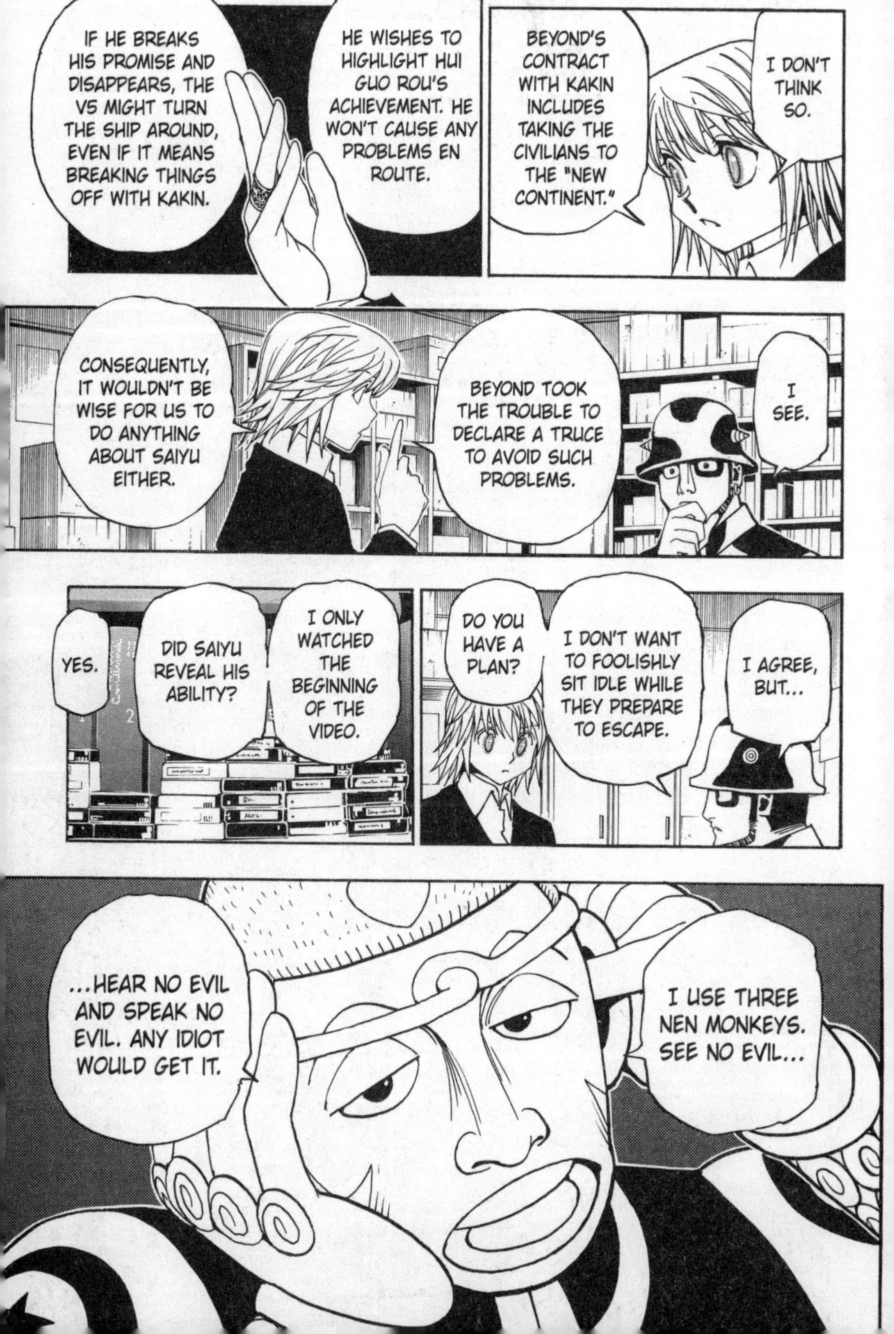
I DON'T THINK SO.
BEYOND'S CONTRACT WITH KAKIN INCLUDES TAKING THE CIVILIANS TO THE "NEW CONTINENT."
HE WISHES TO HIGHLIGHT HUI GUO ROU'S ACHIEVEMENT. HE WON'T CAUSE ANY PROBLEMS EN ROUTE.
IF HE BREAKS HIS PROMISE AND DISAPPEARS, THE V5 MIGHT TURN THE SHIP AROUND, EVEN IF IT MEANS BREAKING THINGS OFF WITH KAKIN.
I SEE.
BEYOND TOOK THE TROUBLE TO DECLARE A TRUCE TO AVOID SUCH PROBLEMS.
CONSEQUENTLY, IT WOULDN'T BE WISE FOR US TO DO ANYTHING ABOUT SAIYU EITHER.
I AGREE, BUT...
I DON'T WANT TO FOOLISHLY SIT IDLE WHILE THEY PREPARE TO ESCAPE.
DO YOU HAVE A PLAN?
I ONLY WATCHED THE BEGINNING OF THE VIDEO.
DID SAIYU REVEAL HIS ABILITY?
YES.
I USE THREE NEN MONKEYS. SEE NO EVIL...
...HEAR NO EVIL AND SPEAK NO EVIL. ANY IDIOT WOULD GET IT.

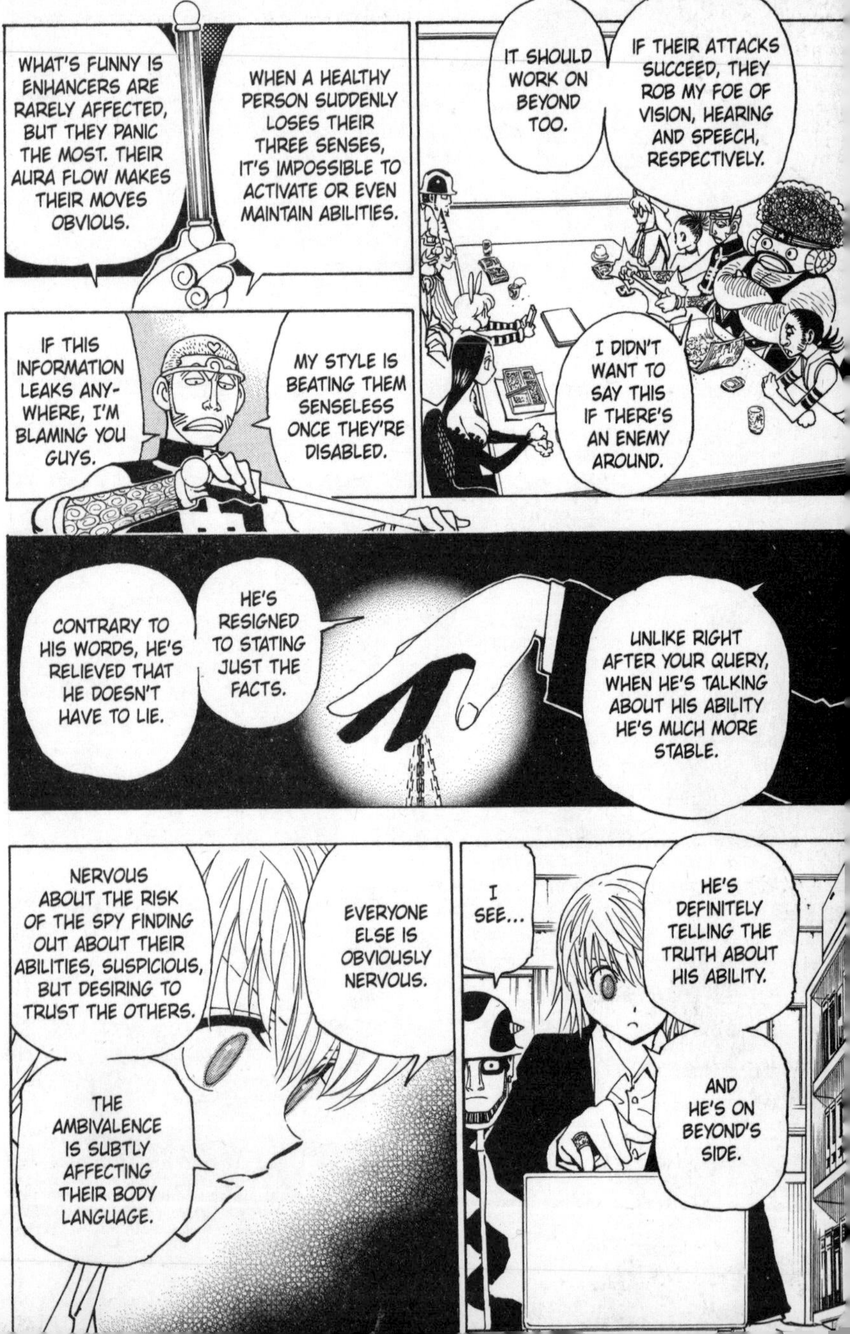
IF THEIR ATTACKS SUCCEED, THEY ROB MY FOE OF VISION, HEARING AND SPEECH, RESPECTIVELY.
IT SHOULD WORK ON BEYOND TOO.
I DIDN'T WANT TO SAY THIS IF THERE'S AN ENEMY AROUND.
WHEN A HEALTHY PERSON SUDDENLY LOSES THEIR THREE SENSES, IT'S IMPOSSIBLE TO ACTIVATE OR EVEN MAINTAIN ABILITIES.
WHAT'S FUNNY IS ENHANCERS ARE RARELY AFFECTED, BUT THEY PANIC THE MOST. THEIR AURA FLOW MAKES THEIR MOVES OBVIOUS.
MY STYLE IS BEATING THEM SENSELESS ONCE THEY'RE DISABLED.
IF THIS INFORMATION LEAKS ANYWHERE, I'M BLAMING YOU GUYS.
UNLIKE RIGHT AFTER YOUR QUERY, WHEN HE'S TALKING ABOUT HIS ABILITY HE'S MUCH MORE STABLE.
HE'S RESIGNED TO STATING JUST THE FACTS.
CONTRARY TO HIS WORDS, HE'S RELIEVED THAT HE DOESN'T HAVE TO LIE.
HE'S DEFINITELY TELLING THE TRUTH ABOUT HIS ABILITY.
I SEE...
AND HE'S ON BEYOND'S SIDE.
EVERYONE ELSE IS OBVIOUSLY NERVOUS.
NERVOUS ABOUT THE RISK OF THE SPY FINDING OUT ABOUT THEIR ABILITIES, SUSPICIOUS, BUT DESIRING TO TRUST THE OTHERS.
THE AMBIVALENCE IS SUBTLY AFFECTING THEIR BODY LANGUAGE.

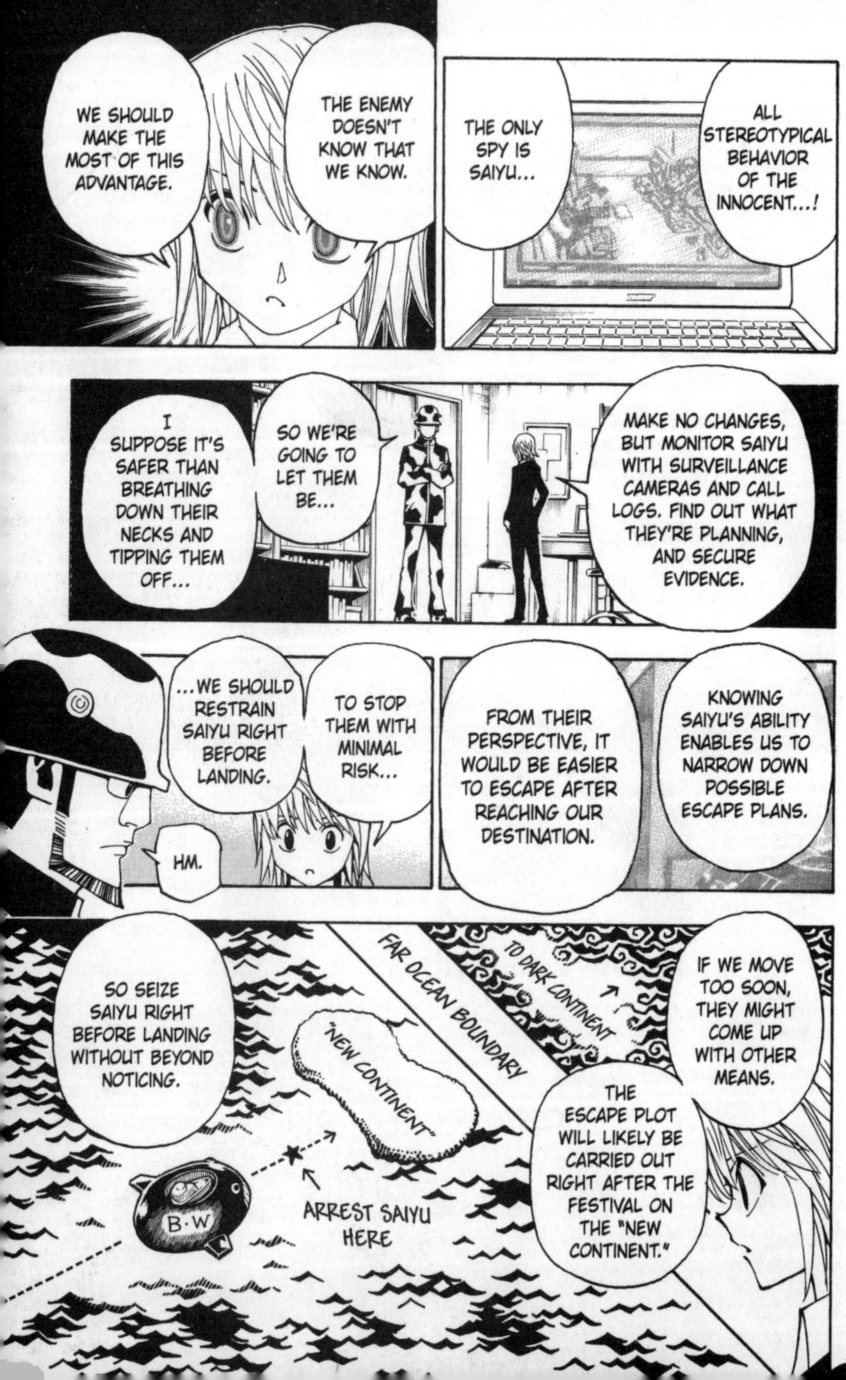
ALL STEREOTYPICAL BEHAVIOR OF THE INNOCENT...!
THE ONLY SPY IS SAIYU...
THE ENEMY DOESN'T KNOW THAT WE KNOW.
WE SHOULD MAKE THE MOST OF THIS ADVANTAGE.
MAKE NO CHANGES, BUT MONITOR SAIYU WITH SURVEILLANCE CAMERAS AND CALL LOGS. FIND OUT WHAT THEY'RE PLANNING, AND SECURE EVIDENCE.
SO WE'RE GOING TO LET THEM BE...
I SUPPOSE IT'S SAFER THAN BREATHING DOWN THEIR NECKS AND TIPPING THEM OFF...
KNOWING SAIYU'S ABILITY ENABLES US TO NARROW DOWN POSSIBLE ESCAPE PLANS.
FROM THEIR PERSPECTIVE, IT WOULD BE EASIER TO ESCAPE AFTER REACHING OUR DESTINATION.
TO STOP THEM WITH MINIMAL RISK...
...WE SHOULD RESTRAIN SAIYU RIGHT BEFORE LANDING.
HM.
IF WE MOVE TOO SOON, THEY MIGHT COME UP WITH OTHER MEANS.
THE ESCAPE PLOT WILL LIKELY BE CARRIED OUT RIGHT AFTER THE FESTIVAL ON THE "NEW CONTINENT."
TO DARK CONTINENT
FAR OCEAN BOUNDARY
"NEW CONTINENT"
ARREST SAIYU HERE
B·W
SO SEIZE SAIYU RIGHT BEFORE LANDING WITHOUT BEYOND NOTICING.

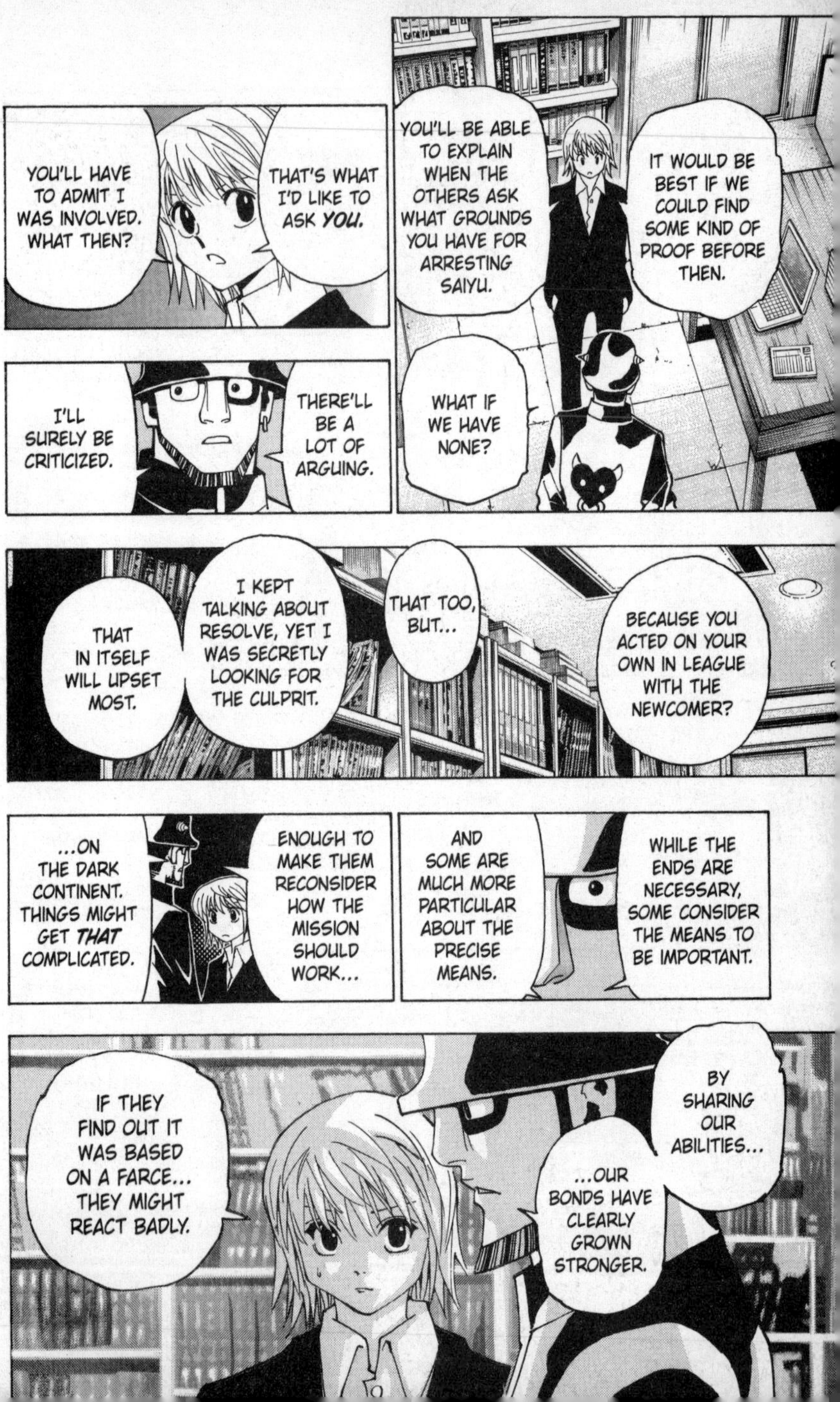
IT WOULD BE BEST IF WE COULD FIND SOME KIND OF PROOF BEFORE THEN.
YOU'LL BE ABLE TO EXPLAIN WHEN THE OTHERS ASK WHAT GROUNDS YOU HAVE FOR ARRESTING SAIYU.
WHAT IF WE HAVE NONE?
THAT'S WHAT I'D LIKE TO ASK *YOU.*
YOU'LL HAVE TO ADMIT I WAS INVOLVED. WHAT THEN?
THERE'LL BE A LOT OF ARGUING.
I'LL SURELY BE CRITICIZED.
BECAUSE YOU ACTED ON YOUR OWN IN LEAGUE WITH THE NEWCOMER?
THAT TOO, BUT...
I KEPT TALKING ABOUT RESOLVE, YET I WAS SECRETLY LOOKING FOR THE CULPRIT.
THAT IN ITSELF WILL UPSET MOST.
WHILE THE ENDS ARE NECESSARY, SOME CONSIDER THE MEANS TO BE IMPORTANT.
AND SOME ARE MUCH MORE PARTICULAR ABOUT THE PRECISE MEANS.
ENOUGH TO MAKE THEM RECONSIDER HOW THE MISSION SHOULD WORK...
...ON THE DARK CONTINENT. THINGS MIGHT GET *THAT* COMPLICATED.
BY SHARING OUR ABILITIES...
...OUR BONDS HAVE CLEARLY GROWN STRONGER.
IF THEY FIND OUT IT WAS BASED ON A FARCE... THEY MIGHT REACT BADLY.

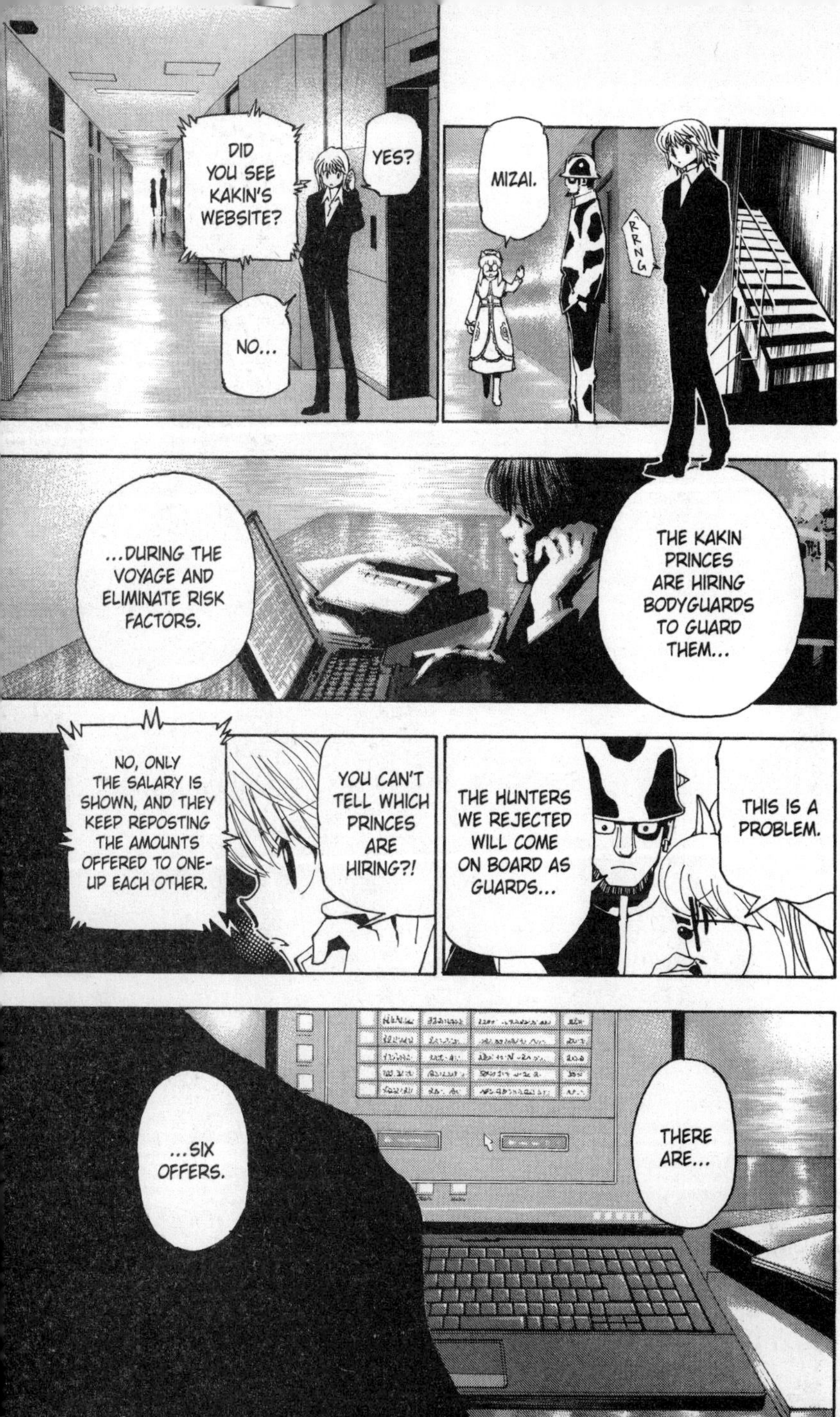
RRNG
MIZAI.
YES?
DID YOU SEE KAKIN'S WEBSITE?
NO...
THE KAKIN PRINCES ARE HIRING BODYGUARDS TO GUARD THEM...
...DURING THE VOYAGE AND ELIMINATE RISK FACTORS.
THIS IS A PROBLEM.
THE HUNTERS WE REJECTED WILL COME ON BOARD AS GUARDS...
YOU CAN'T TELL WHICH PRINCES ARE HIRING?!
NO, ONLY THE SALARY IS SHOWN, AND THEY KEEP REPOSTING THE AMOUNTS OFFERED TO ONE-UP EACH OTHER.
THERE ARE...
...SIX OFFERS.

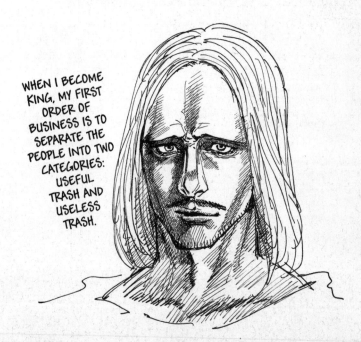

WHEN I BECOME KING, MY FIRST ORDER OF BUSINESS IS TO SEPARATE THE PEOPLE INTO TWO CATEGORIES: USEFUL TRASH AND USELESS TRASH.

Chapter 350: Prince

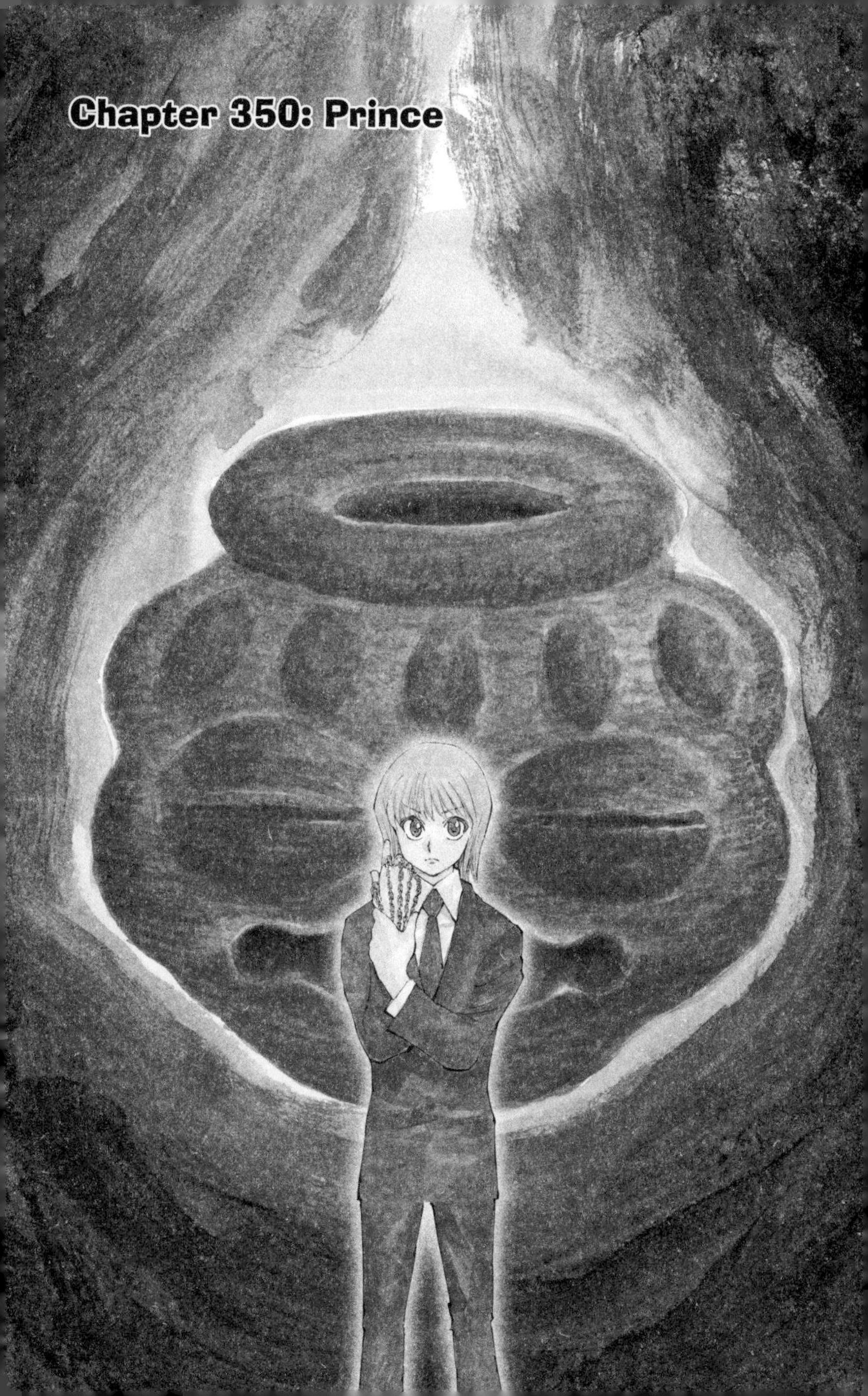

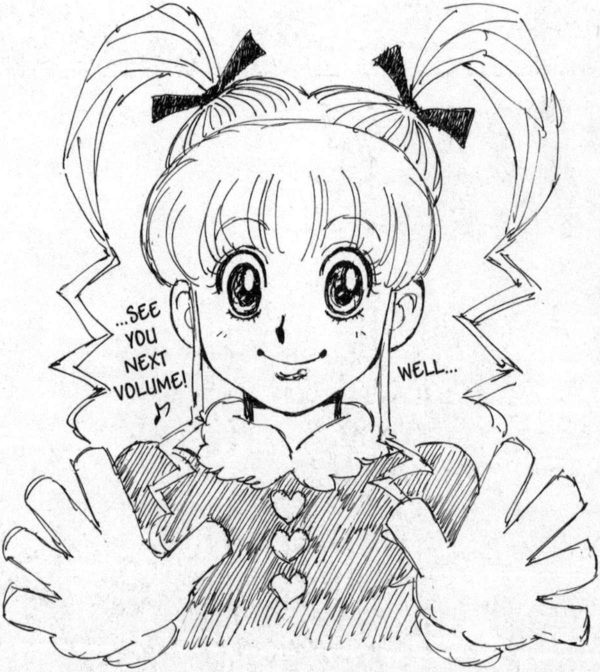
WELL...
...SEE YOU NEXT VOLUME! ♪

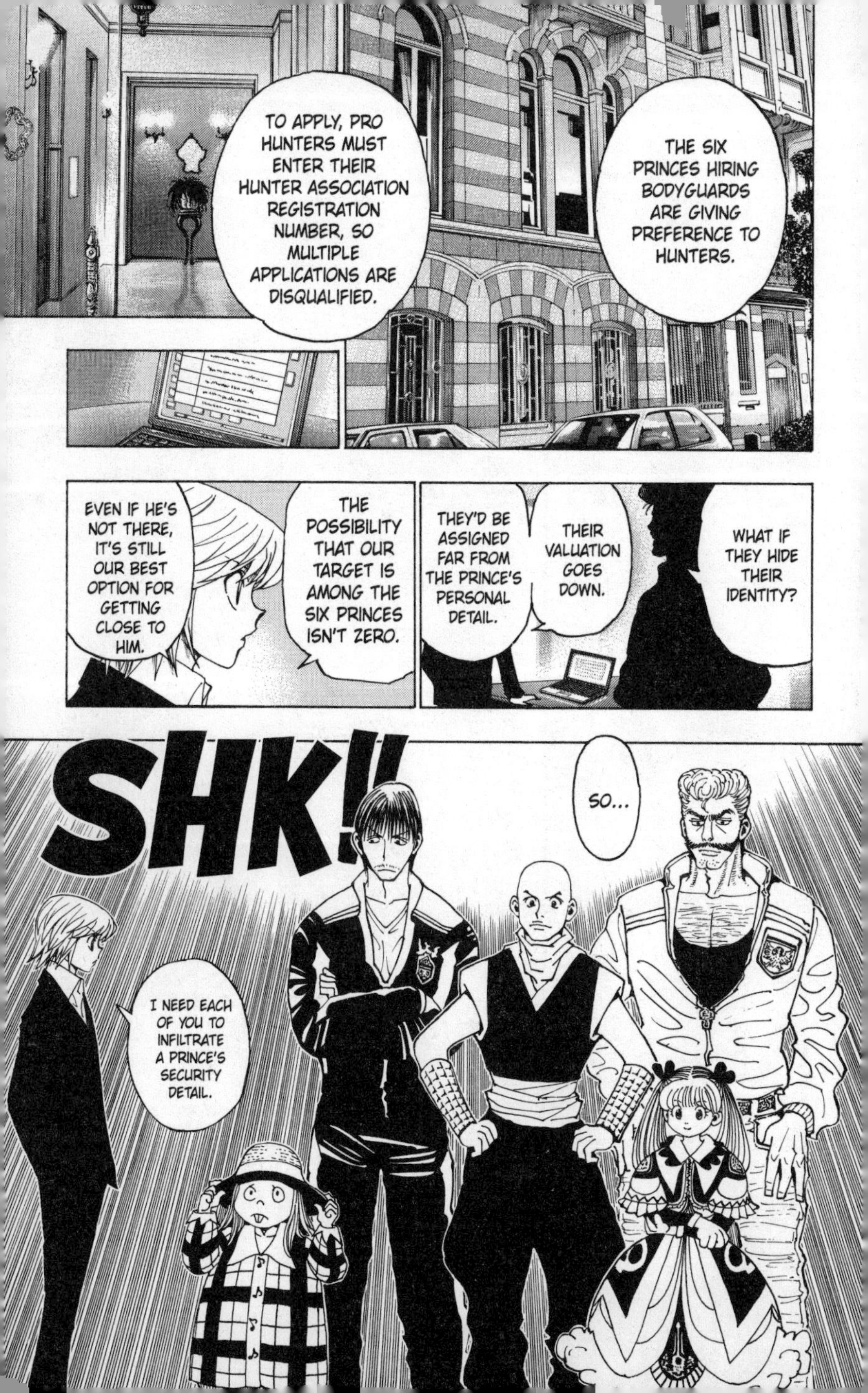
THE SIX PRINCES HIRING BODYGUARDS ARE GIVING PREFERENCE TO HUNTERS.
TO APPLY, PRO HUNTERS MUST ENTER THEIR HUNTER ASSOCIATION REGISTRATION NUMBER, SO MULTIPLE APPLICATIONS ARE DISQUALIFIED.
WHAT IF THEY HIDE THEIR IDENTITY?
THEIR VALUATION GOES DOWN.
THEY'D BE ASSIGNED FAR FROM THE PRINCE'S PERSONAL DETAIL.
THE POSSIBILITY THAT OUR TARGET IS AMONG THE SIX PRINCES ISN'T ZERO.
EVEN IF HE'S NOT THERE, IT'S STILL OUR BEST OPTION FOR GETTING CLOSE TO HIM.
SO...
SHK!!
I NEED EACH OF YOU TO INFILTRATE A PRINCE'S SECURITY DETAIL.

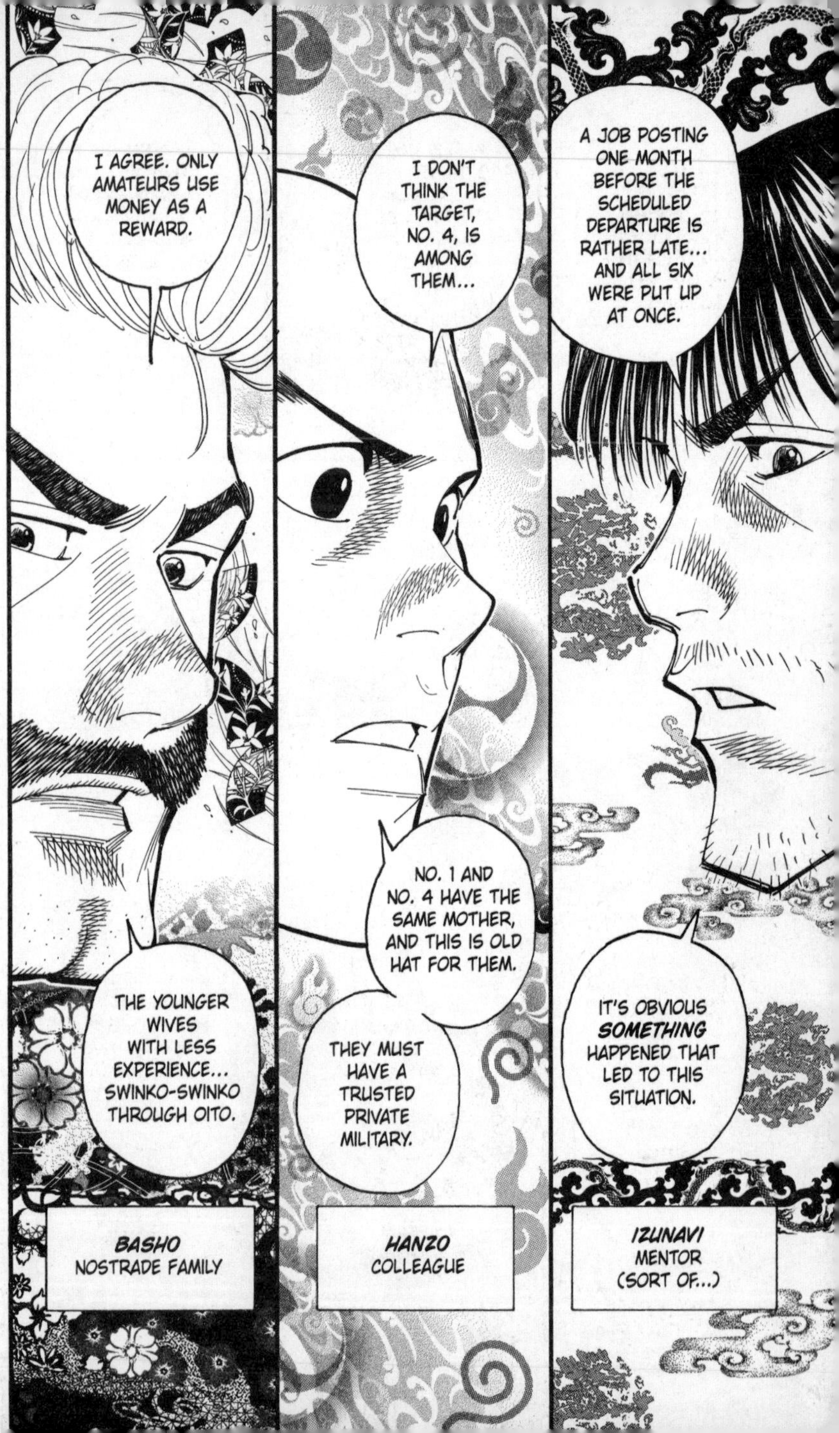
A JOB POSTING ONE MONTH BEFORE THE SCHEDULED DEPARTURE IS RATHER LATE... AND ALL SIX WERE PUT UP AT ONCE.
IT'S OBVIOUS *SOMETHING* HAPPENED THAT LED TO THIS SITUATION.
IZUNAVI
MENTOR (SORT OF...)
I DON'T THINK THE TARGET, NO. 4, IS AMONG THEM...
NO. 1 AND NO. 4 HAVE THE SAME MOTHER, AND THIS IS OLD HAT FOR THEM.
THEY MUST HAVE A TRUSTED PRIVATE MILITARY.
HANZO
COLLEAGUE
I AGREE. ONLY AMATEURS USE MONEY AS A REWARD.
THE YOUNGER WIVES WITH LESS EXPERIENCE... SWINKO-SWINKO THROUGH OITO.
BASHO
NOSTRADE FAMILY

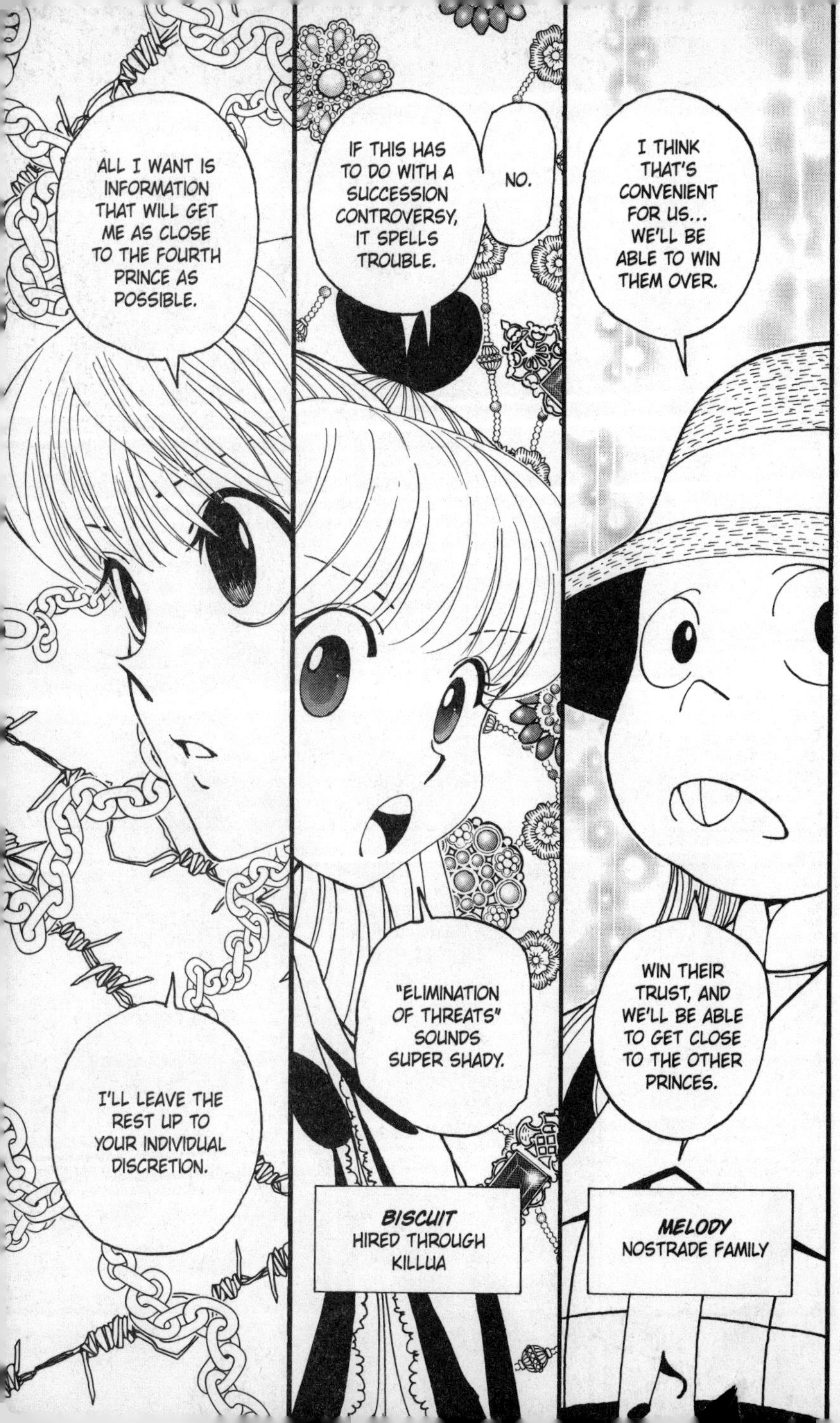

I THINK THAT'S CONVENIENT FOR US... WE'LL BE ABLE TO WIN THEM OVER.
WIN THEIR TRUST, AND WE'LL BE ABLE TO GET CLOSE TO THE OTHER PRINCES.
MELODY NOSTRADE FAMILY
NO.
IF THIS HAS TO DO WITH A SUCCESSION CONTROVERSY, IT SPELLS TROUBLE.
"ELIMINATION OF THREATS" SOUNDS SUPER SHADY.
BISCUIT HIRED THROUGH KILLUA
ALL I WANT IS INFORMATION THAT WILL GET ME AS CLOSE TO THE FOURTH PRINCE AS POSSIBLE.
I'LL LEAVE THE REST UP TO YOUR INDIVIDUAL DISCRETION.

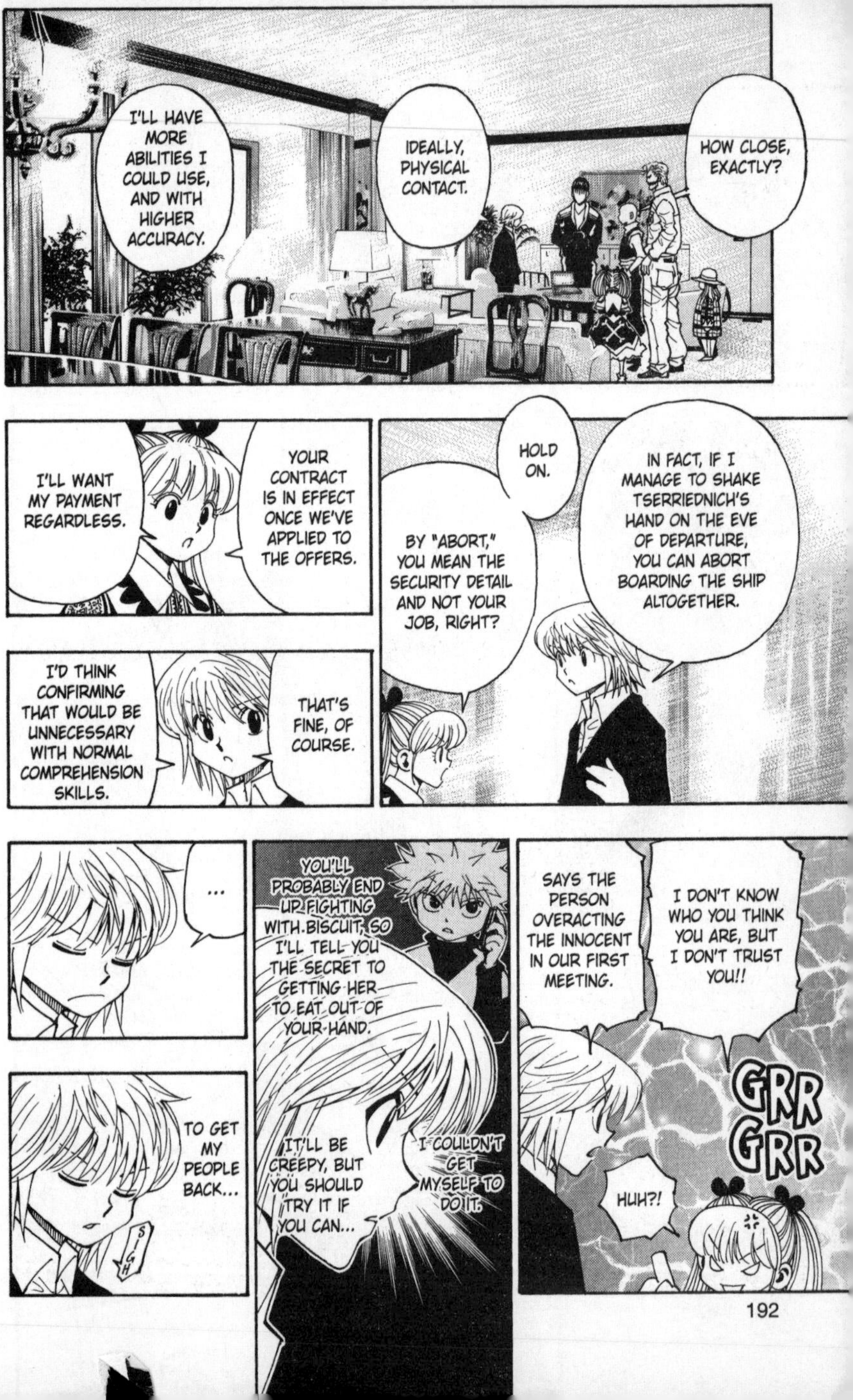
HOW CLOSE, EXACTLY?
IDEALLY, PHYSICAL CONTACT.
I'LL HAVE MORE ABILITIES I COULD USE, AND WITH HIGHER ACCURACY.
IN FACT, IF I MANAGE TO SHAKE TSERRIEDNICH'S HAND ON THE EVE OF DEPARTURE, YOU CAN ABORT BOARDING THE SHIP ALTOGETHER.
HOLD ON.
BY "ABORT," YOU MEAN THE SECURITY DETAIL AND NOT YOUR JOB, RIGHT?
YOUR CONTRACT IS IN EFFECT ONCE WE'VE APPLIED TO THE OFFERS.
I'LL WANT MY PAYMENT REGARDLESS.
THAT'S FINE, OF COURSE.
I'D THINK CONFIRMING THAT WOULD BE UNNECESSARY WITH NORMAL COMPREHENSION SKILLS.
I DON'T KNOW WHO YOU THINK YOU ARE, BUT I DON'T TRUST YOU!!
SAYS THE PERSON OVERACTING THE INNOCENT IN OUR FIRST MEETING.
GRR GRR
HUH?!
YOU'LL PROBABLY END UP FIGHTING WITH BISCUIT, SO I'LL TELL YOU THE SECRET TO GETTING HER TO EAT OUT OF YOUR HAND.
I COULDN'T GET MYSELF TO DO IT.
IT'LL BE CREEPY, BUT YOU SHOULD TRY IT IF YOU CAN...
...
TO GET MY PEOPLE BACK...
SIGH

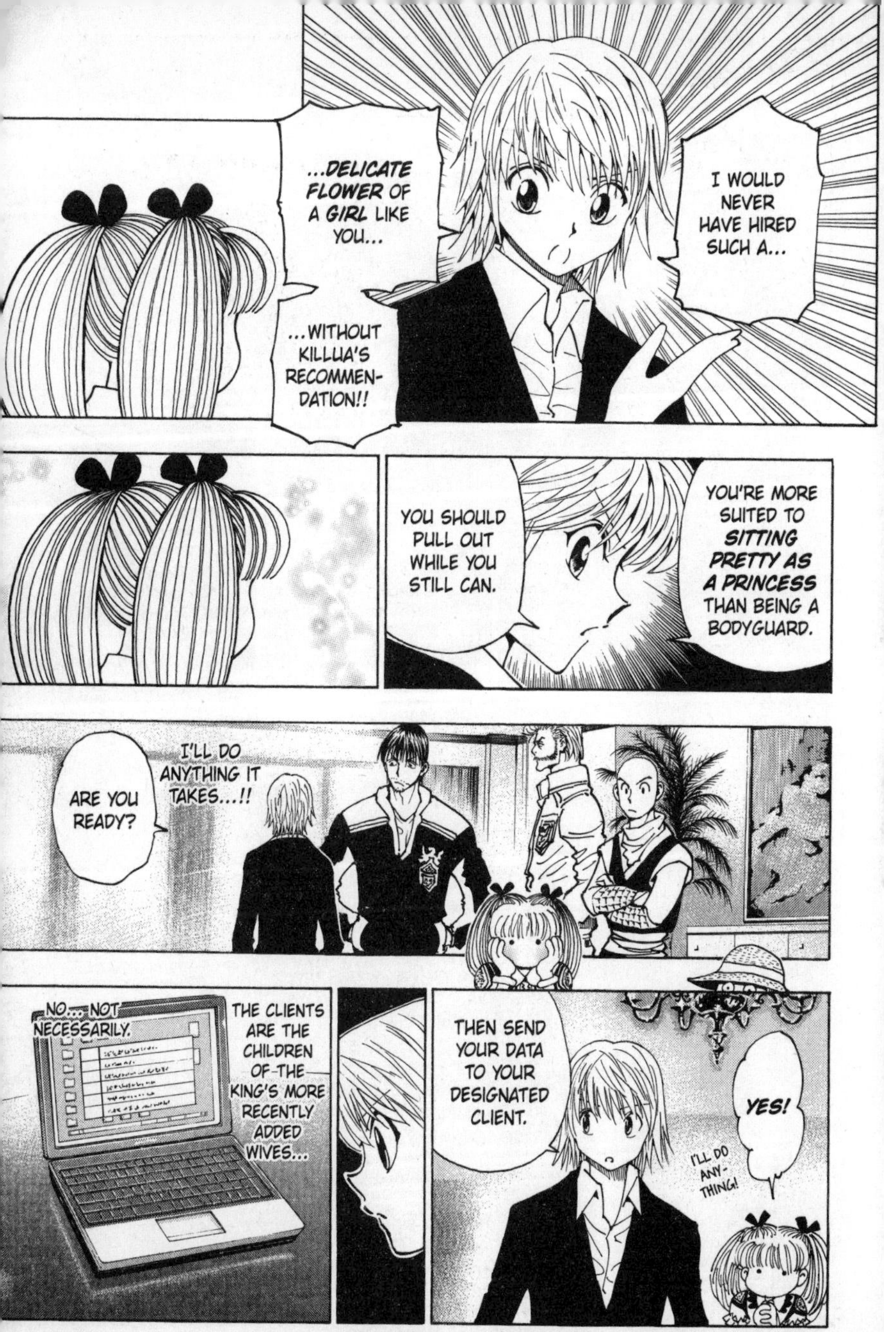
I WOULD NEVER HAVE HIRED SUCH A...
...DELICATE FLOWER OF A GIRL LIKE YOU...
...WITHOUT KILLUA'S RECOMMEN-DATION!!
YOU'RE MORE SUITED TO SITTING PRETTY AS A PRINCESS THAN BEING A BODYGUARD.
YOU SHOULD PULL OUT WHILE YOU STILL CAN.
I'LL DO ANYTHING IT TAKES...!!
ARE YOU READY?
THEN SEND YOUR DATA TO YOUR DESIGNATED CLIENT.
YES!
I'LL DO ANY-THING!
THE CLIENTS ARE THE CHILDREN OF THE KING'S MORE RECENTLY ADDED WIVES...
NO... NOT NECESSARILY.

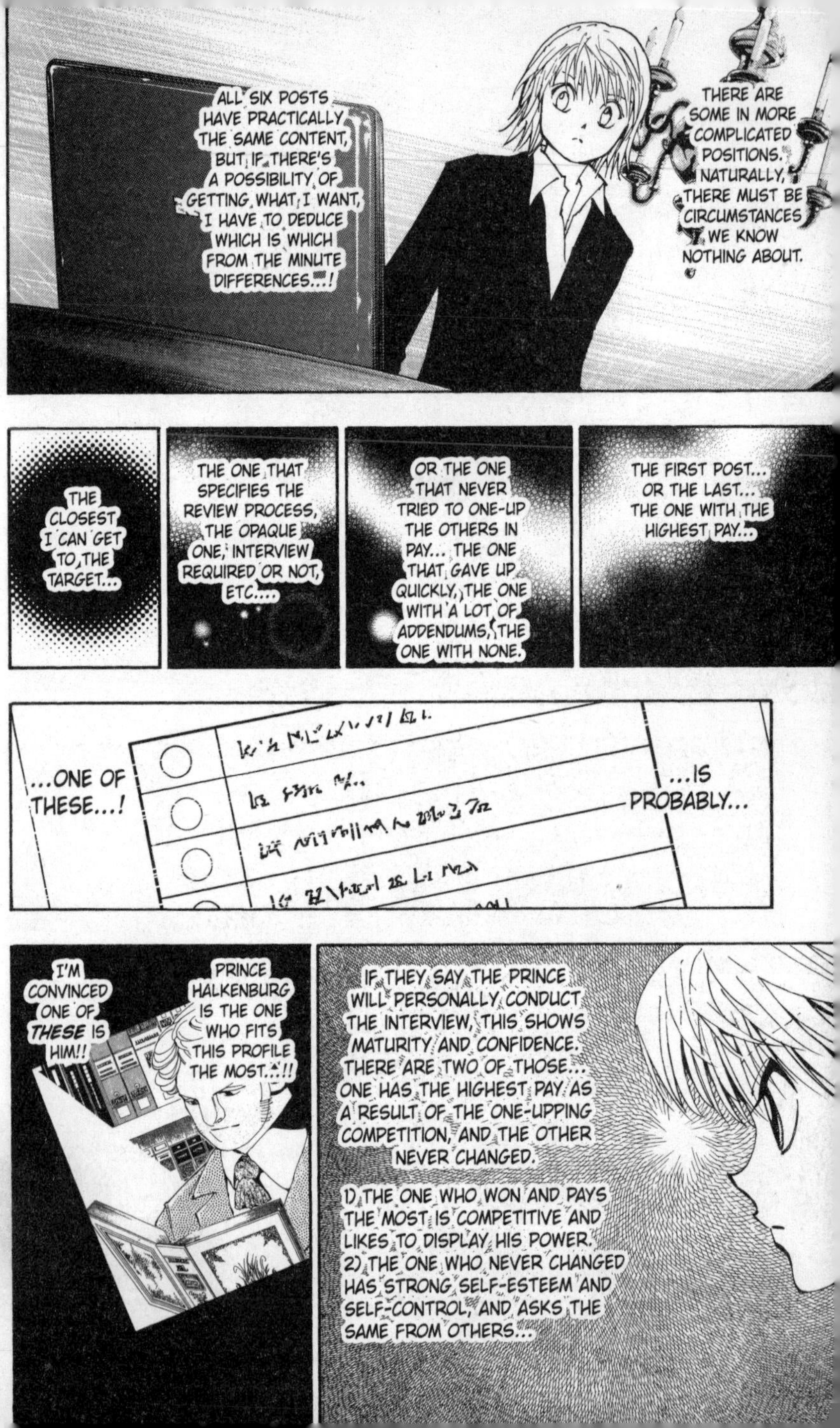
THERE ARE SOME IN MORE COMPLICATED POSITIONS. NATURALLY, THERE MUST BE CIRCUMSTANCES WE KNOW NOTHING ABOUT.
ALL SIX POSTS HAVE PRACTICALLY THE SAME CONTENT, BUT IF THERE'S A POSSIBILITY OF GETTING WHAT I WANT, I HAVE TO DEDUCE WHICH IS WHICH FROM THE MINUTE DIFFERENCES...!
THE FIRST POST... OR THE LAST... THE ONE WITH THE HIGHEST PAY...
OR THE ONE THAT NEVER TRIED TO ONE-UP THE OTHERS IN PAY... THE ONE THAT GAVE UP QUICKLY, THE ONE WITH A LOT OF ADDENDUMS, THE ONE WITH NONE.
THE ONE THAT SPECIFIES THE REVIEW PROCESS, THE OPAQUE ONE, INTERVIEW REQUIRED OR NOT, ETC....
THE CLOSEST I CAN GET TO THE TARGET...
...IS PROBABLY...
...ONE OF THESE...!
IF THEY SAY THE PRINCE WILL PERSONALLY CONDUCT THE INTERVIEW, THIS SHOWS MATURITY AND CONFIDENCE. THERE ARE TWO OF THOSE... ONE HAS THE HIGHEST PAY AS A RESULT OF THE ONE-UPPING COMPETITION, AND THE OTHER NEVER CHANGED.
1) THE ONE WHO WON AND PAYS THE MOST IS COMPETITIVE AND LIKES TO DISPLAY HIS POWER.
2) THE ONE WHO NEVER CHANGED HAS STRONG SELF-ESTEEM AND SELF-CONTROL, AND ASKS THE SAME FROM OTHERS...
PRINCE HALKENBURG IS THE ONE WHO FITS THIS PROFILE THE MOST...!!
I'M CONVINCED ONE OF THESE IS HIM!!

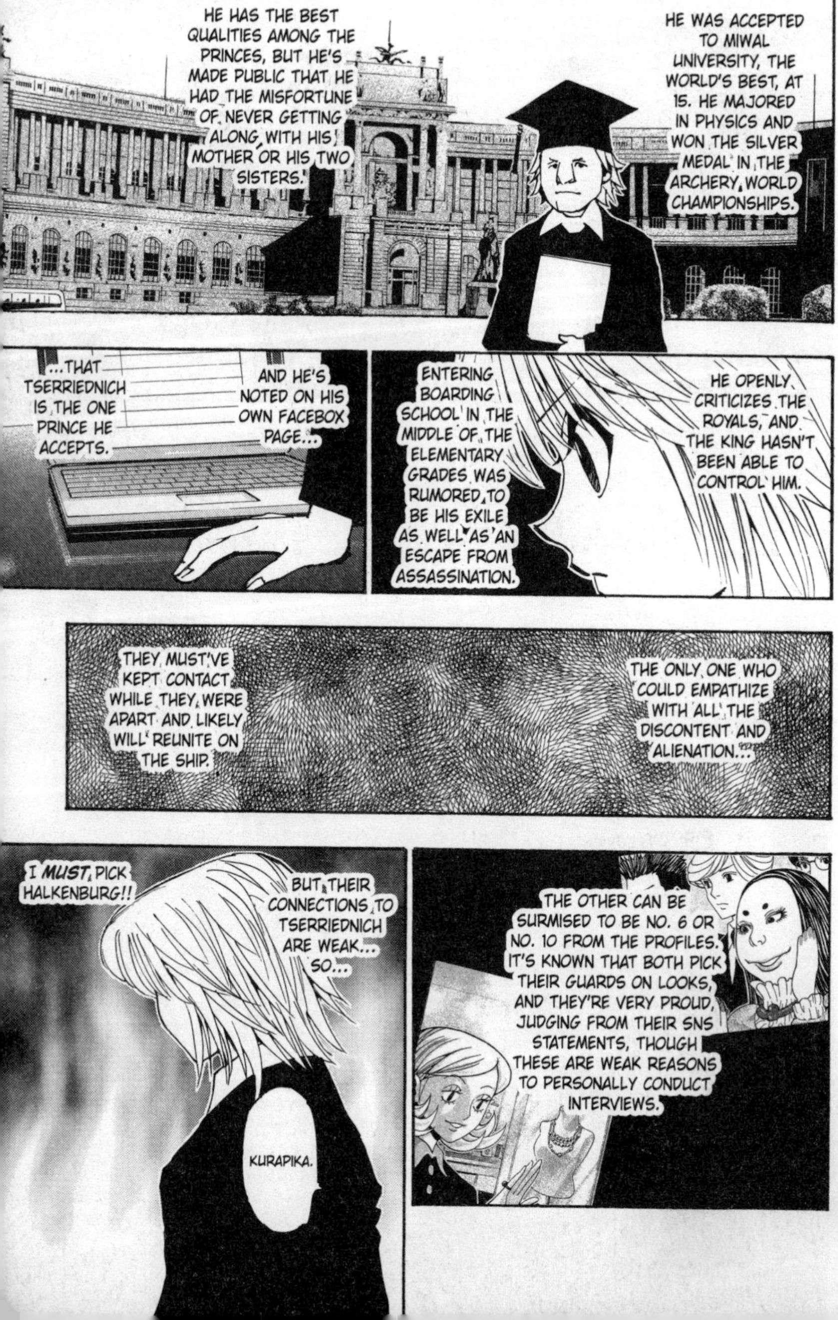
HE WAS ACCEPTED TO MIWAL UNIVERSITY, THE WORLD'S BEST, AT 15. HE MAJORED IN PHYSICS AND WON THE SILVER MEDAL IN THE ARCHERY WORLD CHAMPIONSHIPS.
HE HAS THE BEST QUALITIES AMONG THE PRINCES, BUT HE'S MADE PUBLIC THAT HE HAD THE MISFORTUNE OF NEVER GETTING ALONG WITH HIS MOTHER OR HIS TWO SISTERS.
HE OPENLY CRITICIZES THE ROYALS, AND THE KING HASN'T BEEN ABLE TO CONTROL HIM.
ENTERING BOARDING SCHOOL IN THE MIDDLE OF THE ELEMENTARY GRADES WAS RUMORED TO BE HIS EXILE AS WELL AS AN ESCAPE FROM ASSASSINATION.
AND HE'S NOTED ON HIS OWN FACEBOX PAGE...
...THAT TSERRIEDNICH IS THE ONE PRINCE HE ACCEPTS.
THE ONLY ONE WHO COULD EMPATHIZE WITH ALL THE DISCONTENT AND ALIENATION...
THEY MUST'VE KEPT CONTACT WHILE THEY WERE APART AND LIKELY WILL REUNITE ON THE SHIP.
THE OTHER CAN BE SURMISED TO BE NO. 6 OR NO. 10 FROM THE PROFILES. IT'S KNOWN THAT BOTH PICK THEIR GUARDS ON LOOKS, AND THEY'RE VERY PROUD, JUDGING FROM THEIR SNS STATEMENTS, THOUGH THESE ARE WEAK REASONS TO PERSONALLY CONDUCT INTERVIEWS.
BUT THEIR CONNECTIONS TO TSERRIEDNICH ARE WEAK... SO...
I *MUST* PICK HALKENBURG!!
KURAPIKA.

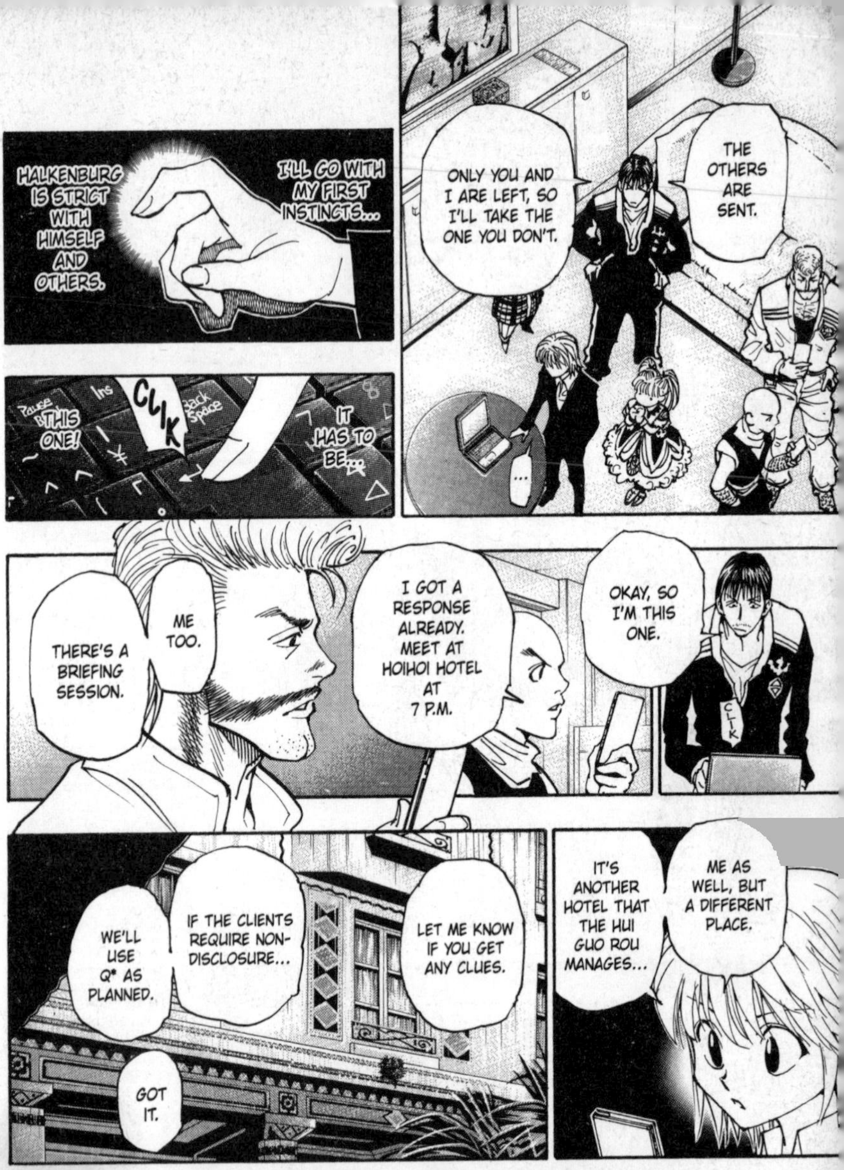
THE OTHERS ARE SENT.
ONLY YOU AND I ARE LEFT, SO I'LL TAKE THE ONE YOU DON'T.
...
I'LL GO WITH MY FIRST INSTINCTS...
HALKENBURG IS STRICT WITH HIMSELF AND OTHERS.
CLIK
IT HAS TO BE...
THIS ONE!
OKAY, SO I'M THIS ONE.
CLIK
I GOT A RESPONSE ALREADY. MEET AT HOIHOI HOTEL AT 7 P.M.
ME TOO.
THERE'S A BRIEFING SESSION.
ME AS WELL, BUT A DIFFERENT PLACE.
IT'S ANOTHER HOTEL THAT THE HUI GUO ROU MANAGES...
LET ME KNOW IF YOU GET ANY CLUES.
IF THE CLIENTS REQUIRE NON-DISCLOSURE...
WE'LL USE Q* AS PLANNED.
GOT IT.

* BY SENDING A NINE-DIGIT CODE TO A PHONE COMPANY HELD BY THE HUNTER ASSOCIATION, YOU CAN SEND AND RECEIVE INFORMATION VIA SPECIAL SOFTWARE CALLED Q. THERE ARE NO LOGS AND NO CALL HISTORY, AND REGULAR WIRETAPPING SYSTEMS CANNOT DETECT THIS METHOD OF DATA TRANSFER.

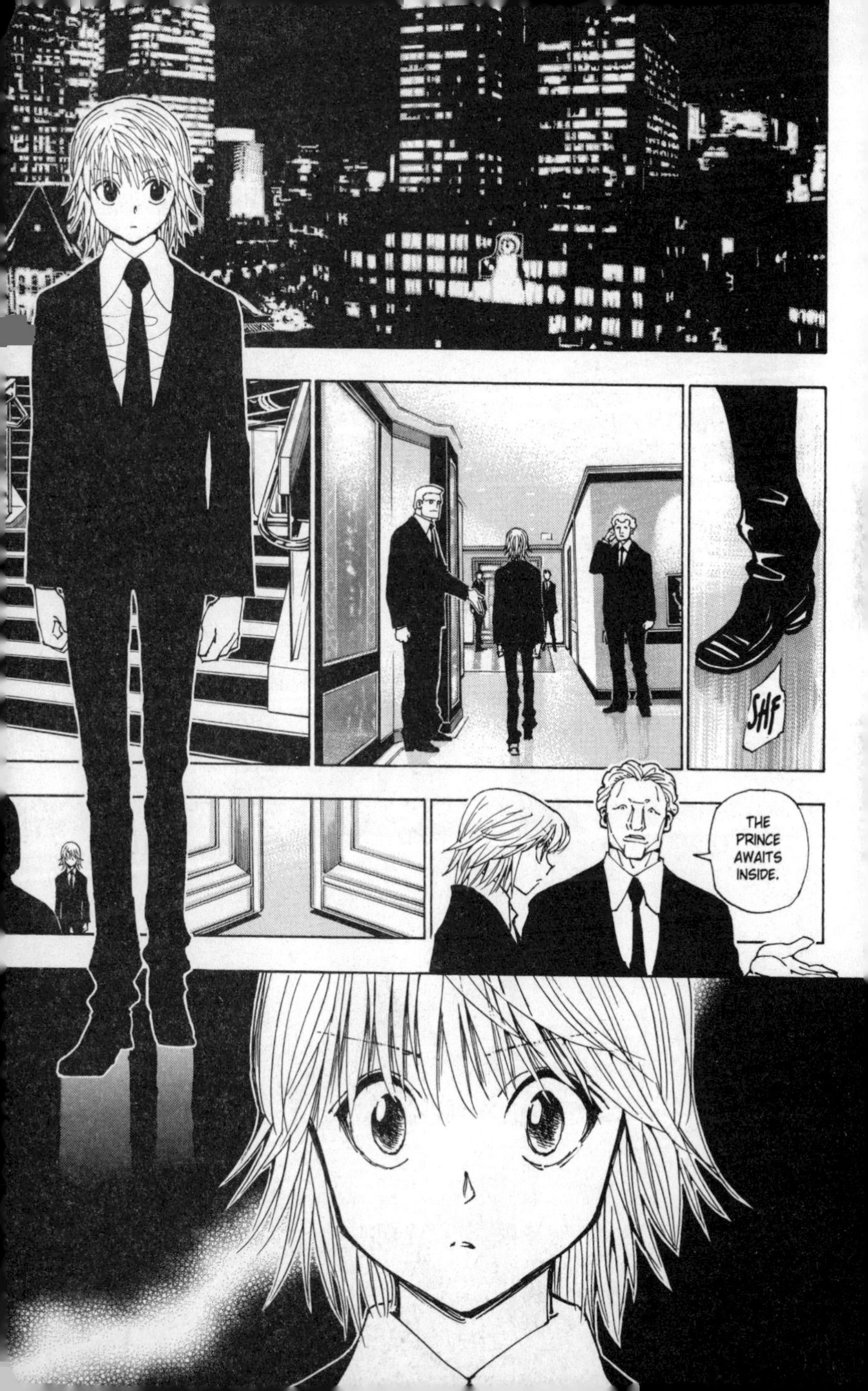
SHF
THE PRINCE AWAITS INSIDE.

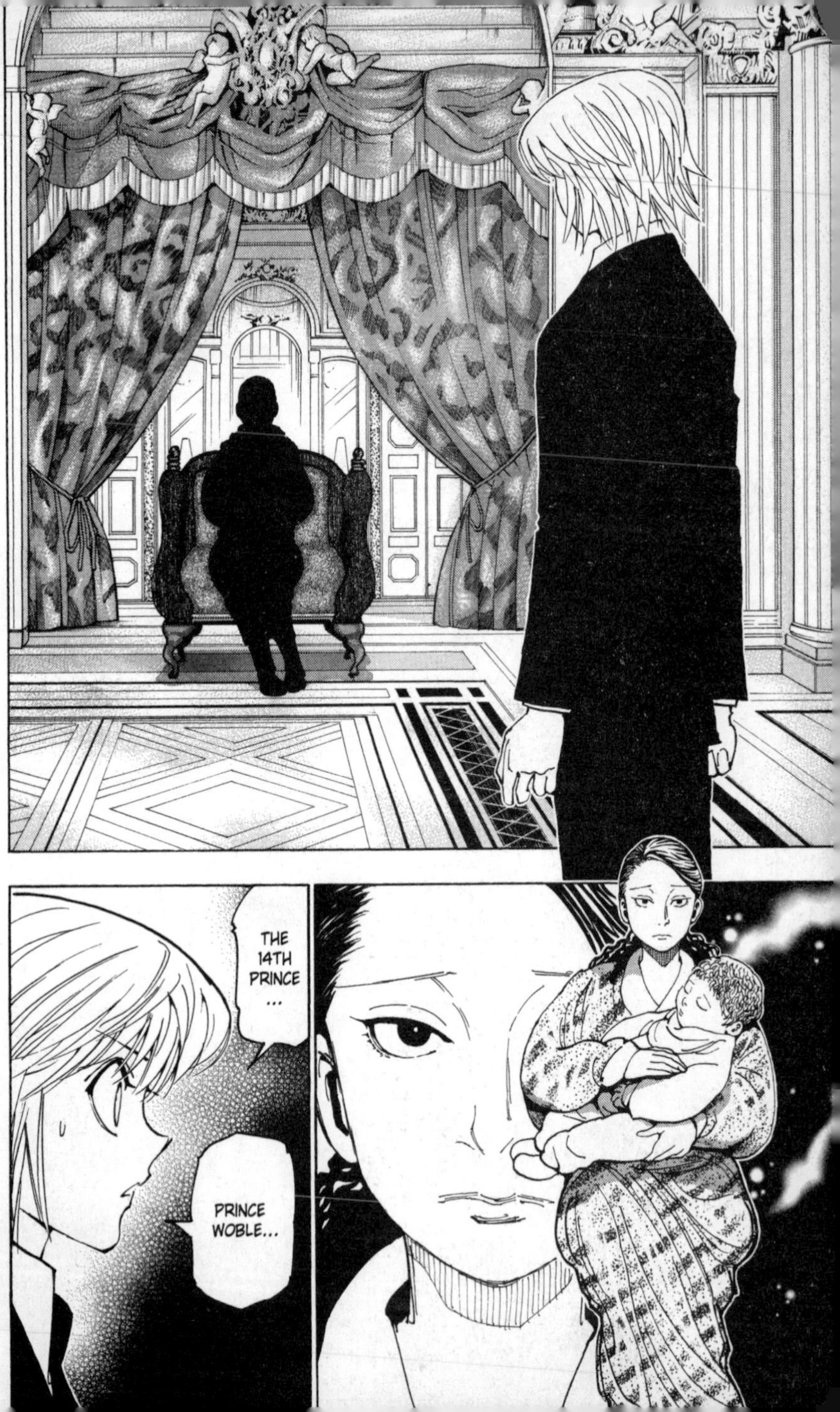
THE 14TH PRINCE ...
PRINCE WOBLE...

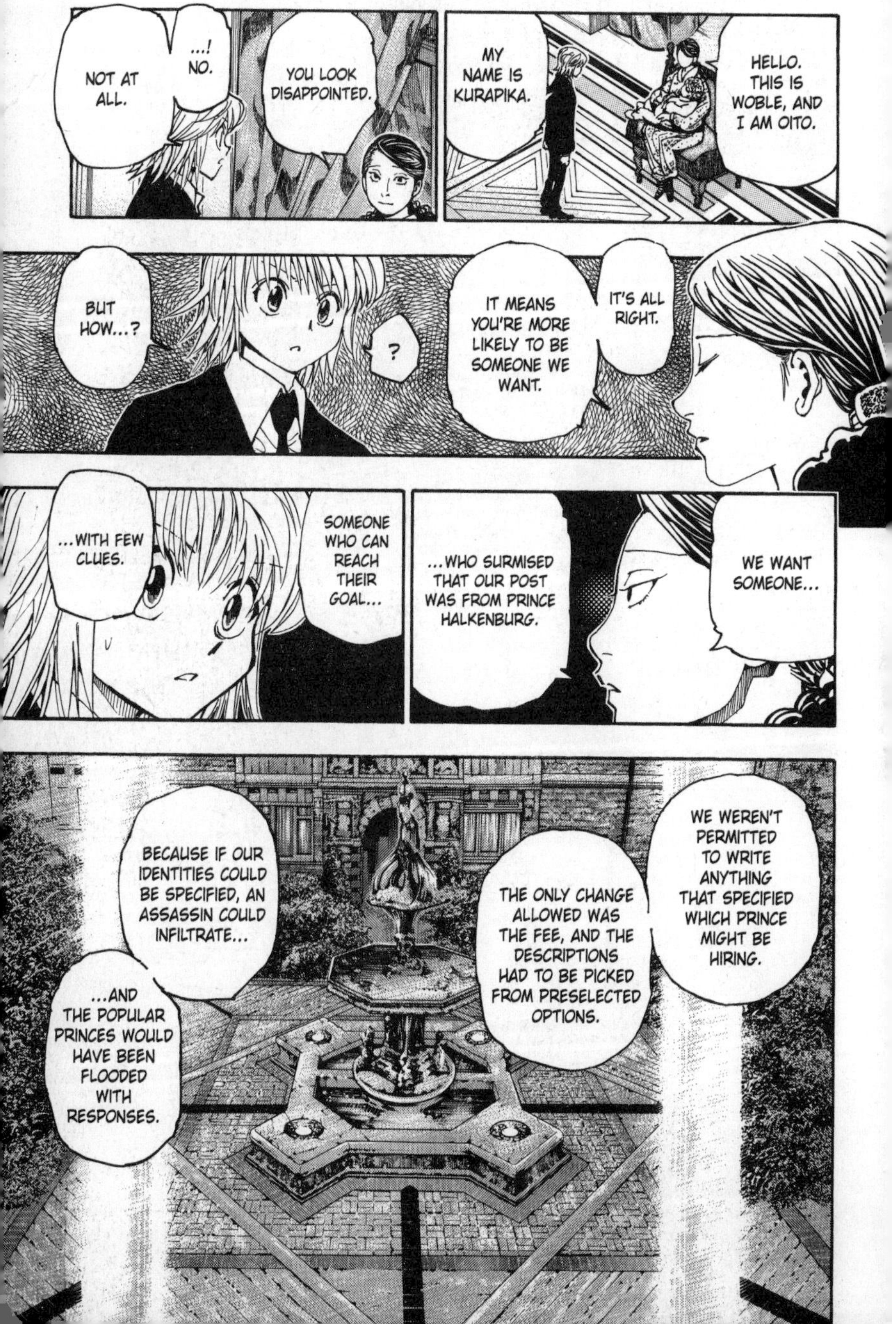
HELLO. THIS IS WOBLE, AND I AM OITO.
MY NAME IS KURAPIKA.
YOU LOOK DISAPPOINTED.
...! NO.
NOT AT ALL.
IT'S ALL RIGHT.
IT MEANS YOU'RE MORE LIKELY TO BE SOMEONE WE WANT.
?
BUT HOW...?
WE WANT SOMEONE...
...WHO SURMISED THAT OUR POST WAS FROM PRINCE HALKENBURG.
SOMEONE WHO CAN REACH THEIR GOAL...
...WITH FEW CLUES.
WE WEREN'T PERMITTED TO WRITE ANYTHING THAT SPECIFIED WHICH PRINCE MIGHT BE HIRING.
THE ONLY CHANGE ALLOWED WAS THE FEE, AND THE DESCRIPTIONS HAD TO BE PICKED FROM PRESELECTED OPTIONS.
BECAUSE IF OUR IDENTITIES COULD BE SPECIFIED, AN ASSASSIN COULD INFILTRATE...
...AND THE POPULAR PRINCES WOULD HAVE BEEN FLOODED WITH RESPONSES.

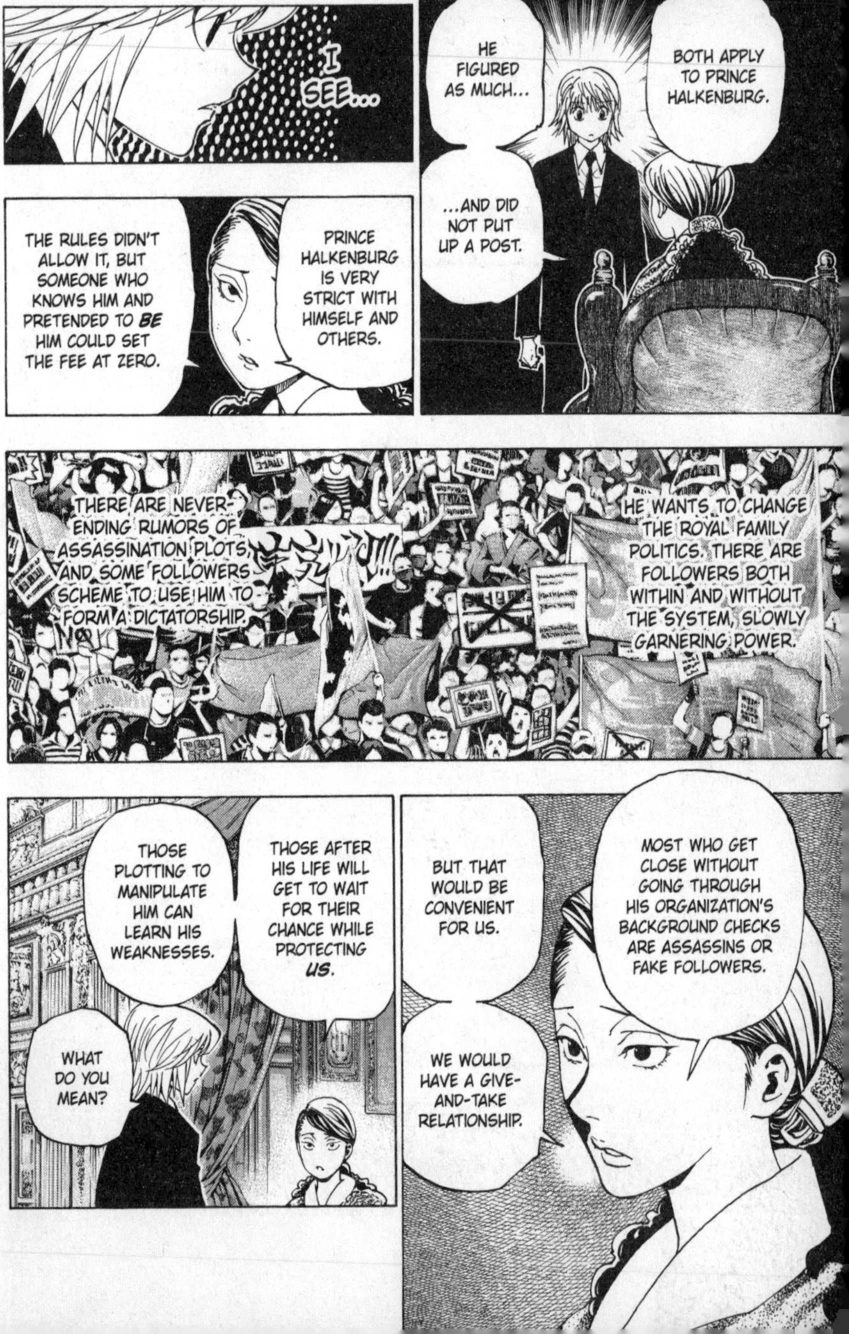
BOTH APPLY TO PRINCE HALKENBURG.
HE FIGURED AS MUCH...
...AND DID NOT PUT UP A POST.
I SEE...
PRINCE HALKENBURG IS VERY STRICT WITH HIMSELF AND OTHERS.
THE RULES DIDN'T ALLOW IT, BUT SOMEONE WHO KNOWS HIM AND PRETENDED TO *BE* HIM COULD SET THE FEE AT ZERO.
HE WANTS TO CHANGE THE ROYAL FAMILY POLITICS. THERE ARE FOLLOWERS BOTH WITHIN AND WITHOUT THE SYSTEM, SLOWLY GARNERING POWER.
THERE ARE NEVER-ENDING RUMORS OF ASSASSINATION PLOTS, AND SOME FOLLOWERS SCHEME TO USE HIM TO FORM A DICTATORSHIP.
MOST WHO GET CLOSE WITHOUT GOING THROUGH HIS ORGANIZATION'S BACKGROUND CHECKS ARE ASSASSINS OR FAKE FOLLOWERS.
BUT THAT WOULD BE CONVENIENT FOR US.
WE WOULD HAVE A GIVE-AND-TAKE RELATIONSHIP.
THOSE AFTER HIS LIFE WILL GET TO WAIT FOR THEIR CHANCE WHILE PROTECTING *US*.
THOSE PLOTTING TO MANIPULATE HIM CAN LEARN HIS WEAKNESSES.
WHAT DO YOU MEAN?

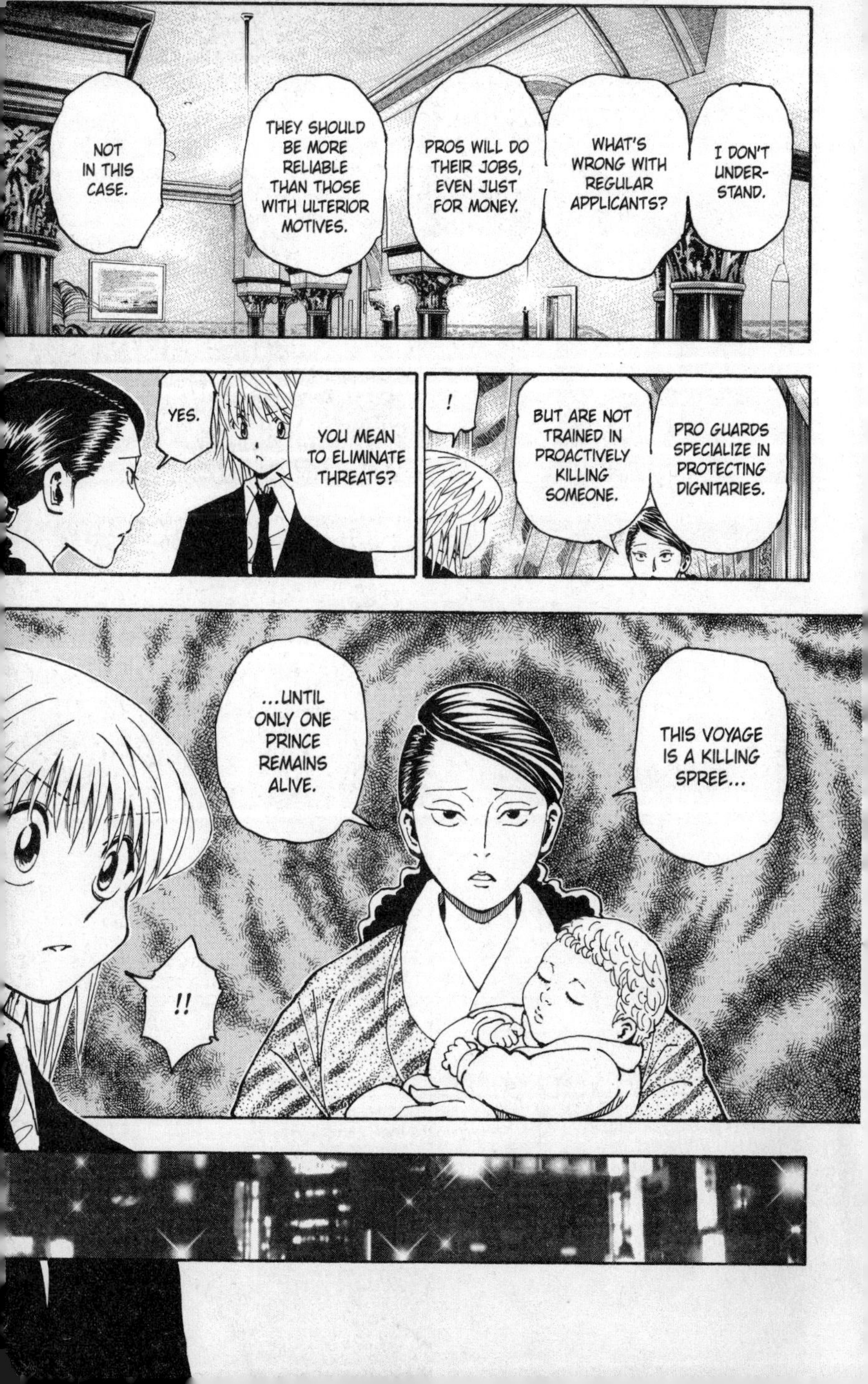
I DON'T UNDER-STAND.
WHAT'S WRONG WITH REGULAR APPLICANTS?
PROS WILL DO THEIR JOBS, EVEN JUST FOR MONEY.
THEY SHOULD BE MORE RELIABLE THAN THOSE WITH ULTERIOR MOTIVES.
NOT IN THIS CASE.
PRO GUARDS SPECIALIZE IN PROTECTING DIGNITARIES.
BUT ARE NOT TRAINED IN PROACTIVELY KILLING SOMEONE.
!
YOU MEAN TO ELIMINATE THREATS?
YES.
THIS VOYAGE IS A KILLING SPREE...
...UNTIL ONLY ONE PRINCE REMAINS ALIVE.
!!

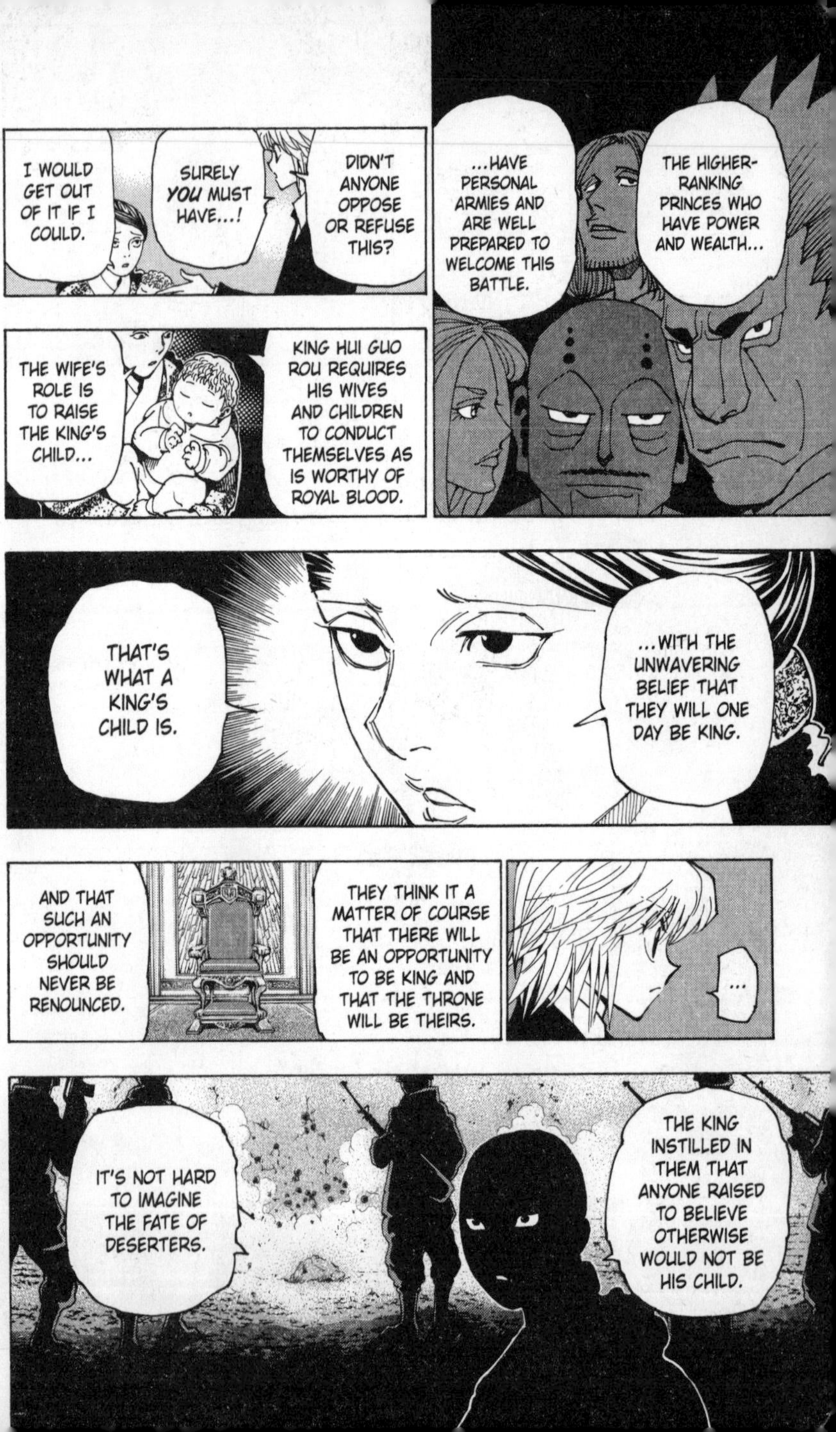
THE HIGHER-RANKING PRINCES WHO HAVE POWER AND WEALTH...
...HAVE PERSONAL ARMIES AND ARE WELL PREPARED TO WELCOME THIS BATTLE.
DIDN'T ANYONE OPPOSE OR REFUSE THIS?
SURELY *YOU* MUST HAVE...!
I WOULD GET OUT OF IT IF I COULD.
KING HUI GUO ROU REQUIRES HIS WIVES AND CHILDREN TO CONDUCT THEMSELVES AS IS WORTHY OF ROYAL BLOOD.
THE WIFE'S ROLE IS TO RAISE THE KING'S CHILD...
...WITH THE UNWAVERING BELIEF THAT THEY WILL ONE DAY BE KING.
THAT'S WHAT A KING'S CHILD IS.
...
THEY THINK IT A MATTER OF COURSE THAT THERE WILL BE AN OPPORTUNITY TO BE KING AND THAT THE THRONE WILL BE THEIRS.
AND THAT SUCH AN OPPORTUNITY SHOULD NEVER BE RENOUNCED.
THE KING INSTILLED IN THEM THAT ANYONE RAISED TO BELIEVE OTHERWISE WOULD NOT BE HIS CHILD.
IT'S NOT HARD TO IMAGINE THE FATE OF DESERTERS.

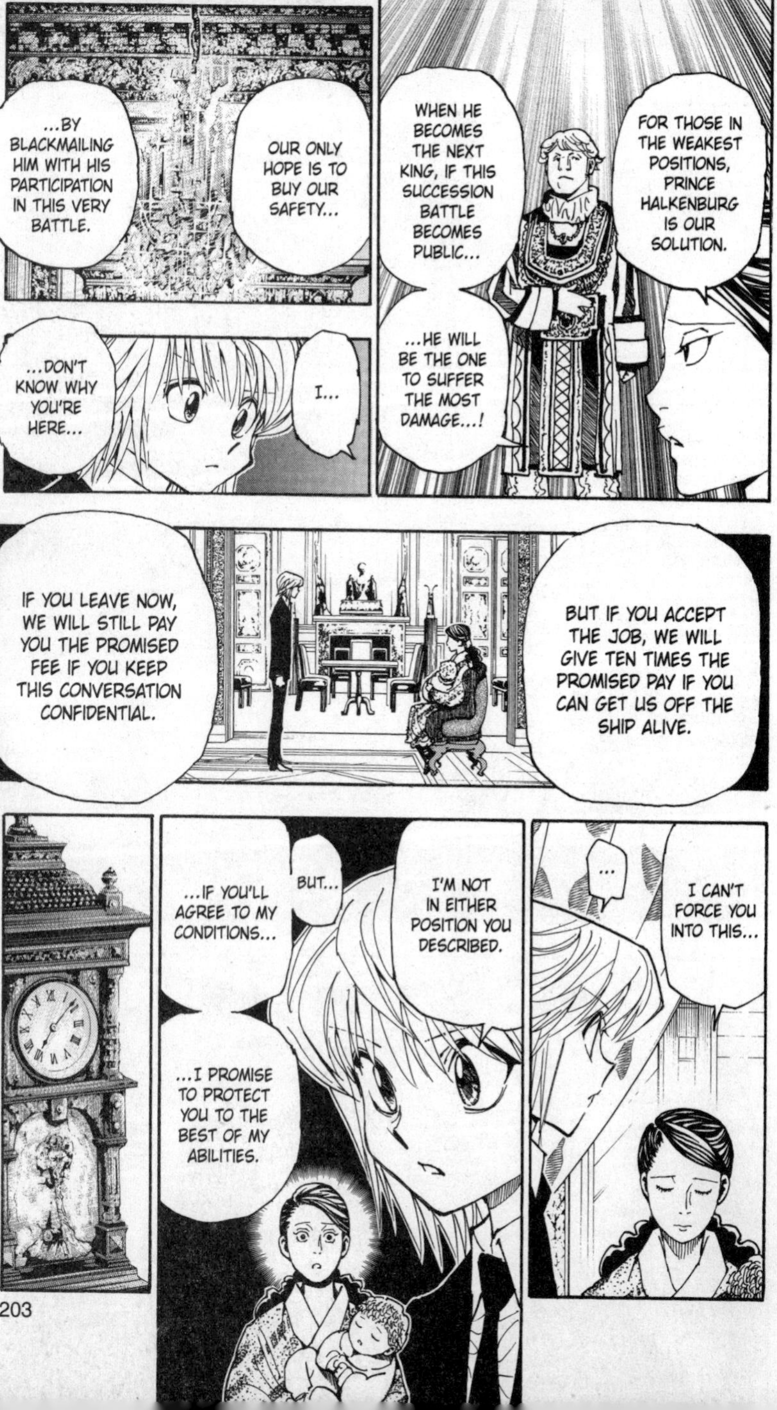

FOR THOSE IN THE WEAKEST POSITIONS, PRINCE HALKENBURG IS OUR SOLUTION.
WHEN HE BECOMES THE NEXT KING, IF THIS SUCCESSION BATTLE BECOMES PUBLIC...
...HE WILL BE THE ONE TO SUFFER THE MOST DAMAGE...!
OUR ONLY HOPE IS TO BUY OUR SAFETY...
...BY BLACKMAILING HIM WITH HIS PARTICIPATION IN THIS VERY BATTLE.
I...
...DON'T KNOW WHY YOU'RE HERE...
IF YOU LEAVE NOW, WE WILL STILL PAY YOU THE PROMISED FEE IF YOU KEEP THIS CONVERSATION CONFIDENTIAL.
BUT IF YOU ACCEPT THE JOB, WE WILL GIVE TEN TIMES THE PROMISED PAY IF YOU CAN GET US OFF THE SHIP ALIVE.
...
I CAN'T FORCE YOU INTO THIS...
I'M NOT IN EITHER POSITION YOU DESCRIBED.
BUT...
...IF YOU'LL AGREE TO MY CONDITIONS...
...I PROMISE TO PROTECT YOU TO THE BEST OF MY ABILITIES.

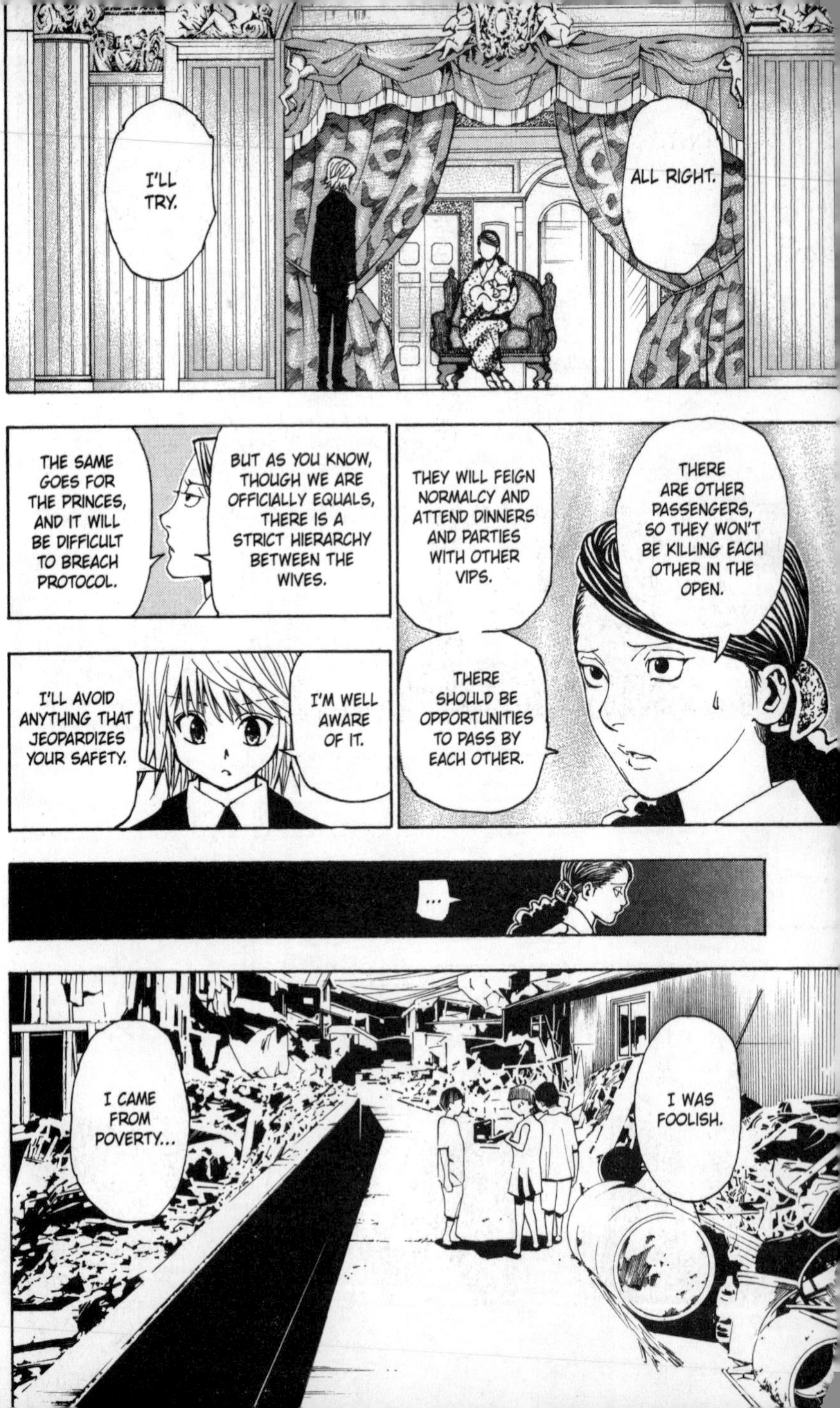
ALL RIGHT.
I'LL TRY.
THERE ARE OTHER PASSENGERS, SO THEY WON'T BE KILLING EACH OTHER IN THE OPEN.
THEY WILL FEIGN NORMALCY AND ATTEND DINNERS AND PARTIES WITH OTHER VIPS.
THERE SHOULD BE OPPORTUNITIES TO PASS BY EACH OTHER.
BUT AS YOU KNOW, THOUGH WE ARE OFFICIALLY EQUALS, THERE IS A STRICT HIERARCHY BETWEEN THE WIVES.
THE SAME GOES FOR THE PRINCES, AND IT WILL BE DIFFICULT TO BREACH PROTOCOL.
I'M WELL AWARE OF IT.
I'LL AVOID ANYTHING THAT JEOPARDIZES YOUR SAFETY.
...
I WAS FOOLISH.
I CAME FROM POVERTY...

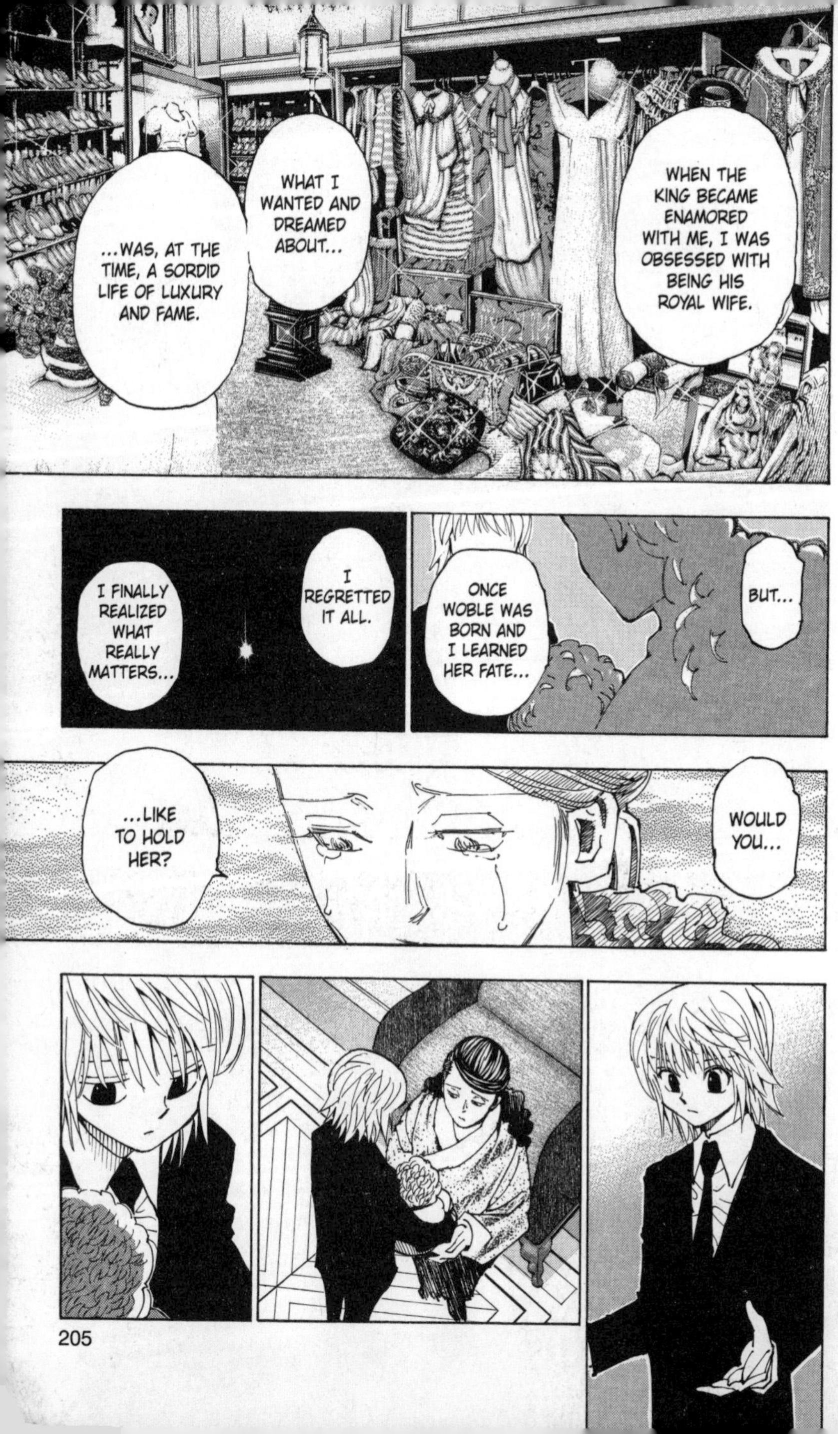
WHEN THE KING BECAME ENAMORED WITH ME, I WAS OBSESSED WITH BEING HIS ROYAL WIFE.
WHAT I WANTED AND DREAMED ABOUT...
...WAS, AT THE TIME, A SORDID LIFE OF LUXURY AND FAME.
BUT...
ONCE WOBLE WAS BORN AND I LEARNED HER FATE...
I REGRETTED IT ALL.
I FINALLY REALIZED WHAT REALLY MATTERS...
WOULD YOU...
...LIKE TO HOLD HER?

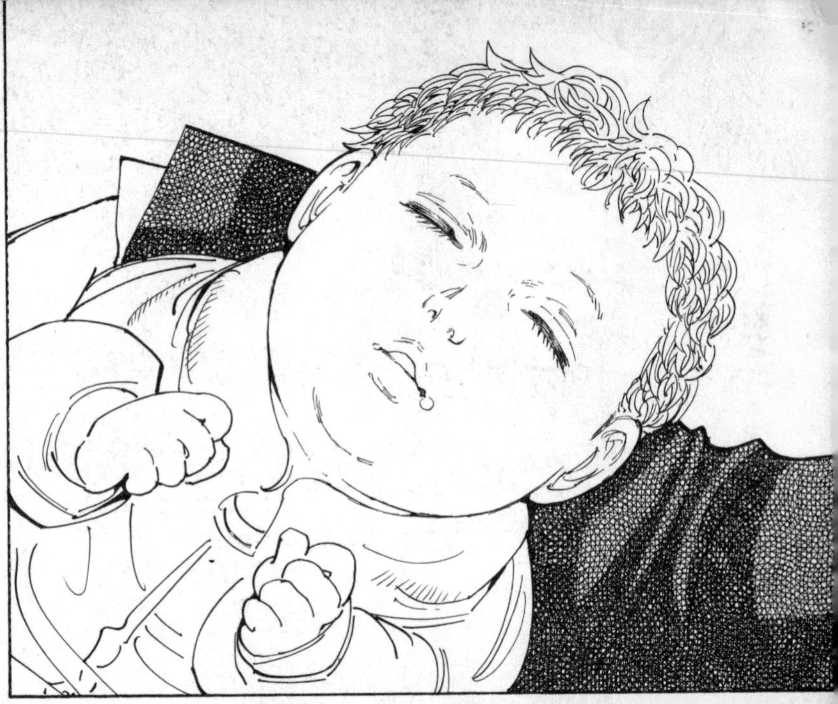
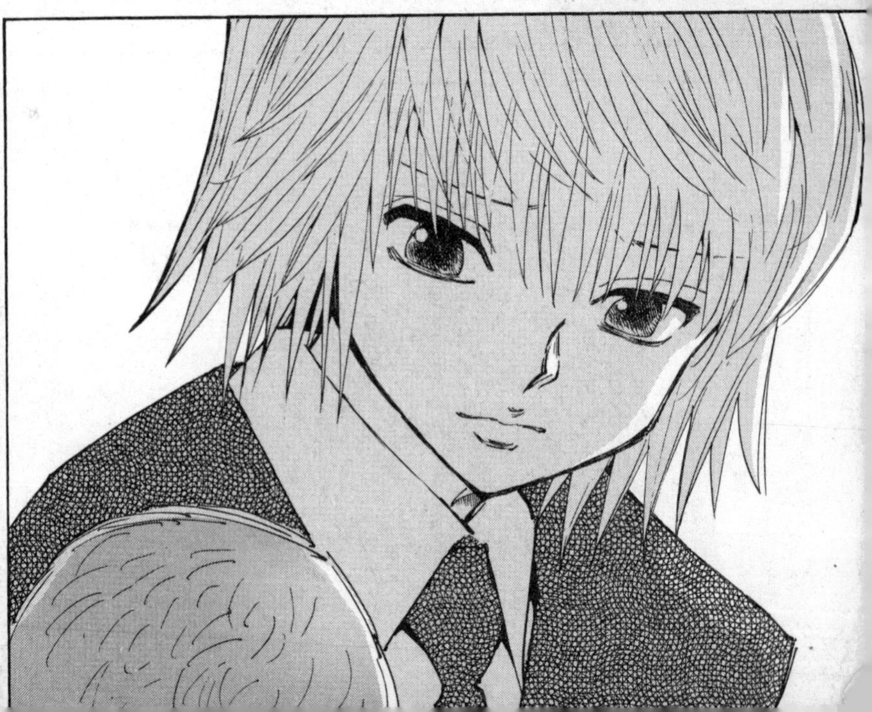

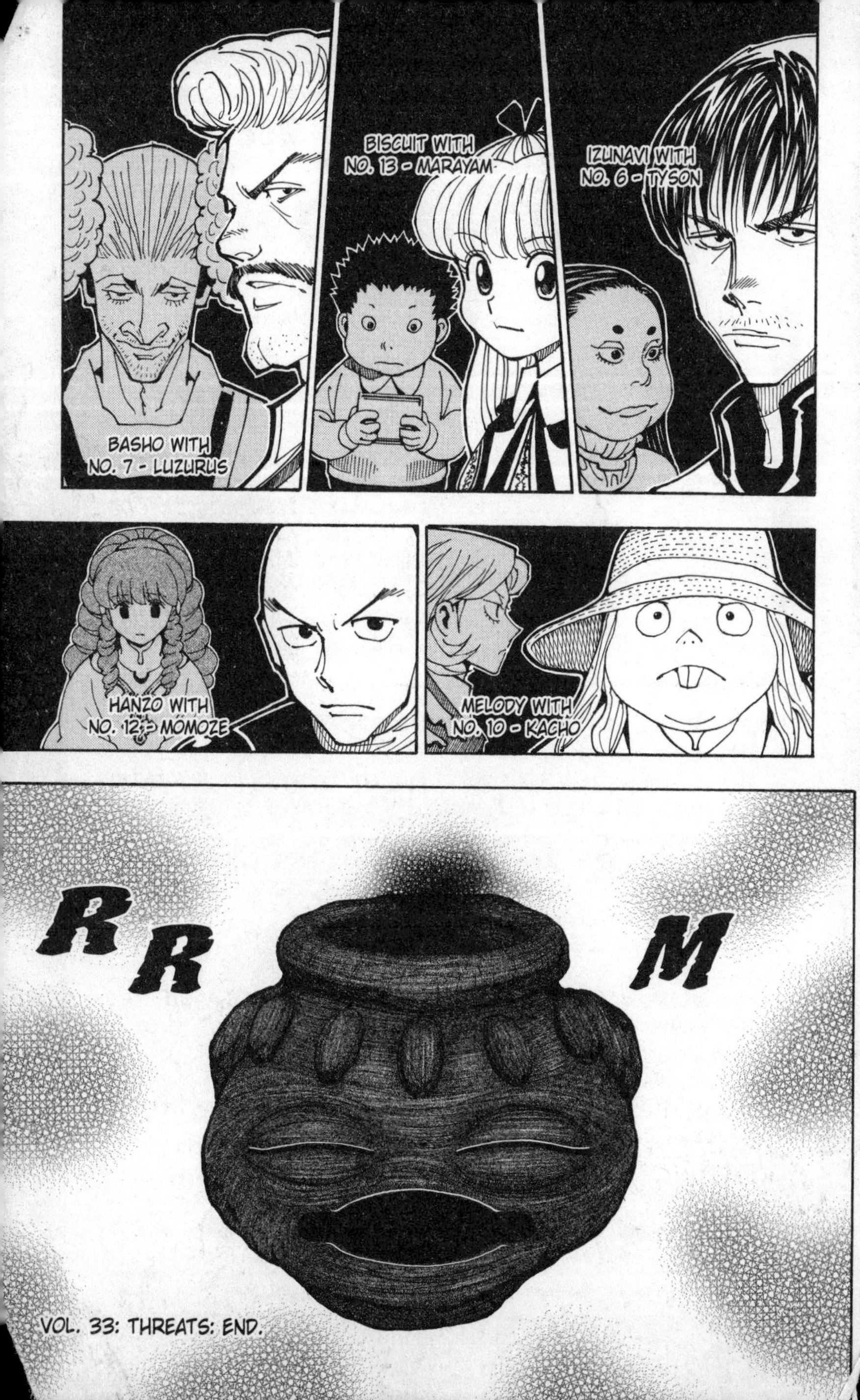
IZUNAVI WITH
NO. 6 - TYSON
BISCUIT WITH
NO. 13 - MARAYAM
BASHO WITH
NO. 7 - LUZURUS
MELODY WITH
NO. 10 - KACHO
HANZO WITH
NO. 12 - MOMOZE
RRM
VOL. 33: THREATS: END.

You're Reading in the Wrong Direction!!

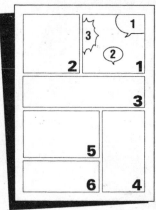

Whoops! Guess what? You're starting at the wrong end of the comic!

...It's true! In keeping with the original Japanese format, **Hunter x Hunter** is meant to be read from right to left, starting in the upper-right corner.

Unlike English, which is read from left to right, Japanese is read from right to left, meaning that action, sound effects and word-balloon order are completely reversed... something which can make readers unfamiliar with Japanese feel pretty backwards themselves. For this reason, manga or Japanese comics published in the U.S. in English have sometimes been published "flopped"— that is, printed in exact reverse order, as though seen from the other side of a mirror.

By flopping pages, U.S. publishers can avoid confusing readers, but the compromise is not without its downside. For one thing, a character in a flopped manga series who once wore in the original Japanese version a T-shirt emblazoned with "M A Y" (as in "the merry month of") now wears one which reads "Y A M"! Additionally, many manga creators in Japan are themselves unhappy with the process, as some feel the mirror-imaging of their art skews their original intentions.

We are proud to bring you Yoshihiro Togashi's **Hunter x Hunter** in the original unflopped format. For now, though, turn to the other side of the book and let the adventure begin...!

—Editor